FAMINE IN
SOUTH ASIA

Famine in South Asia

Political Economy of Mass Starvation

Mohiuddin Alamgir

*Harvard Institute for
International Development*

Oelgeschlager, Gunn & Hain, Publishers, Inc.
Cambridge, Massachusetts

International Standard Book Number: 0-89946-042-9

Library of Congress Catalog Card Number: 80-13708

Printed in the United States of America

Library of Congress Cataloging in Publication Data

Alamgir, Mohiuddin, 1943-
    Famine in South Asia.

    Includes index.
      1. South Asia—Famines. 2. Food supply—Bangladesh. 3. Food prices—Bangladesh. 4. Bangladesh—Rural conditions. I. Title.
HC412.A377   338.1'9'54   80-13708
ISBN 0-89946-042-9

To my parents

Contents

List of Figures

List of Tables

Preface and
Acknowledgments

For a number of years I have tried to understand what causes famine. I find it difficult to accept that after having made so much progress in science and technology, people are unable to feed all of their own kind. It will take many deaths (be it in South Asia, Sahel, or Kampuchea) before world leaders are willing to face this paradox of modern civilization. Unfortunately, though—as this book clearly shows—the problem of foodgrain deprivation that reaches its climax when famine occurs is very complex and not easily soluble.

As an economist, I am aware of my limitations in a study of famine, which calls for a multidisciplinary approach. I have made a modest attempt to throw light on what I consider to be the missing links; it is for my readers to judge how far I have succeeded. I shall not be surprised if purists say that more work should be done on the subject in the future. I have no quarrel with that position, but I must emphasize that the food problem has become so endemic in many regions of the world that only an aggressive action program representing joint national and international efforts can eliminate it. Otherwise, the situation is likely to get worse and the specter of famine will hang over an increasing proportion of the world population.

While working on this book, I received financial and/or institutional support from the Bangladesh Institute of Development Studies, Dacca; Institute for International Economic Studies, Stockholm; Department of City and Regional Planning, Harvard University; Center for Asian Development Studies, Boston University; and the Harvard Institute for International Development. I am grateful to all of them. I have been helped a great deal by discussion with and comments from Professor A. K. Sen, Professor Lance Taylor, Professor Gustav F. Papanek, Professor Anisur Rahman, Mr. Harun Er Rashid, Dr. David Cole, Dr. Richard Goldman, Dr. Peter Svedberg, Dr. Lincoln C. Chen, Dr. S. Liberman, and Dr. Monowar Hossain. Thanks are also due to Professor Rehman Sobhan, Mr. A. A. Abdullah, and Dr. M. Asaduzzaman, who were involved in the original design of the famine survey. I have also been able to improve the analysis and presentation of the book on the basis of comments received from participants in my seminars at the Institute for International Economic Studies, Stockholm; the Christen Michelsen Institute, Bergen, Norway; the University of Antwerp, Belgium; the University of Louvain, Belgium; Harvard University; Johns Hopkins University; Boston University; and the Massachusetts Institute of Technology. Dr. Malcolm Gillis, of the Harvard Institute for International Development, was instrumental in ensuring that the manuscript was finished on time.

Computational work was done by Salimullah, A. B. M. Shamsul Islam, Dilip Kumar Roy, Mizanur Rahman, Mashiur Rahman, Kahn Md. Nabiul Islam, and Karimullah Bhuiyan at the Bangladesh Institute of Development Studies and by Susan Horton at Harvard University. Ms. Horton also commented extensively on earlier drafts of the book, while others were involved in carrying out the field survey under unusually difficult circumstances. I have to admit that, but for their untiring efforts, this book could never have been completed. As is perhaps true of many manuscripts, a large number of people were involved in typing successive drafts, but the final burden was borne by Geraldine Wilson of the Harvard Institute for International Development and my wife, Susan Fuller Alamgir. I am deeply indebted to all of them.

Mohiuddin Alamgir

Chapter 1

Diagnosing Famine

INTRODUCTION: THE CURRENT WORLD SCENARIO

Malnutrition, hunger, starvation, and famine are concerns of many today. Academics, political leaders, administrators, and other professionals have been paying more attention to these problems in recent years than they did in the past. For individual governments and the world community at large, the magnitude (as measured by the proportion of population affected) of these problems has become a matter of embarrassment. Despite advances made by science and technology in different spheres of life, little progress seems to have been made in eradicating signs of malnutrition and starvation from the face of the earth. On the contrary, in many areas of the world, the number of people suffering from starvation is increasing every year. What is a matter of grave concern is that the burden of suffering is unevenly distributed among different regions of the world, different classes of people, and different age groups within each region.

In 1965, 74 percent of the total world population (1.13 billion people) consumed less than Food and Agriculture Organization/World Health Organization (FAO/WHO) calorie requirements, the percentage being highest for Asia and the Far East (82 percent or 736 million people).[1] The

Second Report to the Club of Rome quotes a UNESCO estimate, according to which "between 400 and 500 million children suffered from malnutrition and starvation in 1973."[2] The report itself projects a worsening food supply situation, the prospect for South Asia being particularly gloomy.[3] The United Nations, World Food Conference[4] presented an FAO estimate that showed that 16 percent of the world population had an insufficient protein/energy supply in 1970.[5] The extent of malnutrition varies greatly among regions.[6]

Concern about the world food situation assumed crisis proportions a few years ago when a number of factors combined to produce an unprecedented increase in foodgrain prices (especially cereals) in the world market and considerable shortfall in food supplies in several Third-World countries. In the early 1970s world grain production experienced shortfalls,[7] although by small margins.

Fluctuations around production trends are only natural but the above-mentioned shortfall in the early 1970s was the first in twenty years. Many viewpoints emerged out of this crisis. One extreme view was that the world has almost reached the limit of its ability to provide food for all. Countries with surplus food may soon be unable to meet the demand of all food aid-seeking countries; implying that a large number of people would probably die of starvation.[8]

The "limit" theory finds subtle but sophisticated expression in the Second Report to the Club of Rome, where the authors write:

In summary, the only feasible solution to the world food situation requires:
  1. A global approach to the problem.
  2. Investment aid rather than commodity aid, except for food.
  3. A balanced economic development of all regions.
  4. An effective population policy.
  5. Worldwide diversification of industry, leading to a truly global economic system.
  Only a proper combination of these measures can lead to a solution. Omission of any one measure will surely lead to diaster. But the strains on the global food production capacity would be lessened if the eating habits in the affluent part of the world would change, becoming less wasteful.[9]

Conditions under which a feasible solution can be attained are indeed very stringent given the existing world order. The "new world order" called for by many may change the situation, but this gives rise to a host of new questions that need not be entered into here.

One important point of debate has been the consumption pattern of developed countries or more generally the consumption habits of the rich. In this connection, attention has been drawn to: (1) the impact of the rising prosperity of Europe and Japan on demand for foodgrains and feedgrains;[10] (2) the reluctance of Soviet Russia in 1972/1973 to tighten its belt, instead making one of the largest grain purchases (20.5 million tons of grain including 14.9 million tons of wheat[11]) in history; and (3) the recent trend in Eastern European countries to increase grain consumption more than their grain production.[12] Brown pointed out that, as yet, no nation appears to have reached a level of affluence where its per capita grain requirements stopped rising."[13] Impact of foodgrain consumption of developed countries on that of developing countries has been downplayed by Johnson and Svedberg.[14]

The scenario of immediate global starvation is considered a myth by some.[15] Studies carried out by the U.N. Food and Agriculture Organization suggest that the recent problems are transitory in nature and can be overcome by appropriate action at the regional and global level. In the next two decades average calorie supply per capita in all regions of the world would increase and by the year 2000 it would exceed requirement per capita.[16] While this point is conceded by many authors, they point out that the major problem in the coming years would be lack of purchasing power of many groups of people and/or countries. Thus, in the 1980s and 1990s—as in 1974—countries such as Bangladesh may find themselves unable to import the food they need.[17] In this view, prices of foodgrain play a pivotal role in national and world food economy. In addition to production shortfall and depletion of stock, the foodgrain price increase of the early 1970s in the world market has been attributed to

> Governmental policies in many countries that prevented the price system from rationing the available supplies. In countries with a large fraction of the world's population, grain prices were not permitted to increase to reflect the shortfalls in production and the depletion of grain reserves. Thus, the price-increasing factors were concentrated in the international grain markets, which had to absorb most of the production shortfalls and the expanding world demand.[18]

The question of foodgrain prices in the world market is intimately related to stock and export policy of major suppliers. The price stabilizing effect of the large U.S. and world stock of the 1950s and 1960s has been eliminated by depletion of stocks in the early 1970s and also by the reluctance of the U.S. government to undertake on its own the task of rebuilding stock. Many stabilization schemes are being put forward from various quarters. The alternatives suggested range from complete free trade in foodgrains to an internationally owned and operated food reserve or a nationally owned and internationally coordinated food reserve, the last two being designed largely to protect the interests of the developing countries. Discussions are only at a preliminary stage and consensus is far from achieved.[19]

Whether there is an overt food crisis or not, few will deny that the developing countries of the Third World are under pressure, even during normal years, to ensure adequate nutritional intake for their populations. So far, the thrust of our discussion has been on global availability and prices and their influence on regional availability. The main problem, however, remains the inequitable distribution of economic and political power between different regions as well as between different classes within each region. The confrontation between the rich and poor countries is a reflection of the same between the rich and poor within each country. The global food crisis, therefore, is reflected within individual countries of the Third World in an inability to harness internal resources and make the most of external aid, to achieve a breakthrough in economic development with or without expanded foodgrain production, and to effect an equitable distribution of income that, under normal circumstances, should take care of the problem of malnutrition, hunger, starvation, and famine.[20]

Problems facing developing countries such as Bangladesh are very special although they all now seem to converge into one important symptom—"nutrition crisis" of varying degrees. The international forces discussed above do affect them rather severely, especially because they are trapped within their own domain where internal social, cultural, political, and economic forces have historically interacted in such a manner that they could not release their latent productive potential and thus lagged behind demands of time. Therefore, at a time when the world community was laboring over how to tackle the food crisis, for a number of countries it was translated into staggering figures of human mortality. Notwithstanding the wisdom of scholars and policymakers, the national and international "food systems" failed to avert disaster in countries such as Bangladesh and Ethiopia and did precious little to relieve pressures on people in the Sahelian countries.[21] All of these areas suffered from famine between 1970 and 1974,[22] although in each region it was preceded by a different causal sequence.

It is against the backdrop of the above that the 1974 famine in Bangladesh will be analyzed in Chapter 4. But before the events of 1974 are described and analyzed with the hope of presenting a causal interpretation of the phenomenon, a number of points need be clarified. First, the term famine must be clearly defined. This will be done in the remainder of Chapter 1. Second, to facilitate the analysis of the 1974 famine, it is felt that there is a need to develop a general theoretical framework that will clearly outline the interaction between internal and external factors that may produce a sequence of events leading to famine. Chapter 2 will present the theory of famine. Third, given the nature of social and economic problems facing the famine-prone regions of the

Third World, it is desirable to put a particular occurrence of famine within a proper historic perspective. It is in this context that a brief history of famines in the Indian subcontinent will be presented in Chapter 3. Those occurring in the Bengal region, particularly the great Bengal famine of 1943, will be discussed at greater length. The purpose of this exercise is to establish organic links between different famines.

DEFINING FAMINE

The terms hunger, starvation, and malnutrition do not give rise to problems of definition and interpretation, although some subtle questions still remain to be worked out with respect to the concept of malnutrition. On the other hand, the term famine sometimes seems to be too difficult to define and any interpretation gets highly charged emotionally. Governments and politicians in power avoid the use of this term to describe a situation unless they are forced to do so, while others concerned with hunger and starvation quarrel over when a situation can be described precisely as having turned to a famine. The question here is not only one of political expediency. There is a more fundamental problem related to the definition and causal interpretation (explanation) of famine.

The literature contains many definitions of famine that combine description with a partial and truncated causal sequence. Four different approaches can be identified. The first relates famine to hunger, starvation, and malnutrition. According to this point of view, extreme cases of these should be described as famine. How extreme will be determined by the area and length of period over which the incidence of hunger, starvation, and malnutrition is observed and the number of people affected.[23] The second approach toward defining famine emphasizes excess mortality, thus drawing a line between hunger, starvation, and malnutrition on the one hand, and famine on the other.[24] The third approach does not make a specific distinction between starvation and excess mortality, but proceeds to define famine in terms of extent of external assistance required to alleviate the suffering of the affected population.[25] Finally, there is the approach that looks at famine in terms of a community syndrome consisting of early signals, some societal manifestations leading to starvation, and/or excess mortality on a wide scale.[26]

The multiplicity of definitions of famine indicate that it is a complex socio-economic phenomenon. Its essence cannot be captured within a simple definition. The community syndrome approach, therefore, assumes great importance. Bruce Currey, who studied the 1974 famine in one region of Bangladesh, is one of the first to define famine specifically in terms of a community syndrome. According to him, "Famine might be more effectively defined as the community syndrome which results when social, economic and administrative structures are already under stress and are further triggered by one, or several, discrete disruptions which accelerate the incidence of many symptoms, or crisis adjustments of which one is epidemic malnutrition."[27] This approach will be followed here in presenting a comprehensive definition of famine.

The basic problem with these definitions is that they only present a partial picture in terms of either describing the phenomenon or suggesting a causal sequence. In such a situation, the attempt to combine description with causal analysis could not have been very rewarding. However, as the discussions suggest, essential elements of a comprehensive definition of famine are contained in the above attempts in one form or another. A definition of famine should fulfill the following objectives: First, one should be able to distinguish clearly between a famine and a nonfamine situation. Therefore, emphasis on excess mortality is important. Second, the definition should identify the prior indicators of famine, which will provide a basis for governments and potential victims to be forewarned and relief instruments activated. Finally, it should indicate the immediate cause of a set of famine substates that ultimately lead to excess mortality. A definition fulfilling these objectives will be an appropriate point of departure for developing a causal theory of famine.

Focus on death seems to be very meaningful since it is the ultimate manifestation of famine. Therefore, hunger and starvation, prolonged or not, should not be confused with famine unless they are accompanied by excess deaths. "Excess" refers to death rates above the "normal" observed level in prefamine periods. Admittedly, this concept gives rise to problems and it is impossible to arrive at a solution that will be acceptable to all. Death should not be linked merely to foodgrain shortage. It must be understood that foodgrain shortage, only when translated into prolonged foodgrain intake decline, causes death. Therefore, foodgrain intake decline should be considered as the most proximate cause of famine that operates through the sequence of one or more intermediate steps to bring about the ultimate and essential manifestation of famine—excess deaths. Two points should be carefully noted here. First, one may express foodgrain intake decline in average terms for operational convenience, but it must be understood that the effect of foodgrain intake decline varies from individual to individual depending on a number of environmental parameters.[28] Second, foodgrain intake decline can occur for certain groups of population even without an overall foodgrain shortage.

In this study, famine is considered to represent a general state of prolonged foodgrain intake deficiency per capita giving rise to a number of accompanying substates (symptoms) involving individuals and the community that ultimately lead, directly or indirectly, to excess deaths in a region or in a country as a whole. The substates include: increase in interregional migration, increase in crime, increase in incidence of fatal disease, loss of body weight, changes in nutritional status, eating of alternative "famine foods," mental disorientation, "wandering," uprooting of families, separation of families, transfer of assets, and breakdown of traditional social bonds. Among these, crime, disease, loss of body weight, changes in nutritional status, and eating of alternative "famine foods" can combine to produce significant excess deaths. Following this definition, one can construct a famine syndrome as shown in Figure 1.1.[29]

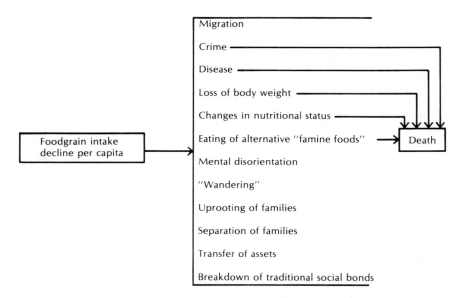

Figure 1.1. The famine syndrome.

Famine is characterized by the presence of the initial and the ultimate state shown in Figure 1.1, but one or more of the substates may be missing from any specific situation under study. One can now distinguish famine from starvation, hunger, and malnutrition, which are associated with poverty. This is not to say that the others are not important, but it is emphasized that in a state of poverty (or affluence, for that matter) famine implies hunger, starvation, malnutrition, and something more—excess death. Unlike other definitions of famine, no attempt has been made here to build a theory of famine. Foodgrain intake decline is mentioned only as a triggering event, but it itself is the subject of a separate causal analysis that provides the foundation of a theory of famine that can be applied to examine any famine including, of course, the 1974 Bangladesh famine. Presentation of the famine syndrome of 1974 will facilitate the unveiling of the root causes and provide links to the world food problem in all its dimensions. The famine syndrome will be discussed in Chapter 5. In Chapter 2 an attempt will be made to construct a theory of famine.

NOTES AND REFERENCES

1. Shlomo Reutlinger, "Malnutrition: A Poverty or a Food Problem?" *World Development* 5(8):716 (1977). Figures for other regions were 77 percent or 190 million people in Africa, 63 percent or 91 million people in the Middle East, and 46 percent or 113 million people in Latin America. The centrally planned economies are not included in these estimates.
2. Mihajlo Mesarovic and Edward Pestel, *Mankind at the Turning Point,* The Second Report to the Club of Rome (New York: E. P. Dutton, 1974), p. 115.
3. For analysis of alternative food scenarios, see ibid., chapter 9.
4. United Nations, World Food Conference, *Assessment of World Food Situation, Present and Future,* Item 8 of Provisional Agenda, November 1974, p. 66.
5. After reassessment of energy and protein "requirements" by an FAO/WHO expert panel, the protein figure for adults was reduced by about one-third. See Food and Agriculture Organization, *Energy and Protein Requirements,* Nutrition Meetings Report, Series 52, 1973.
6. Developed countries, 3 percent; developing countries, 25 percent, including Latin America, 13 percent; Far East, 30 percent; Near East, 18 percent; Africa, 25 percent. On the basis of 1970 population, 462 million people suffered from malnutrition. The above figures exclude centrally planned economies. Note that these figures cannot be directly compared with those for 1965 quoted earlier since the latter referred to calorie deficiency alone.
7. The shortfall is estimated at 1.3, 3.3, and 4.0 percent of long-run production trend (1945/1946–1976/1977) in 1972/1973, 1974/1975, and 1975/1976. See Peter Svedberg, "World Food Sufficiency and Meat Consumption," *American Journal of Agricultural Economics* 60(4):661–666 (November 1978). It is important to note that this period was accompanied by a sharp decline of world and U.S. stock of foodgrain, particularly that held by the United States.
8. This view is taken note of in U.S. Department of Agriculture, Economic Research Service, *The World Food Situation and Prospects to 1985,* Foreign Agricultural Economic Report No. 98, p. v. In a way it reflects what has come to be known as the "triage" theory. According to Gunnar Myrdal, the triage theorists "are merely making the negative point that what little aid is afforded, should not be given to the very poorest countries, but that in regard to them 'nature should be left to take its course' as the most humanitarian solution." He goes on to endorse the stand of the *New York Times,* which calls the triage theory "one of the most pessimistic and morally threadbare intellectual positions to be advanced since the demise of the Third Reich." See Gunnar Myrdal, "The Equality Issue in World Development," in *Les Prix Nobel en 1974* (Stockholm: The Nobel Foundation, 1975), pp. 275–276.

9. Mesarovic and Pestel, *Mankind at Turning Point,* p. 127.
10. See Lyle P. Schertz, "World Food: Prices and the Poor," *Foreign Affairs* 52(1):513–514 (October 1973). It has been observed, though, that increased absorption of feedgrains does not necessarily reduce consumption of foodgrain. See Dale E. Hathaway, "Food Prices and Inflation," in *Brookings Papers on Economic Activity,* I (Washington, D.C.: Brookings Institution, 1974) pp. 90–94.
11. D. G. Johnson, *World Food Problems and Prospects,* Foreign Affairs Studies 20 (Washington, D.C.: American Enterprise Institute for Public Policy Research, 1975), p. 27. See also Hathaway, "Food Prices," pp. 85–90 and Schertz, "World Food," p. 514.
12. Johnson, *World Food,* p. 31.
13. Lester R. Brown, "The Next Crisis? Food," *Foreign Policy* 13:5 (Winter 1973/1974). Brown is of the opinion that "the world food economy is undergoing a fundamental transformation, and that food scarcity is becoming chronic. The soaring demand for food, spurred by continued population growth and rising affluence, has begun to outrun the productive capacity of the world's farmers and fishermen," ibid., p. 3. See also Lester R. Brown and Erik P. Eckholm, *By Bread Alone* (New York: Praeger, 1974). Brown and Eckholm favor reduced consumption by the rich to feed the poor. Both the Second Report to the Club of Rome and Cocyoc declaration expressed concern about the general pattern of overproduction and overconsumption in the West. (UNEP/UNCTAD Symposium on "Patterns of Resource Use, Environment and Development Strategies," October 1974).
14. Johnson, *World Food,* p. 31; Svedberg, "World Food Sufficiency," pp. 661–666.
15. Thomas T. Poleman, "World Food: Myth and Reality," *World Development* 5(5–7):383–386 (May–July 1977).
16. United Nations, World Food Conference, *The World Food Problem—Proposals for National and International Actions* (Rome: Food and Agriculture Organization, 1974); United Nations, World Food Conference, *Agriculture Towards 2000* (Rome: Food and Agriculture Organization, 1979).
17. Emma Rothschild, "Food Politics," *Foreign Affairs* 54(2):287 (January 1976).
18. Johnson, *World Food,* p. 3. Pricing policies of the Soviet Union and other Eastern European countries and the variable import levies of EEC countries have been criticized by Johnson (pp. 33–34).
19. For some discussion on the subject, see Johnson, *World Food,* pp. 51–59; Tim Josling, "Grain Reserves and Government Agricultural Policies," *World Development* 5(5–7):603–611 (May–July 1977); R. S. Weckstein, "Food Security: Storage vs. Exchange," *World Development* 5(5–7):613–621 (May–July 1977); Marian Radetzki, "Stock-holding for the Stabilization of the World Food Market," *SE Banken Quarterly,* No. 4, Stockholm 1975.
20. Issues of inequality at the national and international level have been focused by Myrdal, "Equality Issue"; Susan George, *How the Other Half Dies: The Real Reasons of World Hunger* (London: Penguin, 1976); Jonathan Power and Anne-Marie Hollenstein, *World of Hunger* (London: Maurice Temple Smith, 1976); and Solon Barraclough, "Agricultural Production Prospects in Latin America," *World Development* 5(5–7):459–476 (May–July 1977).
21. The Sahelian countries are Chad, Niger, Upper Volta, Mali, Senegal, and Mauritania.
22. The Ethiopian famine claimed about 100,000–200,000 lives in the 1972–1974 period; see United Nations Research Institute for Social Development, *Famine Risk and Famine Prevention in the Modern World: Studies in Food Surplus under Conditions of Recurrent Scarcity,* Geneva, June 1976. Masefield quotes a figure of 50,000–100,000 in the period 1971–1973. See G. B. Masefield, *Famine: Its Prevention and Relief* (Oxford: Oxford University Press, 1963), pp 112–117. For Bangladesh the author estimates a mortality figure of over one million in the period August 1974–February 1976. Details are presented in Chapter 4.

23. Examples of this approach can be found in Masefield, *Famine*, p. 2; B. M. Bhatia, *Famines in India 1860–1965*, 2nd ed. (New Delhi: Asia Publishing House, 1976), p. 1; A. Keys, A. Henschel, O. Michelson, and H. L. Taylor, *The Biology of Human Starvation*, vol. II (Minneapolis: University of Minnesota Press, 1950), p. 784; and Arthur Lukyn Williams, *Famines in India: Their Causes and Possible Prevention* (London: Henry S. King, 1876), pp. 14–15.

24. This approach was adopted by Masefield, *Famine*, pp. 3–4; Jean Mayer, "Management of Famine Relief," *Science* 188:572 (May 9, 1975); W. R. Aykroyd, *The Conquest of Famine* (London: Chatto and Windus, 1974), p. 1; G. Blix, Y. Hofvander, and B. Vahiquist, eds., *Famine: A Symposium Dealing with Nutrition and Relief Operations in Times of Disasters* (Uppsala, Sweden: Almquist and Wiksell, 1971), p. 190; United Nations Research Institute for Social Development (UNRISD), *Famine Risk in the Modern World*, Geneva, August 1975; and D. G. Johnson, "Famine," in *Encyclopaedia Britannica*, Fourteenth edition (1973), p. 58. Social characterization of famine is made in the UNRISD document, which states that a famine occurs when many people in the same place and at the same time lack resources to provide them with command over foodstuff, for example, adequate income, interpersonal solidarity, and so forth, and institutional aid can no longer cope with the situation. On the other hand, Johnson introduces the social-class dimension in the definition of famine by pointing out that starvation deaths occur mainly among the poor. Both UNRISD's and Johnson's definitions reflect partial representation of a community syndrome associated with famine although the authors themselves do not articulate it properly.

25. UNRISD, in its definition, did use this criterion, although its major emphasis was elsewhere. Other examples of this approach can be found in the characterization of famine by FAO as quoted in Masefield, *Famine*, p. 5; and in Hari Shanker Srivastava, *The History of Indian Famines 1858–1918* (Agra: Sri Ram Mehra, 1968), p. 290. The origin of famine codes in India can be traced back to the government's appreciation in the late nineteenth century that famine represents a situation where widespread suffering of the people will continue in the absence of private and/or publicly organized relief. However, the relief criterion was formally incorporated only in 1915 when the government of India declared that famine was a situation where full relief work was necessary. A scarcity situation was characterized by the need for "some" relief and test works but not "full" relief works. It may be added here that the first famine code was formulated in 1877 by the Famine Commissioner of Mysore. It was later adopted and elaborated by the Madras Famine Commission of 1880 and gradually provinces were encouraged to formulate their own famine codes modeled around the Mysore–Madras one.

26. See Bruce Currey, "The Famine Syndrome: Its Definition for Preparedness and Prevention in Bangladesh," *Ecology of Food and Nutrition* 7:87 (1978). He quotes A. E. Taylor, who says "famine is like insanity, hard to define but glaring enough when recognized."

27. Currey, "Famine Syndrome," p. 87. Earlier, the Bengal Famine Code portrayed famine as a community syndrome although the task of full articulation was not completed. Under this code, at a time of apparent foodgrain scarcity, the district officers were asked to watch for the following symptoms: contraction of private charity, contraction of credit, feverish activity in the grain trade, increase in crime, unusual movement of flocks and herds in search of pasturage, wandering of people, and increased activity in emigration. See Kali Charan Ghosh, *Famines in Bengal 1770–1943* (Calcutta: India Associated Publishing Co., 1944), p. 3

28. See F. E. Viteri and O. Pineda, "Effects on Body Composition and Body Function. Psychological Effects," in *Famine: A Symposium Dealing with Nutrition and Relief*

Operations in Times of Disasters, G. Blix, Y. Hofvander, and B. Vahlquist (Uppsala, Sweden: Almquist and Wiksell, 1971), pp. 25–40; and Keys, Henschel, Michelson, and Taylor, *Biology of Human Starvation,* pp. 783–826.

29. In this context it will be interesting to note the tests of severity of famines suggested by Masefield, *Famine,* p. 12. His tests include number of deaths, occurrence of cannibalism, inability of the living to bury the dead owing to the weakness of the former and number of the latter, and migration enforced by famine.

Chapter 2

From the Definition to a Theory of Famine

The literature has done a lot to improve our understanding of the causal sequence of events leading to famine, although no systematic attempt has been made to develop a general theory of famine. There has been a tendency to present an oversimplified analysis of famine. By and large, three approaches have emerged so far. The first indicates that famine is caused by foodgrain availability decline, the second attributes it to lack of purchasing power, and the third combines the two. A. K. Sen has formalized the lack of purchasing power in terms of what he calls failure of exchange entitlements. His paper has added a new dimension in that a rigorous analytic framework has been presented to study famines, although he admits that "the exchange entitlements approach provides a *structure* for analyzing famines rather than presenting a particular theory of 'ultimate' explanation."[1]

Detailed studies of past famines reveal that a large number of factors can combine to produce one or more causal sequences initiating the crisis. Thus, even though some of these studies finally emphasize one sequence or another, they recognize the complexity of the phenomenon under consideration.[2] Since the concern of most authors has centered on particular instances of famine, they were able to reflect in only a limited way on the causal sequence of famine. They made no attempt to study famine in more general terms so as to be able to incorporate all admissible causal sequences in logical order within a broader analytic framework. Some authors, however, have presented useful check lists of causes of famine without building a consistent theory of famine.[3] Sen's contribution was a departure from this practice in that he provided a structure for analyzing famines.

TYPOLOGY OF FAMINE

Before proceeding any further with the construction of a general theory of famine, it may be worthwhile to discuss a typology of famine. Three types of famine can be identified from history: (1) general famine, (2) local/regional famine, and (3) class famine. Taking the national boundary as a point of reference, famine as a general phenomenon will imply a situation in which all classes of people in all regions are affected, although the time sequence may differ between regions and between classes of people. The great famine of 1344–1345 in India was of this type.[4] A later example is the 1975 famine of Cape Verde Island. In the recent decades the 1944 Dutch famine approached this dimension due to a war-created blockade of supplies.

In a local/regional famine only a part of a country, but all groups of people within it, is affected. The 1630 Indian famine of Deccan is an example.[5] The final category includes those famines in which only specific groups/classes of people are affected without any reference to the geographic area of concentration. Historically, this has been the most important type of famine and, in the modern world, most of the famines are of this nature. In a class famine the burden of foodgrain intake deficiency per capita and excess mortality falls primarily on the weaker sections of the population with little staying power. The great Bengal famine of 1943 falls into this category, and so does the 1974 Bangladesh famine.[6] Another famous example of "class famine" is the great Irish potato famine of 1846–1847.[7] Different countries can be affected by different types of famine depending on their initial condition and the particular causal sequence leading to the famine. Once we present the general framework, it will be clear which sequence leads to which type of famine.

THEORY OF FAMINE

A theory of famine should integrate the chains of causation that may lead to famine under different situations, and it should also explain the process of postfamine adjustment of the individuals and the society.

In essence, one needs a combined theory of economy and society to understand how they function under normal circumstances, which shocks induce a chain of reactions leading to famine, what happens during a famine, and finally whether the economy and the society adjusts back to the original position or to a new position. Although such a theory should be applicable to all countries of the world at all times, the emphasis here will be primarily on the famine-prone regions of the Third World in modern times. More specifically, since the theory will be applied to study the 1974 famine in Bangladesh, the scenarios considered will be those of Bangladesh and other comparable regions. As will be clear from the presentation below, the framework itself can be extended to study famines elsewhere in the world.

It is important that such a theory helps to resolve the somewhat contradictory views presented on the possibility of famine in the modern world. In addition, there is the more important task of assisting governments and relevant agencies to develop effective famine forewarning, prevention, and relief systems. This is a very important consideration because, given the social structure of different Third-World countries with consequent distribution of political and economic power combined with the international division of resources and power, it is unlikely that mere application of modern technology, transport, and organization (even assuming that such adaptation was possible everywhere) would eliminate famine. However, it is also unlikely that famine as defined here will be as frequent as it was in the nineteenth and earlier centuries in some regions of the world such as India, China, and Russia.[8]

The more likely outcome is that, under the prevailing circumstances, quasi-famine situations (understood as widespread hunger and starvation) will affect an increasingly larger number of people of the Third World, famine occurring only occasionally as a result of breakdown of the existing equilibrating forces. This is closely related to the phenomenon of "Below Poverty Level Equilibrium Trap," which is being experienced by many Third-World countries in recent decades. The author has elaborated this concept elsewhere in the context of Bangladesh.[9] The equilibrium depicts a situation where the majority of the population are caught between the poverty line and the famine line.[10] This is the result of a historic process in which certain internal social forces have combined with external forces to arrest development of productive forces and to adopt policies that tended to aggravate the problem of inequality and poverty. The state of equilibrium referred to is defined with respect to the famine line in the sense that, if some forces act to raise the income level of the poor above the famine level, there are opposing forces that quickly react by pushing it down to the famine level. For a country like Bangladesh, however, the situation is further compounded by a high population growth rate and the impact of international factors such as oil crises, foodgrain price increases, and depletion of world foodgrain reserves, and so forth. Internally, the trap is sustained by certain laws of motion operating in the society.[11] In relation to this equilibrium trap, famine is a disequilibrium situation that occurs only when a number of exogenous forces combine to produce a shock of considerable magnitude under the pressure of which the existing institutions give in, at least temporarily.[12]

A FAMINE-PRONE ECONOMY

To appreciate the above viewpoint of famine, let us consider a typical famine-prone country such as Bangladesh and, more specifically, examine what happens at any point in time in such a society. The economy is primarily rural; rice cultivation is the most important production activity. There is also nonrice producing agricultural activity. In addition, there is nonagricultural production activity. Land is given; other capital stock is growing very slowly but for any given period of production can be regarded as fixed. The population growth rate of working age is higher than the population growth rate itself, which is quite high.[13] The distribution of land and other assets is highly skewed. Land is cultivated mainly under owner-management and on a crop sharing basis.[14] Agricultural laborers work as family labor and/or hired (permanent or casual) labor. Crops are mostly consumed by the producing units, roughly one-fifth to one-third entering the market.[15] The land-use pattern between different activities is determined by subsistence requirements and relative prices of output.

Production technology adopted in the three sectors reflect relatively high labor intensity in rice and nonrice rural production activities but somewhat higher capital intensity in relation to internal factor endowments for nonagricultural production activity. But in all sectors, the scope for further substitution is limited; this along with a low rate of capital accumulation produces a low rate of employment growth.[16] Land being limited and population and labor force increasing, pressure on land increases.[17] Thus, in the land market, a large number of potential tenants are bidding for limited land; on the other hand, in the labor market, a reserve army of unemployed and underemployed laborers is competing for rare job opportunities.[18] Capital market is characterized by isolated (delinked) organized and unorganized markets, inaccessibility of organized market to majority of rural population, dichotomy of the unorganized market between "survival" and "nonsurvival" borrowing, and, of course, overall scarcity of capital reflected mostly in high cost of capital.[19] As indicated before, the situation is compounded by the underlying social structure characterized by a low level of productive forces and exploitative production relations that have generated a set of laws of motion sustaining a very low level of living in which the majority of the population seem trapped.

Land Market

Land and labor being the two most important factors, a large part of the income of households originates from them, particularly in the rural areas. Land and labor are mostly devoted to rice production and other agricultural activities. Labor in rural areas is somewhat undifferentiated in the sense that there is little or no formal training of agricultural labor. In the land market, the two bargaining parties are the landowners and the potential tenants. For the landowners, two options are available. They may rent out a portion of the land under a sharecropping arrangement,[20] or they may keep it under their own management.[21] On the other hand, tenants can either lease land or can offer themselves as wage laborers. The landowners also can hire themselves out as wage laborers. In a more general way, the situation can be visualized as land and labor transactions between two contending parties, one with surplus land relative to family labor and the other with surplus labor relative to owned land.

Much literature discusses the existence and extent of sharecropping in the rural areas of developing countries.[22] In the context of Bangladesh, different studies have highlighted the following factors: (1) the farming unit is too small for economic operation, in which case the owner either rents his land or leases additional land; (2) the farm area is either too large or too fragmented for efficient management by the owner so that he rents a portion of his landholding; (3) the household does not have access to adequate fixed and working capital (in terms of absolute availability as well as cost) and is forced to rent a part or the whole of its landholding; (4) the household may have more fixed capital and labor than can be efficiently used on the land owned, in which case it leases additional land; (5) the farm belongs to an absentee landlord who cultivates it through a sharecropper; and (6) the owner may not have an adequate supply of family labor and is, therefore, forced to rent a part of his landholding. Zaman [23] found (1) and (2) to be important factors in two areas of Bangladesh. Hossain [24] found evidence for all of these factors, but he favored the nature of rice agriculture and of land distribution as the two most important factors explaining existence of sharecropping. On the other hand, using micro-level data, he shows that the amount of net land rented by individual households has a significant positive relationship with their land and labor endowments. It has also been argued, in the context of Bangladesh, whether or not sharecropping is socially desirable. Zaman[25] is of the opinion that sharecropping is efficient and socially desirable. Jabbar[26] questions this position, while Hossain[27] discusses alternative viewpoints and provides some evidence to suggest that it "lends support to the Marshallian proposition that sharecropping is an 'inefficient' form of tenurial arrangement."

The upshot of the above viewpoints is that under the prevailing situation of rural areas in countries like Bangladesh, transaction in land-use rights takes place through the institution of sharecropping to the benefit of both parties involved. Each party tries to maximize total income from land and labor, subject to the various constraints operating on the system. Other things remaining the same, relative prices of land and labor determine allocation of land between family labor and hired labor. The price of land can be expressed in terms of crop-share to tenants with a hypothetical range between 0 (owners get it all) and 100 (tenants get it all). The land market can now be depicted in Figure 2.1 in terms of two offer curves derived from the allocation exercises carried out by the contending parties under alternative parametric variation of the price. The horizontal axis represents percentage of land sharecropped (1) and the vertical axis crop-share going to tenants (c), also in percentage terms the maximum in each case being one hundred. The offer curves of the landowners and tenants are marked as *0* and *T* respectively. These curves show that at zero crop-share to tenants the landowners would like to rent out all land while the potential tenants would take none. At the other extreme, when tenant's crop-share is 100 percent the situation will be exactly opposite. Under normal market operations, the distribution of land between owner cultivation and sharecropping would be determined by the market clearing crop-sharing arrangement *C*. But, in reality, conditions of sharecropping are determined, among others, by social and institutional norms. The usual outcome is 50 percent crop-share with the tenant bearing the entire cost of cultivation.[28] At this level excess demand for land exists even though with this arrangement, given the productivity of land, the income of the tenant falls short of poverty level. Historically, in many regions, this level of crop-share was observed to be sticky downwards—that is, the downward adjustment of the crop-share did not take place easily. So, for all practical purposes, one might say that the offer curve of the tenants is truncated at this level, which suggests that the institutional norm coincides with the market clearing price. Therefore, to a certain extent, area sharecropped depended on the position of the offer curve of owners. Similarly, one can set an upper limit to what the tenants can sharecrop given their resource base including labor power.

It is important to note here that the institutional crop-share comes under two types of pressures. With population growth and growing pauperization (reflected in the increasing number of landless households) in the society T curve moves to the right and with the diffusion of new technology O curve moves to the left as it becomes more profitable for the owners to cultivate land under their own management. Both of these trends have the effect of lowering the market clearing crop-share arrangement, which, in turn, tends to lower the institutional share. This has been observed in many countries.[29]

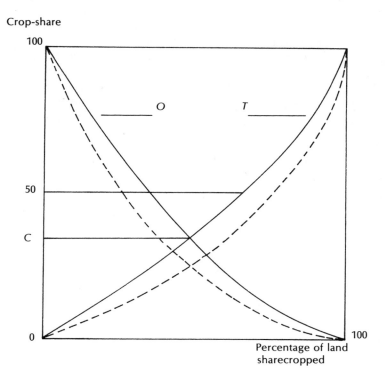

Figure 2.1. Land market.

Labor Market

The labor market can be differentiated between agricultural labor and nonagricultural labor. The respective labor supply and demand curves are shown in Figures 2.2 and 2.3. In Figure 2.2, w_F represents famine wage level below which the laborer cannot maintain the desired level of work effort.[30] Some labor will be available at this wage level. Wage rate will have to rise to draw labor supply beyond L_F. L represents the maximum supply of labor at any point in time. The labor supply curve $S(L_R)$ represents roughly the situation prevailing in a country such as Bangladesh.[31] Underlying this supply schedule is the utility maximization process of individuals with respect to income and leisure and also aggregation of individual labor supply into the community labor supply schedule. Income, as mentioned before, originates from sale of labor power as well as from family labor applied on land and crop-share, if any. For the moment we ignore the nonagricultural income component of rural households because, for the majority, this is small.

The demand curve for labor $D(L_R)$ reflects the production technology characterized by nonsubstitutability between labor and capital beyond a certain point. Here we run into some problems because of seasonal variation in labor demand as well as labor supply. The demand and supply schedules in Figure 2.2 can be considered a normal working period of the labor market, which has to be distinguished from the peak labor market period. We now find that the marginal condition for profit

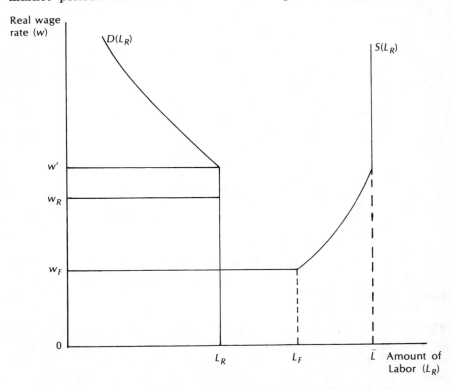

Figure 2.2. Agricultural labor market.

maximization, although not strictly applicable because of the discontinuity involved, dictates a wage level w' with excess labor supply, while the market equilibrium wage is obviously w_F, which is the famine wage. However, actual wage rate w_R is determined from time to time through a process of social arbitration, but a link is maintained on the upward side with the market clearing wage rate and the general market environment during the peak periods and on the downward side with, of course, the famine wage w_F.

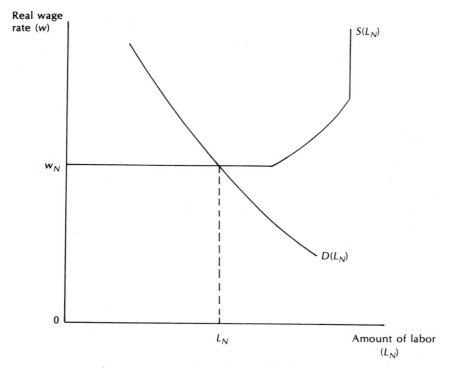

Figure 2.3. Nonagricultural labor market.

During the peak period, the demand curve shifts to the right and the supply curve to the left, the former due to increased need for labor at some crucial stages of crop production and the latter due to withdrawal of labor from the market to meet part of the demand of the family farm. The new supply and demand schedules produce a market clearing wage rate for a limited period during the year, the level itself may be above, below, or equal to w' depending on the relative shift of the two curves. One important reason why some employers will maintain a link with the peak period wage rate in determining the off-peak period wage rate is that they would like to ensure labor supply during the peak period. As a matter of fact, the apparent excess payment in wages over the minimum possible $(w_R - w_F)$, does not necessarily represent pure interpersonal transfer of income on account of factional, kinship, or dependency considerations alone, although these do enter into the picture under precapitalist agrarian relations. This excess payment could very well be the opportunity cost in terms of production loss due to nonavailability of labor during the peak period.[32]

Clearly, at w_R there is excess supply of labor; w_R is usually observed to be not very far above poverty level, it may even be below in many years. It is significant to note in the context of the current study that there is an excess supply of labor $(L_R L_F)$ even at w_F. This group represents pure destitutes, who have to fight for bare survival even during an average year. Their situation becomes precarious in off-peak months. In recent years specialized works programs have been implemented in some countries, including Bangladesh,[33] to alleviate the suffering of this group. But the situation becomes untenable and assumes famine dimensions when there is a drastic shortfall in employment opportunities during lean months of the year indicated by a leftward shift in $D(L_R)$. Historically, many famines in the Indian subcontinent have been associated with lack of employment and limited efforts have been made by the government to create additional employment through relief works. The preoccupation of Indian famine codes (referred to above) with management of relief works in times of famine is quite understandable.[34]

To extend the analysis further, it may be noted that w_R fluctuates depending on the variation of L_F and $\bar{L}$ over time, which is related to population and labor force growth and also to the possibility of shift of labor from agricultural activity to nonagricultural activity. Such a shift, which affects $S(L_N)$ in Figure 2.3, will, to a certain extent, depend on employment opportunities in the nonagricultural activity given by $D(L_N)$ and the prevailing market determined wage rate w_N. $S(L_N)$ is thus comparable to $S(L_R)$ but w_N is a shade above w_R. The difference represents the transfer cost between the two sectors. This sector, too, normally carries excess labor supply at wage level w_N. The excess is absorbed partially in self-employment in nonformal sectors with very low return for labor, that is, the urban destitute is one of the first victims of a famine.

Capital Market

We shall be concerned primarily with the rural capital market, which is segmented on both the lenders' side as well as the borrowers' side. Supply of funds in the capital market being, by and large, short of the total requirements of the different classes of borrowers, the terms of loans are usually dictated by lenders. Rural households borrow primarily for current consumption or current capital expenditure. The majority of consumption loans are "survival" loans (pure consumption or distress loans) for low-income households. All types of loans are obtained from three sources: organized institutions such as agricultural banks and cooperatives, friends and relatives, and professional moneylenders and traders. Other intermediate groups supplying credit may be identified, and groups may overlap. Let us examine more closely the three markets and their characteristics.

Organized credit institutions obtain their capital from various governmental sources. Historically, these institutions have not been able to mobilize a significant amount of resources from within rural areas to carry out credit operations on their own. The total capital base is relatively small; in general, these institutions account for less than one-fifth of total loans negotiated in a year. The interest rate is fixed at a low level by central and cooperative bank regulations. Loans are primarily meant for capital expenditure, but usually a significant part leaks into consumption. The borrowers in this market are mainly large and medium farmers. Small farmers, landless laborers, and other low-income households have little or no access to this market. Figure 2.4 shows the situation prevailing in the organized capital market in rural areas at any

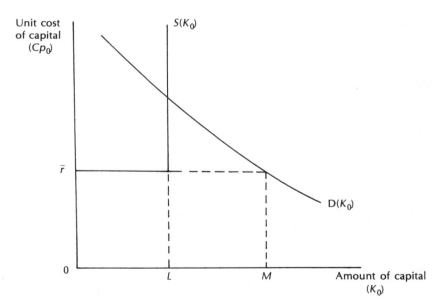

Figure 2.4. Organized capital market in rural areas.

point in time. Supply of capital is fixed at OL and at the ruling interest rate $O\bar{r}$ there is excess demand for capital of the amount LM. Clearly, these institutions are unable to satisfy the needs of the deficit families. The problem is not only lack of funds but also of the inefficiency and inequity of these institutions and the people involved in their management. This comment is particularly relevant for the functioning of rural cooperatives.[35] Unfortunately, the cooperatives are an important channel through which the government provides emergency loans to the famine-affected households in rural areas.

The unorganized rural capital market accounts for about four-fifths of the total loans negotiated. Friends and relatives provide about one-fifth of the total loans, and they constitute a special category of lenders in that they charge little or no interest. Both low-income and middle-income households fall back on this source from time to time to tide them over difficult periods of relatively short duration. The problem is that the supply of this type of capital is relatively inelastic and the market itself functions on the basis of nonprice considerations, such as patron-client relationship and other forms of social relations that bind the contracting parties. During a period of distress, this market provides a cushion for potential deficit families, but in times of a disaster these sources tend to dry up sooner than expected.

The portion of the unorganized rural capital market dominated by professional moneylenders and traders requires careful analysis to understand how it works, particularly in explaining the prevalence of usurious interest rates.[36] There are two segments of this market, one catering to "survival" loans and the other to "nonsurvival" loans. In these segments, both marketable and nonmarketable securities are used as collateral,[37] the latter being more prevalent among poorer groups. As can be seen from Figure 2.5, demand for "survival" loan $D(K_s)$ is characterized by a perfectly inelastic segment. During any year, depending on the extent of the deficit of poor households, the amount of "survival" loan required is given by OQ but above a unit cost of Or_s^1 some households start dropping out of the market, and we get the elastic segment AB. Supply of credit $S(K_s)$ is also inelastic, implying that an increase in the amount of capital supplied is associated with acceptance of relatively more risky collateral compared with the previous unit. The lower bound $O\bar{r}_s$ is given by the opportunity cost of capital elsewhere in the economy.[38] The unit cost of capital for this part of the unorganized market is then Or_s^2 at which the amount of "survival" loan funds utilized is OP. Thus, in a strict market interpretation, supply equals demand, but, in reality, PQ amount of survival requirement remains unfulfilled. Like previous examples, households falling in this zone are destitute. In a scarcity or famine period the demand curve shifts to the right (basic survival requirement

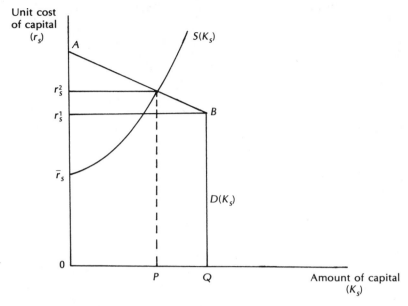

Figure 2.5. Unorganized capital market in rural areas for survival loans.

increases) and the supply curve shifts to the left implying an increase in the number of destitute households and an increase in the unit cost of survival loans. As will be seen later, data from earlier famines as well as the 1974 Bangladesh famine support this analysis.

The unorganized rural capital market for "nonsurvival" loans, which includes loans for capital expenditure in agriculture and related activities, is shown in Figure 2.6. The market clearing unit cost of capital is Or_{ns}, and $O\bar{r}_{ns}$ is the same as $O\bar{r}_s$ in Figure 2.5. The vertical segment in the supply curve shows the upper limit on the availability of internal finance at any point in time. On the other hand, OT represents the maximum amount of capital required for optimum utilization of other resources (particularly land) in production. The supply of capital at any price apparently falls short of this limit under the existing technology and propensity to save in rural areas.

Product Markets

In the three product markets (rice, other agricultural products, nonagricultural products), prices are determined by simple demand and supply considerations. For a given level of income and money supply, demand for nonrice products and nonagricultural products can be taken

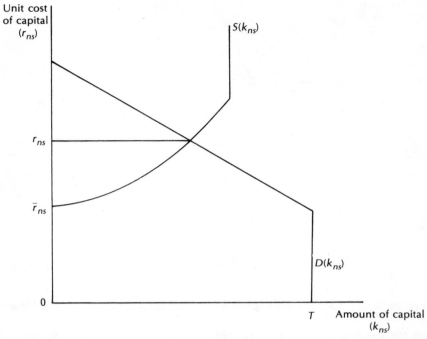

Figure 2.6. Unorganized capital market in rural areas for nonsurvival loans.

to be a function of prices. Supply is given by cost considerations that are derived, among others, from production conditions. Other things remaining the same, supply of the product in the market is a function of price. For rice, the situation needs to be investigated more closely because of its importance for survival in these countries. Some producers of rice consume a part and sell a part. But the majority of rural households are either in deficit in varying degrees or produce just enough for their own consumption (subsistence). For surplus households, own consumption has a pure survival component and an income- and price-induced component. A higher production will imply a higher real income and will increase own consumption. On the other hand, market price will determine how much of the output in excess of the pure subsistence requirement will be marketed. Thus, given the production level and prices of other commodities, marketed supply of rice will be a function of its own price.

On the other hand, given the production level and wages, demand for rice will also be a function of price. The participants in this market are surplus farmers on the supply side, and deficit farmers and wage earners on the demand side. The rice market is shown in Figure 2.7. $D(f)$ and $S(f)$ represent demand for and supply of foodgrains (rice). 00″ shows the maximum possible market supply given production level and the pure subsistence requirement of surplus households. The situation is sometimes compounded by government interventions in terms of internal and external procurement of rice and its sale in the domestic market at a subsidized price under the rationing system, which raises the real income of those who can avail themselves of this facility. In Figure 2.7, 00′ is the rationed supply and $0P_r$ is the rationed price. To the extent that the system of rationing is effective in the sense that people buy as much as they can at rationed price and no rice from the rationing system leaks into the free market, the market price itself will be determined by supply and demand, although the extent of transaction is reduced by the amount of rationed supply, as shown in Figure 2.7.

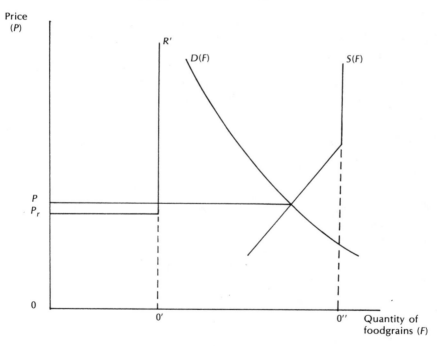

Figure 2.7. Foodgrain market.

Famine Syndrome Revisited

The above system of production activities and market relations with little or no change in technological endowments in the countries under consideration produces a quasi-equilibrium solution with a low level of real income per capita that, in turn, implies a low level of foodgrain intake per capita, the factor that was earlier observed to be very closely related to the initiation of a famine syndrome. Over the years, values of other variables change, but income per capita and foodgrain intake per capita tend to fluctuate between poverty and famine level. As the previous analysis indicated, this equilibrium, at any point in time, is associated with excess supply of some factors such as labor and excess demand for others such as land and capital. The essential economic characteristics of the solution are price differentials between segmented markets for final products and factors of production and nonmarket clearing prices.

In a normal year, social arbitration, patron-client relationships, kinship bond, and occasional intervention from the government and international agencies keep the system from sliding below a crisis point in terms of decline in real income per capita, and consequent fall in foodgrain intake per capita. The relationship between the two is shown in Figure 2.8. An upper limit to per capita foodgrain intake is indicated by $\bar{f}$. For simplicity, the relationship is assumed to be linear. The structure of a famine-prone economy enunciated above indicates that per capita income of a major segment of the population fluctuates between poverty level (y_p) and famine level (y_f) which implies foodgrain intake between f_p and f_f. This outcome can be projected into Figure 2.8(a), which shows a hypothetical relationship between the death rate and foodgrain intake. As foodgrain intake persists between the above-mentioned critical bounds or approaches f_p, the death rate starts rising above normal level indicated by d_n in Figure 2.8(a), but apparently the difference with the norm does not become very pronounced until f falls below f_f. This is where the famine syndrome is initiated. However, as indicated in Figure 1.1, the transition from foodgrain intake decline below critical level into the famine zone characterized by excess mortality is not necessarily a direct one. The society passes through a number of famine substates before entering the excess mortality zone. It remains to be discussed, however, which chain of events cause a decline in foodgrain intake per capita in such an economy.

CAUSAL SEQUENCES LEADING TO FOODGRAIN INTAKE DECLINE PER CAPITA

As shown in Figure 2.8, foodgrain intake decline can occur due to a drop in real income. But there are other factors that may directly affect the existing level of foodgrain intake. From Figure 2.9 one can easily see

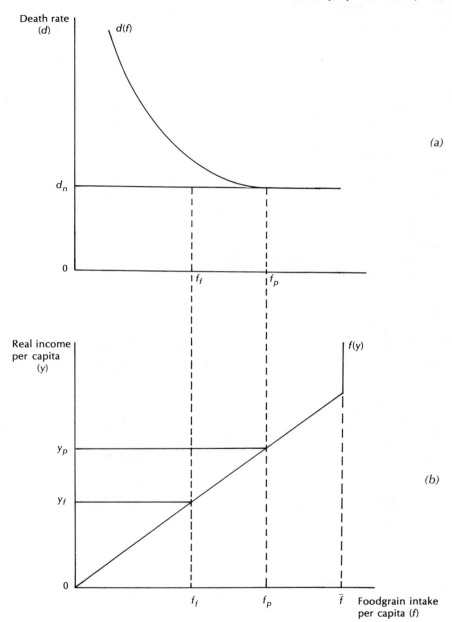

Figure 2.8. (a) Famine syndrome; (b) real income and foodgrain intake.

that the other immediate factors causing a drastic fall in foodgrain intake include a sharp fall in foodgrain availability per capita, a sharp increase in foodgrain prices, absence of social security, and inadequate institutional arrangements to cope with the effect of a food shortage. A certain amount of interaction between these factors is also indicated. The relative importance of each of these factors may differ depending on the situation under consideration, yet any analysis of famine must include a careful investigation of all of them.

Famine as a general phenomenon may occur through a combination of foodgrain availability decline per capita and inadequate institutional arrangements to cope with the effect of food shortage. This type of famine, therefore, is unlikely to occur in modern times except under exceptional circumstances such as war. Even in the past there were not many instances in which general famine occurred. Similarly, famine as a local/regional phenomenon can occur through foodgrain availability decline per capita, inadequate institutional arrangements to cope with the effect of food shortage, and real income decline per capita. Finally, famine as a class phenomenon can occur through any one or a combination of situations depicted in Figure 2.9. The world has perhaps witnessed more of this type of famine than the other two. It may be mentioned here that experience varies regarding the relationship between loss of body weight and death.[39] But it seems inevitable that for death to occur on a large scale within a relatively short period as experienced during a famine, the average observed figure for foodgrain intake must fall much below the national level of f_f (or else for intake to be close to f_f for an extended period prior to famine, which is true for the poor). Such a drastic decline in foodgrain intake is likely to be concentrated among the poorer sections of the population for whom no institutional support exists to replace that once provided by the traditional society in times of emergency.

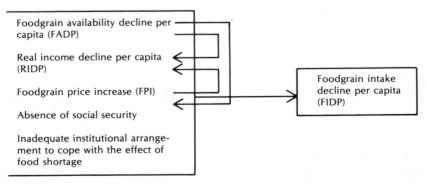

Figure 2.9. Factors causing foodgrain intake decline per capita.

Foodgrain Availability Decline Per Capita

Other things remaining the same, a decline in foodgrain availability for a consuming unit will reduce its intake. In a purely subsistence economy, where each accounting unit consumes what it produces (except saving for input requirement), a famine may occur from availability decline precipitated by production shortfall, and each unit will be affected to the extent of availability shortfall. In an exchange economy, availability shortfall will imply shortfall in own production and/or shortfall in the amount that could be obtained through exchange. However, for purposes of analysis, the conventional definition of availability needs to be extended to include geographical distribution, interclass distribution, and seasonal distribution. From the point of view of famine analysis, these dimensions of availability are important. It is also necessary to distinguish between the stock and flow concepts of availability. On the one hand, one should know what the stock of foodgrains was at different points in time before and during the famine. On the other hand, it is also important to capture the flow variables. The famine intervention policies should be directed toward both. For the country as a whole, stock of foodgrain at time period t is given by

$$S(t) = Q(t-1) + M(t-1) + A^P(t-1) + A^G(t-1)$$
$$+ A^T(t-1) - C(t-1) - X(t-1) - L(t-1) \tag{2.1}$$

where

$S(t)$	= stock at the beginning of period t
$Q(t-1)$	= net production during period $t-1$
$M(t-1)$	= imports during period $t-1$
$A^P(t-1)$	= private stock carryover from period $t-2$
$A^G(t-1)$	= government stock carryover from period $t-2$
$A^T(t-1)$	= trading stock carryover from period $t-2$
$C(t-1)$	= consumption during period $t-1$
$X(t-1)$	= exports during period $t-1$
$L(t-1)$	= leakage from the system during period $t-1$.

Production is considered as net, after account has been taken of seed, feed, and wastages. Leakage here refers to smuggling or some unforeseen loss. For a particular region, the above relationship should be modified slightly. We use superscript R to refer to a region.

$$S^R(t) = Q^R(t-1) + O^R(t-1) - I^R(t-1) + A^{PR}(t-1) + A^{TR}(t-1)$$
$$+ M^R(t-1) - C^R(t-1) - X^R(t-1) - L^R(t-1) \qquad (2.2)$$

where

$O^R(t-1)$ = government offtake in region R during period $t-1$

$I^R(t-1)$ = internal procurement in region R during period $t-1$.

Here offtake from government stocks is relevant since neither imports nor government stock carryover can be related directly to any specific region, although probably one could refer to a policy parameter α_R, which will represent the fraction of imports preassigned to region R and also to A^{GR}_{t-2}, which will stand for government stock carryover from period $t-2$ located in region R. If a region does not have a government storage facility, this term will be zero. M and X now refer to interregional trade flows.

For any household, stock at the beginning of the period t will be given by

$$S^H(t) = Q^H(t-1) + R^H_m(t-1) - R^H_x(t-1) + A^H(t-1) + E^H_M(t-1)$$
$$- E^H_X(t-1) - C^H(t-1) - I^H(t-1) + O^H(t-1) + G^H(t-1)$$
$$+ w^H_m(t-1) - w^H_x(t-1) - L^H(t-1) \qquad (2.3)$$

where

$R^H_m(t-1)$ = produce share rental receipt by household H in period $t-1$

$R^H_x(t-1)$ = produce share rental payment by household H in period $t-1$

$E^H_m(t-1)$ = receipt from other units (household or trading) through market exchange by household H during period $t-1$

$E^H_x(t-1)$ = transfer to other units through market exchange by household H during period $t-1$

$G^H(t-1)$ = gifts and credit received (net) in kind by household H during period $t-1$

$w^H_m(t-1)$ = wages received in kind by household H during period $t-1$

$w^H_x(t-1)$ = wages paid in kind by household H during period $t-1$

$O^H(t-1)$ = purchase from government offtake by household H during period $t-1$.

Availability during a period of time considered as a flow will be given by the following.

At the national level,

$$F(t) = Q(t) + M(t) - S(t) - X(t) - L(t) \tag{2.4}$$

$$\text{or} \quad = Q(t) + S^P(t) - \triangle S^P(t) - \triangle S^T(t) + O(t) - I(t) - X(t) - L(t) \tag{2.5}$$

$$f(t) = F(t)/P(t) \quad \text{or} \quad F(t)/\bar{P}(t) \tag{2.6}$$

where

$S(t)$ = net changes in total stock during period t

$\triangle S^P(t)$ = net changes in private stock during period t

$\triangle S^T(t)$ = net changes in trading stock during period t

$S^P(t)$ = private stock at the beginning of period t

$P(t)$ = mid-period population during period t

$\bar{P}(t)$ = mid-period adjusted (for adult equivalence) population during period t

$f(t)$ = foodgrain availability per capita during period t.

Emphasis here is placed on determining the amount that is available for consumption, whether actually consumed or not. Therefore, current production, private stocks, and government offtake add to current availability and increase in trading stock, internal procurement, exports, and leakages reduce it. However, one should be careful about double counting. For example, if a part or the entire amount of $I(t)$ is exported then this should be deducted from $X(t)$. During periods of crisis, knowledge about population size adjusted for age-sex composition, may turn out to be crucial from the point of view of organizing famine relief. For a given P, a bottom heavy population (that is, high proportion of children) will require less foodgrains. It is also important to realize that if an acute shortage appears, the children are likely to be the first victims, if not for any other reason than inequitable distribution of foodgrains within the family. This has been observed during normal times as well as during famines.[40]

At the regional level foodgrain availability can be defined as

$$F^R(t) = Q^R(t) + O^R(t) - \triangle S^R(t) + M^R(t)$$
$$- X^R(t-1) - I^R(t) - L^R(t) \tag{2.7}$$

or $\quad = Q^R(t) + O^R(t) + S^{PR}(t) - \triangle S^{PR}(t) - \triangle S^{TR}(t) + M^R(t) - X^R(t)$

$\qquad - I^R(t) - L^R(t)$ $\hfill (2.8)$

$$f^R(t) = \frac{F^R(t)}{P^R(t)} \qquad \text{or} \qquad \frac{F^R(t)}{\bar{P}^R(t)} \hfill (2.9)$$

For a typical household, foodgrain availability can be defined in terms of potential flow within the command of the household. Therefore,

$$F^H(t) = Q^H(t) + S^H(t) + R_m^H(t) - R_x^H(t) - I^H(t) + G^H(t) + w_m^H(t)$$

$$- w_x^H(t) - L^H(t) + \bar{O}^H(t) - E_x^H(t) + \left[P_{Fx}^H(t) \cdot E_x^H(t) \right.$$

$$+ Y_{NF}^H(t) + W_R(t)L_R^H(t) + \sum_{i=1}^{n} P_{Ki}K_i(t) + W_N(t)L_N^H(t)$$

$$\left. - P_r(t)\bar{O}^H(t) \right] / P_F(t)$$

$\hfill (2.10)$

$$f^H(t) = \frac{F^H(t)}{P^H(t)} \qquad \text{or} \qquad F^H(t) / \bar{P}^H(t) \hfill (2.11)$$

where $\bar{O}^H(t)$ = amount of government distributed foodgrain assigned to household H during period t

$\quad P_{Fx}^H(t)$ = sale price of foodgrain during period t

$\quad Y_{NF}^H(t)$ = nonfoodgrain income of household H during period t

$\quad W_R$ = wage-rate (money) in rural activity during period t

$\quad W_N$ = wage-rate (money) in nonrural activity during period t

$\quad L_R^H(t)$ = wage employment in rural activity for household H during period t

$\quad L_N^H(t)$ = wage employment in nonrural activity for household H during period t

$\quad K_i(t)$ = amount of asset i available for sale during period t

$\quad P_{Ki}$ = sale price of capital asset i during period t

$\quad P_r(t)$ = price of government distributed foodgrain during period t

$\quad P_F(t)$ = purchase price of foodgrain during period t.

In the above, time reference t can be so adjusted as to enable one to analyze the seasonal dimension of the problem. Foodgrain availability, real income and foodgrain prices have often been found to observe certain seasonal patterns, and, if there are exogenous shocks occurring during the lean season, chances are that the situation will assume catastrophic proportions, and many people will be victims of famine. Relationships (2.5), (2.8) and (2.10) provide a basic framework to analyze famine. They combine all the elements in Figure 2.9 that may precipitate a famine. A shortfall in $F^H(t)$, $F^R(t)$, and $F(t)$ is an indication of a general famine. Regional famine can occur with no change in $F(t)$ but with a sharp decline in $F^R(t)$ and $F^H(t)$, while a class famine can occur with or without a decline $F(t)$ and/or $F^R(t)$, the important characteristics in this case being that decline in $F^H(t)$ is limited to specific groups.

Shortfall or decline should be measured in relation to the nonfamine normal period. Therefore, a slightly modified definition of foodgrain availability in terms of command over flow of foodgrains has provided us with a powerful tool to study famine. A sharp decline in foodgrain availability per capita will necessarily result in a decline in foodgrain intake per capita and lead to a sequence of events culminating in excess deaths (Figure 1.1 and Figure 2.8). Clearly, this can happen with foodgrain availability decline as conventionally measured—refer to relation (2.5) and (2.8)—real income decline, and sharp increase in food prices. Also, the other two factors are entered into the above relations through mechanisms of transfer embodied in government foodgrain distribution and gifts and credit. One could, as we attempt to do for the 1974 Bangladesh famine, use the above three relationships to determine the extent to which each factor was responsible for initiating the famine syndrome and which classes of people suffered most. One can also, if one wants to, use this framework to predict what can happen in the future and where government and relevant agencies can possibly intervene to prevent a recurrence of famine.

However, a complete analysis will require further penetration in terms of causal analysis so that each one of the components on the right hand side of (2.5), (2.8), and (2.10) can be predicted with a certain degree of confidence. Let us first concentrate on (2.5) and (2.8) only. Figure 2.10 shows that a decline in $F(t)$ or $F^R(t)$ can be caused by any combination of a given number of factors. In addition to the elements contained in relationships (2.5) and (2.8), Figure 2.10 identifies several other structural factors that could not be directly incorporated in those expressions.

Foodgrain Production

At the national level, foodgrain production is determined by land availability, crop yield, natural environmental factors, and the socio-political and administrative environment. At the household level, social

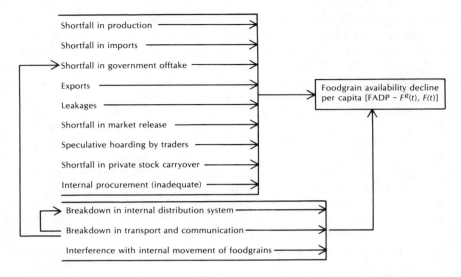

Figure 2.10. Causal sequences of foodgrain availability decline per capita.

structure reflected in tenurial status, size of landholding, and other assets (such as agricultural implements, draft power, and so forth) are factors affecting production. One can now say that foodgrain availability decline may occur due to a shortfall in production, which can be caused by natural factors, low crop yield, war, civil commotion, inefficient government management, and changes in agrarian structure (Figure 2.11).

Natural factors causing shortfall in foodgrain production include flood, drought, excessive rainfall, earthquake, volcanic eruption, cyclone, wind storm, river erosion, changes in the course of river, water logging, salinity, tidal bore, frost and snow, crop disease, crop pest and locust, livestock disease, and epidemic. Flood may be caused by river siltation and/or excessive rainfall, while flood itself sometimes causes changes in the course of a river. Shortfall in river water flow will lead to the problem of salinity intrusion in the lower reaches of the river. Excessive withdrawal of ground and surface water is likely to aggravate the situation (Figure 2.12). Deforestation of mountain slopes leads to fast surface runoff of rainwater, increasing the risk of flooding of plains. Surface runoff creates two additional problems; it results in loss of top soil, which reduces productivity of land on the upper slopes and it causes siltation of rivers and streams in the plains, which compounds the flood problem. Similarly, drought may be caused by deforestation of the plains. Apparently, natural disaster is purely an exogenous shock to the system,

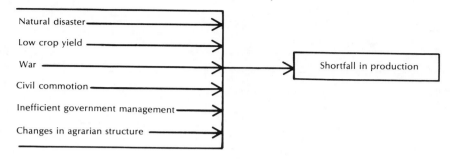

Figure 2.11. Factors causing shortfall in production.

and it can occur quite unexpectedly with such an intensity that the existing institutions fail completely to cope with the situation. Despite sustained efforts by scientists, prediction of natural calamities remains a very difficult task. The existing forewarning systems are sometimes useful to avoid direct loss of human lives and property damage, but so far as reducing the impact on standing or stored crops is concerned, nothing much can be done within a very short period. Prevention in such cases requires long-run measures. Unfortunately, most famine-prone areas of the world today are also areas frequented by natural disasters.

Crop Yield

Crop yield is a function of rainfall, irrigation water, fertilizer, other inputs, labor, supervision, and draft power. Therefore, a decline in crop yield originates from a shortfall of any one of these factors. Shortfall in rainfall can affect crop yield directly or indirectly by reducing the supply of water for irrigation. Irrigation may also be adversely affected by interruption of water flow in the main channel as a result of withdrawal in the upper reaches (which sometimes causes interregional or international disputes), depletion of ground water reserve, breakdown of irrigation equipment and nonavailability of fuel. Inefficient management at various levels often leads to breakdown of irrigation equipment and sudden scarcity of fuel.

Similarly, inefficient management and shortage of credit may adversely affect the supply of irrigation water, fertilizer, other inputs, and draft animals. The situation is further compounded by the skewed distribution of power and resources, which leads to low crop yield, output, and income for certain groups in the society, laying the foundation for or aggravating a class famine situation. Availability of credit

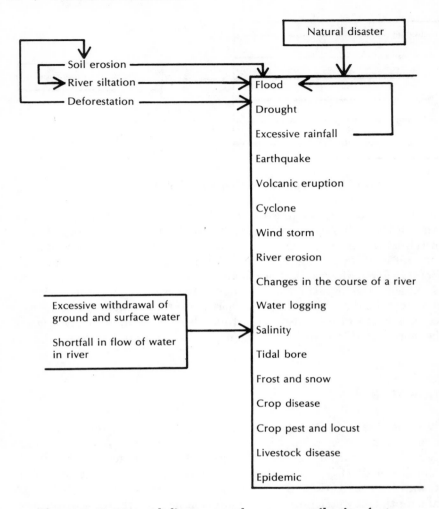

Figure 2.12. Natural disasters and some contributing factors.

reflects the internal resource position of rural society, intersectoral flow of funds through government and private channels, and, above all, the influence of government policies with respect to allocation of resources between the foodgrain sector and other sectors. Needless to say, the overall resource position of the country will depend on the effectiveness of instruments for mobilization of domestic and foreign resources. On the other hand, supply of fertilizer and other inputs to ultimate users may decline due to production shortfall, import shortfall, and distribution bottlenecks. Shortage of imported inputs (for example, fertilizers and pesticides) may seriously affect production. Natural disaster, war, and so forth, affect production of inputs and create distribution bottlenecks; they also lead to shortage of labor, inadequate supervision, and shortage of draft animals. A sudden change in agrarian structure could upset the balance in a manner such that all factors are adversely affected. The causal sequence with respect to low crop yield is shown in Figure 2.13.

Foodgrain Import

Imports are a function of domestic production, population, total foreign exchange resources, import prices, and government policy. However, import planning and the international supply situation also figure prominently in the determination of imports. Therefore, a shortfall in imports may occur due to inadequate foreign exchange resources, sharp increases in import prices, supply shortage in the international market, poor import planning, and government policy with respect to allocation of foreign exchange between purchase of foodgrains and inputs for foodgrain production, on the one hand, and imports of other items, on the other. Lack of foreign exchange resources may arise from poor export performance, inadequate foreign capital inflow, and unusual international price movements. Import price rise and supply shortage in the international market are caused by any one or a combination of such factors as production shortfall in exporting countries, depletion of world stock, increased world absorption, domestic policies of exporting and other importing countries, increased cost of production, and international inflation. Some of these issues were referred to in Chapter 1. The import sequence is presented in Figure 2.14.

Other Causes of Foodgrain Availability Decline

The causes of a shortfall in production, as indicated in Figure 2.11, can also be responsible for breakdown of the internal distribution system, breakdown of transport and communication, speculative hoarding by traders, shortfall in market release, and shortfall in private stocks carryover. Trading stock and market release are also influenced by the rate of inflation, rate of increase of foodgrain prices, previous period's production level, status of standing crop, and prolonged retention of marketable foodgrain by farmers. Shortfall in government offtake can be caused by inadequate stock and storage carryover and unforeseen storage loss or destruction. Poor planning and government policy may both affect foodgrain stock while natural disaster, war, and so forth will lead to storage loss. Furthermore, government offtake may be directly affected

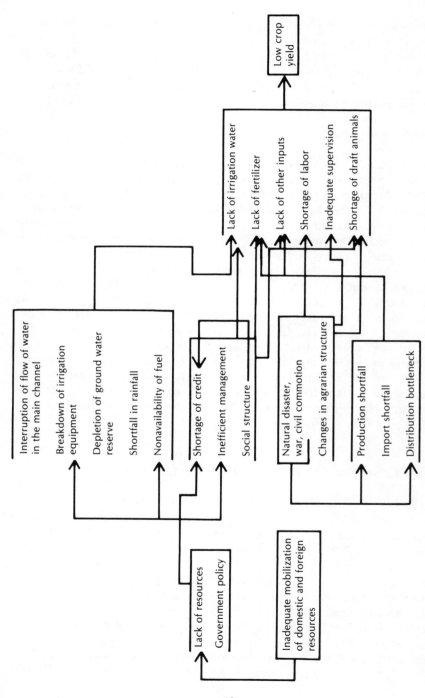

Figure 2.13. Casual sequences explaining low crop yield.

40

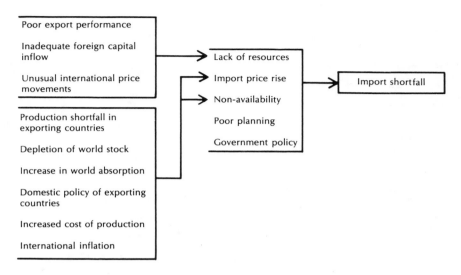

Figure 2.14. Causal sequences leading to import shortfall.

by breakdown of transportation and communication systems. Leakages through smuggling are caused by price differentials between neighboring countries, maintenance of an artificial exchange rate at home, inadequate border policing, and general lack of confidence in the economy, giving rise to a tendency for capital flight. War and inefficient government management feed into this process. Government policy and price differentials are responsible for exports across boundaries of nations and regions. Export of foodgrains can clearly aggravate a simple shortage situation into a famine. Government policies of internal procurement and interference in the internal movement of foodgrains may worsen the situation during shortage, precipitating a famine. The above causal sequences leading ultimately to foodgrain availability decline per capita are shown in Figure 2.15.

Real Income Decline and Foodgrain Price Increase

Relationship (2.10) shows that foodgrain availability, understood broadly, is also linked with the real income of households and foodgrain prices. In other words, a decline in $F^H(t)$ may be contributed to by real income decline and foodgrain price increase. In addition, a fall in the value of saleable assets may also adversely affect the situation. Real income is affected by output, level of economic activity, employment, rate of inflation, real wages, demand, terms of trade, and social (agrarian)

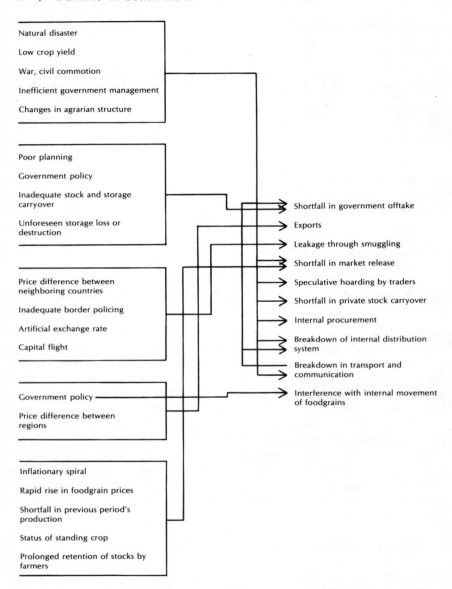

Figure 2.15. Other causes of foodgrain availability decline.

structure. Output, particularly of the nonfoodgrain type, may be affected by government policy and inefficient management in addition to the factors already considered. Similarly, disruption in normal economic activity and fall in employment may be caused by natural disaster, war, and so forth and also by shortfall in demand, which, in turn, is caused by shortfall in output. It is well known that shortfall in output also contributes to inflation. Monetary expansion and international inflation may add to domestic inflation, and all of these are affected by government policy. Inflation leads to a fall in real wages, which is also contributed to by shortfall in demand. Government policy has a direct bearing on intersectoral terms of trade.

The other factor, foodgrain price increase, is caused by foodgrain availability decline $(F(t), F^R(t))$, incidence of panic purchase by consumers, increases in cost of imports, increase in money supply, and government policy. It will be necessary to carefully analyze the foodgrain market. For prediction of foodgrain prices one can estimate a price equation while the problem is more complex in the case of real income. One may either extrapolate the values of certain determinants of income or construct a simple model to determine employment and wage level that, along with prices, will give real income. The relevant causal sequences for real income and foodgrain price are shown in Figure 2.16.

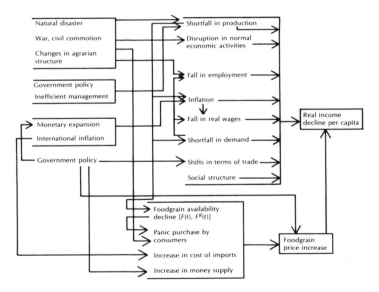

Figure 2.16. Causal sequences leading to real income decline per capita and foodgrain price increase.

restored, the society is confronted with the outcome of a few processes that have both positive and negative impacts on foodgrain availability per capita. Admittedly, the outcome on balance is quite uncertain, but the recent history of the societies under consideration indicates that any gain is unlikely to be sustained over a long period of time. Given the fact that following famine, the society is basically back to the operational framework represented in Figures 2.2 through 2.8, one can only predict the restoration of the original equilibrium.

The causative analysis of famine presented in Figures 1.1 and 2.9 through 2.17 can now be summarized in Figure 2.18. Alternative causal sequences contribute to factors that immediately lead to the famine syndrome consisting of foodgrain intake decline, famine substates, and excess deaths to which society reacts in certain ways, and adjustment processes set in to restore the original low-income–low-foodgrain intake equilibrium.

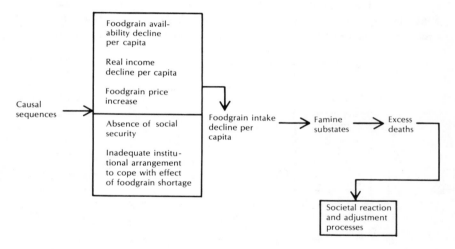

Figure 2.18. Summary view of causal sequences of famine.

SOME HYPOTHESES AND POSSIBLE SCENARIOS

The analytical framework presented to study famine can be applied widely, although specific cases may require some modification of the basic structure. In the present context, it will be necessary to carry out a fairly elaborate analysis to identify the causal sequence in a typical famine-prone region of the Third World, such as Bangladesh, and also to indicate the nature, timing, and point of intervention by the government and other concerned institutions. Out of a large number of hypotheses that emerge from the causal sequences described, a few should be singled out because of their importance in the literature. It is a strong feature of the framework presented here that these hypotheses emerge naturally, and they can be put to test for ultimate acceptance or rejection in a given situation.

1. The most obvious hypothesis is that a famine is caused by a serious shortage in the total availability of foodgrains and substitutes. This, of course, will apply to all types of famine. One can then proceed to examine whether all the famines of the past occurred due to food shortage or whether there were instances of famine without food shortage.

2. A second hypothesis would call for the examination of the proposition that famine can occur from lack of purchasing power or, to use Sen's terminology, from a sharp deterioration of exchange entitlement.[41] A shift in exchange entitlement reflects a shift in the balance of class power in the society that may lead to class famine. One can examine the trend of real income of various classes in the society to determine whether there was a significant decline during the period under consideration. In addition, one can look at the market for assets to establish how far people were able to sustain themselves through liquidation of assets.

3. Substitution of market and exchange economies for a subsistence economy introduces many new factors that may contribute to initiation of foodgrain scarcity or famine. This view needs to be moderated to the extent the existence of market lessens the probability of purely local famines by allowing distribution of output to areas hit by temporary disaster and/or by allowing the deficit households to sell labor power and assets to buy others' surplus. However, history of famines indicates that once major crisis signals are triggered off, markets tend to feed on one another and lead the situation to a point of no return. The crisis moderating role of the market comes only as a part of the postfamine adjustment process.

4. A hypothesis related to (2) and (3) is presented by Sen. The possibility of famine increases with "the emergence of labor-power as a commodity, with neither the protection of the family system or peasant agriculture, nor the insurance of unemployment compensation—nor, of course, the guarantee of the right to work at a living wage."[42] One can put forward a corresponding hypothesis that in modern times, a simple food shortage is aggravated into a famine due to the breakdown of traditional dependency relations. While it is not very difficult to see the logic of the arguments underlying these hypotheses, their validity is difficult to establish because of lack of data. The reason we emphasize these

POSTFAMINE ADJUSTMENT OF THE SOCIETY

Famine is caused by a decline in foodgrain availability as given in relationships (2.5), (2.8), and (2.10). One can also refer to the corresponding per capita relationships. From the above, it is apparent that a large number of causal sequences may lead to the famine syndrome. However, it is contended here that possibly more than one sequence operate simultaneously, reinforcing one another so as to finally cause excess deaths—a disequilibrium situation. During famine, a set of forces gets underway to establish a new equilibrium for the society and economy. However, while certain parameters change as a consequence of famine (for example, population is reduced), the society basically reverts back to the low-income–low-foodgrain intake equilibrium as shown in Figure 2.8. The process of adjustment to the original equilibrium through a sequence of events is shown in Figure 2.17.

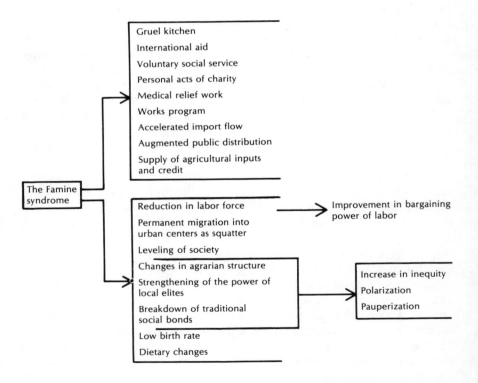

Figure 2.17. Postfamine adjustment processes.

As excess mortality from starvation and related diseases occur, the national government and international agencies take measures, though often belated and ineffective, to help the affected population. The measures include government-sponsored gruel kitchens (free cooked food distribution centers), emergency international aid and relief support, voluntary social service temporarily establishing an interpersonal resource transfer mechanism, personal acts of charity, medical relief work, work programs, acceleration of imports, augmented public distribution at subsidized prices, and emergency supply of agricultural inputs and credit. The time lag after which each of these relief instruments comes into operation depends on the situation under consideration, particularly on the sensitivity of the government to catastrophe and human suffering. By and large, such relief efforts continue until the government believes that the worst is over in terms of human mortality. In Bangladesh, during 1974, gruel kitchens were operating on a regular basis between October and November, while starvation is known to have occurred long before and after this period.

The famine syndrome indicates a number of processes in the society that facilitate restoration of the low-income–low-foodgrain intake equilibrium. Excess deaths reduce the labor force, thus improving the bargaining power of labor in certain localities. However, this gain is very short-lived; it is wiped out by new additions to the labor ranks through the process of pauperization and marginalization (owing to distress sale of assets) in rural areas, and permanent migration into urban centers as squatters. The power of the local elites is clearly enhanced since they gain command over a greater amount of productive resources and inequities in the society become even more pronounced. A general famine, however, can bring about a leveling of the society, while any type of famine causes leveling within the lowest stratum, which becomes even more homogeneous. Following famine, the agrarian structure tends to undergo changes. In the context of Bangladesh, some argue that the process of pauperization and polarization strengthens the semifeudal mode of production in agriculture although there is an opposing view that in modern times famine opens up a new vista for capitalist penetration in agriculture. The process of breakdown of the traditional social bonds continues, eliminating an informal support mechanism without replacing it with anything new. Sometimes a slow change in dietary pattern sets in, which may simplify the famine relief work or improve the normal foodgrain availability situation. Introduction of wheat in rice-eating regions is a case in point. Finally, famine reduces the birth rate and increases the death rate, thus having a long-run decelerating effect on high population growth regions with consequent positive impact on foodgrain availability. With normal production activities hypotheses is that they have important welfare implications for societies in transition. The issue is, is it so "bad to be traditional?" as some would like us to believe.

5. There are three contending hypotheses regarding the relationship between agrarian structure and famine in the Third World. These are (a) famine in modern times strengthens semifeudalism in agriculture; (b) famine facilitates penetration of capitalism in agriculture; and (c) penetration of capitalism in agriculture increases the possibility of famine. An examination of these hypotheses will require analysis of the mode of production dominating the agricultural sector and the laws of motion operating in the society. However, empirical tests may be devised to compare the situation before and after famine to determine the extent to which any one of the above assertions can be validated. But purely mechanistic tests may be misleading if they fail to reveal the dialectics of antagonistic classes in the society.

6. The more unequal the distribution of income generating assets, the greater the probability of intensity of famine. A class famine situation is triggered off or accentuated by an exogenous shock more easily if the command over productive assets is unevenly distributed. Empirically this can be tested with both longitudinal and cross-sectional data.

7. A region characterized by a low level of productive forces and a high rate of population growth is relatively more susceptible to famine. This is rather obvious and many instances can be found in history. While in the short run nothing much can be done on either front, long-run measures will have to be initiated to remove them as causes of famine.

8. Exploitative production relations aggravate the effect of a famine. Other things remaining the same, share croppers, tenants, and wage laborers are squeezed more during or prior to famine than at normal times by landowners, moneylenders, and other exploitative elements in the society. This is reflected in the postfamine societal adjustment sequence described above. It can be empirically established that the weaker sections of the population suffer specifically from a famine because of their poor bargaining position. Data on land sales, indebtedness, real-wage levels, and so forth can be analyzed to test this hypothesis.

9. Destabilizing price speculation in foodgrains can lead to or worsen a famine situation. This can be demonstrated very easily. A foodgrain price spiral will very soon reach a crisis point and in a short time will victimize the large section of the population that depends on the market for foodgrains.

10. Lack of seasonal or spatial arbitrage mechanisms can create and/or accentuate a famine situation. This is again easily verified. Seasonality in availability has, in many cases, created severe, although

temporary, distress. On the other hand, regional price differentials due to absence of smooth interregional flow of foodgrains can cause regional famine.

11. Uncoordinated world production, consumption, and storage policies will make the famine-prone regions of the world even more vulnerable to the hazards of famine. This has been observed in the international foodgrain crisis of recent years, reflected in unusual stock and price movements.

NOTES AND REFERENCES

1. A. K. Sen, "Starvation and Exchange Entitlements: A General Approach and Its Application to the Great Bengal Famine," *Cambridge Journal of Economics* 1(1):35 (March 1977).
2. See B. M. Bhatia, *Famines in India 1860–1965*, 2nd ed. (New Delhi: Asia Publishing House, 1967); Hari Shanker Srivastava, *The History of Indian Famines 1858–1918* (Agra: Sri Ram Mehra, 1968); R. A. Dalyell, *Memorandum on the Madras Famine of 1866* (Madras: Central Famine Relief Committee, 1867); Vaughan Nash, *The Great Famine and Its Causes* (London: Longmann, Green, 1900); Romesh C. Dutt, *Open Letters to Lord Curzon on Famines and Land Assessments in India* (London: Kegan Paul, Trench, Trubner, 1900); Prithwis Chandra Ray, *Indian Famines: Their Causes and Remedies* (Calcutta: Cherry Press, 1901); and Satischandra Ray, *An Essay on the Economic Causes of Famine in India and Suggestions to Prevent Their Frequent Recurrence* (Calcutta: Calcutta University, 1909).
3. W. R. Aykroyd, *The Conquest of Famine* (London: Chatto and Windus, 1974); G. B. Masefield, *Famine: Its Prevention and Relief* (Oxford: Oxford University Press, 1963); Arthur Lukyn Williams, *Famines in India: Their Causes and Possible Prevention* (London: Henry S. King, 1876); Walter H. Mallory, *China: Land of Famine* (New York: American Geographical Society, 1926); and C. Walford, "The Famines of the World: Past and Present," *Journal of the Statistical Society* 41(3):433–526 (September 1978).
4. Walford writes of "a famine, supposed to have extended more or less over the whole of Hindustan. Very severe in the Deccan. The Emperor Mahommed, it is said, was unable to procure the necessaries for his household," *Famines of the World*, p. 439.
5. See Irfan Habib, *The Agrarian System of Mughal India* (London: Asia Publishing House, 1963), pp. 102–104; and Aykroyd, *Conquest of Famine*, p. 52.
6. Sen, "Starvation and Exchange Entitlements."
7. Aykroyd, *Conquest of Famine*, pp. 31, 52.
8. See Walford, *Famines of the World*; Bhatia, *Famines in India*; Srivastava, *History of Indian Famines*; A. Loveday, *The History and Economics of Indian Famines* (London: G. Bell and Sons, 1914); Habib, *Agrarian System*; Aykroyd, *Conquest of Famine*; Mallory, *China*; and W. A. Dando, "Man-Made Famines: Some Geographical Insights from an Exploratory Study of a Millenium of Russian Famines," *Ecology of Food and Nutrition* 4:219–234 (1976).
9. M. Alamgir, *Bangladesh, A Case of Below Poverty Level Equilibrium Trap* (Dacca: Bangladesh Institute of Development Studies, 1978).
10. These concepts are discussed in ibid., pp. 2–3. See also M. Alamgir, "Some Analysis of Distribution of Income, Consumption, Saving and Poverty in Bangladesh," *Bangladesh Development Studies* 2(4):882 (October 1974).

11. In the context of Bangladesh these laws include increasing concentration of land-holding, inheritance laws resulting in subdivision and fragmentation of landholding, increasing landlessness, asset transfer, progressive deterioration of exchange entitlement, urban domination and disintegration of joint family, kinship, and community bonds. See Alamgir, *Bangladesh*, pp. 90–122.

12. Under normal circumstances, certain amounts of interpersonal and public transfer of resources provide limited support to the people below the poverty line. But governments of many Third-World countries, including Bangladesh, have so far failed to overcome social and political barriers and undertake fundamental reforms that will increase the command of the poorer groups of population over productive resources (for example, land and capital).

13. This is due to age distribution. Labor force growth, however, is lagging behind growth of working age population mainly because the labor force participation rate has shown a declining trend in recent years. See M. Alamgir, "Population Growth and Economic Activity of the Population in Bangladesh," a contribution to the country monograph on *Population Situation—Bangladesh*, prepared under the auspices of ESCAP/Bangladesh (forthcoming).

14. M. Alamgir, "Some Aspects of Bangladesh Agriculture: Review of Performance and Evaluation of Policies," *Bangladesh Development Studies* 3(3):261–300 (July 1975).

15. See M. Alamgir, *Famine 1974: Political Economy of Mass Starvation in Bangladesh*, Statistical Annexe, Part II, Dacca: Bangladesh Institute of Development Studies, 1977 (mimeo.); and F. Tomasson Jannuzi and James T. Peach, *Report on the Hierarchy of Interests in Land in Bangladesh*, U.S. Agency for International Development, Washington, D.C., September 1977.

16. Iftikhar Ahmed, "Employment in Bangladesh: Problems and Prospects," in *Economic Development of Bangladesh within the Framework of a Socialist Economy*, E. A. G. Robinson and Keith Griffin, eds. (London: Macmillan, 1974), pp. 241–250.

17. Alamgir, *Bangladesh*, pp. 93–101.

18. Ibid., pp. 29–32.

19. On characteristics of capital market in rural areas of South Asia, see Amit Bhaduri, "On the Formation of Usurious Interest Rates in Backward Agriculture," *Cambridge Journal of Economics* 1:341–352 (1977). See also Alamgir, *Bangladesh*, pp. 35, 75; M. Asaduzzaman and M. Hossain, "Some Aspects of Agricultural Credit in Bangladesh," Research Report (New Series), No. 18, Bangladesh Institute of Development Studies, Dacca, 1975; and M. Hossain, "Farm Size, Tenancy and Land Productivity: An Analysis of Farm Level Data in Bangladesh Agriculture," *Bangladesh Development Studies* 5(3):308–311 (July 1977).

20. Various surveys carried out in Bangladesh revealed that sharecropping was the single most important tenancy arrangement other than owner farming. See Alamgir, *Famine 1974*, p. 122; Hossain, "Farm Size," p. 301; and Raquibuz M. Zaman, "Sharecropping and Economic Efficiency in Bangladesh," *Bangladesh Economic Review* 1(2):149 (April 1973); and Jannuzi and Peach, *Hierarchy of Interests*, Table D-IV in Appendix.

21. Management implies the landowners retain physical control and all options. In terms of use, they may cultivate land themselves or through hired labor. On the other hand, they may also decide to keep a portion unutilized. It may be added that in a sharecropping arrangement, sometimes management options (input use and cropping decisions) are vested in the landlord.

22. See for example, P. K. Bardhan and T. N. Srinivasan, "Cropsharing Tenancy in Agriculture: A Theoretical and Empirical Analysis," *American Economic Review* 61(1):48–64 (1971); C. Bell, "Alternative Theories of Sharecropping: Some Tests Using Evidence from Northeast India," *Journal of Development Studies* 13(4):317–346 (1977); S. N. S. Cheung, *The Theory of Share Tenancy* (Chicago: University of Chicago

Press, 1969); D. M. G. Newbery, "The Choice of Rental Contract in Peasant Agriculture," in *Agriculture in Development Theory*, L. G. Reynolds, ed. (New Haven: Yale University Press, 1975), pp. 109–137; and J. D. Reid, Jr., "The Theory of Share-Tenancy Revisited Again," *Journal of Political Economy* 85(2):403–432 (1977).

23. Zaman, "Sharecropping and Economic Efficiency," pp. 153–154.
24. Mahbub Hossain, "Factors Affecting Tenancy: The Case of Bangladesh Agriculture," *Bangladesh Development Studies* 6(2):139–162 (Summer 1978).
25. Zaman, "Sharecropping and Economic Efficiency," pp. 159–160.
26. M. A. Jabbar, "Sharecropping and Economic Efficiency in Bangladesh—Comment," *Bangladesh Development Studies* 3(2):253–259 (April 1975).
27. Hossain, "Farm Size," pp. 292–296, 332.
28. For evidence on Bangladesh, see Hossain, "Farm Size"; and Government of Bangladesh, Bureau of Statistics, *Statistical Pocket Book of Bangladesh 1978* (Dacca: Bureau of Statistics, December 1977), p. 124.
29. Admittedly, this analysis is a simplified representation of a very complex phenomenon, but it is hoped that it throws light on the vulnerability of the tenants under the prevailing socio-economic environment of rural areas.
30. The wage productivity relationship has been found by many authors. See H. Leibenstein, "The Theory of Under-Employment in Backward Economies," *Journal of Political Economy* 65(2):91–103 (1957); D. Majumdar, "The Marginal Productivity Theory of Wages and Disguised Unemployment," *Review of Economic Studies* 26(71):190–197 (1959). Labor is measured here in terms of standard (at normal efficiency level) work unit (say, mandays or manhours).
31. Existence of famine wage rate in rural Bangladesh was recognized when a government sponsored works program, called Food-for-Work, employed workers at a wage rate (in foodgrain units) considered to satisfy basic survival requirements. For more on this, see M. Alamgir, "The Experience of Rural Works Programme in Bangladesh," in *Planning for Effective Public Works Programmes: Case Studies from Bangladesh, India and Pakistan* (Bangkok: U.N. Economic and Social Commission for Asia and the Pacific, 1979), pp. 11–68.
32. These and other related issues are discussed in H. Leibenstein, *Economic Backwardness and Economic Growth* (New York: Wiley, 1957), pp. 58–76; Mazumdar, "Marginal Productivity Theory," pp. 190–197; Hossain, "Farm Size," pp., 301–308; Edward J. Clay, "Institutional Change and Agricultural Wages in Bangladesh," *Bangladesh Development Studies* 4(4):00–00 (October 1976). For evidence on differential wages such as indicated by w_F and w_R, see Alamgir, "Rural Works Programme in Bangladesh," pp. 55–57. The situation depicted here seems to parallel capitalist firm behavior—for example, treating labor as a quasi-fixed factor—retaining idle or overpaid labor during some periods is a hedge against uncertain future needs. The fact that wages are not totally fixed by the external market is because in capitalism the firm creates internal labor markets to compensate for inefficiencies of the external one. I am grateful to Susan Horton for pointing this out to me.
33. See Alamgir, "Rural Works Programme in Bangladesh," pp. 11–68; A. K. Sen, *Employment, Technology and Development* (Oxford: Clarendon Press, 1975), pp. 135–145; World Bank, *Public Works Programs in Developing Countries: A Comparative Analysis*, Staff Working Paper No. 224, February 1976.
34. Bhatia, *Famines in India*; Srivastava, *History of Indian Famines*; Dalyell, *Madras Famine of 1866*; Nash, *Great Famine*; William Digby, *The Famine Campaign in Southern India 1876-1878* (London: Longmann, Green, 1878); *Report of the Indian Famine Commission 1901* (Calcutta: Office of the Superintendent of Government Printing, India, 1901).
35. See A. Abdullah, Mosharaff Hossain, and Richard Nations, "Agrarian Structure and

the IRDP: Preliminary Consideration," *Bangladesh Development Studies* 4(2):209–266 (April 1976); Alamgir, "Aspects of Bangladesh Agriculture," pp. 291–293.

36. Bhaduri, "Formation of Usurious Interest." The exposition given here has been influenced by his presentation.

37. Bhaduri identifies the following items being offered as collateral in this market: standing crops, free labor, already encumbered land, revision of tenurial condition, and so forth. See ibid., p. 343. Standing crops and land are marketable securities but the others are not.

38. Here we differ from Bhaduri by recognizing an exogenously given opportunity cost of capital for the lender.

39. For some discussion on the fatal degrees of weight loss, see Aykroyd, *Conquest of Famine*, pp. 13–14.

40. Ibid., p. 16. See also Lincoln C. Chen, "An Analysis of Per Capita Foodgrain Availability, Consumption and Requirements in Bangladesh: A Systematic Approach to Food Planning," *Bangladesh Development Studies* 3(2):93–126 (April 1975); Kamaluddin Ahmad (ed.), *Nutrition Survey of Rural Bangladesh* (Dacca: Institute of Nutrition and Food Science, December 1977), pp. 54–69.

41. Sen, "Starvation and Exchange Entitlements."

42. Ibid., p. 56.

Chapter 3

Indian Famines of the Past

In this chapter we shall selectively discuss a few famines of the past that are relatively better documented in order to bring out the causes, effects (on the economy and the society), and the actions taken by the government to remedy the situation. This is done with a view toward putting the 1974 Bangladesh famine in historic perspective as well as to see how far the framework presented in Chapter 2 can be applied in studying past famines. More attention will be given to famines in Bengal than in other regions. Two periods will be separately dealt with —pre-British and British India. There is not much detailed information available concerning famines during the first period, only some general references by historians.

FAMINES IN PRE-BRITISH INDIA

Walford,[1] writing in 1878, provides a list of seventeen famines that occurred in pre-British India. Loveday,[2] on the other hand, mentions forty. There is not much to quarrel about since the variation may simply be due to the differences in the sources consulted by the respective authors or in their definitions of famine. The authors do not indicate clearly which criterion they used to distinguish between a famine and a nonfamine situation. These numbers can be compared with a list of twenty-four localized famines between 1474 and 1670 presented in a history volume edited by Majumdar.[3] Discussing famines in Mughal, India, Habib[4] gives reference to as many as twenty-eight famines and local scarcities.

One of the most noted famines in ancient India occurred in Kashmir in 917–918, and is attributed to drought. The mortality is said to have been high.

> One could scarcely see the water in the Vitasta (Jehlem), entirely covered as the river was with corpses soaked and swollen by the water in which they had long been lying. The land became densely covered with bones in all directions, until it was like one great burial-ground, causing terror to all beings. The king's ministers and the Tantrins (guards) became wealthy, as they amassed riches by selling stores of rice at high prices. The king would take that person as minister who raised the sums due on the Tantrin's bills, selling the subjects in such a condition.[5]

This was evidently a class famine precipitated by foodgrain availability decline, combined with foodgrain price increase.[6] Excess mortality was a natural outcome since, as Loveday mentions, there is no evidence of steps being taken by the government to mitigate the distress.[7]

It is interesting to note that the state sometimes attempted to protect the residents of the capital city even if it meant suffering elsewhere in the country. Alauddin Khilji introduced a system of rationing in Delhi. Grain stores were created, and during famines a limited quantity was supplied at fixed prices. Many centuries later the British government tried to protect the residents of Calcutta from the great famine in 1943, using a similar program.[8]

Loveday was very critical of Alauddin Khilji's policy of interfering with the natural course of trade. According to him, the 1344–1345 famine during the reign of Mohammad Bin Tughlag can be attributed to the excessive land taxes that ruined the cultivators. Successive droughts from 1343 to 1345 only took the final toll, which was inevitable. He acknowledges, however, as do other authors, that the emperor took some action to help those affected. The measures adopted included advancing of loans and sinking of wells to provide cultivation, encouraging migration (people migrated to Bengal), bringing uncultivated land under cultivation, selling of provisions to people of Delhi (for six months) at fixed price, and distributing cooked food. This was perhaps one of the first instances when cooked food was distributed as relief. In more recent times, this has become a mainstay of famine relief. Another early example of remedial action was during the 1396 famine in southern India when "Sultan Mahmud kept a train of ten thousand bullocks on his own account, constantly going to and from Malava and Gujarat for grain, to supply his stricken kingdom of Bahmini."[9] The famine itself was described as severe, caused by prolonged drought. Apparently, it caused high mortality.[10]

Authorities on medieval India suggest that the condition of the peasantry was only a shade better than what it is today. The end of the period witnessed a decline in the standard of living under the pressure of feudal surplus extraction.[11] Habib, who examined the living conditions of the peasantry in Mughal India, concludes that the ordinary people lived in relative poverty. As for food, he says, "If we take only the middle and poorer strata of the Indian peasantry today, the change in diet would seem to have been inconsiderable."[12] In a normal year, apart from scattered incidences of extreme hardship, people generally were not in grave danger, as was the case when they were hit by vagaries of nature (for example, drought or flood) or man-made exigencies such as war. A number of severe famines have been recorded during the reign of Akbar. These famines were mostly localized, although in some instances the people affected were said to have suffered terribly. In discussing the famine of 1555 to 1562, Habib makes reference to people eating seeds of Egyptian thorn, wild dry grass, and cowhides, and, on the authority of Badauni, he mentions cannibalism. Other years of famine during this period were 1574–1575 in Gujarat and 1595–1598 in northern India (Kashmir and Lahore) due to failure of rain. Like other famines, human sufferings were great but, as Habib cautions, historians sometimes get carried away with their descriptions of famines. Two things should be noted. First, during these famines foodgrain price increase was enormous and therefore people who had to procure it on the market became particularly vulnerable. Second, Akbar adopted some short- and long-term measures to help the famine victims. He instituted free distribution of food, provided employment in fort building, and appointed a Special Famine Officer. Collection of tax in kind (foodgrain) to build up emergency stock, a food kitchen, and a viable administrative framework to supervise famine relief became part of his long-term policy to combat famine. Notwithstanding the reservations expressed by some authors, we find that many governments of the past came to acknowledge the need to intervene in the market in order to protect the potential victims of famine. As we shall see later, this was a much debated point throughout the British period. It should be pointed out, however, that (although not much data is available) because of limited transportation and storage facilities and also of limited resources to spend on relief, the magnitude of actual relief afforded to people could not have been very significant in relation to the total population affected.[13] This fact had to be reckoned with, no matter how well intentioned a government may have been.

According to contemporary accounts, a departure was made by Shahjahan in extending relief beyond capital following the great famine of 1630–1632, which is considered by some to be the most destructive of all recorded calamities. The areas affected were Golconda, Ahmednagar, Gujarat, and parts of Malawa. The major cause of the famine was the failure of rain, but it was partly attributable to the difficulty of grain transport due to demands placed by Emperor Shahjahan's army encamped at Burhanpur.

Foodgrain prices were prohibitive and people resorted to migration to other areas to escape famine but with little success. Habib says that, "Of all the provinces affected Gujarat suffered the most heavily. Three million of its inhabitants are said to have died during the ten months preceeding October, 1631; while a million reportedly perished in the country of Ahmadnagor."[14]

Shahjahan mounted one of the best known (until then) relief efforts in history. Loveday found it comparable only to the relief measures of Mohammad Bin Tughlag about three hundred years earlier. The three major actions taken were distribution of cash among the poor, free distribution of cooked food among the needy, and remission of taxes. The last mentioned measure needs some elaboration since it was followed up in the nineteenth century by the British government on the recommendation of the famine commissions. The Mughal land revenue system provided for relief in tax payments during bad years, but the peasants were obliged to pay arrears in later years. Large remissions were allowed in famines (for example, during 1630–1632).

The next noteworthy famine occurred in 1660. It actually started in 1658, and difficulties were experienced in certain regions even after 1660. War of succession and failure of rain were the main causes of the trouble that engulfed Sind, Punjab (Agra, Delhi, Lahore), and Gujarat. The suffering of the people is recorded by historians in the words of Muhammad Rajwiny, who writes:

Life was offered for a loaf of bread, but none would buy; rank was to be sold for a cake, but none cared for it. For a long time dog's flesh was sold for goat's flesh and the pounded bones of the dead were mixed with flour and sold. Destitution at length reached such a pitch that men began to devour each other and the flesh of a son was preferred to his love. The numbers of dying caused obstruction in the roads.[15]

Awrangzeb, who was otherwise considered a conservative ruler by some contemporary historians, apparently rose to the occasion in providing relief to famine-affected areas. His efforts were appreciated by the Famine Inquiry Commission of 1880.

A severe, localized famine occurred in Dacca, the capital of Bengal, during 1662–1663, "the distress from which was intensified owing to the interference with the transport of foodgrains by official exactions and obstructions on the routes."[16] This famine occurred when Mir Zumla, the Mughal Viceroy of Bengal, went on an expedition to the neighboring province of Assam. According to historian Roy, "Hundreds and thousands of *souls perished* due to famine. The prices of grain soared sky high owing to the high rate of *zakat*, the virtual supervision of movements of grain traders on account of internal insecurity, the grasping habits of the 'chawkidars,' and the oppression of the 'rahdars' (toll collectors)."[17] Here we get an example of how administrative excesses can complicate a situation. Historically, governmental authorities have taken a different view of interference with trade, depending on the situation under consideration. In 1943, the Bengal government was very upset about the surplus states' restriction on movement of grain out of the state, while it put certain restrictions of its own on movements within Bengal.[18]

Passing reference is given to two other famines because not much detailed information is available. The first occurred in 1677 affecting Hydrabad and the cause was attributed to excessive rain. The second was in 1687 and was caused by siege during war in Golconda. Both rich and poor are said to have suffered greatly. Historians in general have said that, during the second half of the reign of Awrangzeb, war related difficulties multiplied and the situation assumed critical dimensions when a natural calamity visited any region. Extensive references can be found to the great Deccan famine of 1702–1704, which was associated with drought. Mortality is placed at over two million. Nothing much is known of the relief efforts by the government. This period coincided with the decaying era of the great Mughal empire.

Keeping in view the weakness of documentation, the following observations can be made about famines in pre-British India: (1) Famines visited India periodically; (2) Most famines were localized; (3) "Years of large scale mortality might have been few, but when they did come around, the amount of depopulation could have been frightful";[19] (4) Bengal, as a region, was largely free from famine; (5) Drought was the most important cause associated with famine; (6) Famine initiated large-scale migration of population from one region into another. Redistribution of population was often associated with the upsetting of balance of basic economic activity (that is, agriculture); (7) Most famines were class famines, although one instance of general famine (1344–1345) and another of regional famine (1630) were recorded; (8) Government policies sometimes increased the intensity of suffering of the famine victims; (9) Government in some instances provided famine relief.

FAMINES IN BRITISH INDIA

Let me repeat what I have said elsewhere.

"India was visited more frequently by famines of greater intensity and wider coverage in the colonial epoch as compared with earlier periods. . . . What is important to note is that famine and death occurred even when there was a unified administrative superstructure and a much improved transport network as compared with, say, Moghul India. In addition to the usual physical factors, it was found that manipulation of foodgrain stocks by traders, inaction on the part of the government, exports of foodgrains even in years of apparent scarcity, and gradual decline in income and employment opportunities for agricultural laborers and small farmers often made a bad situation worse."[20]

There will probably be little debate over this general statement but authorities on famines in India, particularly those during the British rule, differ regarding frequency, intensity, causes, mortality, and possible remedies. As expected, the scope for different opinions exists because facts are not well documented, although beginning with the 1860s exclusive literature on Indian famines proliferated with contributions from both Indian and European authors.

Drawing on an excellent work by F. C. Danvers of the India Office (1877), Walford lists thirty-one famines and scarcities between 1769–1770 and 1877–1878, and of these he considers twenty as being severe. Loveday's list includes twenty-nine famines between 1770 and 1907. The Famine Commission of 1901 says that, during the East India Company's rule (1765–1858), India suffered twelve famines and four severe scarcities, and, from the beginning of direct rule up to 1900, there were seven famines and one severe scarcity.[21] Using the historic sketches provided by the Famine Commissions of 1880 and 1898, Romesh Dutt says, "Excluding severe scarcities, often confined to limited areas, there were eighteen famines between 1770 and 1878; and if we add to this list the subsequent famines of 1889, 1892, 1897, and 1900 we have a sad record of twenty-two famines within a period of 130 years of British rule in India."[22]

Ghosh, who was primarily concerned with famines in Bengal, says that "during British Rule, India has had twenty-two 'Famines' excluding severe 'scarcities.' Famine was not declared by the Government in 1943, although the conditions were more severe than in most of the previous famines in India. Out of these twenty-three, Bengal suffered in seven either alone or along with some other province or provinces in 1770, 1783, 1866, 1873–74, 1892, 1897, and in 1943."[23]

Srivastava draws attention to fourteen famines between 1858 and 1918 and Bhatia discusses thirty-four major famines and scarcities in different parts of India over the period 1860 to 1943. Many of these covered all of India and were responsible for very high mortalities. However, mortality figures are not always accurate. Two different estimates of mortality are available for nineteenth-century India. The sources place mortality figures at 1.0, 0.5, and 5.0 millions for the first three quarters, but they differ significantly over the mortality figure for the fourth quarter, one mentioning 15 million[24] and the other 26 million.[25] In the twentieth century, the Deccan famine of 1905–1906 is said to have claimed over two hundred thousand lives, and the mortality figure for the 1943 great Bengal famine is placed as high as 3.5 million by some.[26]

Famine of 1770

The worst recorded famine of the eighteenth century occurred in Bengal in 1770. Failure of rain was the main cause. The suffering of the people was not relieved by the rain in 1770 that followed drought of the year before because that rain was excessive and caused overflowing of rivers, which damaged standing crops. Both the people and the administration (East India Company) were not prepared for such a calamity. Official estimates in 1772 suggest that about one-third of the population (or about 10 million people) perished in this famine.[27] People's suffering was enhanced due to administrative inefficiency, absence of any relief measures worth the name,[28] and above all the greed of the company officials, who indulged in profiteering in foodgrain.

To make a difficult situation desperate, the government refused to reduce land tax. The region was depopulated and agricultural production and revenue collection subsequently fell, which prompted the government in 1772 to resort to providing incentives such as reduction of land tax and advances to induce cultivators to migrate from other regions to Bengal. The important impact of this famine was to raise the consciousness of the British public to the plight of the common man in India and the state of the British administration. According to Dutt, this led to "the Regulating Act of 1773 . . . passed by the parliament to improve the administration."[29] From the point of view of this study, the importance of this famine lies in the fact that this was the first time Bengal was affected by a catastrophe of such magnitude. It had a tremendous impact on the society and the economy of the region. After having enjoyed perpetual plenty, Bengal became a famine-prone region.

From the scanty descriptions available, we can try to place the 1770 famine within the general framework presented in Chapter 2. In terms of typology, it was a class famine, but considering rural and urban areas separately, it approached a regional famine in that the rural population was affected across the board. The causal sequence seems to have run the following course: A natural calamity (drought) led to a shortfall in production and in the absence of substantial import (either through private or government channels) overall availability declined sharply. This was combined with a sharp price increase and, since there was obviously neither a social security benefit nor any institutional arrangement to cope with the drastic fall in foodgrain availability, the famine syndrome was initiated culminating in excess mortality. The period of maximum intensity was June to September. People expected to get some relief after the rain of 1770. But, as mentioned above, heavy rain created further difficulties for the famine-affected people. In the postfamine era, Bengal found itself with surplus land and shortage of labor, to which the government reacted by adopting measures for effecting redistribution of population.

As we shall see later, a variation of this sequence is applicable to other famines of eighteenth- and nineteenth-century India. The changes that occurred over time were the following: (1) Depopulation occurred at times but consequent shortage of labor became only a temporary phenomenon, given the ever-increasing size of the agricultural labor force, due to population growth and alienation of peasants from land, and very slow growth of employment opportunities in nonagricultural sectors;[30] (2) With improved transport and communication, famine-relief effort, on the one hand, and speculative trading opportunities, on the other, were facilitated;[31] (3) The importance of long-distance trade (exports and imports) and related factors for internal foodgrain balance increased;[32] (4) Lack of purchasing power emerged as an important factor aggravating a crisis;[33] (5) Internal social structure, particularly the relations of production in agriculture, continued to have an adverse effect on productive efficiency and inequality in the distribution of food resources increased over time;[34] and (6) Government policies during normal times as well as during immediate prefamine, famine, and postfamine situations produced mixed results for the well-being of the people.[35]

Famine of 1783

The next serious famine, known as the 1783 famine, was actually staggered between 1781 and 1783. Madras was hit hard by crop failure and Mysore by the effects of war. In the north, famine was caused primarily by crop failure due to drought. Extent of mortality is unknown. Bengal proper was not affected (Bihar, which was included in the Bengal province at that time, was affected). This famine was noteworthy because of the attempt by the government to meet the distress situation through various administrative measures, although admittedly they were not very successful, and, in some cases, certain measures increased the hardship of the people.[36] Walford quotes Danvers, "Early in 1781 the Government of Madras took steps to regulate the supply of grain . . . in January, 1782, a public subscription was raised for the relief of the poor, to which the government contributed. *This was the origin for the relief of the native poor, known as the Monegar Choultry.* Early in October the government deemed it necessary to take the supply of rice and foodgrain into their own hands."[37] Specific measures adopted by the Madras government include remission of import duties on grain, appointment of a "Grain Committee" with powers to fix price and quantity sold, forcing traders to declare stocks, sale of foodgrains under government account, and deportation of paupers to northern districts. This was the first government attempt at fixing the rice price; at a later stage it came out in favor of complete control of the grain trade. But such attempts were no more successful in 1782 than they were years later in 1942 in Bengal.[38] The government was forced to relax rules to accommodate demand of the trading community.

On the other hand, in northern India no positive policy was adopted by the government to relieve distress during famine. The government only ordered district administrators to collect information on prices and stores and to prohibit hoarding. In addition, an embargo was forced on export of grain, which apparently hurt Madras. Warren Hastings is reported to have said that the drought induced suffering in the north during this period that was further aggravated by a defective administration. An interesting outcome of this famine was the decision by Hastings to construct permanent foodgrain storage facilities in Bengal and Bihar to prevent future famines. Although one was built in Bankipure, it was never put to use and no further construction of storage facilities was undertaken by the government.[39] This measure can again be contrasted with the recommendation of the Foodgrain Policy Committee in 1943 to create a central foodgrain reserve and also with the current international debate on international grain reserve (particularly the need for an emergency stock to prevent serious food shortage in the Third World). Bihar having been seriously depopulated, the government asked officers to encourage emigration from Lucknow and Benares to Bihar, a measure similar to the one adopted in 1772.

A passing reference may be given to the famine of 1790–1792, which affected Bombay and Madras, particularly the latter. Nothing much is known about the causal sequence that led to the famine or the exact mortality. Apart from the relief measures already referred to in connection with earlier famines in British India, "relief was afforded by employing the poor in public works."[40] Wages were paid in foodgrain. The effort was apparently moderate, but this marked the beginning of relief works in famine under British India.

Famines between 1800 and 1825

A number of famines occurred during the first quarter of the nineteenth century. The most notable among them were the Bombay, Madras, and northern Indian famine of 1802–1804, the Madras famine of 1807, the Bombay and Madras famine of 1812–1814, and the Madras famine of 1823. During this period British territorial domination of India was expanding and the administrative machinery of the East India Company was settling down. This period was also marked by alienation of the common people from the government and the emergence of rent-receiving intermediaries in certain regions created by permanent settlement of land. Even when settlement was made directly with the ryot (cultivator), the interest of the government did not extend beyond rent collection. The peasantry was subjected to various forms of surplus extraction, legal rent, illegal exactions, and interest payment on wars. Increasing indebtedness became a new dimension of rural life. Basically, this period witnessed the disintegration of village community structure and both land and labor became a commodity. Merchant capital slowly penetrated into the grain economy and a majority could obtain their means of sustenance only after a share of their income was expropriated in the form of profit in grain trade. Famine became a very frequent phenomenon; drought, excessive rain, or war-related disruption would precipitate a crisis. The government, although it attempted from time to time to adopt various types of relief measures, was not very effective in relieving the suffering of the affected people. Long-term preventive measures were not seriously considered during this period.

The famine syndrome followed a very familiar pattern. It was mainly localized, although not as localized as it was in some instances in pre-British India. Greater integration of the administrative and trade structures meant that the impact of famine in one region could be felt in another because of interregional trade and redistribution of population through migration. A drought will normally lead to crop failure and thus reduce availability. Since the peasantry are forced to surrender their entire surplus during a good year, very little is left in their barns to tide them over a bad year. Grain traders' activity increased prices enormously during famines. The peasantry during such a crisis have no alternative source of income, so they are unable to purchase grain. On some occasions grains were not available at any price. Because of an inadequate transport network, import of grain from other areas either by the traders or by government always took time, which added to the suffering of the people. The period under consideration saw the emergence of a strong "free trade" lobby within the government. Therefore, except in 1807 when the government of Madras "conceived it necessary to purchase, guaranteeing a minimum price to importers",[41] a policy of nonintervention with private trade in grains was followed. The result on the whole was disastrous.

The severity with which drought affected foodgrain production is not surprising in view of the lack of supplementary irrigation facilities. Those in existence from pre-British India had degenerated by the beginning of the nineteenth century because of lack of maintenance. Only half-hearted attempts were made to undertake irrigation works following the 1802–1804 famine. It is no wonder that one of the major concerns expressed by many authorities in the late nineteenth century was expansion of irrigation facilities.[42]

The government made no attempt to develop a comprehensive famine relief and prevention policy. It only responded with ad hoc relief measures once a crisis struck a region. No principle evolved in the early nineteenth century from the administration of famine relief. The only policy pursued consistently was that of free trade. However, two other things had emerged out of experimental work programs: no relief should be given without getting some work in return, and relief should not be given in kind because it interfered with the free working of the grain market. But, as in 1823, the Madras government opened food kitchens to those who were unable to work.[43] In the 1802–1804 famine, the government allowed some revenue remission and advanced *taccavi* (distress) loans to cultivators. Neither of these measures actually added up to much. A new dimension was added to famine relief when the government set up hospitals for famine victims. Accounts of famine during this period reveal that the government always failed to recognize the severity of the calamity in time, and, on occasion, it refused to acknowledge the phenomenon even when it was at the doorstop. This reaction is not only typical of British rule, but has prevailed throughout the nineteenth and twentieth centuries. In fact, we shall see later that the 1974 Bangladesh famine was not officially declared until it was almost too late. We have already mentioned that in 1943 the Bengal government refused to declare famine, although the death toll ultimately exceeded three million.

Famines between 1826 and 1858

During the remaining years of the East India Company's rule (1826–1858), India suffered two major famines—in 1832–1833 and 1837–1838. The 1832–1833 famine most seriously affected the northern districts of the Madras presidency. It is better known as the "Guntor Famine" because of "the fearful loss of life which took place in the Guntor district."[44] The cause of this famine is not quite clear, although one can find some mention of failure of rains "in 1832 in the Eastern Ghats affecting the coastal districts from Madras northward."[45] However, there is consensus that the famine caught the Madras government by surprise and nothing much could be done to save lives. Mortality was very high, and it was concentrated in a limited area.[46] Social disruption was complete, "as the country was reported to be infested by bands of marauders which daily increased in number, owing to the alarming rise which had taken place in the price of food."[47] The government concentrated its effort on inducing traders to increase importation of foodgrains and to encourage southern districts to export foodgrains. At no stage was the idea of a direct intervention in the market by the government entertained. General relief measures were adopted along the same lines as before.

Failure of rain precipitated a severe famine in northern India in 1837 that supposedly affected 113,000 square miles with a population of twenty-eight million. A vivid picture of this famine emerges from the following quote by Loveday:

> Indeed, the whole social structure became a chaotic ruin. Internal trade was cumbered with burdensome duties, the cultivators fled because the landlords endeavored to collect rents for the payments of taxes, the intended remission of which the Government neglected to announce; the applications for work at Bishour exceeded the work to be done; and finally riots broke out and the military had to be called in to assist. The Commission of 1880 estimated the mortality conservatively at 800,000; but such estimates are of questionable value. It is more enlightening to read that 'the river, owing to the sluggishness of the stream, became studded with dead bodies.'[48]

Relief efforts were sluggish and inadequate. In fact, during the entire period of East India Company rule, "there were no permanent famine officials, there were no codes, there were no regular reports on crops."[49] One good thing that came out of the 1837 famine was the construction of the Ganges Canal, which contributed through irrigation facilities to softening the impact of drought in 1859–1860.[50]

Famine of 1860

The first famine after the introduction of direct rule in India occurred in 1860 and covered the northwestern provinces and Punjab. This famine is attributed to the after-effects of disturbances in 1857 and failure of rain during 1858–1860. The famine lasted about two years and claimed 200,000 lives. According to Baird Smith, who investigated this famine at the request of the Bengal Chamber of Commerce,[51] the immediate causes were reinforced by the long-term adverse effect of land revenue demand on the rural economy. As pointed out earlier, the question of land revenue assessment under British rule was taken up vigorously by historian Romesh Dutt. This was strictly a class famine and one of the main problems associated with it was lack of employment opportunity. Loveday quotes Baird Smith, who was of the opinion that "our famines are rather famines of work than of food."[52] Importance of irrigation for India was appreciated during this famine. Many authorities point out that fatalities would have been higher but for extension of irrigation facilities that took place during the previous twenty years. People could easily emigrate from famine-affected areas into irrigated areas without imposing undue burden on the host regions as in times of earlier famines.

The 1860 famine had profound impact on foreign trade as reflected in the concern expressed by the Calcutta Chamber of Commerce. Unlike other famines, one does not come across influences of social tension; it seems people suffered quietly. There was, however, an increase in petty crimes. Government relief measures primarily included gratuitous relief and relief works. In general, relief was inadequate, but it was better organized. The Indian government acknowledged organization of famine relief as an official responsibility. The first poorhouse was set up during this famine and became a model for other poorhouses in later years. Other measures added were special relief works for "Purdanashen" women (women who observe "purdah") and advances to cultivators for the purchase of seed and cattle. The most distressing thing was that there was no departure from free-trade doctrine, even when it was clear that speculation in grain trade increased prices enormously.

In contrast to earlier famines, an inquiry into the causes of the 1860 famine was carried out by Baird Smith. Unfortunately, his major suggestions were not immediately followed up. In particular, his recommendation to extend permanent settlement to unirrigated regions was rejected by the British government in England, although it was endorsed by Viceroy Lord Canning. The desirability of this measure was also advocated by authors such as Romesh Dutt and Prithwis Ray. It is somewhat ironic that Baird Smith found transferability of land and other property to be a good cushion against starvation since they could be converted into cash, but he failed to focus on the long-term impact of this on alienation in rural society, which accelerates the growth of agricultural labor in India.

Famine of 1866

In 1866, Orissa, parts of Bengal, Bihar, and Madras suffered a severe famine known as the "Orissa Famine." Apparently, Orissa was the worst victim of this famine. Beginning in late 1865, these regions suffered a significant decline in foodgrain availability that lasted the better part of 1866. There was a shortfall in production due to failure of rain in 1865. This was combined with depletion of stocks in the preceding two years through excessive exports to Bombay from Orissa in 1864 and 1865. Although, on the whole, there were no excessive exports from Madras during 1864–1866 as compared with earlier years, the absolute amount exported was high relative to the production level in 1865–1866, which added to the existing difficulty. In addition, there was some export of grain out of famine-affected districts. However, the situation reached crisis proportions when the government ignored the early warnings of local officers and refused to take measures to augment supply by imports on private (by providing necessary incentives) or government account. Furthermore, the government was still blindly adhering to the liberal principles of political economy, which led to its not taking any steps to arrest the abnormal rise in prices. Orissa fell into greater distress because it was isolated from the rest of the country due to its extremely bad transportation and communication system.

The general socio-economic condition of the population reveals different trends in different regions in the decade preceding the famine. Orissa is said to have been suffering from the effect of high land revenue assessment and also at the time of famine there was uncertainty because the region was awaiting the award of fresh settlement following the end of the thirty-year settlement. Destruction of the salt industry had earlier (1863) added to the employment problem. The famine-affected areas of Bengal and Bihar had been experiencing a decline in the real wage of agricultural laborers, which obviously reached below famine level as the height of the crisis approached. As for Madras, Dalyell says, "On the whole, then, it is impossible to arrive at any other conclusion, than that the mass of the population of the Madras Presidency have considerably progressed in wealth, during the ten years previous to the famine of

1866."[53] In the case of agricultural laborers, he specifically mentions that there was no decline in real wages received by them.[54]

Some estimates of mortality are available for the 1866 famine. Figures quoted are about one million in Orissa, 450,000 in Madras, and 135,000 in Bihar.[55] Nothing is known about the extent of mortality in Bengal but from the evidence available it seems to be moderate. All relief efforts were belatedly undertaken and have been described as poorly administered. The only thing worth mentioning is the system of village relief under which assistance was provided to the distressed people at their own places of residence, after careful official inquiry, but the total number of people thus relieved was very small (21,774).[56] It was essentially a class famine, although if Orissa is treated separately, then the famine can perhaps be characterized as general in the sense that it "affected all classes of people."[57]

In other areas the burden of suffering fell heavily on agricultural laborers, village artisans, professional beggars, nonagricultural classes, people on fixed salaries, at low rates. In Madras, "the Mussulman population were stated to have suffered severely, in many districts, owing, probably, to a large proportion of them being dependents of noble families, and subsisting on meager monthly allowances."[58]

In order to investigate the causes of the 1866 famine and suggest remedial measures, a Famine Commission [59] was appointed by the government of India. This was the first official body of its kind with extensive powers of enquiry. After an elaborate analysis of the famine, the commission suggested the following important measures for consideration by the government: liberal assessment of land revenue; removal of intermediaries from land; strengthening of land occupancy rights; improvement in the terms of existing settlement; expansion of railways, lands, and roads; and improvement of irrigation systems. Important omissions were measures to extend permanent settlement and to control exports of foodgrains. But the commission approved of imports, if necessary. However, no suggestion was made for any major deviation from the free-trade principle under any circumstances. Some principles of famine relief and its management emerged from the deliberations of this commission. But no one took the initiative to formulate a Famine Code. The success of the Orissa commission perhaps lay in the creation of a "panic famine" in 1873–1874 when the government overreacted to a mild scarcity situation in Bengal and Bihar.

From the point of view of studying famine in Bangladesh in modern times, the 1866 famine highlights a number of facts that are of considerable interest. (1) After a lapse of about eighty years, Bengal suffered a famine. More importantly, this famine represented the culmination of a worsening trend of the condition of small cultivators and agricultural laborers in Bengal since the beginning of the nineteenth century. This trend, sustained by the existing precapitalist production relations in agriculture, has been continuing in the twentieth century. (2) The government in 1866 had very little means at its disposal to collect agricultural statistics or systematic information on rainfall, so it was difficult to forewarn (predict) the possibility of famine. (3) Proliferation of administrative tiers of the government implied that important decisions concerning the life of the people were taken by authorities who were far removed from them. The suffering of the people in 1866 was increased many times due to the conflicting assessment of the situation by local administrators, on the one hand, and the divisional commissioner, Board of Revenue, and the central government, on the other. Delayed response to a crisis by the central government seems to have become a pattern since then. (4) Blind adherence to the principle of free trade can only worsen a crisis that develops out of natural or artificial scarcity of feedgrains. Direct governmental intervention in the market in any one or a combination of the following forms may be unavoidable in the face of a famine: internal and external procurement on government account, direct sale in the market, supportive measures to encourage procurement on private account but with adequate safeguards for uninterrupted market release, direct action to enforce dehoarding, price control, introduction of a selective rationing system for distribution of subsidized or free foodgrains. (5) Relief works at cash wage is meaningless if foodgrains cannot be made available to workers at a price that was used to calculate the cash wage.

Famine of 1876–1878

In the latter half of the nineteenth century India suffered severe famines during 1876–1878, 1896–1897, and 1899–1900. The mortality is estimated at five and a quarter million in 1876–1878 and half a million in 1899–1900.[60] No figure is available for 1896–1898. In each case, a drought causing shortfall in production causing shortfall in availability causing decline in foodgrain intake has been superimposed on a socio-economic environment characterized by cultivators being subjected to surplus extraction in the form of excessive rental and interest payment by the landlord and other intermediaries (in permanently settled areas), by the government (in ryotwari areas where revenue settlement was made directly with the ryots), and by the money lender (in all areas). Some protection against landlords was afforded to tenants through various acts, but it was not very significant. The moneylender who was almost a nonentity in village life at the beginning of the century, became an important institution. "We have made the money-lender, once the village servant, into the village master; we have turned him from a useful agent into a blood-sucker; and we have stood as Shylock's friend whenever he came into court to enforce his hand."[61] The impact of the growing inequity in rural India, given the existing social relations and nature of state power, has been ably summarized by Bhatia:

> The unequal distribution of incomes between various classes in Indian agriculture had a three-fold effect. In the first place, it reduced the cultivator's share in the produce of the land to the level of wages of ordinary laborers in the village and left the producer little better than the farm laborers and artisans in facing the vicissitudes of seasons. Secondly, it prevented the accumulation of capital in the hands of the cultivator for carrying out improvements in land. Thirdly, it destroyed all incentives of the cultivator for hard work and improvement of methods of production. The State, of course, was not directly responsible for either the poverty of the cultivating class or for the backwardness of the agricultural industry but the circumstances which led to these results were the creation of the laws and the system of administration introduced in the country by the British.[62]

According to Srivastava, one additional factor that affected the well-being of many in the south during the period under consideration was the slump in the cotton market following the end of the Civil War.[63] The first signs of famine were observed in Madras. Later it spread to Bombay and Mysore. Lack of emergency discretionary power at the regional and local level was more obvious during this famine than in any other. Famine broke out with all its evil manifestations in Madras even before the first round of correspondence between district administration, provincial government, central government, and London could be completed. On a number of issues such as large projects vs. small projects for relief work, government grain purchase, rates of wage on relief works, and land revenue remission, there was a difference of opinion between the government of Madras and the government of India.[64] Needless to say, these issues are no less important today than they were a century ago.

During the 1876–1878 famine, the major concern of the Indian government in organizing famine relief was the cost of such relief. The government apparently did not want to repeat the costly mistakes of "panic famine" of 1873–1874, but this policy was pushed too far, particularly by its special delegate to famine areas, Sir Richard Temple, lieutenant-governor of Bengal, who liberally interpreted the instructions given him in a letter[65] from the Secretary of State to the government of India. The government of India had earlier expressed its concern for economy in a dispatch to the Secretary of State in which it said, "While the necessity of preventing, as far as practicable, death by starvation is paramount, the financial embarrassment which must in any case arise, will be most difficult to overcome, and any departure from the most rigid economy, or from the principles in dealing with famine which experience has confirmed as sound, only aggravate it to a degree which cannot be estimated."[66]

On the question of large vs. small works, the government of India favored the latter and initially forced the Madras government to go along with this decision by limiting the size of expenditure on each project. At a later stage, however, the central government reversed its stand and allowed organization of large relief works. This question comes up before concerned authorities today during famine periods as well as in normal times when special programs are designed to provide employment to the rural and urban poor. Basically, the question boils down to developing appropriate institutions for designing and implementing various types of projects. Apart from the question of finance, technical and administrative supervision of projects becomes a matter of important consideration in deciding upon the nature and size of projects to be undertaken. The question from the point of view of a country like Bangladesh today is not one of choice between the two alternatives considered in 1876–1878; rather, it is one of finding an appropriate combination of the two after carefully taking into account all environmental considerations.

Grain purchase by the government became a hotly debated point during this period when it was disclosed that the Madras government had arranged with a private dealer to hold on its behalf a small amount (30,000 tons)[67] of grain with the idea of using it to soften market pressure if necessary. The government of India disapproved and rejected all arguments put forward by the Madras government in its favor. As we have already indicated, some sort of intervention in the market by the government is unavoidable in a crisis. This has been an accepted position in recent years to the extent that the government controls the foodgrain market partially even during a normal period. It is important to note that when private dealers play an influential role in the foodgrain market, government should intervene only in a selective way so as not to create famine in the market, which will ultimately hurt the poor more than the rich. The government's responsibility lies, as recognized by many authorities on famines in India in the late nineteenth century, in taking appropriate measures to improve the supply of foodgrains to and purchasing power of the famine-affected population. The tragedies of earlier famines and also the 1974 Bangladesh famine clearly indicate that the governments concerned failed in this basic objective, and millions of lives were lost.

The essence of the wage controversy was the following: The Madras government was employing adult male labor at one and a half pounds of foodgrain per day, a rate that Sir Richard Temple thought was excessive because it would encourage more people to seek relief work than was justified by their actual need. At his insistence, the rate was reduced to one pound but this gave rise to bitter controversy.[68] While the newly imposed rate achieved the objective of saving money for the government exchequer, the cost in terms of human suffering mounted, and the government of India ultimately relented as it came under pressure from home (England) and various quarters within India. It is interesting to note that theoretically both positions had some merit. The Madras government thought reduction of wage level would be disastrous because the laborers shared their ration with other members of the family, while Sir Richard assumed that the amount was meant exclusively for the consumption of the working members while other members of the family would resort to alternative sources including gratuitous relief. Given the state of general relief measures available, Sir Temple's assumption was unrealistic. On the other hand, if he had been correct in his assumption, then a lower wage rate to ration the limited wage fund to the absolutely needy would have had certain undeniable merit. But as we know, his and the government of India's concern was not rationing as such, but minimizing cost. In addition, there was prolonged debate over the adequacy of the "Temple Ration" on nutritional considerations between Sir Temple and Dr. Cornish, sanitary commissioner of Madras.[69] A similar debate has arisen in Bangladesh in recent years concerning the level of wages and nature of payment (cash or kind) in test relief works and the Food-for-Work program. As mentioned earlier, the current practice is to make payment in kind (wheat) at a rate less than the prevailing market wage. There is no denying the fact that both of these measures had a screening (rationing) effect on the people who approached for work, and at the same time it stretched the fund to provide more employment than would otherwise have been possible.

The final point debated was the recommendation by Sir Richard Temple to suspend only land revenue (to be collected later) and not to allow general remission as desired by the Madras authorities. The Madras government presented a strong case with the government of India and was able to make a favorable impression on the viceroy, although this only led to remission in special cases. It is interesting to note that the government of India accepted the argument, among others, that "the Madras ryot is very heavily taxed."[70] Apart from the fact that there has always existed a difference in the level of awareness at various tiers of the government regarding the difficulties faced by the common man from time to time, there often emerged fundamental differences in the conceptualization of the basic problem that gave rise to bitter controversy over measures to be adopted for tackling the crisis when it occurred. In these debates, however, we should also include the contributions of other groups (social scientists, politicians, medical and nutrition experts, and engineers).

The upshot of all this was a very poor famine relief effort during 1876–1878. According to the Famine Commission of 1901, "In this famine, relief was to a large extent insufficient, and to a large extent imperfectly organized; the insufficiency being largely due to the inability of private trade, hampered by want of railways and communication, to supply the demand for food."[71] On the other hand, following this famine, a number of advances were made in famine policy that were more relevant for later years. The viceroy chose Mysore to start reorganization of famine administration. For the first time, a famine commissioner was appointed. Mr. C. A. Elliot, the famine commissioner, prepared a famine code "containing detailed instruction for the administration of relief of all kinds."[72] This apparently represented a milestone in the development of famine administration in India, and it was the basis for the famine codes prepared subsequently. The code indicated that "the backbone of the famine policy is the employment of all suitable applicants for relief on large works of permanent utility, superintended by professional officers of the Public Works Department."[73] A clear preference for large works as opposed to small works was shown. The reference to the utility of the work undertaken is connected with the earlier controversy regarding the size of the works, which essentially boiled down to differences of opinion with respect to the productivity of different types of work done. This is a very familiar topic in all discussions of rural and urban public works programs that have been undertaken in many Third World countries, including Bangladesh in the 1960s and 1970s. The code suggests that no applicant should be rejected if he/she satisfies the distance test, the wage test and the task-work test.[74] The code provided classification of workers and outlined the duties of various officials (officer of Public Works Department, civil officer, and medical officer). Other provisions of the code were for: a relief camp, treatment of special cases, rates of wages in Public Works Department relief work, and village inspection and relief.

A Famine Commission [75] was appointed in 1878 "whose enquiries for the first time reduced the system of the administration of famine relief and whose report has powerfully influenced for good agrarian and administrative reform in India during the last twenty years."[76] The commission was concerned with both famine relief and measures of a preventive nature. It reiterated the position that the state was responsible for providing relief in times of famine. Suggested relief measures included large works of permanent utility, village relief, distribution of cooked food to the disabled, remission and suspension of revenue, and *taccavi* loans for seed and cattle. As for preventive measures, the commission emphasized the need to improve conditions so that agricultural production would be enhanced, protection would be afforded against unforeseen natural calamity, and the interest of the poor peasants would be protected. In this spirit, reorganization of the Department of Agriculture, collection of vital and agricultural statistics, expansion of irrigation and railways, and enactment of laws to protect peasants from the oppressive hold of the landlords and moneylenders, were recommended. It is, however, important to note that, because of their continued reliance on free trade, neither the commission nor the government of India saw the need to establish emergency food stock[77] and to adopt measures to tackle the chronic unemployment of the landless agricultural laborers.

The most important outcome of the 1880 commission was the consolidation of the 1877 Mysore Famine Code into a Provisional Famine Code for India in 1883, which was to be used as the model for provincial governments to frame their own famine codes. Madras was the first to act on this. Other provincial governments were asked to follow the principles of the Madras Famine Code until they framed their own. The famine codes addressed directly the question of famine relief and not its prevention. According to the codes, the stages involved in preparation and administration of relief included watching signals of distress, designing relief works, administering works at the initial stage of difficulty, declaring famine, appointing a famine commissioner, and, finally, instituting full relief operation on the basis of the principles laid down in the code. Some of the important aspects that deserve attention are the emphasis placed on monitoring of basic information, promotion of village organization, and allowance made for the government to procure and sell foodgrains at rationed prices when private channels of trade failed to ensure supply.

Famine of 1896–1898

The famine codes went through successive revisions in the light of minor experiences until they were put to a proper test during the famine of 1896–1898, which affected Bihar, Bengal, Bombay, Madras, North Western Provinces, Oudh, Central Provinces, and Punjab. As mentioned earlier, failure of rain was the triggering factor although its effect was further aggravated in Bombay, Madras, and Bengal by excessive export of foodgrains. Food prices increased manyfold and though foodgrain was physically available in the market, it was beyond the reach of the majority of the population. The government of India was not in favor of allowing provincial governments to directly interfere in the market to reduce prices. It rejected a proposal by the Bengal government to provide loans to private traders to import foodgrain. Only in limited areas was the intervention of the government in the free market tolerated. Relief works were organized along the lines suggested in the famine codes, with certain marginal changes regarding classification of laborers and the mode of wage payment. With regard to the latter, a new system known as the piece-work system was evolved and implemented in North Western Provinces, Central Provinces, and Bengal.

A famine commission, headed by Sir J. B. Lyall, was appointed in December 1897. Unlike other commissions, the major concern of the 1898 Commission (as it was popularly known) was to examine the effectiveness of provincial famine codes in alleviating distress of the affected population. According to the 1901 Famine Commission, "The very elaborate enquiry into its results conducted by the Commission of 1898 completely vindicated the principles laid down in 1880, and demonstrated the success which a system of relief based upon them could achieve. Wherever there was failure, it was due not so much to defects in the system of relief as to defects in the administration of it."[78] The commission continues, "But, while confirming the principles enunciated by the Commission of 1880, the Commission of 1898 departed from them in recommending a more liberal wage and a freer extension of gratuitous relief. Moreover, their repeated warnings against any measures of relief involving an element of risk were, in effect, an invitation to recede from the strictness, or, as we prefer to call it, the prudent boldness, of the former policy."[79] As for specific achievement of the 1898 Commission, Srivastava says, "Its recommendation for the relief of hill and tribal people, diversion of Famine Insurance Grant from railways to irrigation works, appreciation of Charitable Relief fund, and policy towards the projects of Princely States had all great effect on the future famine policy."[80]

From our point of view, the 1898 Famine Commission made an extremely important observation on the condition of the laboring class of India.

This section is very large and includes the great class of day-laborers and the least skilled of the artisans. So far as we have been able to form a general opinion upon a difficult question from the evidence we have heard and the statistics placed before us, the wages of these people have not risen in the last twenty years in due proportion to the rise in prices of their necessaries of life. The experience of recent famine fails to suggest that this section of the community has shown any larger command of resources or any increased power of resistance. Far from contracting, it seems to be widening, particularly in the more congested districts. Its sensitiveness of liability to succumb, instead of diminishing, is possibly becoming more accentuated.[81]

This statement is confirmed from the figures available for index of real wages (1883 = 100), which shows a decline from 91 in 1884–1888 to 81 in 1904–1908.[82]

Famine of 1899–1900

The nineteenth century in British India came to a close with another drought-related famine that engulfed twenty-eight million people over an area of 189 thousand square miles. Central Provinces, Berar, Bombay, Ajmer and Merwara, and the Rajputna states were most severely affected. Authorities on this famine have noted a number of peculiar features.[83] First, many areas were affected simultaneously by crop famine, fodder famine, and water famine. The result was not only excess human mortality, but also heavy cattle mortality, estimated at two million heads. Second, the number of persons on relief during this famine far exceeded those in earlier famines. As a matter of fact, since this famine occurred even before people could recover from the effects of the 1896–1898 famine, a large number of people were forced on relief at a very early stage. Third, unlike other famines, the number of people on relief steadily increased during the entire course of this famine. Fourth, cultivators constituted a significant proportion of relief-seekers, which was never before the case. We have already noted the high mortality in the famine. This occurred even when provincial governments, according to the 1901 Commission, indulged in excessive relief distribution. One can take it either as a poor commentary on famine administration or as a reflection of poor perception on the part of the 1901 Commission of the need for famine relief during 1899–1900. The major areas of expenditure were relief works, gratuitous relief, advances, and suspension of revenue. Large works programs constituted the backbone of relief policy. Provincial governments were directed not to adhere to the liberal wage recommendation of the 1898 Commission if they thought it was too high and in most provinces the principle of the minimum wage was abandoned.

A commission was appointed under the chairmanship of Sir A. P. MacDonnell in 1900[84] to look into the experiences of the famine relief administration, to examine "the questions of the collection of the land revenue and the grant of advances to agriculturalists" and to give recommendations regarding "treatment of future famines."[85] This commission emphasized the need for standing preparations that consisted of systems of intelligence, effective relief works programs, food reserves of government establishment, and reserves of tools and plants. The commission thought it was important to help people overcome depression through moral impetus, which could be provided through early actions regarding enlistment of nonofficial agencies (that could help in famine relief), advances, and remission of revenue. It then provided a list of steps that should follow the early actions. These included preparation and publication of a comprehensive plan, liberal preparations in advance of pressure, appointment of a famine commissioner, and creation of a thoroughly efficient accounts and audit establishment. The commission listed the danger signals associated with famine, which we have considered earlier, and left it up to the local government to satisfy itself as to when actions were warranted. To increase the effectiveness of the measures adopted, the commission suggested that an order should be followed. First-stage relief included organization of private charity, test works, and establishment of poorhouses to receive early destitutes. In the second stage, in which scarcity is said to have turned into famine, test works were to be converted into relief works and, at the same time, distribution of gratuitous relief was to be started. It is interesting to note that the Famine Commission felt that it was "impossible to fix in formal language exactly the point where conditions of scarcity cease, and where conditions of famine begin."[86] Then the commission proceeded to enumerate class of works, organization and management of works, and rates of wages. It favored village works and recommended abolition of minimum wage for the able bodied on public works. As for protective measures, the commission recommended supervision and remission of land revenue on a more liberal basis than before. It also suggested "establishment of some organization or methods whereby cultivators may obtain, without paying usurious rates of interest, and without being given undue facilities for incurring debt, the advances necessary for carrying on their business."[87] Appreciating the need for advances, the commission recommended certain measures to go along with the Land Improvements Loans Act (XIX of 1883) and the Agriculturalists' Loans Act (XII of 1884).[88] A number of recommendations of the 1901 Famine Commission concerning relief measures were incorporated into famine codes in later years.

THE GREAT BENGAL FAMINE OF 1943

India remained relatively free of famine from the beginning of the twentieth century until 1943 when Bengal was hit by a devastating famine. From the summary profile of past famines in Bengal as presented in Table 3.1, one can see that the 1943 famine was one of the worst in terms of excess mortality. During the early part of the century a few local scarcities and a famine were recorded in 1905–1906 and 1907–1908. The latter affected the United Provinces of Agra and Oudh. It was caused by drought, which led to considerable shortfall in foodgrain output. Prices rose sharply but, on the whole, excess mortality was low. People were able to migrate to other areas.[89] Bhatia[90] points out a few changes in relief policy during this famine period. Laborers in works programs were paid at the prevailing market rate. The "distance test" evolved earlier was abandoned, and employment was offered near the workers' residence. Gratuitous relief, grants of loans, and remission of land revenue were offered on a more liberal basis than before.

Bengal suffered from famines less frequently than many other parts of India (for example, Bombay, Madras, Central Provinces), but whenever one occurred the intensity was severe measured by human mortality and suffering. The famine of 1943 was no exception. It is important to realize that as 1943 approached, Bengal was led into a position where a majority of the population became very vulnerable to exogenous shocks. What made the people, particularly the peasants, so vulnerable was the continued deterioration of their social and economic status, a trend that had set in at the beginning of the nineteenth century. Per capita net output in India declined between the turn of the century and the early 1940s.[91] Separate figures of total output are not available for Bengal. But from the work of Blyn we know that per capita all-crop output in greater Bengal (Bengal, Bihar, and Orissa) showed a declining trend in all decades between 1891 and 1941 except 1901–1911, when there was a slight increase of 2 percent.[92] As for per capita foodgrain output, Blyn indicates a total decline of 38 percent in greater Bengal during 1901–1941.[93] The picture is somewhat mixed if one analyzes the data on rice output of Bengal during 1928–1941 as provided by the Famine Inquiry Commission of 1944. The index of per capita output fluctuated between 100 in 1941 and 154 in 1933 when it had reached its peak.[94] However, it is clear that overall prosperity declined in the second half of the decade as compared with the first. There is supporting evidence to prove this hypothesis.

The average food situation in Bengal was satisfactory during 1900–1941 except during three years—1928, 1936, and 1941—when there was shortfall in production. Actually, up to the mid-1930s, Bengal was a net exporter of rice, but it became a net importer beginning in 1934.[95] Bengal continued to export foodgrains irrespective of the internal supply position. It was part of the overall strategy of the British government to supply its other colonies with foodgrains, and no interruption in this flow was allowed even in periods of scarcity and distress within India.[96]

Movement of aggregate indexes does not truly reflect the trend of well-being of different classes in the society. In Bengal, during the late nineteenth and throughout the twentieth century leading up to the 1943 famine, the number of landless laborers and sharecroppers multiplied. To begin with, with the emergence of British rule in Bengal, the peasantry was subjected to feudal and colonial exploitation, but other classes, such as rich farmers, intermediary interests in land, traders, and money lenders, emerged in a dominant position in rural society. Thus, rural Bengal witnessed the ascendance of semifeudal production relations in agriculture during the latter part of British rule in India.[97]

The growth of sharecropping as well as the size of the laboring class can be traced back to the emergence of private ownership of land that followed the permanent settlement between the *Zemindars* (landlords) and the British government in 1793. Rack-renting, subinfeudation, and usurious interest rates all became a common feature of Bengal agriculture. The sharecroppers were subjected to a very high rent—one-half of the produce. The Famine Commission of 1944 observed. "The number of *bargadars* (sharecroppers) is increasing rapidly and in consequence a large and increasing proportion of the actual cultivators posses no security of tenure."[98] The process was further accelerated with the loss of land by cultivators through sale and mortgage foreclosure.[99] It is not surprising that the landless peasants whose existence was not even officially recognized in 1842[100] turned out to be a very important class among the rural population in the 1920s and 1930s in Bengal. Writing on the condition prevailing in Faridpur district in east Bengal (presently Bangladesh), during the first decade of this century, J. C. Jack remarks that "the landless laborer so common in England is unknown in Faridpur and very rare anywhere in Eastern Bengal."[101] This may be a slight overstatement since evidence from Comilla (Brahmanbaria subdivision) and Dacca districts place the proportion of agricultural laborers to the total population at around 15 percent.[102] In any case, census returns for Bengal show this ratio to be 4.8, 10.0, 17.7, and 33.2 percent in 1901, 1911, 1921 and 1931 respectively. Almost doubling of the proportion of agricultural laborers between 1921 and 1931 is indeed remarkable.[103]

As for real wages of laborers, the period 1900–1940 was characterized by an upward trend for industrial workers,[104] but the same was not true of agricultural workers. Ghose provides a long time series for West Bengal that shows that the real-wage index of agricultural laborers declined from 100 in 1916 to 64 in 1941.[105] As we shall see later, the declining trend in purchasing power of the agricultural laborers continued and is considered to have sharply aggravated their suffering during the 1943 famine. But agricultural laborers were not alone in facing deterioration of their economic position. There were an increasing number of households whose landholding was not sufficient to provide means of subsistence. According to the 1939 Bengal Land Revenue Commission, about half of the holdings in Bengal were below subsistence level. The nature of the shift in the economic condition of peasants during several decades leading up to the 1943 famine can be clearly seen from the two pieces of evidence provided by Ramkrishna Mukherjee and Karunamoy Mukerji. Ramkrishna Mukherjee provides some data on increasing polarization in terms of landownership in six villages of Bogra district of East Bengal during 1922–1941. He further demonstrates that during this period "16 percent of the total households have changed to the worse and 11 percent to the better."[106] Karunamoy Mukerji, on the other hand, uses data for the Faridput district generated by himself and by J. C. Jack to show that "families in comfort" fell from 49.5 percent to 4.7 percent of the total from 1908 to 1944 respectively; "below comfort" from 28.5 percent to 5.9 percent; "above want" from 18 percent to 17.2 percent. But those "in want" rose from 4 percent to 72.1 percent.[107]

The situation in Bengal prior to the great 1943 famine can be summarized in the words of the 1944 Famine Commission:

Even in normal times, however, considerable numbers among the poorer classes live on the margin of subsistence because they do not grow enough food and do not earn enough money to buy the amount of food they need. Food shortage in this sense may, and does, exist even when crops are good and prices low, and works are abundant, and are exported. It is the result, not of a shortage in the total supply of food, but of lack of purchasing power in the hands of the poorer classes, that is, of their poverty.[108]

From the beginning of the twentieth century, Bengal turned into a region characterized by a large proportion of the population leading a quasi-famine existence. Occurrence of a severe famine of the type experienced in earlier centuries was averted only because there were no major natural calamities, on the one hand, and to a somewhat improved system of government vigilance over minor instances of scarcity on the other. In addition, the system of interpersonal transfer of resources continued, which sustained the equilibrium above excess mortality until

1943. The overall supply position was satisfactory except for a few years when a major catastrophe was averted by (1) drawing down of old stocks of foodgrains; (2) early consumption of new winter (*aman*) crop; and (3) curtailment of consumption. Existing free-trade policy worked quite well in the sense that traders were able to take advantage of local/regional scarcities by moving foodgrain from one place to another whenever market signals called for it. However, this did not necessarily ensure an adequate foodgrain intake for all since, at the ruling market price, the implicit purchasing power was unevenly distributed between various classes in the society. But the most important thing to realize here is that neither the private trading channels nor the governmental machinery was prepared to tackle a situation in which natural functioning of the economy and the society breaks down under the pressure of exogenous shocks. Working of endogenous forces, was we noted earlier, had created a situation, vulnerable to major outside shocks, more so because existing institutions were unwilling or unable to prepare themselves to protect the society from disaster of the type we are considering here.

This is the result of an alien administration and increasing inequity in the distribution of economic and political power. The dominant classes (feudal and semifeudal interests) in the society joined hands with the administrative elite to exploit the peasantry and workers. It is interesting to note that members of the alien ruling elite were sensitive to the possibility of internal hierarchical balance being upset through over-stretching of the processes of exploitation of the common people. Thus we see proliferation of various committees and commissions deliberating from time to time over problems of famine, rural indebtedness, land revenue and settlement policy, state of agriculture, and so forth. The reports produced contained very valuable insights into the problems of Indian agriculture, but not much action followed on their recommendations. During the nineteenth century, the emerging philosophy of the government was to do just enough to avoid peasant revolts of the Deccan type, which prompted it to appoint a Deccan Riots Commission and to avoid, if possible, huge excess mortality in famine, a concern that led it to emphasize formulation of famine codes. However, at no stage was there any serious effort to eliminate the basic causes of famine. More importantly, as the events of the few years preceding 1943 suggest, the government was reluctant to do anything beyond a certain point in terms of administrative, financial, and philosophical commitment to avert human suffering and excess mortality. Bhatia correctly says that "The Bengal famine was a tragedy in unpreparedness."[109] The famine was a tragedy indeed, but the unpreparedness was deliberate. It only reflects, on the one hand, a level of government indifference to the well-being of the people and, on the other, government's reluctance to "overcommit" (indeed, by its own narrowly conceived criteria) itself in the work related to famine prevention and relief. As we shall see shortly, the situation prevailing in Bangladesh was no different. It may sound odd, but the fact remains that the ruling elite of Bangladesh in 1974 was no less indifferent to the suffering of the people than the British government was in 1943. The same classes of people in the same region who were left to themselves to die because of lack of food and related diseases in 1943 were met roughly with the same situation thirty years later.

In the light of what has been said, further elaboration of the causes of the 1943 famine may sound academic, nevertheless it is very important for understanding the 1974 Bangladesh famine and attempting to develop a famine forewarning, prevention, and relief framework for the future. Two major causal hypotheses have been put forward regarding the 1943 famine. The Famine Inquiry Commission of 1944 and other contemporary writers seem to have argued that the famine was caused primarily by a shortfall in availability.[110] On the other hand, Sen attributes it to failure of exchange entitlements "which include the opportunities the market offers to a person to exchange other commodities into food."[111] Notwithstanding the assertion made by Sen that " 'food availability decline' seems to fail altogether in explaining famine,"[112] we must insist that both explanations have some merit and a proper understanding of the 1943 famine requires that we apply the general framework presented in Chapter 2 and test some of the hypotheses that emerge from it. In the modern world, famine represents a complex socio-economic phenomenon and as such, the search for *the* explanation as opposed to others is not likely to be very rewarding. As Sen himself points out, it is important to understand the general interdependencies that hold in the market economy. This naturally suggests that a famine of the dimension of the one in Bengal in 1943 should be analyzed in terms of a causal sequence where a number of factors make their own contributions and the task of the investigator is to reveal, if possible, the relative importance of each. In this context, it is somewhat of an oversimplification to present one single hypothesis of famine causality.

Sen shows that as compared with the average for 1938–1940, there was a shortfall in foodgrain availability per capita in 1941 and 1943.[113] Aggregate data actually suggests that the situation in 1943 was a shade better than 1941. But in terms of absolute availability in different districts and to different classes, the above data presents a somewhat misleading picture. Many districts suffered more relative to others because physical availability was affected by the "denial policy,"[114] favorable treatment of Calcutta as opposed to the rest of Bengal,[115] barriers on interdistrict movement of foodgrains,[116] late arrival of imports into Bengal,[117] inefficiency of the administration in storage and distribution of foodgrains to districts,[118] and panic hoarding by producers, consumers, and traders.[119]

These factors were carefully analyzed in the context of at least one district (Faridpur) by Mukerji.[120] His evidence, combined with the data provided by the Famine Inquiry Commission on dispatches of foodgrains to districts by the government, suggest that between April and October of 1943, many parts of Bengal witnessed a drastic shortfall in foodgrain availability per capita, which is not entirely captured by the aggregate annual index of per capita foodgrain availability calculated by Sen.[121] We have ignored here the question of carryover of rice stocks, which gave rise to considerable controversy among authors on the 1943 famine. We are somewhat sympathetic to the view contained in a dissenting note by a member of the Famine Commission in 1944, Mr. M. Afzal Hossain, that there probably was no carryover of previous production of rice at the end of 1942.[122] There was, therefore, a sharp decline in foodgrain availability in both stock and flow terms as defined by relationships (2.1), (2.2), (2.4), (2.6), (2.7), and (2.9) of Chapter 2. Here national level is equated with all of Bengal and regional level with districts. At the regional level, clearly, the decline in availability was unevenly distributed.

We do not intend to suggest that decline in physical availability explains everything, but its importance cannot be overlooked. Actually, in the context of our general analytic framework, the 1943 famine was a textbook famine in the sense that all factors identified in Figure 2.10 as causing foodgrain intake decline were operative. Foodgrain prices showed an increasing trend beginning in 1939, but the increase was much sharper between 1942 and 1943 as compared with earlier years.[123] Then the evidence provided by Sen clearly shows that there was a drastic fall in real income and relative prices of exchangeable (into food items) commodities of a large segment of rural population including agricultural laborers, fishermen, barbers, transport workers, paddy huskers, and so forth.[124] As was pointed out earlier, even in normal times a large number of families belonging to these groups live from hand to mouth. In the absence of formal social security arrangement, they are sustained over the years by informal charity and other types of interpersonal transfer of resources. At the time of the 1943 famine, this institution broke down under the pressure of rapidly changing circumstances. "Village charity, customarily in the form of gifts of rice, dried up not only because rice was in short supply, but also because it had become an expensive commodity. Those dependent on charity were thus soon reduced to starvation."[125]

Finally, the government had earlier supplied famine relief as its responsibility, but it was unwilling to develop an institutional arrangement to cope with the initial effects of foodgrain shortage that, in the situation prevailing in 1943 Bengal, would have required a large scale intervention in the market affecting import, export, procurement, and distribution. In fact, the crisis was unfolding as early as 1939 with the start of the war, and many ominous signs[126] were observed in the succeeding years, but the government failed to react to these in time. The government was conditioned, historically, to react only after foodgrain intake decline had taken considerable toll in terms of excess mortality.

In the years following the 1943 famine, many authors, including the Famine Inquiry Commission, have rightly criticized the government for delayed action, but little did they appreciate that the real tragedy lay in the fact that famine prevention was never seriously considered as part of the government's responsibility. The famine codes detailed the measures of relief and their administration, but indirectly they have been responsible for delayed action since there was emphasis on a "wait and see" policy. In addition, the determination of the time to declare famine was left entirely at the discretion of local authorities, who were often reluctant to take the final step for fear of not being able to cope with the demand for action placed on them by various provisions of the Famine Code.

Putting together all of the factors discussed so far, it can be asserted that the great Bengal famine of 1943 occurred due to a sharp decline in per capita foodgrain availability as defined broadly in relationships (2.10) and (2.11) of Chapter 2, which subsume the contending hypotheses presented by Sen and others. In order to complete the chain of causation, we can follow through the sequence presented in Figures 2.11 through 2.17. A number of factors leading to foodgrain availability decline per capita ($f(t)$ and $f^R(t)$) as shown in Figure 2.11 have already been commented on. We shall therefore concentrate on others. As compared with the year before, there were very moderate arrivals of rice and wheat into Bengal during the last quarter of 1942 and first quarter of 1943.[127] Import flow received a serious setback with the fall of Burma.[128] During the height of the crisis, the Bengal government and private traders were unable to procure rice and wheat from surplus states because of an embargo placed on exports from these states and also because of the inability of the central government to implement in time the "Basic Plan" which was designed to coordinate procurement and distribution throughout India according to availability in and requirement of different states.[129] Furthermore, despite the symptoms of a deepening crisis, there was a small amount of net export of rice from Bengal in 1942.[130] It has been suggested by many that the unprecedented price rise during late 1942 and early 1943 led to a reduction in market release by producers.[131] Finally, early in 1942, pressure was created in local availability by procurement under "Denial Policy" of the government.[132]

We next consider real income decline and foodgrain price increase as factors contributing to foodgrain intake decline. Data compiled by Sen indicate only a moderate increase in money wages of unskilled agricultural laborers as opposed to a very sharp increase in prices of foodgrains from September 1942 to December 1943.[133] This reflects a poor employment situation, which is not surprising in view of the fact that the historic process of pauperization and, hence, increase in numbers of landless agricultural laborers was further accelerated during this period through transfer of assets. In certain areas mild relief was available due to employment generated by war-related construction activities.[134] Furthermore, fall in output of the winter rice crop affected the income and employment of paddy huskers. Sen correctly points out the adverse effect of the "Boat Denial Policy" and shortfall in demand due to overall economic distress on the income and employment of fishermen, rural transport workers, craftsmen, barbers, and so forth.[135]

Unprecedented rise in foodgrain prices played a very important part in initiating the 1943 famine. On the supply side, shortfall in physical availability contributed to price rise. Here, physical availability should be looked at as a flow rather than a stock concept. On the demand side, panic purchase,[136] influx of Burmese refugees,[137] and general inflationary pressure in the economy pulled foodgrain prices up.[138] Both supply and demand situations were compounded by the Midnapore cyclone sending out the signal for impending crisis, failure of government price control measures,[139] ill-conceived and poorly executed internal procurement schemes of the government,[140] and general callousness shown by the central government of India[141] and the home government of Britain,[142] and finally the political difficulties at the state level faced by Bengal.[143] Thus we get the complete causal sequence of the 1943 famine in which a large number of factors played their own part. Admittedly, all factors were not equally important and probably the famine would have occurred even if a few among those discussed had actually been nonoperative. Given the present state of our knowledge, it would be presumptuous to attempt to estimate precisely the relative contribution of each factor.

The most important mark of the 1943 famine on the population of Bengal was the huge excess mortality, which at that time was estimated at 2.7 million by K. P. Chattopadhayay[144] and 1.5 million by the Famine Inquire Commission.[145] Both of these figures are somewhat arbitrary and extend only up to June 1944. In estimating famine mortality, Sen emphasized sensitivity of estimates to the time coverage. He shows that excess mortality continued many years after 1943 and arrives at his own estimates, varying between 2.62 million and 3.05 million during the 1943–1946 period, under alternative assumptions.[146] His estimates of excess mortality are based on registered deaths in West Bengal districts corrected for assumed underregistration. He did not estimate famine mortality for East Bengal, which is now Bangladesh.[147] Indeed, he merely used a figure of 1.714 million quoted in the Census of Pakistan 1951 reports and alternatively, he assumed that excess mortality in East Bengal was twice that in West Bengal,[148] which produced two estimates of excess mortality in East Bengal—1.816 million and 2.032 million under his assumptions A and B, respectively.[149] An alternative figure of 1.864 million is quoted by Khan.[150] But the basis of this estimate is not very clear. On the whole, excess mortality in Bangladesh due to the 1943 famine can be placed at 2 million. Sen makes the important point that there was neither a sex bias nor an age bias as compared with normal mortality. This is relevant in considering the growth and age composition of the population in the future, particularly in view of the fact that there is a general belief that famines in the past have caused a reduction in the birth rate in India. The Famine Inquiry Commission of 1944 said "there is no reason to doubt that births were greatly reduced in the Bengal Famine."[151]

As mentioned earlier, the 1943 famine was a prime example of class famine. Figures on mortality and distribution clearly reveal that the hard-hit groups were the agricultural laborers, fishermen, and other similar occupational groups.[152] The rate of destitution increased sharply during the famine.[153] It is not surprising that the famine led to further polarization in the rural society of Bengal as reflected in increased concentration of landholding, increased landlessness, and sharecropping, all of which are related to land transfer that took place during the famine period.[154] Loss of plough and cattle, through transfer and mortality, also affected the economic status of a large number of families in rural Bengal. Survey data compiled by Mahalanobis et al. shows that 14.4 percent of the families owning plough and cattle in April 1943 lost them between that period and April 1944. The figure for "agricultural labor" and "agriculture and labor" were 28.5 and 12.6 percent respectively.[155] On the whole, deterioration of the economic status of different classes in the society during the 1943 famine has been well documented by Mahalanobis et al., Mukherjee, and Mukerji.[156]

It is of particular interest to be able to see separately the effect of the 1943 famine on East Bengal, now Bangladesh. Mahalanobis et al. provides evidence for the whole of Bengal. It is not possible to get a separate picture for East Bengal. But the studies by Mukherjee and Mukerji cover two districts, Bogra and Faridpur, which are now included in Bangladesh. In the five surveyed villages of Faridpur, 13.7 percent of the population died of starvation and of diseases resulting from starvation; 28.5 percent of the families became destitutes, the rate of destitution being highest (52.4 percent) among agricultural laborers. This class also suffered most in the sense that, of the families turned destitutes, 77 percent were wiped out during 1943. Proportion of pure landless families (those with no landholding) in total increased from 29.9 percent on January 1, 1943, to 36.7 percent on January 1, 1944. Area under sharecropping increased from 16.1 percent to 16.5 percent of the total area under cultivation. Mean acreage of "owned and cultivated" land per family in each group below ten acres seems to have declined while that in the group above ten acres nearly doubled. The number of documents registered for sale of land (of the value of Rs. 100/- and upwards) increased from 14,783 in 1939 to 50,321 in 1943 in Faridpur. In the survey villages of the same district, Mukerji found that during 1943, 47.71 percent of the families transferred land, and the amount of land involved was 49.56 percent of total land owned in January 1943. As for Bogra, Mukherjee observes, "Out of the 232 households in 1942, the economic condition has deteriorated in 39 cases, that is, for 17 percent of the total households, and it has improved in 20 cases, that is, for 9 percent of the total number. Thus under a fine scrutiny a net 8 percent of the total households are seen to have gone down the ladder during 1942–44."[157] He further observes, "The specific feature of the change in the economic structure during 1942–44 is thus obvious. Hereby the differentiation has been further accentuated, leading to sharp polarization. The slightly inflated group at the top, which controls the vast mass of the people at the bottom, is being swelled more and more and having a gradually weaker link through the middle layer."[158]

The overall situation prevailing in East Bengal during 1945 can be visualized by analyzing the classification of subdivisions according to severity of famine as determined by two different departments of the Bengal government. Both clearly reveal great severity of famine in East Bengal as compared with the rest of the province. In terms of districts, Dacca, Tipperah, Chittagong, Noakhali, and Rangpur were particularly hard hit. This is also brought out by the course of mortality as revealed in the Famine Commission report.[159] Rangpur, Chittagong, Noakhali, and Tipperah were among the first districts experiencing a rise in death rather early in May and June 1943, with Chittagong having the highest mortality. Relating the degree of foodgrain scarcity to excess mortality, the commission points out,

> Chittagong, Dacca, Faridpur, Tipperah and Noakhali, normally deficit areas, were unquestionably seriously short of supplies in the famine year.

The excess mortality recorded in these districts in 1943 was in general considerably higher than the buying areas. It ranged from 51.1 percent in Faridpur to 121.0 percent in Chittagong, the excess in Tipperah, Dacca, and Noakhali being 118.6, 88.7, and 95.9 percent respectively.[160]

Dacca, Rangpur, and Tipperah were among four districts (including Malda) that continued to suffer severely from excess mortality in the first six months of 1944.

Available evidence shows that following the 1943 famine, Bengal made an adjustment back to low income–low foodgrain intake equilibrium, which characterized the economy and society prior to the famine. The route taken to achieve this adjustment was the familiar one, depicted in Figure 2.18 of Chapter 2. As the famine distress unfolded in the form of excess mortality, migration, wandering, disintegration of families, and the long trek of people into cities, particularly Calcutta, the Bengal government was forced to react by organizing relief measures. The relief efforts were summarily characterized as inadequate and belated by all concerned including the Famine Commission. Since the government did not declare famine, it was unable to appoint a famine commissioner with plenary powers. Instead, a relief commissioner was appointed in September 1943. Relief was afforded by way of gratuitous relief in the form of gruel, uncooked foodgrains and cash; test relief works wages; agricultural loans; and sale of foodgrains at cheap rates to the poor. Medical and voluntary relief work were also organized. The Famine Commission of 1944 was particularly critical of the quality and quantity of the medical assistance and pointed out that many lives could have been saved by timely action.[161]

However, as relief efforts continued in one form or another up to the end of the year (medical relief continued well into 1944), Bengal received large supplies of rice and wheat from outside and reaped a bumper harvest itself. Excess mortality slowly started to taper off although, as we mentioned earlier, the normal rate did not return until 1951. Available data also suggests that despite reduction in labor force due to excess mortality, neither winter rice output nor wages at that time and in subsequent periods was affected, an outcome consistent with our expectation regarding the impact of famine-induced pauperization in the state of the rural labor market. We have already commented upon the process of polarization observed in rural areas during the famine.

The combined effect of the operation of these processes has been the strengthening of the semifeudal production relations in Bengal agriculture. This view is also supported by Mukherjee, who studied very closely the social relations in rural East Bengal during the early 1940s.[162]

Like the previous instances of famine in British India during the late nineteenth century, a Famine Inquiry Commission[163] was appointed.

The commission presented a *Report on Bengal* in May of 1945. We have already quoted extensively from that document, which was later followed up by a *Final Report* containing in-depth discussion of all the issues related to food problems in India and recommendations for a future course of action. The effort of this commission was perhaps the best in this series although it should be recognized that it had the benefit of being able to draw upon earlier reports. In another report published in 1948, the government of India outlined the actions taken on the recommendations of the commission.[164] We shall very briefly sketch some of the important recommendations of the Famine Inquiry Commission along with immediate follow-up actions, if any, by the government.

1. The commission suggested that a "Grow More Food" campaign should be continued vigorously, and an appropriate administrative mechanism should be provided for its execution. The government of India reorganized the Ministries of Agriculture and Food at the Centre.

2. For deficit areas with difficulties of internal distribution, "full monopoly" of the government in procurement and distribution of food-grains was recommended. However, it was pointed out that this scheme would not be a practical proposition for Bengal where a limited monopoly should be considered. Nothing much came of this recommendation because "the Government of India . . . has since decided to embark upon a policy of progressive decontrol."[165]

3. The commission reiterated the need for accurate statistics on acreage and crop yield. Its recommendations regarding plot-to-plot enumeration to determine acreage and random sample surveys of yield were accepted by the government and, accordingly, special grants were made to respective state governments to carry out the work.

4. An important departure from the past was a recommendation for creating a reserve of 500,000 tons of foodgrains. This was accepted in principle by the government of India.

5. The question of size and growth of population received considerable attention. The commission said that although the rate of population growth in India had been less rapid than in certain other countries, "India, in relation to the existing stage of her industrial and economic development, is overpopulated,"[166] but added:

> While the fact that there is a serious population situation must be recognized, the primary problem is that of under-development of resources, both agricultural and industrial. The belief is expressed that it is possible, by a variety of means, to produce not only enough food to meet the needs of the growing population at subsistence level, but enough to effect an improvement in the diet of the people.[167]

It is to the credit of the commission that it was able to delineate a few important areas of population research. The government of India appeared to be in sympathy with the sentiment expressed by the Famine Inquiry Commission but in terms of specific actions, its approach was inexplicably cautious.[168]

6. On the question of nutrition, after analyzing the data on per capita income and the composition of a well-balanced diet, the Famine Inquiry Commission came to the conclusion that the average person cannot afford a balanced diet, and improvement of diet is not possible "without a great increase in the production of protective foods and simultaneous increase in purchasing power."[169]

7. The commission made a very far-reaching recommendation in saying that "the State should recognize its ultimate responsibility to provide enough food for all: not only to prevent starvation but to improve nutrition and create a healthy and vigorous population. All the resources of Government must be brought to bear to achieve this end in view."[170] The response of the government was cool and calculated. It said, "The general recommendation has been accepted but the methods of applying these principles will change in light of the overall situation."[171] But clearly this is begging the question. The issue here is not merely one of matching demand with supply, but actually touches upon a fundamental philosophy that needs to be clearly understood. This calls for adherence to the principle that each citizen of a country should have the right to control resources adequate to provide for his/her minimum needs at least. Unfortunately, past and present governments, with few exceptions, have failed to accept this philosophy, hence, the above reaction of the government of India.

8. For improvement of food production and nutrition, the Famine Inquiry Commission recommended expansion of irrigation facilities, increased use of manures and fertilizers, protection against pests and diseases and, wherever applicable, introduction of mechanization. In addition, specific recommendations were made to improve livestock, fisheries, production of fruits and vegetables, and agricultural research and organization.

9. Given the extensive problem of subdivision and fragmentation, the Famine Inquiry Commission recommended that land consolidation be actively undertaken by provinces along the lines of Punjab and Central Provinces. In this context the commission felt that "some limitation on the existing rights of unrestricted transfer is necessary and desirable in order to prevent an increase in fragmentation."[172] Land being a provincial subject, the central Ministry of Agriculture could do little more than draw the attention of provincial governments to these matters.

10. With respect to the tenurial system, the commission was of the opinion that "the terms of tenancy should be such that either the occupancy-right-holder provides the facilities necessary for efficient cultivation, or the non-occupancy tenant holds on conditions as to duration of tenancy and rent which provide adequate incentive for efficient cultivation."[173]

11. The commission was divided on the question of the crop-sharing system. Sir Manilal Nanavati suggested that the crop-sharing system should be abolished and the state should acquire the land of large landholders for resale on reasonable terms to landless cultivators and small landholders. Alternatively, he suggested registration to fix cash rents to lands held on the crop-sharing system and to confer occupancy rights on the tenants. Other members of the commission disagreed because they were not convinced that such changes would increase efficiency and also because a large amount of capital outlay and subsidization would be necessary to effect the transfer.

12. The commission was noncommittal about reforms in permanently settled areas. It suggested that problems of these areas should be carefully investigated.

13. In agricultural finance, the commission correctly assessed that the private money lender would continue to play an important role but that the system needed to be improved. Following the Punjab model, legislation was recommended to have money lenders licensed, to regulate interest rates by law, and to establish adequate machinery for administering the licensing system.

14. In its discussion on rural development organizations, the Famine Inquiry Commission rejected the idea of "collective farming" (Russian-type) and "joint farming" and came out in favor of multipurpose village cooperative societies with unlimited liability and the federation of such societies into multipurpose cooperative unions with limited liability.

15. Finally, a very thoughtful recommendation put forward by the commission was that "farm workers should also be encouraged to organize themselves, in order that they may enjoy reasonable wages which would be conducive to increased efficiency and production."[174] In this context the commission emphatically pointed out that "the aim of agricultural development is not merely an increase in production; it also includes the allotment of a larger share of such production for the benefit of the weaker members of society. The economic position of the weakest section of the agricultural community, the agricultural laborers, must also be improved."[175] One cannot but admire the forthrightness of the statement, since it represents the crux of the famine problem in Bengal, but the question remains as to who will initiate such a mobilization involving a large segment of the population?

Table 3.1. Past Famines in Bengal

Year	Popularly Attributed Cause	Mortality	Remarks
1662–1663	Interference with the transport of foodgrains by official exactions and obstructions on the routes.	Hundreds and thousands of souls perished.	A localized famine affecting primarily Dacca. Prices of foodgrains soared sky high.
1769–1770	Drought followed by flood	One-third of population or 10 million people	Suffering of the people intensified due to greed of East India Company officials, who formed a ring for the purpose of raising the price of grain.
1783	Drought	No estimate available	Bengal proper was not affected. Bihar, a part of greater Bengal, was partially affected. Warren Hastings, governor of Bengal, considered construction of permanent foodgrain storage facilities, with a view to preventing future famines. Nothing much came of this.
1866	Drought	135,000	Severely affected districts were Bankura, Nudea, Hugli. Twenty-four Parganas, an area of 9126 square miles and a population of over 6 million. A famine commission was appointed to inquire into the causes.
1873–1874	Drought	No famine deaths	This famine is known as "scare famine."
1891–1892	Failure of rains	No estimate available	Local scarcity affecting districts of Muzaffarpur, Darbhanga, Monghuyr, Bhagalpur, Purnea and Dinajpur, a population of 4 million in Bengal and Bihar.
1896–1897	Failure of rains	Loss of life	

(cont.)

Table 3.1 (continued)

Year	Popularly Attributed Cause	Mortality	Remarks
1943	Indifferent rain, "Midnapore Cyclone," fall of Burma, cutting off imports; difficulties created by speculation and hoarding.	3 million	This famine has been described as a tragedy in unpreparedness. All subdivisions of Bangladesh were affected with various intensities.

Sources: Atul Chandra Roy, *History of Bengal, Mughal Period* (Calcutta: Nababharat Publishers, 1968), pp. 256–257; Irfan Habib, *The Agrarian System of Mughal India* (London: Asia Publishing House, 1963), p. 107; W. W. Hunter, *Annals of Rural Bengal* (London: Smith, Elder, 1868), 3rd ed., pp. 19–60 and Appendixes A and B; Satischandra Ray, *An Essay on the Economic Causes of Famine and Suggestions to Prevent Their Frequent Recurrence* (Calcutta: Calcutta University, 1909), table of memorable Indian famines; Kali Charan Ghosh, *Famines in Bengal 1770–1943* (Calcutta: India Associated Publishing Co., 1944), pp. 7–8; Hari Shanker Srivastava, *The History of Indian Famines 1858–1918* (Agra: Sri Ram Mehra, 1968), pp. 238–240; A. K. Sen, "Starvation and Exchange Entitlement: A General Approach and Its Application to the Great Bengal Famine," *Cambridge Journal of Economics* 1 (1): 33–59 (March 1977).

NOTES AND REFERENCES

1. C. Walford, "The Famines of the World: Past and Present," *Journal of the Statistical Society* 41(3):436–442 (September 1978).
2. A. Loveday, *The History and Economics of Indian Famines* (London: G. Bell and Sons, 1914), pp. 135–137.
3. R. C. Majumdar, ed., *The History and Culture of the Indian People* (Bombay: Bharatya Vidya Bhaven, 1970) vol. 8, pp. 734–737.
4. Irfan Habib, *The Agrarian System of Mughal India* (London: Asia Publishing House, 1963).
5. As quoted in Loveday, *History and Economics of Indian Famines*, p. 11.
6. Ibid., p. 135.
7. Srivastava refers to Kautilya, who in his *Arthashastra* gives an account of measures to be adopted by the King in times of famine to relieve the suffering of the people. The measures include migration, encouragement of agriculture, and taxation of the rich to help the poor. See Hari Shanker Srivastava, *The History of Indian Famines 1858–1918* (Agra: Sri Ram Mehra, 1968), p. 14.
8. Famine Inquiry Commission, 1944, *Report on Bengal*, (New Delhi: Manager of Government Publications, 1945), pp. 30–31, 63–65.
9. Loveday, *History and Economics of Indian Famines*, p. 23.
10. Srivastava, *History of Indian Famines*, pp. 55–56.
11. Time and again many authors have referred to excessive revenue extraction. See M. Alamgir, *Bangladesh, A Case of Below Poverty Level Equilibrium Trap* (Dacca: Bangladesh Institute of Development Studies, 1978), pp. 48–50.
12. Habib, *Agrarian System*, p. 94.
13. Probably nothing much was done by way of providing relief to the famine victims outside the capital. See Loveday, *History and Economics of Indian Famines*, p. 23.
14. Habib, *Agrarian System*, p. 22.
15. As quoted in Prithwis Chandra Ray, *Indian Famines: Their Causes and Remedies* (Calcutta: Cherry Press, 1901), p. 6.
16. Habib, *Agrarian System*, p. 107.
17. Atul Chandra Roy, *History of Bengal, Mughal Period* (Calcutta: Nababharat Publishers, 1968), pp. 256–257. Italics in original.
18. Famine Inquiry Commission, 1944, *Report on Bengal*.
19. Habib, *Agrarian System*, p. 109.
20. Alamgir, *Bangladesh*, p. 63.
21. *Report of the Indian Famine Commission 1901* (Calcutta: Office of the Superintendent of Government Printing, India, 1901), p. 1.
22. Romesh C. Dutt, *Open Letters to Lord Curzon on Famines and Land Assessment in India* (London: Kegan Paul, Trench, Trubner, 1900), p. 1.
23. Kali Charan Ghosh, *Famines in Bengal 1770–1943* (Calcutta: India Associated Publishing Co., 1944), p. 3.
24. Majumdar, *History and Culture of Indian People*, vol. 9, p. 837.
25. B. P. Maheswari, *Industrial and Agricultural Development of India Since 1914* (New Delhi: S. C. Chand, 1971), p. 8.
26. These figures are quoted from B. M. Bhatia, *Famines in India 1860–1965* (New Delhi: Asia Publishing House, 1967), pp. 263, 324. For detailed analysis of mortality in the 1943 famine, see A. K. Sen, "Famine Mortality: A Study of the Bengal Famine of 1943," mimeographed, London School of Economics, August 1976.
27. W. W. Hunter, *Annals of Rural Bengal* (London: Smith, Elder, 1868), 3rd ed., pp. 19–60 and Appendixes A and B; Walford, "Famines of the World," p. 519. Srivastava

points out that this famine was not entirely due to rain as some authors claim, Srivastava, *History of Indian Famines*, p. 20n. For an account of this famine and comments on contemporary views, see Charles W. McMinn, *Famine, Truths—Half Truths—Untruths* (Calcutta: Tharker Spink, 1902).

28. From Arthur Lukyn Williams, we learn the following about actions taken by the government. "At an early period of the crisis, unsuccessful attempts were made to procure grain from abroad, and general instructions were published against the hoarding of grain, and against all sales or purchases of the article at any other place than the public markets. The utmost endeavors were used to bring to market all the produce which the country contained, and large subscriptions were raised for the relief of the distressed to which Europeans and natives contributed with equal liberality. In Moorshedasad alone 7,000 persons were fed for several months, but the devastation was so widespread that no general alleviation of the distress was possible," *Famines in India: Their Causes and Possible Prevention* (London: Henry S. King, 1876), p. 4. Loveday was, however, critical of relief efforts, which he thought were "unwise, unorganized and ungenerous," *History and Economics of Indian Famines*, p. 32.

29. Dutt, *Open Letters to Lord Curzon*, p. 2.

30. See R. Palme Dutt, *India Today* (London: Victor Gollancz, 1940), pp. 201–234; Kamal Kumar Ghose, *Agricultural Laborers in India, A Study in Their Growth and Economic Conditions* (Calcutta: India Publications, 1969), pp. 1–59; Surendra J. Patel, *Agricultural Laborers in Modern India and Pakistan* (Bombay: Current Book House, 1952), pp. 1–63; and Karunamoy Mukerji, *The Problem of Land Transfer* (Shantiniketan: Visva-Varati Press, 1957), pp. 1–90.

31. Alamgir, *Bangladesh*, p. 64.

32. Bhatia, *Famines in India*; Famine Inquiry Commission, 1944, *Report on Bengal.*

33. Bhatia, *Famines in India*; Famine Inquiry Commission, 1944, *Report on Bengal.*

34. Alamgir, *Bangladesh*; Ramkrishna Mukherjee, *The Dynamics of a Rural Society* (Berlin: Akademie-Verlag, 1957); Dutt, *India Today.*

35. Dutt, *Open Letters to Lord Curzon*; Williams, *Famines in India*; Vaughan Nash, *The Great Famine and Its Causes* (London: Longmann, Green, 1900); Ray, *Indian Famines*; Satischandra Ray, *An Essay on the Economic Causes of Famine in India and Suggestions to Prevent Their Frequent Recurrence* (Calcutta: Calcutta University Press, 1909); *Report of the Indian Famine Commission 1901*; Famine Inquiry Commission, 1944, *Report on Bengal*; Famine Inquiry Commission, 1944, *Final Report* (Madras: Manager of Government Publications, 1945); Bhatia, *Famines in India*; Srivastava, *History of Indian Famines*; Dadabhai Naoroji, *Poverty and Un-British Rule in India*, 1st India ed. (Ministry of Information and Broadcasting, Government of India Press, 1962).

36. Loveday, *History and Economics of Indian Famines*, pp. 34–36; Dutt, *Open Letters to Lord Curzon*, pp. 2–3; Srivastava, *History of Indian Famines*, pp. 21–22; R. A. Dalyell, *Memorandum on the Madras Famine of 1866* (Madras: Central Famine Relief Committee, 1867), pp. 12–17.

37. Walford, "Famines of the World," p. 443. Italics in original.

38. Famine Inquiry Commission, 1944, *Report on Bengal*, pp. 36–41.

39. Ray, *Economic Causes of Famine*, table on Memorable Indian Famines.

40. Walford, "Famines of the World," p. 444.

41. As quoted in Srivastava, *History of Indian Famines*, p. 24.

42. See, for example, Sir A. Cotton, "The Madras Famine," in *Famine in India* (New York: Arno Press, 1976) pp. 1–35; Williams, *Famines in India*, pp. 100–126; and Baird Smith as quoted in Srivastava, *History of Indian Famines*, pp. 51–52.

43. See W. R. Aykroyd, *The Conquest of Famine* (London: Chatto and Windus, 1974), p. 23; Dalyell, *Madras Famine of 1866*, pp. 20, 30.

44. Dalyell, *Madras Famine of 1866,* p. 32.
45. Ibid., p. 33; Srivastava, *History of Indian Famines,* p. 25.
46. Dalyell gives a mortality figure of 150,000 in the Guntor district with a population of half a million, *Madras Famine of 1866,* pp. 40–41.
47. Ibid., p. 32.
48. Loveday, *History and Economics of Indian Famines,* p. 41. The burden of the existing oppressive fiscal system has also been highlighted by Baird Smith. See Srivastava, *History of Indian Famines,* p. 26.
49. Loveday, *History and Economics of Indian Famines,* p. 47.
50. Ray, *Economic Causes of Famine,* table on Memorable Indian Famines; Bhatia, *Famines in India,* p. 62.
51. The Chamber of Commerce wanted to find remedies against drastic fall in demand for British goods following the 1860 famine. See Srivastava, *History of Indian Famines,* p. 50; Bhatia, *Famines in India,* p. 61n. The mortality figure mentioned here is attributed to Baird Smith.
52. Loveday, *History and Economics of Indian Famines,* pp. 46–47.
53. Dalyell, *Madras Famine of 1866,* p. 79.
54. Ibid., pp. 72–73. According to Dalyell, agricultural laborers being paid largely in kind at the same rate as before were not affected by the rise in prices of agricultural commodities during the ten years prior to 1866.
55. Srivastava, *History of Indian Famines,* p. 81n.
56. Ibid., p. 76.
57. Ibid., p. 80.
58. Dalyell, *Madras Famine of 1866,* p. 109.
59. Srivastava, *History of Indian Famines,* pp. 87–91. Members of the commission were Colonel Morton and Mr. H. L. Dampiers, and George Campbell was the chairman.
60. Ray, *Indian Famines,* p. 8. For 1900 alone the 1901 Famine Commission estimates excess mortality of 1.5 million. Unofficial estimates put it at 3.25 million for the famine and related diseases. *Report of the Indian Famine Commission 1901,* para. 203; Bhatia, *Famines in India,* p. 261.
61. Nash, *Great Famine,* p. 222.
62. Bhatia, *Famines in India,* p. 159.
63. Srivastava, *History of Indian Famines,* p. 129.
64. These issues are discussed in William Digby, *The Famine Campaign in Southern India 1876–1878* (London: Longmann, Green, 1878), vol. I, pp. 2–3, 9–10, 28–33, 90–91; vol. II, pp. 167–174; Loveday, *History and Economics of Indian Famines,* pp. 59–60; Srivastava, *History of Indian Famines,* pp. 130–134; Bhatia, *Famines in India,* pp. 94–96.
65. The letter is reproduced in Digby, *Famine Campaign,* vol. II, pp. 397–405.
66. Ibid., vol. I, p. 50.
67. In the interested trading circles, the amount rumored was much higher, as much as ten times this amount. See ibid., vol. I, p. 33.
68. The new ration (wage rate) was nicknamed the "Temple Ration."
69. A detailed account of this debate can be found in Digby, *Famine Campaign,* vol. II, pp. 175–210.
70. Ibid., vol. I, p. 91.
71. *Report of the Indian Famine Commission 1901,* para. 6.
72. Digby, *Famine Campaign,* vol. II, p. 482.
73. Ibid., p. 483.
74. These tests show respectively, "that he is willing to labour at a distance from his home, not returning there at night, but being hutted on the work. . . . that he receives a wage calculated to provide a bare subsistance for himself, but not enough to support any

non-working member of the family. . . . that he performs a daily task proportional to his strength," Ibid., p. 483.

75. The commission was presided over by Sir John Strachey. Mr. C. A. Elliot was appointed secretary to the commission.

76. *Report of the Indian Famine Commission 1901,* para. 7.

77. On the question of state storage of foodgrains, the government of India categorically rejected a suggestion by two dissenting members of the Strachey commission. See Bhatia, *Famines in India,* pp. 182–183.

78. *Report of the Indian Famine Commission 1901,* para. 8.

79. Ibid., para. 9.

80. Srivastava, *History of Indian Famines,* p. 239.

81. As quoted in Dutt, *Open Letters to Lord Curzon,* pp. 14–15.

82. Alamgir, *Bangladesh,* p. 251.

83. See *Report of the Indian Famine Commission 1901,* paras. 15–20; Bhatia, *Famines in India,* pp. 215–252.

84. Other members were F. A. Nicholson, J. A. Bourdillon, and Sayam Sunder Lal.

85. *Report of the Indian Famine Commission 1901,* para. 11.

86. Ibid., para. 48.

87. Ibid., para. 288.

88. The measures include exemption of increase of assets from assessment to revenue, reduction of rate of interest and liberalization of conditions of security. Ibid., paras. 316–318, 323.

89. See Srivastava, *History of Indian Famines,* pp. 296–299; Bhatia, *Famines in India,* pp. 265–270.

90. Bhatia, *Famines in India,* pp. 268–269.

91. Alamgir, *Bangladesh,* p. 62n; Bhatia, *Famines in India,* p. 312.

92. George Blyn, *Agricultural Trends in India, 1891–1947: Output Availability and Productivity* (Philadelphia: University of Pennsylvania Press, 1966), p. 122.

93. Ibid., p. 102.

94. Famine Inquiry Commission, 1944, *Report on Bengal.* Figures calculated on the basis of output data on p. 215 and population figures on p. 183. Per capita availability of foodgrains shows a similar pattern during the period under consideration.

95. Ibid., pp. 213, 215.

96. Ghosh, *Famines in Bengal,* pp. 27–32; Bhatia, *Famines in India,* pp. 38, 137, 219, 317.

97. Alamgir, *Bangladesh,* pp. 50–56; Mukherjee, *Dynamics of Rural Society,* p. 53.

98. Famine Inquiry Commission, 1944, *Report on Bengal,* p. 6.

99. Mukerji, *Problem of Land Transfer,* pp. 1–100; Mukherjee, *Dynamics of Rural Society,* p. 39, 39n. Many other authors commented on how land became a transferable commodity in Bengal and what implications it had for changing social relations in agriculture. For example, M. Azizul Haq, *The Man Behind the Plow* (Calcutta: The Book Company, 1939), pp. 298–312; Krishnakali Mukerji, "The Transferability of Occupancy Holdings in Bengal," *Bengal Economic Journal* 1(3):247–266 (January 1917) and 2(1):22–43 (January 1918).

100. Patel, *Agricultural Laborers in Modern India,* p. 9.

101. J. C. Jack, *The Economic Life of a Bengal District, A Study* (London: Oxford University Press, 1927), p. 84.

102. See J. M. Pringle, "Agricultural Distress in Brahmanbaria," *Bengal Economic Journal* 1(3):271 (January 1917).

103. Ghose, *Agricultural Laborers in India,* p. 36. Dutt draws attention to a substantial increase in the number of noncultivating landlords or rent receivers between 1921 and 1931. See Dutt, *India Today,* p. 217.

104. Alamgir, *Bangladesh,* p. 65.

105. Ghose, *Agricultural Laborers in India,* p. 185.

106. Ramkrishna Mukherjee, *Six Villages of Bengal* (Bombay: Popular Prakashan, 1971), pp. 190–207.

107. These are somewhat subjective criteria developed by J. C. Jack. According to him, " 'Comfort,' . . . implied a condition in which the material necessities of life could be fully satisfied; 'indigence' (want) . . . implied a condition in which the family had just sufficient to keep itself alive and no more; and two classes intermediate between these extremes, one labeled 'below comfort,' in which the income and material conditions approximated more nearly to those of families living in indigence, and the other labeled 'above indigence,' in which the income and material conditions approximated more nearly to those of indigent families." Jack, *Economic Life of a Bengal District,* p. 73. A more objective analysis of the economic condition of the rural population in Bogra district was carried out by Mukherjee. He shows that 29 percent of the households had per capita income below 'food level' which is defined in terms of a minimum nutritional requirement. See Mukherjee, *Six Villages of Bengal,* pp. 158, 173.

108. Famine Commission, 1944, *Report on Bengel,* p. 12. In this statement there is an implicit recognition of the relationship (2.10) given in Chapter 2 as a basis for analyzing famine.

109. Bhatia, *Famines in India,* p. 302. Historically, as we noted earlier, the British government's financial commitment to famine relief has been constrained by its excessive concern for economy.

110. To be fair to the Famine Inquiry Commission, it should be noted that they also recognized that "out of the total supply available for consumption in Bengal, the proportionate requirements of large sections of the population who normally buy their supplies from the market, either all the year round or during a part of the year, were not distributed to them at a price which they could afford to pay." Famine Inquiry Commission, *Report on Bengal,* 1944, p. 77.

111. A. K. Sen, "Starvation and Exchange Entitlements: A General Approach and Its Application to the Great Bengal Famine." *Cambridge Journal of Economics* 1(1):55 (March 1977).

112. Ibid.

113. Ibid., p. 41. Shortfall in availability in 1943 was due primarily to shortfall in *aman* (winter rice) output caused by indifferent rain and the devastating Midnopore cyclone of October 1942.

114. Under this policy, orders were issued on May 1, 1942, to remove all boats with carrying capacity of ten persons or more to deny easy mobility to the Japanese, who were posing a threat on the frontier of Bengal. According to the Famine Inquiry Commission of 1944, "The extent to which the movement of rice was impeded, it is impossible to frame an estimate." Famine Inquiry Commission, 1944, *Report on Bengal,* pp. 26–27. According to Mukerji, "External supply to the district (Faridpur) in 1942 was very greatly hindered in consequence of the 'Boat Denial' policy of the Government." See Karunamoy Mukerji, *Agriculture, Famine and Rehabilitation,* (Shatiniketan: Visva Varati, 1965), p. 45. See also Ghose, *Agricultural Laborers in India,* pp. 52–55.

115. Sir Manilal Nanavati, a member of the Famine Inquiry Commission of 1944, emphasized this point. Famine Inquiry Commission, 1944, *Report on Bengal,* pp. 101–102.

116. Ibid., pp. 16–17, 190–194; Mukerji, *Agriculture, Famine and Rehabilitation,* p. 45.

117. Mukerji, *Agriculture, Famine and Rehabilitation,* pp. 41–54; Sen, "Starvation and Exchange Entitlements," p. 40.

118. Famine Inquiry Commission, 1944, *Report on Bengal,* p. 104.

119. Sen, "Starvation and Exchange Entitlements," p. 50; Ghosh, *Famines in Bengal*, pp. 33–38; Mukerji, *Agriculture, Famine and Rehabilitation*, pp. 46–47.

120. Mukerji, *Agriculture, Famine and Rehabilitation*, pp. 1–218.

121. Sen, "Starvation and Exchange Entitlements," p. 41. For each year from 1938 through 1943, the index of per capita foodgrain availability was as follows: 1938, 129; 1939, 120; 1940, 123; 1941, 100; 1942, 130; 1943, 109.

122. Famine Inquiry Commission, 1944, *Report on Bengal*, pp. 179–187. See also Government of Bengal, Civil Supplies Department, *Report of the Foodgrain Procurement Committee, 1944* (Alipore: Bengal Government Press, 1944), pp. 26–27.

123. Data from two sources may be quoted.

Year	Foodgrains Price Index	Year	Index Number of Wholesale Prices of Cereals in Calcutta (1914—100)
1939–40	100	1939	86
1940–41	109	1940	99
1941–42	160	1941	112
1942–43	385	1942	157
1st half of 1942–43	385	1943	396

Source: For col. 2, Famine Inquiry Commission, 1944, *Final Report*, p. 484; Sen, "Starvation and Exchange Entitlements," p. 43. For col. 4, Mukerji, *Agriculture, Famine and Rehabilitation*, p. 106, Table 20.

124. Sen, "Starvation and Exchange Entitlements," pp. 42–49.

125. Famine Inquiry Commission, 1944, *Report on Bengal*, p. 67.

126. Some of these include: successive crop failures beginning in 1938, fall of Burma, rising trend in rice prices, and the Midnapore cyclone.

127. Famine Inquiry Commission, 1944, *Report on Bengal*, pp. 28, 31, 54, 189n, 214–222.

128. Bhatia, *Famines in India*, pp. 322–323. Between 1935–1936 and 1939–1940, Bengal imported an average of approximately 377,200 tons of rice and paddy from Burma. See *Report of Foodgrains Procurement Committee*, p. 26.

129. Famine Inquiry Commission, 1944, *Report on Bengal*, pp. 21–24, 44–54, 90–92.

130. Ibid., p. 215.

131. Bhatia, *Famines in India*, p. 321; Sen, "Starvation and Exchange Entitlements," p. 50.

132. Famine Inquiry Commission, 1944, *Report on Bengal*, pp. 25–26.

133. Sen, "Starvation and Exchange Entitlements," p. 44.

134. Ibid., p. 51.

135. Ibid., p. 45, 48, 51.

136. Famine Inquiry Commission, 1944, *Report on Bengal*, p. 18.

137. Bhatia, *Famines in India*, p. 321.

138. Sen, "Starvation and Exchange Entitlements," p. 5.

139. Famine Inquiry Commission, 1944, *Report on Bengal*, pp. 27–30, 38–41; Bhatia, *Famines in India*, p. 327.

140. Famine Inquiry Commission, 1944, *Report on Bengal*, pp. 36–38, 58–59, 85–98; Bhatia, *Famines in India*, pp. 328–331.

141. Famine Inquiry Commission, 1944, *Report on Bengal*, pp. 105–106; Sen, "Starvation and Exchange Entitlements," p. 54; Bhatia, *Famines in India*, p. 339; T. G. Narayan, *Famine Over Bengal* (Calcutta: The Book Company, 1944) pp. 73–89.

142. Sen, "Starvation and Exchange Entitlements," p. 53; Narayan, *Famine Over Bengal*, pp. 90–101. The Churchill government was reluctant to allow other nations (for

example, the United States) to come to the aid of Bengal. See M. S. Venkatramani, *Bengal Famine of 1943, the American Response* (Delhi: Vikas Publishing House Pvt., 1973).

143. This was primarily reflected in the lack of cooperation between the governor of Bengal and his cabinet headed by A. K. Fazlul Huq. For a detailed account of the politics of famine administration during this period, see Bhatia, *Famines in India*, pp. 236–237; Famine Inquiry Commission, 1944, *Report on Bengal*, p. 105; Ghosh, *Famines in Bengal*, pp. 236–237 and Appendix C; Narayan, *Famine Over Bengal*, pp. 20–34, 47–72.

144. Sen, "Famine Mortality," pp. 5-6.

145. Famine Inquiry Commission, 1944, *Report on Bengal*, p. 110. Dr. Aykroyd, who was responsible for this estimate, later admitted that it was an understimate. See Aykroyd, *Conquest of Famine*, p. 77.

146. Sen, "Famine Mortality," pp. 1-10. He mentioned that normal death rate was not restored until 1951.

147. Ibid., p. 9.

148. Ibid., p. 10.

149. Under assumption A, the average mortality of 1941 and 1942 is taken as "normal" and under assumption B, the 1942 figure is taken as "normal." Ibid., p. 7.

150. Masihur Rahman Khan, "Bangladesh Population During the First Five Year Plan Period (1973–1978): An Estimate," *Bangladesh Economic Review* 1(2):188 (April 1973).

151. Famine Inquiry Commission, 1944, *Report on Bengal*, p. 112.

152. Sen, "Starvation and Exchange Entitlement," pp. 46–49; Sen, "Famine Mortality," pp. 18–19; Mukerji, *Agriculture, Famine and Rehabilitation*, p. 178; Tarakchandra Das, *Bengal Famine (1943) as Revealed in a Survey of the Destitutes in Calcutta* (Calcutta: University of Calcutta, 1949), pp. 67–69; P. C. Mahalanobis, Ramkrishna Mukherjee, and Ambika Ghosh, "A Sample Survey of After-Effects of the Bengal Famine of 1943," *Sankhya* 7(4):360–361 (1946).

153. According to Mahalanobis, Mukherjee, and Ghosh, the process of destitution had set in before 1943, "After-Effects of the Bengal Famine," pp. 357, 362.

154. Ibid., pp. 375–383; Das, *Bengal Famine (1943)*, pp. 70–74; Mukerji, *Agriculture, Famine and Rehabilitation*, pp. 58–59, 178–179; Mukerji, *Problem of Land Transfer*, pp. 45–66, 111–138; Mukerji, *Six Villages of Bengal*, pp. 216–219.

155. P. C. Mahalanobis, Ramkrishna Mukherjee, and Ambika Ghosh, "After-Effects of the Bengal Famine," pp. 284–390.

156. Ibid., pp. 365–371; Mukerji, *Six Villages of Bengal*, pp.175–188; Mukerji, *Agriculture, Famine and Rehabilitation*, pp. 55–57.

157. Mukherjee, *Six Villages of Bengal*, p. 186.

158. Ibid., p. 187.

159. Famine Inquiry Commission, 1944, *Report on Bengal*, pp. 112–115.

160. Ibid., p. 114. "Buying areas" refer to those districts considered as surplus by the Bengal government.

161. Ibid., p. 69.

162. Mukherjee asserts that, during the British period, the agrarian economy of Bengal was semifeudal. He refutes the viewpoint that appropriation of land from the peasantry and growing number of sharecroppers are signs of the emergence of capitalism in agriculture. See *Dynamics of Rural Society*, pp. 53–54.

163. The commission was headed by J. A. Woodhead. Members were S. V. Ramamurty, Manilal B. Nanavati, M. Afzal Hossain, and Dr. W. R. Aykroyd.

164. Government of India, Ministry of Food, *Report Showing Action Taken by Central and Provincial Governments on the Recommendations Made by the Famine Inquiry*

Commission in their Final Report (Delhi: Manager of Publications, 1948).
165. Ibid., p. 4.
166. Famine Inquiry Commission, 1944, *Final Report*, pp. 102–103.
167. Ibid., p. 104.
168. *Action Taken by Central and Provincial Governments on Recommendations Made by Famine Inquiry Commission*, pp. 10–11.
169. Ibid., p. 12.
170. Ibid., p. 13. In making this statement, the Famine Inquiry Commission had gone far beyond the limit set by previous commissions, who only asserted that famine was the government's responsibility.
171. Ibid., p. 13.
172. Famine Inquiry Commission, 1944, *Final Report*, p. 265.
173. Ibid., p. 273.
174. Famine Inquiry Commission, 1944, *Report on Bengal*, p. 68.
175. Famine Inquiry Commission, 1944, *Final Report*, p. 324.

Chapter 4

Bangladesh Famine of 1974

INTRODUCTION

In this chapter we look closely at the 1974 Bangladesh famine. We shall first discuss the nature of the data used in this study.[1] This will be followed by a section detailing the prelude to the crisis, that is, outlining events leading to the 1974 famine. More specifically, we will discuss the development of the Bangladesh economy and the society from the 1950s through the 1970s. A short description will be added in this section on the incidence of natural disasters (floods and cyclones) in Bangladesh during its recent history. Natural disasters assume great importance because many social and economic characteristics of Bangladesh have been molded by the occurrence of natural calamities at regular intervals. It is, however, interesting to note that, while both floods and cyclones are known to have caused death and destruction, none of the recorded major famines of this region has been attributed to either. However, in 1770 drought was followed by flood so that the expected yield of the winter crop could not be realized, thus aggravating the famine. But the 1974 Bangladesh famine was associated with, among other factors, a severe flood. In addition, the cyclones of December 1970 and 1973[2] left many areas and groups of population (for example, coastal fishing communities) especially vulnerable to further exogenous shocks.

101

Following this, the profile of the 1974 famine is presented. Then we focus our attention on some famine substates about which we have detailed information. The final section discusses famine mortality.

DATA—NATURE AND SOURCE

This study of the 1974 famine is based on the data obtained from a survey carried out in eight villages and eight *langarkhanas* (gruel kitchens—free cooked-food distribution centers) of Bangladesh during November of 1974. In addition, time series data on acreage, production, stock, procurement, import, government offtake, price of food grains (rice and wheat), and other relevant items were collected from secondary sources. Data on wages of agricultural laborers were obtained from the Directorate of Agriculture. Most of the nonsurvey data was obtained from either secondary published sources or directly from related organizations. Care has been taken to remove inconsistencies of data from various sources.

The famine survey was carried out by the Bangladesh Institute of Development Studies (BIDS), Dacca, during the later period of the famine, and the data collected related to the periods from July 1973 to June 1974 and from July to October 1974, prior to and corresponding with the flood and famine of 1974. The sample of observations include 1774 households in eight villages and 788 inmates of eight *langarkhanas*. "Households" were defined as consisting of members who ate from the same kitchen and who operated productive assets as a single unit. The choice of villages was not random. Observing a close correspondence between the intensity of flood (measured by maximum depth and period of innundation) and the intensity of famine (measured by reported incidents of starvation-related deaths and the proportion of population seeking relief in *langarkhanas*), the districts of Bangladesh were divided into famine areas and nonfamine areas. Those districts suffering maximum depth of inundation, six feet and above in a period of three months and above with the proportion of population seeking relief in *langarkhanas* being 5 percent and above were classified as famine districts. The remaining districts were classified as nonfamine districts. Districts classified accordingly are shown in Table 4.1.

Admittedly, the above classification of districts is somewhat arbitrary. In fact, at the time the survey was conducted, we were very hard pressed for time because we wanted the investigators to get to the field before the height of the famine was over. In addition, prior to the survey, we did not have detailed information available at our disposal except for the newspaper accounts of the famine in various parts of the country and what was revealed from a small preliminary survey of destitutes in Dacca, the capital city of Bangladesh. The concerned government agency at the center, the Ministry of Food, Relief and Rehabilitation, was reluctant to cooperate with our study.[3] It was therefore impossible to obtain a more elaborate classification of districts according to the degree of famine intensity as was done during the 1943 famine. Our own survey and information obtained later revealed that all districts of Bangladesh suffered from famine to a certain extent in 1974 but there remained a difference in the intensity of suffering in the two areas grouped separately in Table 4.1.

Table 4.1. Classification of Districts of Bangladesh into Famine and Nonfamine Areas as Used for Selection of Survey Villages

Famine (3)	Nonfamine (16)
Mymensingh	Bogra
	Comilla
Rangpur	Chittagong Hill Tracts
	Dinajpur
Sylhet	Jessore
	Khulna
	Pabna
	Rajshahi
	Barisal
	Chittagong
	Dacca
	Faridpur
	Kushtia
	Noakhali
	Patuakhali
	Tangail

Four villages were selected from famine areas, and four from non-famine area. As for famine areas, the most affected unions (lowest administrative unit consisting on an average of fifteen villages with populations between 15,000 and 30,000) were first chosen in consulation with the district authorities and then the nearest village from the union headquarters where a gruel kitchen was operating was selected. A second village was selected from Rangpur (being the hardest hit of all districts), thereby giving us four villages from three famine districts. The second village in Rangpur and all four villages in nonfamine areas were selected from among those about whom we had prior information from other surveys carried out by BIDS. This is why we selected a village from a relatively prosperous area of Sylhet that was otherwise a famine-stricken district. We also used the same field staff members who had been associated with earlier surveys to carry out the famine survey. This enabled us to obtain very intimate accounts in these areas, and there was little problem in establishing rapport with the interviewees. In any case, the field investigators secured assistance of locally recruited enumerators from among college students or school teachers in each area. Survey questionnaires were administered to all households in selected villages. The sample villages cannot be said to be strictly representative of the country as a whole, but given the fact that, apart from covering famine and nonfamine areas, the villages are scattered over all four important geographical regions of Bangladesh (Northwest, North, Northeast, and South and Southwest) and the total number of observations is quite reasonable, we do make some general observations that should be treated with caution.

At about the same time that the village surveys were undertaken, 788 inmates of eight *langarkhanas* were also interviewed. Of the eight *langarkhanas*, four were in rural areas and four in urban areas. Three of the four rural *langarkhanas* were located in the three famine-area villages, while the fourth was taken from a nonfamine-area village. Urban *langarkhanas* selected for this study were from among those located in the corresponding district headquarters of the rural *langarkhanas* except that instead of choosing one from Sylhet we chose the Mirpur *langarkhana* in Dacca. Mirpur was selected because Dacca, the main urban center of the country, has had a tremendous pull on the destitutes and potential migrants from other areas, and this process was accelerated during the 1974 famine. Therefore, a sample of inmates of a *langarkhana* in Dacca was expected to capture a cross section of migrants from different parts of the country, revealing additional information that could not have been available from other places. In each of the *langarkhanas* selected, between ninety and a hundred inmates were chosen at random. Professional beggars were avoided. A list of sample villages and *langarkhanas* with number of observations is given in Table 4.2, and their locations are shown in Figure 4.1

PRELUDE TO CRISIS

The Period Before 1970

The 1943 Great Bengal Famine left behind a deep impression on the economy and society of Bangladesh. Almost all districts were affected, some very severely. As the low-income–low-foodgrain intake equilibrium

Table 4.2. Sample Villages and Langarkhanas

	Thana	District	Number of Observations
Villages			
Famine area			869
Ramna	Chilmari	Rangpur	294
Gaorarong	Sunamganj	Sylhet	235
Kogaria	Gobindaganj	Rangpur	179
Kellakata	Dewanganj	Mymensingh	161
Nonfamine area			905
Nazirpur	Bauphal	Patuakhali	363
Laskarpur	Kulaura	Sylhet	227
Komorpur	Satkhira	Khulna	178
Charbaniari	Bagerhat	Khulna	137
All villages			1774
Langarkhanas			
Rural area			388
Bagerhat	Bagerhat	Khulna	91
Chilmari	Chilmari	Rangpur	102
Dewanganj	Dewanganj	Mymensingh	95
Sunamganj	Sunamganj	Sylhet	100
Urban area			400
Khulna	Kotwali	Khulna	101
Rangpur	Kotwali	Rangpur	101
Mymensingh	Kotwali	Mymensingh	97
Mirpur	Mirpur	Dacca	101
All *langarkhanas*			788

was restored through the postfamine societal adjustment processes discussed in Chapter 3, partition of India took place and East Bengal gained independence as East Pakistan, a part of Pakistan. The most significant impact of the partition was massive in-and-out migration across international frontiers, which continued throughout the 1950s and 1960s.[4] The basic characteristics of rural areas did not change. It is true that in 1950 the *Zemindari* system—under which land was permanently settled with landlords who paid land revenue annually to the government —was abolished, but the mass of peasantry continued to suffer at the hands of rich farmers, moneylenders to whom the peasants and agricultural laborers had to surrender surplus in the form of high share rental, high interest on loans, excessive markups on marketed commodities, and low return on the sale of labor power.[5]

During the 1950s and 1960s many resources were transferred from East to West Pakistan,[6] which accounted for a slow economic growth rate in

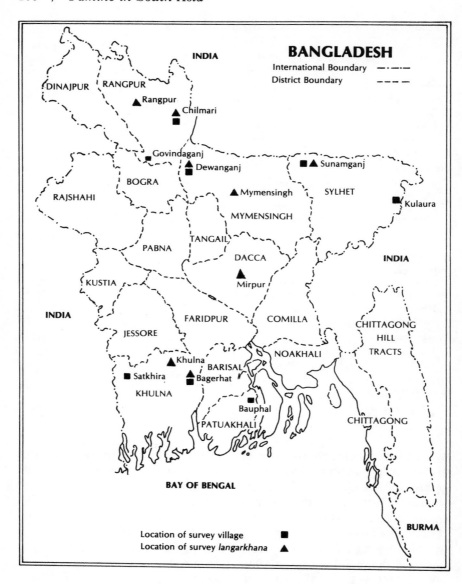

Figure 4.1. Location of survey villages and langarkhanas.

East Pakistan. Over the period 1949/1950 to 1969/1970, the Gross Domestic Product of Bangladesh at constant 1959/1960 factor cost increased at an annual compound rate of 3.3 percent, the rate being much lower for 1949/1950 to 1959/1960, only 2.3 percent per annum. The corresponding figures for the agricultural sector were 2.2 percent and 1.5 percent respectively.[7] These figures may be contrasted with the population growth rates of 1.9 percent and 2.5 percent per annum for the 1951–1961 and 1961–1970 periods.[8] Real income per capita declined for both agricultural and rural populations between the early 1950s and late 1960s.[9] Analyzing the long-term trend in real wages of agricultural laborers in Bangladesh, it is found that, with some fluctuations over the period, the index of real wage stood at 124 (1966 = 100) in 1970 as compared with 112 in 1949. However, the overall purchasing power of agricultural laborers declined because the total number of days employed declined, due to slow growth of the agricultural sector and a relatively high rate of population and labor force growth. Additional employment generated in the nonagricultural sectors was insignificant. The trend of the index of real wage earnings of urban laborers is similar. Throughout the 1950s and 1960s the levels of real wage earnings for both rural and urban laborers fluctuated between poverty level and famine level. Available data indicates that during the 1960s both the proportion and number of people below poverty level increased.[10]

According to the special inquiry made in 1939 at the insistence of the Bengal Land Revenue Commission, the average landholding of agricultural families was 4.38 acres. Data for 1960 and 1968 place the figures for Bangladesh (East Bengal) at 3.5 and 3.2 acres, respectively. On the other hand, in 1939 it was found that 75 percent of households owned 5 acres or less in Bengal, the corresponding figures for 1960 and 1968 in Bangladesh being 77 percent and 83 percent. Available evidence also suggests that concentration of landholding in rural areas in Bangladesh increased between the 1940s and 1950s, but there was no appreciable change during the 1960s. Similarly, the proportion of families living mainly or entirely as sharecroppers during these three periods were found to be 12.2, 39, and 34 percent respectively. Therefore, the number of families susceptible to pressure from the landlord class increased significantly over the 1940s and the 1950s, the proportion in the late 1960s showing a declining trend although the absolute number continued to rise. It is difficult to present data on the long-term trend of landlessness because the definition of landlessness has changed from time to time. We have access to some data that suggests that the percentage of landless households to total households increased between 1951 and 1961, the worsening trend continuing throughout the 1960s.[11]

Clearly, the majority of the Bangladesh population lived in poverty during the 1950s and 1960s even though there was no period of drastic fall in the standard of living or foodgrain intake per capita comparable to that of 1943. The domestic production of rice and wheat was not sufficient to meet domestic demand; substantial import of rice and wheat was necessary throughout the entire period. The rate of growth of rice output has not kept much ahead of population growth. The per capita production of rice was higher in 1950–1955 than in 1955–1960, and it improved only slightly during 1965–1969. Per capita availability of foodgrains shows considerable fluctuation over the period 1950–1970.[12] After reviewing different estimates by different authorities, the Famine Inquiry Commission of 1944 came to the conclusion that, in Bengal, general average consumption of all cereals was somewhere between fifteen and seventeen ounces per capita per day.[13] In only one year out of twenty (1950–1951 to 1969–1970) was this range reached in Bangladesh (as measured by availability).[14] There is considerable disparity in per capita consumption of cereals between different income groups. Available data suggest that in periods of lower availability per capita, people in lower income groups were forced to reduce consumption more than those in upper income groups. In the rural areas, during the 1960s, per capita consumption in low-income families has been consistently declining irrespective of availability per capita.[15] In some urban areas, the cereal consumption levels of households were protected through a system of rationing.[16]

During the 1950s and 1960s, Bangladesh experienced general scarcity of foodgrains in almost all years if measured by any objective norms, but, as we discussed earlier, the low foodgrain intake status was one of the general characteristics of the country. In two years, however, there were significant shortfalls in foodgrain availability per capita, which were also reflected in the accompanying price movement. First, in 1955–1956 annual per capita availability of foodgrain declined to 226 pounds as compared with the average of 288 pounds during 1950–1955. The second shortfall was experienced three years later in 1958–1959 when the availability figure stood at 230 pounds.[17] Shortfall in *aman* production accounts for the shortfall in availability in 1955–1956, while in 1958–1959 both *aman* and *aus* were short.[18] Floods caused damage to crops in both years.[19] Although there were reports of localized, intense suffering, the situation did not quite reach famine dimensions. Society adjusted to scarcity by simply reducing the average consumption level. Thus, while the retail price of medium quality rice increased by about 36 percent in 1955–1956 over the year before, it was only about 3 percent above the average for 1950–1956. On the other hand, in 1958–1959 the rice price increased by 5 percent over the year before but it was 13 percent above the average for the previous five years (1953–1958).[20]

Given the overall state of poverty in the country, the slow process of further pauperization and polarization continued unnoticed except that from time to time natural calamities such as floods or cyclones created a crisis atmosphere and the government then provided temporary support to the affected population either from its own resources or from donations from other governments and international agencies.

A number of factors have combined to make Bangladesh one of the most flood-prone regions of the world in recent decades. Normally, an area of about 26,000 square miles out of a total of 55,000 square miles is flooded to a depth of greater than one foot during a year, more specifically, during the monsoon season (May through September). One-third of the total area is flooded to a depth greater than three feet and 15 percent to a depth greater than six feet, which is considered the level beyond which life and property are seriously threatened.[21] Over the years both the settlement and the cropping patterns have adjusted to this situation.

This fact of nature is bad enough in that it does not allow Bangladesh fuller utilization of its land resources, but the situation was further compounded by above normal flooding occurring rather frequently during the 1950s and the 1960s. According to the Bangladesh Water Development Board the following factors explain the intensification of floods in Bangladesh: (1) low general topography; (2) high monsoon flood through principal channels; (3) situation of the offtake of the principal distributaries from the Ganges-Padma and the Brahumaputra; (4) overbank spilling of the rivers; (5) effects of flood-control measures in the upper reaches (located in India) of the rivers; (6) high intensity of rainfall within the country; (7) strong backwater effects of tides of the Bay of Bengal; (8) rise of the mean sea level (during monsoon); (9) backwater effect of the principal channels on one another at their confluence; (10) tropical features controlled by geological factors; (11) effect of the 1950 earthquake; and (13) peak-flood synchronization in the Ganges and the Brahmaputra.[22] In addition, the carrying capacity of the rivers and streams of Bangladesh has been declining due to siltation over the years.

The history of floods is not very well documented. Mujumdar mentions a severe flood in 1585–1586.[23] In the 1770 flood in Bengal, which followed the drought of the previous two years, the rain caused further damage to the famine stricken people. Calcutta was struck by flood in 1773. Change of the course of the Teesta River is attributed to severe flood that affected the districts of Dinajpur and Rangpur in 1787.[24] Bengal was hit again by flood in 1814 when the Norbudda River overflowed its banks, damaging villages, inhabitants, and cattle.[25] From the beginning of the twentieth century to 1938 a number of floods were recorded by Azizul Huq.[26] Many of these were localized inundations although damage was considerable; particularly in terms of crop loss. Extensive areas were affected by the

1918 floods over great parts of the Rajshahi division, 1922 floods over North Bengal, and 1931 floods over Rangpur, Rajshahi, Pabna, and Bogra. The districts of Jessore and Mymemsingh[27] were apparently hard hit by floods in 1938. Frequency of floods and the extent of flood damage increased manyfold beginning in the mid-1950s as compared with earlier years. Severe (measured in terms of loss of life and property) floods occurred in 1954, 1955, 1956, 1962, 1963, 1968, and 1969.[28] Successive catastrophes of this type left the poor peasants poorer by forcing them to draw on past savings if any, get into further debt, or in extreme cases, sell assets (mainly land). Loss of cattle added to the problem of the cultivating class. Agricultural laborers and fishermen experienced drastic drops in income since their source of employment was disrupted. Famine did not break out on any of these occasions because the government was able to provide adequate relief in time to avoid excess death due to starvation, and also, despite the impact of these disasters, market availability and price of foodgrains never reached a danger point except in the two years mentioned earlier. But, by and large, the resistance to famine weakened during these years in the flood-prone areas of Bangladesh. A list of past floods along with areas affected is presented in Table 4.3.

In addition to floods, Bangladesh has been visited by many severe tropical cyclones, which are usually formed in the Bay of Bengal. These cyclones had devastating effects on life and property "in the coastal districts of Khulna, Patuakhali, Barisal, Noakhali and the off-shore islands like Bhola, Hatiya, Sandwip, Ramgati, Kutubdia, etc."[29] Historic records, as presented in Table 4.4, show that cyclones mostly occur during May and from September to December. They are characterized by extremely high wind velocity and tidal surge. For the recorded period, cyclone frequency increased in the 1960s as compared with earlier periods, which, of course, may be partly attributed to better documentation of recent cyclones. Between 1960 and 1969, Bangladesh was struck by seven severe cyclonic storms[30] that claimed over 62,000 human lives and caused high cattle mortality. The total damage was estimated at Taka 1353 million. While all classes of people in the affected regions suffered in terms of mortality, crop loss and property damage, the fishing community was particularly hard-hit in terms of loss of earning members of the family, boats, and fishing equipment. After each cyclone, the surviving fishermen took quite a while before they were able to function normally again in earning their livelihood. During early years, there was hardly any cyclone preparedness in the country. Storm warning systems were rudimentary but they improved after the occurrence of several cyclones in the early 1960s. By the late 1960s, Bangladesh was equipped with storm warning radar and weather satellite service. However, major

Table 4.3. Floods in Bangladesh up to 1970

Year	Area affected	Remarks
1585–1586	Not known	Called the "Meghna Flood."
1770	Bengal	"Great flood in the Eastern Provinces (Bengal) by which much of the benefit which would have followed a two years' drought was diverted."[a]
1773	Calcutta	Great destruction.
1787	Dinajpur, Rangpur, Sylhet, Jessore, and Central Bengal	"By this disaster, the late crops, which , after all previous disasters were fast getting into ear, were in a great measure destroyed over larger tracts of the country."[a]
1814	Bengal	Great overflow of Narbudda river.
1915	Comilla	464 square miles in Brahmanbaria overflooded.
1916	Feni, Patuakhali, Pirojpur, and Bhola	Winter rice crop damaged.
1918	Rajshahi division	Damage to crops and homestead greatest in Rajshahi and Bogra districts.
1922	North Bengal	Great loss of crops, cattle, and houses in Rajshahi and Bogra. In Rajshahi alone 12,000 square miles flooded. The flood caused crop failure to the extent of 75 percent of 222,605 acres.
1931	Rangpur, Rajshahi, Pabna, Bogra	Extensive damage to crops, cattle, houses, and property of the people in the affected area.
1932	Kurigam and Gaibandha subdivision of Rangpur district	654 square miles affected.
1954	14,200 square miles	Widespread losses of lives and property.
1955	19,500 square miles	
1956	Not known	
1962	14,400 square miles. Crop damage in the districts of Bogra, Dacca, Rangpur, Rajshahi, Faridpur, Sylhet, and Comilla reported.	A large number of human lives and livestock were reported lost.
1963	13,600 square miles. Damages to crops to the extent of 20 percent in the districts of Sylhet, Pabna, Chittagong, and Chittagong Hill Tracts.	A large number of human lives and livestock were reported lost.

Table 4.3. (continued)

Year	Area affected	Remarks
1968	14,400 square miles. Crops to the extent of 75 percent damaged in Chittagong, Dinajpur, Rangpur, Sylhet, Bogra, Pabna, Kushtia, Mymensingh, Noakhali, and Chittagong Hill Tracts. Over 900,000 tons of paddy damaged.	Mortality: 126 human lives and 12,324 livestock; 107,622 homesteads completely destroyed and 112,620 partially damaged.
1969	16,000 square miles. Extensive damages to crops in Comilla, Sylhet, Noakhali, Faridpur, Kushtia, and Chittagong.	A large number of human lives and livestock were reported lost.
1970	16,400 square miles. Crop damage reported in Sylhet, Mymensingh, Dacca, Comilla, Rangpur, Bogra, Pabna, Noakhali, Faridpur, Kushtia, Barisal, Chittagong, Patuakhali, and Rajshahi. About 1.3 million tons of paddy damaged.	Mortality: 87 human lives and 6882 livestock; 134,225 homesteads completely destroyed and 637,790 partially damaged.

Sources: C. Walford, "The Famines of the World: Past and Present," *Journal of the Statistical Society* 41(3):451–467 (September 1978); M. Azizul Huq, *The Man Behind the Plow* (Calcutta: The Book Company, 1939), pp. 21–26; Government of Bangladesh, Water Development Board, *Annual Report of Flood in Bangladesh 1974* (Dacca: Water Development Board, April 1975), pp. 10-11; Government of East Pakistan, Water and Power Development Authority, *Interim Report of East Pakistan 1970* (Dacca: Water and Power Development Authority, 1971), pp. 1-50.

[a]C. Walford, "The Famines of the World: Part and Present," *Journal of the Statistical Society* 41(3):460, 461 (September 1978).

problems remained in terms of protective measures against the devastating consequences of cyclones. The Pakistan government did very little by way of instituting a comprehensive program for construction of coastal shelters, embankment, and afforestation, although a considerable amount of voluntary and official relief activities were initiated following cyclones, which, of course, was always too late in terms of reducing direct human and animal casualties. Although general suffering in different regions and for different groups of people had been intense during the period under consideration, neither flood nor cyclone directly led to famine as defined here. However, under the impact of natural calamities, the staying power of the poorer members of the population declined further.

The Period 1970 and After

The situation in Bangladesh took a sharp turn for the worse beginning in 1970. Throughout the 1960s serious political polarization took place between East and West Pakistan on the question of regional autonomy and regional disparity. By the late 1960s normal economic activities, particularly in nonagricultural sectors, were interrupted by political currents that reached their peak in late 1968 and early 1969. Things settled down for a while when the army took control in March of 1969. But by mid-1970 political tension between the two wings of the country reached a new height with the revival of active politics around the upcoming general election scheduled for December of 1970. Meanwhile, Bangladesh, for the third successive year, was struck by a severe flood during July-September 1970. As Table 4.3 shows, the area affected by this flood exceeded that in any other flood during the 1950s and 1960s, although the maximum period of inundation was less than in both the 1954 and 1955 floods.[31] The flood seriously damaged the prospect of winter (*aman*) crop among other things. There was significant loss of assets in terms of damage to households, loss of land due to erosion and damage to flood control embankments, and the transportation and communication system.

Even before the people of Bangladesh had a chance to recover from the initial impact of the 1970 flood, the coastal belt of Barisal, Khulna, Patuakhali, Noakhali, and Chittagong was hit by the worst cyclonic storm of the century on November 12 and 13 of that year. Direct human mortality is officially placed at 200,000. Unofficial estimates put it near a million. Cattle mortality is just described as innumerable, since no count was ever taken. The areas affected were literally strewn with bodies of men and animals. The maximum wind speed was estimated at about 138 miles per hour in Chittagong and the height of tidal surge was estimated to be in the range of 10 to 30 feet.[32] The tremendous surge height is attributed to the fact that the cyclone apparently reached its maximum intensity during high tide. According to Dr. A. M. Chowdhury, "Nearly 90% of the marine fishermen suffered heavy losses. It is estimated that some 46,000 inland fishermen operating in the cyclone affected region lost their lives. Some 9,000 fishing boats were destroyed during the cyclone."[33] He also indicates that warning for this cyclone was received well in advance—at least four days before it hit the Bangladesh coast. The government failed to respond to the gravity of the situation. As a

Table 4.4 Information about Destructive Cyclones in Bangladesh for the Period 1876–1975

Category of Cyclones	Date of Occurrence/Duration			Location over Which it Passed	Wind Speed in mph	Height of Tidal Surge in Feet	Area (Districts) Affected	Loss of		Total Damage in Terms of Million Taka
	Year	Month	Day					Human Life	Cattle-head	
Severe cyclonic storm	1876	October to November	30 1	Meghna Estuary	N.A.	10–45	Chittagong, Noakhali Barisal and Patuakhali	2,000,000	N.A.	N.A.
Cyclonic storm	1895	October	—	Sundarban	N.A.	N.A.	Khulna	N.A.	N.A.	N.A.
Severe cyclonic storm	1897	October	24	Chittagong	N.A.	N.A.	Chittagong	32,000	N.A.	N.A.
Severe cyclonic storm	1919	September	22–25	Barisal	N.A.	N.A.	Barisal and Dacca	3,500	38,950	N.A.
Cyclonic storm	1926	May	—	Cox's Bazar	N.A.	N.A.	Chittagong	N.A.	N.A.	N.A.
Cyclonic storm	1941	May	—	Eastern Meghna	N.A.	N.A.	Noakhali and Comilla	N.A.	N.A.	N.A.
Cyclonic storm	1958	October	21–24	Barisal-Noakhali	55	6	Patuakhali, Barisal Comilla and Noakhali	N.A.	N.A.	N.A.
Severe cyclonic storm	1960	October	9–10	Eastern Meghna	70/80	10	Noakhali, Patuakhali and Barisal	3,000	N.A.	N.A.
Severe cyclonic storm	1960	October	30–31	Chittagong	130	20	Chittagong and Noakhali	5,149	N.A.	168.900
Severe cyclonic storm	1961	May	9	Eastern Meghna Estuary	Comilla 92 Dacca 90	8–10	Comilla, Noakhali and Barisal	11,468	N.A.	300.859
Severe cyclonic storm	1963	May	28–29	Sitakundu	Chittagong 125 Cox's Bazar 102	8–12	Chittagong and Noakhali	22,000	1,000,000	245.151
Severe cyclonic storm	1965	May	11–12	Barisal	Dacca 100	12	Barisal and Noakhali	19,279	N.A.	523.597
Severe cyclonic storm	1965	December	14–15	Cox's Bazar	Cox's Bazar 130 Chittagong 60	8–10	Chittagong	873	N.A.	523.597
Severe cyclonic storm	1966	September	29	Sandwip	Chittagong 90	10–22	Noakhali and Chittagong	853	N.A.	115.086
Severe cyclonic storm	1970	October	23	Khulna-Patuakhali coast	N.A.	N.A.	Khulna, Patuakhali and Barisal	N.A.	N.A.	—

73

114

Table 4.4 (continued)

| Category of Cyclones | Date of Occurrence/Duration | | | Location over Which it Passed | Wind Speed in mph | Height of Tidal Surge in Feet | Area (Districts) Affected | Loss of | | Total Damage in Terms of Million Taka |
	Year	Month	Day					Human Life	Cattle-head	
Severe cyclonic storm	1970	November	12–13	Meghna Estuary	Chittagong 138	10–30	Entire coastal belt of Barisal, Patuakhali, Khulna Noakhali and Chittagong	200,000	Innumer-able	1176.589
Severe cyclonic storm	1973	December	6–9	Sundarban coast	50/60	5–6	Barisal, Patuakhali, and Khulna	N.A.	N.A.	951.481
Severe cyclonic storm	1974	November	24–28	Chittagong	100	10–12	Chittagong and Noakhali	28	1,000	980.810

N.A. = not available
Source: Government of Bangladesh, Storm Warning Centre, Dacca.

115

matter of fact, nothing much was done in terms of initiating relief effort for the cyclone victims until quite a few days after it had occurred, when reports started coming in on the devastating impact of the cyclone.

As if the successive floods of 1968, 1969, and 1970 and the severe cyclonic storm of 1970 were not enough, the people of Bangladesh were forced into a civil war following the general election in December of 1970 in which they overwhelmingly voted in favor of their demand for regional autonomy. The Awami League party won a majority in the National Assembly but the central ruling elite, dominated by the armed forces, refused to transfer power to it. All attempts by the Awami League (majority party) leadership to arrive at a compromise with the central authority regarding transfer and share of state power failed. The final response of the central authority was calculated genocide against the people of Bangladesh beginning in March of 1971.

We noted earlier that the impact of natural disasters had a region and class bias. Certain areas were hit harder by floods and cyclones than others; poor peasants, agricultural laborers, and fishermen suffered relatively more intensely from a natural disaster as compared with other groups of the population. The socio-political catastrophe of 1971 revealed a similar class bias in terms of relative suffering of various groups of population. The major brunt of mortality due to army operations was borne by poor peasants and the urban working class. Among the people who escaped to India, the poorer majority landed in refugee camps while the Awami League leadership and the major section of other petit-bourgeois groups established themselves in the relatively secure environment of Calcutta. Within Bangladesh, a section of the affluent classes in both urban and rural areas collaborated with the occupation army while the rest of the population suffered throughout 1971 until Bangladesh was liberated on December 16, 1971.

As the year 1971 progressed, there was widespread fear among national and international observers that the country would be faced with a severe famine. The early prediction was based on an assessment of the impact of natural calamities of the previous year that left Bangladesh one million tons short in *aman* production as compared with the year before.[34] Observers were also concerned because, initially following the army crackdown, import flow into the region had ceased and distribution of existing stocks had slowed down. In addition, it was also feared that the war would interrupt normal production activity.[35] Furthermore, 1971 witnessed another flood that affected 14,000 square miles in the districts of Dacca, Comilla, Chittagong, Rajshahi, Pabna, Faridpur, Kushtia, Khulna, and Jessore. Flood casualties were estimated at 120 human lives and 2327 livestock. About 229,535 homesteads were completely destroyed and 363,444 were partially damaged. Loss of crops (paddy) was placed at

306,150 tons.[36] During the calendar year 1971 domestic availability of rice declined by about 11 percent as compared with 1970. We agree with Bose that a serious famine possibility was averted because the population to be fed during 1971 was about 14 percent[37] lower than the estimated figure for January 1, 1970, implying that estimated per capita availability remained above the famine level although it was, as in many other years, below poverty level. Food grain availability per capita in 1971 remained at about the same level as in 1970 even after making allowances for the fact that people who crossed over to India carried some rice with them. Bose estimated this figure to be about 50,000 tons.[38] This was also reflected in the level of foodgrain prices, which remained stable between 1970 and 1971.[39] However, there was some decline in real wages of agricultural laborers and unskilled urban workers,[40] which was probably absorbed by reduction of the overall consumption level of these groups, particularly consumption of nonfood items.

Although a famine was averted in 1971, there is no denying the fact that the majority of the Bangladesh population (including those taking refuge in India) suffered a drastic drop in their standard of living. This general trend was accelerated in the years following liberation of the country. Bangladesh emerged from the 1971 war with a shattered economy and an unsettled population. The task of rehabilitation was enormous. According to the United Nations, the material damage suffered by the country during the war amounted to about $1200 million, consisting of loss of fixed physical assets (particularly the transportation system), damage to agricultural potential, and rehabilitation requirements.[41] Thanks to the massive inflow of foreign assistance, the task of rehabilitating returning refugees and other floating population was accomplished early but the general economic activities could not be restored to a normal level even two years after independence.

It seems the government could not tackle the problems related to economic management and civil administration very efficiently. There were allegations of widespread corruption at all levels of the administration during the period preceding the 1974 famine. Economic activity lagged behind the levels reached in prewar years. The downward spiral of real income and employment continued. The worst victims of this process were industrial workers, small peasants, agricultural laborers, and low-paid, fixed-income earning groups. In contrast, gains were made by those classes that constituted the dominant group and who were also either part of or closely linked to the ruling elite. To this group belonged the bureaucratic managers of nationalized enterprises.[42] They were usually inexperienced and performed very poorly.

Inefficiency and corruption in the administration apart, Bangladesh was faced with a number of additional problems following liberation.

First, there was lack of experience in running a national government. Almost overnight a set of provincial government functionaries had to adjust to a new and higher level of responsibility. Second, a large part of foreign exchange resources had to be diverted to financing current consumption (both private and public), thus financing of investment and raw material imports suffered, leading to serious underutilization of installed capacity.[43] Third, internal resource mobilization through taxation remained unsatisfactory.[44] Fourth, Bangladesh experienced a shortfall in the winter rice crop in 1972 as a result of drought.[45] Fifth, the transport network was not functioning fully until the end of 1973 and even then with a drastic reduction in the carrying capacity of the railways.[46] Sixth, prices of all imported supplies increased sharply in the international market between 1972 and 1974.[47] Seventh, Bangladesh was hit by another severe cyclone in December of 1973 (Table 4.4), which affected the coastal belt of Barisal, Patuakhali, and Khulna. The estimated damage was about Tk. 951 million.[48]

The situation prevailing in Bangladesh as 1974 approached can be best understood if reference is made to certain indexes presented elsewhere.[49] The index of real income per capita stood at 87 in 1972–1973 as compared with 100 in 1969–1970. Similarly, over the same period, the index of agricultural and industrial production declined to 84 and 66 respectively. There was an unprecedented expansion of money supply. According to its narrow definition, total money supply increased from Tk. 3875 million on December 1971 to Tk. 8079 million in December of 1973, an increase of over 100 percent in two years. Shortfall in production combined with an increase in money supply created tremendous inflationary pressure in the economy. Wholesale price indexes of agricultural and industrial products increased from 100 in 1969–1970 to 188 and 255 respectively in 1972–1973. The cost of living for industrial workers increased by more than 100 percent during the same period and for agricultural laborers the increase was about 150 percent. Real wages of agricultural and industrial laborers went down by 24 and 48 percent, respectively between 1970 and 1973. Indeed, the living standard of the majority of the population in Bangladesh had about reached a crisis low point by the end of 1973.

PROFILE OF THE 1974 FAMINE

January–March 1974

An analysis of consumer expenditure survey data shows a very low foodgrain intake per capita for the poorest 12 percent of the population (863 calories per capita a day).[50] As a matter of fact, one wonders how they have been surviving at all, considering that they have very little else to supplement their intake of cereals. The good harvest of the 1973-1974 winter rice crop did not seem to have changed the situation at all since, in spite of it, rice prices showed an upward trend. This indeed was an important signal for the impending crisis but no one seemed to have paid much attention to it. The government made a half-hearted attempt to procure winter rice but it was a failure. This was admitted by the Food Minister in the National Assembly on February 1, 1974. As we shall see later, in the light of the development of a severe famine during this year, the failure of the government to procure a substantial quantity of *aman* rice from surplus farmers turned out to be an important factor in accentuating the suffering of the people. The increasing price of rice during February and March drew expressions of concern from various quarters. In Dacca, the average retail price of coarse quality rice increased from TK. 93 per maund (= 82.29 pound) in November 1973 to TK. 127 per maund in March 1974, an increase of 36 percent. Similarly, the price increase in Sunamganj was 62 percent between December 1973 and March 1974. Other places showing a high rate of price increase over the same period include Rangpur (63 percent), Bhairab Bazar (57 percent) and Netrokona (57 percent). These figures were calculated from monthly averages of weekly price quotations collected by the Directorate of Agricultural Marketing in selected centers of Bangladesh.

It is not surprising that, by the end of March 1974, leading newspapers in the country were reporting that people were eating alternative "famine foods." It was also reported that begging and promiscuity were increasing. Lack of food and employment was forcing people to leave villages for cities and towns. From our field survey we learned that widespread starvation started in the Rangpur district in March. A member of the National Assembly from that area, Mr. Karimuddin Mia confided to an associate (with whom our field investigator had intimate discussions) that he would not be surprised if by September and October of the year 25 percent of his constituents would die of starvation. "I am going to Dacca to see if I can stir up anybody to pity them," he said. The outcome of his mission to Dacca is unknown to us but his prediction subsequently turned out to be correct.

The usual response of the government was either that the reported worsening of the food situation was exaggerated or that there was no reason for undue alarm since the administration was in full command of the situation. Following a review of the food situation in the country in a high level official meeting held on March 28, the Food Minister "assured" the nation that the rising price of rice was only temporary, that the existing stock of rice was satisfactory, and that more rice was being procured from abroad.[51] Two days later the Food Minister reiterated his earlier statements. He claimed that the price rise was due to manipulation by traders and revealed that adequate food would be made available through the open market and the modified rationing system. At this point rice dealers made a gesture by increasing the supply in the Dacca market but at the retail market the price increased by TK. 2/3 per maund in the course of a day or two. Wholesale rice dealers then decided to sell rice directly to consumers to help ease the situation in the capital. The government was encouraged by this development and made an announcement that the rice supply in the market was increasing and that *the upward trend of rice price had been arrested.*[52] This statement appears unjustified in the light of the actual development of the price situation between March and April of 1974 as reflected in official data.

April 1974

April was characterized by a highly unstable rice price; in certain areas it was reported that the price was increasing by the hour. Even a normally surplus area like Jamalpur recorded a very high price, which was about 72 percent above the level prevailing a year before. In addition, the supply of rice into the market became very uncertain. In early April, district authorities in Barisal carried out a drive against hoarding by seizing rice from the traders and selling it in the open market at moderate prices. While it provided temporary relief to the people, it "scared away" rice from the market, which naturally caused tremendous hardship to the people in that area. These were simple *ad hoc* measures not backed by well-coordinated national or regional plans. Similarly, an attempt at price fixing dried up supply channels to the market in Rajshahi. There were protests in the country when abnormally high prices were reported in early April. For example, in parts of Netrokona subdivision in Mymensingh district rice was selling at Tk. 192 per maund although official data showed that the average price for the entire month of April in that subdivision was Tk. 149 per maund. There was a tremendous rush for wheat at the distribution centers in that area. At this time the rice traders in Dacca claimed that there was sufficient rice in the city for three months. In a statement to the press on April 4, the secretary of the Dacca Rice Merchants Association indicated that the stock situation was also good in the traditional supply centers, such as Dinajpur, Patuakhali, Bogra, and Banaripara (Barisal). However, he did not comment on the price situation.

In spite of the repeated assurances by government officials and rice traders alike, the actual market supply situation was reported to be very tight during the first three weeks of April in almost all parts of Bangladesh, including Banaripara (Barisal) where, according to the secretary of the Dacca Rice Merchants Association, the stock situation was good. This was clearly reflected in the price quotations at various places as reported in the *Daily Ittefaq*. Besides, most of the districts reported a low government stock position[53] and, in many areas under modified rationing, distribution of foodgrains was either stopped temporarily or drastically reduced.[54] On April 17 the Food Minister announced that every month 200,000 tons of foodgrains were being imported from abroad. Recorded import figures show that between November 1973 and June 1974, the 200,000 mark of import arrival was reached only in May of 1974.[55] We shall explore these questions in greater depth in Chapter 6.

Fluctuation of rice price apart, there were continued reports of starvation, starvation deaths, suicide, and eating of alternative "famine foods" from Netrokona, Chandpur, Pabna, Gaibandha, Jamalpur, Bonarpara (Rangpur), Sayedpur, and Kurigram. Extreme instances of eating alternative "famine foods" were reported from all over the country especially from Jamalpur, Gaibandha, Netrokona, and Raipur (Noakhali). As rice became scarce people ate potatoes, sweet potatoes, and *khichuri* (a mixture of rice and lentils). But soon prices of these items soared and they were out of the reach of the majority of the affected population. The people were forced to eat *kochu* (arums), *kalar thor* (plantain saplings), *shaks and leaves,* rice husk, and rice water.[56] During our field survey, we learned that banana trees, roots of arums, and leaves of any remotely edible plants were exhausted by July in Kurigram and Gibandha subdivisions of Rangpur district. Rice water, which is normally thrown away, became a commodity and was being sold in the open market at a price reported to be TK 0.12 per seer (2.06 pounds) in Rangpur. Starvation and eating of alternative "famine foods" led to epidemics of diarrheal diseases in many areas. People started moving from rural to urban areas.

The suffering of the people was greater in areas where the employment situation was a problem. During our field survey, we were told by respondents that many day laborers turned into beggars. Theft, dacoity, and destroying railway cars carrying foodgrains increased. At the same time, the country was experiencing a "salt famine." In addition, it was alleged that foodgrain smuggling into neighboring India was taking place. The "salt famine" was apparently a purely artificial phenomenon created by traders in February of 1974 and continued for quite some time until the government made arrangements for importing salt from Pakistan and India and for its distribution through the rationing system. As the salt price skyrocketed, it became quite profitable to smuggle foodgrains into India and obtain salt in return as it was very cheap there. However, presumably the magnitude of smuggling of foodgrains into

India during the period under consideration was much greater than what could be explained by the "salt exchange." We shall go into this question later. In any case, the government downplayed the smuggling issue during the early months of the crisis. On the basis of reports received from border areas, opposition politicians and the public in general seemed to agree that smuggling of essentials from Bangladesh to India was partly responsible for the suffering of the people. They were equally concerned with the activities of traders.

By mid-April we find that the influential *Daily Ittefaq* and a respected elderly political leader, Maulana Bhashani, had declared that a man-made famine was in the offing and demanded that action be taken against hoarders and smugglers. From the evidence presented here and the information we collected during our field survey, it seemed that their concern at that point was well justified.[57] The situation in certain areas of Kurigram in Rangpur had already reached a point of desperation, so much so that a few *langarkhanas* were opened at the initiative of local social workers and streams of people from villages starting crowding them.[58] Local authorities from various parts of the country sent in urgent requests to the central government in Dacca for help in the form of an emergency supply of rice and cash grants for test relief works, but the response was not very encouraging. In Jamalpur one *langarkhana* was opened under local leadership, but it could not be sustained for long due to lack of government support.[59]

The most damaging event of the month was the occurrence of a flash flood in Sylhet and localized hailstorms and heavy rains in Sirajganj, Magura, Narail, Netrokona, and Daudkandi. This flood was an early signal for the worst flood of the century that would come in full fury beginning in July of 1974. The early flood caused extensive damage in parts of Sylhet district in the northeast of the country. According to the Water Development Board, "Heavy rainfall in and around the district, high stage in the Barak-Surma-Kushiyara system and flash discharges through the Monu, Juri, Khowai, Lungla, Korangi, Sutang, Piyan, Jadukata and numerous revulets and drainage congestion due to high stage in the upper Meghna caused flooding in this district."[60] The *boro* rice, which would have been harvested in another two weeks, was almost entirely destroyed. Estimates by the Water Development Board reveal that over 168,360 acres of *boro* crop were completely destroyed and over 170,580 acres partially destroyed—the total crop loss being put at 149,695 tons.[61] Our field survey in Sylhet area (Sunamganj) showed that almost all households were affected by this flood and loss of cattle was enormous. The problem was more serious for areas where *boro* was the only crop (the low-lying *bil* and *haor* areas of the district). Cultivators in these areas were left without any support and heavy sale of assets was reported following the flood. The problems created by hailstorms, heavy rain, and flash flooding during this month can be summarized as follows: (1) *boro* and *china irri* crop was damaged; (2) *aus* and *jute* cultivation was affected; (3) in many areas rice and *jute* seedlings were destroyed and replanting was made difficult because of heavy rain; and (4) crops in low-lying areas were damaged and cultivation of such areas was difficult because of flooding.

May–August 1974

The foodgrain situation eased somewhat during May due to new arrivals of rice in the market and to army action. The price of rice declined by 5 to 20 percent in May as compared with April in different parts of the country and remained at the same level during most of June. But the intensity of army action could not be sustained for too long because it was in conflict with the interest of friends and supporters of the ruling Awami League party. The result was that the decline in rice price was only short-lived and the general state of difficult food supply in the market returned soon. Distribution of foodgrains through the government rationing system became irregular again. In response to criticism of the government's handling of the situation from various quarters, the Food Minister assured the people on June 17 that a regular and uninterrupted supply of full rations would be maintained. During the preceding few weeks, ration shops could not supply all items to the ration card holders, because they apparently did not receive a full supply of goods from the government. It should be pointed out that the ration shop owners often diverted rationed items into the open market.

During this period Bangladesh also experienced heavy rainfall and a devastating flood, which gave rise to untold human misery. In addition to heavy local rainfall within Bangladesh, there was spillover from heavy rainfall over the vast catchment area of the rivers of Bangladesh, most of which (93 percent) lie outside the country. Table 4.5 indicates that in almost all areas of Bangladesh actual rainfall exceeded the normal level by over 50 percent during some part of the April–October period in 1974, with the maximum concentration in July. The flood that followed was claimed to be the worst in the last one hundred years. *The Report on Floods* shows that, as compared with the floods of 1954 and 1955, the peak flood at Bahadurabad was higher, and at Bhairab Bazar the same as in 1955, while at the other two stations it was slightly lower than both the 1954 and 1955 floods. But considering Bangladesh as a whole, flood water remained above danger level for a much longer period in 1974 as compared with 1954 and 1955. More importantly, water level hydrographics prepared by the Bangladesh Water Development Board show that, during the 1955 flood season, there was only one peak, indicating a relatively slow rise in the water level at all stations. The corresponding

Table 4.5. Variation over Normal Rainfall in Different Stations of Bangladesh in 1974

Station	200 Percent and Above	100–199 Percent	50–99 Percent
Dacca	—	July	—
Mymensingh	—	July, October	—
Barisal	—	July, September	April
Chittagong	June	September	July
Comilla	—	April, July	September
Sylhet	—	—	April, July, October
Rangpur	—	July	—
Dinajpur	—	April, July	May
Rajshahi	—	—	—
Bogra	—	April	—
Pabna	—	—	April, July
Jessore	—	September	July, August, October
Khulna	—	August	—

Source: Government of Bangladesh, Water Development Board, Annual Report on Flood in Bangladesh 1974, April 1975.

number in 1974 was five at Bahadurabad, two at Hardinge Bridge, two at Goalundo, and four at Bhairab Bazar.[62] At Bahadurabad there were also four periods when flood water was above the danger level for an extended period of time. The 1974 flood had the following effects on the economy and society: (1) The flood water damaged standing boro and aus rice and interfered with the planting of aus and aman. Areas such as Kurigram in Rangpur district, which were hit by three different peak floods in June, July, and September, faced difficulty with replanting; (2) Normal life was disrupted and economic activities were reduced thus shrinking employment opportunities in rural areas; (3) Houses were damaged and families were uprooted from their normal places of residence; (4) In many areas, stored paddy was lost; (5) Both human and cattle lives were lost; (6) Although an accurate estimate is not yet available, the Water Development Board reported that there was considerable loss of land due to river erosion during the flood. This was confirmed by many interviewees during our field survey. Table 4.6 presents a summary of the flooded area and damages due to the 1974 flood. Table 4.7 does the same for our survey villagers and langarkhana inmates. The difference between famine and nonfamine villages in terms of cultivated operational landholding affected by flood can be seen very clearly in Table 4.7. The langarkhana inmates, who represent uprooted destitute families with very little landholding to begin with, seem to have been almost completely wiped out by the flood. We found many in this group who had lost their land due to river erosion, particularly in Chilmari thana of Rangpur district.

Table 4.6. Area Flooded and Damage to Properties and Life in 1974

District	Area of the District (sq. miles)	Total Area Affected by Flood (sq. miles)	Maximum Depth of Inundation (ft.)	Period of Inundation (months)	No. of Persons Affected	No. of Human Lives Lost	No. of Cattle Heads Lost	Crops Damaged (acres)	Houses Damaged Fully	Houses Damaged Partially
Mymensingh	5,060	3,308	15	4	5,065,576	353	3,118	1,819,200	114,532	185,111
Sylhet	4,785	3,500	13	3	4,003,000	96	6,818	1,453,220	144,695	247,816
Comilla	2,594	2,296	10	2	2,976,442	372	6,028	1,849,809	17,480	123,310
Noakhali	1,855	1,070	6	2	1,759,800	356	3,552	951,841	14,391	55,591
Rangpur	3,704	983	7	4	1,700,000	8	1,748	361,841	100,000	63,839
Faridpur	2,694	1,845	7	3	2,640,138	140	1,510	693,474	104,829	263,120
Bogra	1,502	292	10	1	505,000	4	143	15,000	1,780	1,361
Barisal	2,554	1,445	8	2½	1,442,797	37	13,163	452,452	26,219	10,384
Pabna	1,877	961	11	5	1,070,800	6	259	685,959	20,980	23,380
Dacca	2,882	2,214	10	4	3,161,862	211	1,909	669,340	44,135	305,798
Chittagong	2,705	468	13	3	787,769	355	5,910	243,669	15,298	64,285
Tangail	1,301	936	12	3½	726,350	—	55	124,480	980	5,283
Khulna	4,652	15	—	2	480,000	9	1,300	44,773	2,323	9,360
Rajshahi	3,654	804	8	2½	339,450	36	850	196,450	6,958	9,485
Jessore	2,547	—	—	—	441,580	1	273	42,900	551	1,251
Kushtia	1,371	40	—	—	650,500	2	165	43,425	202	986
Patuakhali	1,688	17	4	—	465,223	—	91	130,000	121	12,673
Dinajpur	2,609	82	4	1	707,034	—	73	47,898	159	398
Total	55,126	20,277			29,898,320	1,988	46,405	9,825,394	615,633	1,383,431

Source: Government of Bangladesh, Water Development Board, *Annual Report on Flood in Bangladesh 1974,* April 1975; Government of Bangladesh, Ministry of Relief and Rehabilitation.

125

Table 4.7. Cultivable Area Affected by Flood as Reported by Sample Villagers and Langarkhana Inmates

Area	Number of Households	Affected Households		Total Cultivable Operational Landholding (acres)	
		No.	%	All Families	Families Affected
Total villages	1774	561	31.62	3111.16	907.13
Famine villages	869	341	39.24	1170.02	562.37
Nonfamine villages	905	220	24.31	1941.14	344.76
Ramna, Rangpur	294	159	54.08	347.48	179.21
Gaorarong, Sylhet	235	91	38.72	221.38	213.66
Kogaria, Rangpur	179	5	2.79	323.23	4.98
Dewanganj, Mymensingh	161	86	53.42	277.93	164.52
Nazirpur, Patuakhali	363	185	50.96	894.42	280.08
Laskarpur, Sylhet	227	—	—	326.45	—
Komorpur, Khulna	178	—	—	571.53	—
Charbaniara, Khulna	137	35	25.55	148.74	64.68
Langarkhana					
Bagherhat	91	57	62.64	51.64	50.55
Mymensingh	97	3	3.09	13.47	—
Dacca	101	33	32.67	36.92	29.99
Khulna	101	10	9.90	5.72	5.72
Chilmari, Rangpur	102	30	29.41	16.03	12.97
Dewanganj	95	19	20.00	49.28	25.71
Rangpur	101	14	13.86	8.97	15.31
Gaorarong, Sylhet	100	17	17.00	23.09	7.42

aPercentages may exceed 100 due to double cropping.

It would be premature to attribute the 1974 Bangladesh famine entirely to the flood, but there is no denying that the flood accentuated human suffering that was already in evidence, and all those families who were living well below poverty level, finally succumbed to the pressure. By the end of July, the scenario in all flood-affected regions of the country, was flood leading to loss of human and cattle life, loss of agricultural land and crops, loss of homestead, and loss of employment, all of which combined to lead to starvation and outbreak of epidemic diseases (particularly cholera), the situation being further compounded by shortage of fresh drinking water and prevalence of high prices of all essentials. This nearly completed the famine syndrome depicted in Figure 1.1 in Chapter 1. By the beginning of August reports of excess deaths poured in from all over the country, particularly from the areas severely hit by the flood, such as Rangpur district. Our field investigator

Table 4.7 (continued)

| Cultivable Operational Landholding Affected (acres) by Flood | | | | Total Land Affected as % of Total Cultivable Operational Holding a | Total Land Affected as % of Cultivable Operational Landholding of Families Affected |
| | Aman | | Total Land Affected | | |
Aus	Partial Damage	Total Damage			
530.51	9.25	632.51	1172.27	37.68	129.23
136.57	5.65	558.05	906.69	77.49	161.23
393.94	3.60	74.46	472.00	24.32	136.91
189.23	17.19	179.21	385.63	110.98	215.18
—	—	213.66	213.66	96.51	100.00
—	4.32	0.66	4.98	1.54	100.00
136.57	1.33	164.52	302.42	108.81	183.82
270.30	3.60	9.78	283.68	31.72	101.29
—	—	—	—	—	—
123.64	—	64.68	188.32	126.61	291.16
28.27	—	22.28	50.55	97.89	100
—	—	—	—	—	—
18.11	—	11.88	29.99	81.23	100
0.69	—	3.32	4.01	70.10	100
7.44	—	5.56	12.97	80.91	100
13.80	—	11.91	25.71	52.17	100
6.65	—	8.66	15.31	170.68	100
0.33	—	7.09	7.42	32.14	100

in that area learned that by the middle of July, the death toll began to rise sharply. Using the reference of a local member of the National Assembly, Mr. Siddique Hossain, a cable was sent to Prime Minister Sheikh Mujibur Rahman apprizing him of the current situation in the following words, "People dying of starvation, please arrange free dole." No reply was received, and it is alleged that the prime minister expressed his displeasure over this cable to Mr. Hossain, and added that he was well aware of what was going on in different parts of the country.

Since we did not have access to the official briefings received by the prime minister or other relevant agencies, we cannot comment on the extent of knowledge the central government had of the crisis faced by the people of Bangladesh. However, certain actions of the government indicated its callousness in the face of the suffering of the people. Rangpur town was crowded with migrants from flood-affected areas of the district and occasionally dead bodies could be seen lying on the street. To relieve the distress of the people, local social workers opened a *langarkhana* in the town with some wheat obtained from the district administration at a controlled price. A couple of days later, the Deputy Commissioner of Rangpur cancelled the allotment of wheat for the *langarkhana*, referring to an instruction he received from Dacca saying that the government did not want to encourage the establishment of *langarkhanas* and, therefore, no wheat would be made available at a controlled price for this purpose. The *langarkhana* in question, however, continued to operate with contributions from the members of the local business community.

The stability of rice prices observed from May to July was disturbed, and there was a sharp increase in the price of rice in August as compared with earlier months. Prices increased in all sixty centers at which data are collected regularly by the Directorate of Agricultural Marketing. The extent of price increases between July and August apparently exceeded that between any previous two months beginning with November of 1973. This came at a time when the flood was at its worst in most places, and income and employment generating opportunities were at their minimum in rural areas as compared with any previous year. More importantly, a prolonged period of very low foodgrain intake, beginning in 1968, had left the members of the poor families physically weak. Foodgrain price hikes forced them to reduce their consumption below an acceptable level. The situation became even more precarious as the flood caused deterioration of the physical environment, in ways conducive to the spread of various types of diseases.

By the end of August, the whole of Bangladesh turned into an agonizing spectacle of confusion and human suffering. With the addition of the flood, it was 1943 re-enacted. Streams of hungry people (men, women, and children), who were nothing but skeletons, trekked into towns in search of food. Most of them were half-naked. Events such as husbands deserting wives and children, or wives doing the same, parents trying to sell children, mothers killing babies out of frustration and anguish, man and dog fighting for a piece of bone, women and young girls turning to prostitution became very commonplace. We were all personally witnessing these things in despair. There was very little support available for the destitutes in urban centers except for some private charity, which was almost negligible even after taking account of the few privately organized and financed *langarkhanas* and government-sponsored flood relief centers.[63] Long travels had depleted the victims' energy even further and after a few days of "wandering" around the streets of the city they simply collapsed and died. In Rangpur town alone as many as fifty to seventy unclaimed bodies were reported to have been spotted every day during August of 1974. In Dacca, Anjuman Mufidul Islam, a Muslim organization, collected 127 bodies for burial in August 1974.[64] I myself saw an average of three to five unclaimed bodies a day in August on my way to my office, which was only a five minute walk from my place of residence in Dacca. The month of August was punctuated with a statement from the Food Minister, who said that the country's food gap (consumption requirement less production) for the year 1974–1975 originally estimated at around 1.7 million tons would now be increased by an additional 1.3 million tons minimum, which he attributed to the damage caused by flood. It seemed the flood had provided an excellent excuse to the administration to escape its own responsibility in the handling of the food crisis and its failure to avert the famine. However, there is no denying the fact that any government would have found it a very challenging task to tackle the food crisis in the face of the devastating flood. One can only speculate on how much human suffering could have been avoided by a more efficient and prompt response to the crisis.

September–December 1974

In the beginning of September another flood hit six districts in the north and northwest. However, it did not stay above the danger level for too long. By the end of September, flood water began receding from all parts of Bangladesh for the final time. Famine and epidemic had by then broken out in full fury as the water drained away. Government estimates put deaths from cholera, smallpox, diarrhea, and dysentery at 1300 in September.[65] The number of starvation deaths as quoted in official and nonofficial reports increased manyfold. Four hundred and forty such deaths were reported by government sources in Dewangang thana of Mymensingh district. In Islampur of the same district 170 starvation deaths occurred in three days during September. The Bangladesh government sent out an emergency appeal to international agencies for 0.6 million tons of foodgrain by October and a further 0.15 million tons by December of 1974 to meet the situation arising out of the flood.[66]

Increasing incidence of starvation deaths, reports of unclaimed bodies from all over the country, and the capital city of Dacca itself being crowded with famished people and strewn with dead bodies for the third month in a row (July, August, September) finally forced the government to acknowledge the gravity of the situation. On September 24, 1974, the prime minister admitted that famine conditions prevailed in the country. He ordered an immediate opening of 4300 *langarkhanas* up to the union level. The food minister declared at the same time that a total of 2.5–3.0 million people would be given bread daily in the *langarkhanas*.

Two vagrant homes (poorhouses) were opened in Dacca. The *langar-khanas* began operation on the first of October. But the presence of *langarkhanas* for the next two months (they were closed down by the end of November) could not significantly reduce excess mortality. People continued to die inside and outside of the *langarkhanas*. This was because the physical condition of the famine-affected people was by then so deteriorated that they could not be saved anyway. Besides, as we shall see later, the conditions in the *langarkhanas* (lack of sanitation, and so forth) were not always ideal for preventing deaths.

Rice price continued to increase very sharply in September and October before it declined slightly in November and December. The government completely failed to contain the upward trend of rice price throughout 1974. On September 23, the food minister declared that rice dealers were manipulating prices to earn more profit. He assured the nation that steps would be taken to bring down prices. The next day he came out again with a warning for the rice traders, "Rice price must come down in 4 days; appropriate measures will be taken against hoarders." In order to discourage hoarding by consumers and traders, the following measures were taken by the government: (1) hoarding of foodgrains beyond family requirement for two months was prohibited (October 5); (2) dealers were asked to declare excess rice/paddy stock by October 16 (October 5); and (3) it was decided that traders would not be allowed to retain rice/paddy in their possession for more than twenty days from the date of purchase (October 11). These measures did not produce the expected results. The retail price of rice (coarse) increased by 40 percent between August and October of 1974. Naturally, the situation continued to be very grim as starvation deaths mounted. On October 8, the prime minister said, "Crisis is temporary," although by all accounts thousands of people were dying every day. The death rate jumped sharply in the city of Dacca. On an average eighty-four persons a day were dying of hunger during October. From October 1 to October 11, 806 bodies were buried at Azimpur (the main graveyard of the city) and another 190 at Jurain (a suburban graveyard). Deaths were reportedly due to starvation, malnutrition, cholera, and dysentery.[67] Unclaimed bodies buried in Dacca by Anzumane Mofidul Islam were on the increase every month; figures show that as late as December there were about thirty such burials a day. Excess death continued between September and November 1974, a period when an average 4.3 million people were being fed daily in 5862 *langarkhanas*. Our field investigators reported excess mortality in November when they were carrying out village and *langarkhana* surveys. With the arrival of larger shipments of rice from abroad starting in November of 1974, and also with the arrival of the winter crop in the market, the situation eased somewhat. The government had actually closed down *langarkhanas* in many places before the winter harvest so that people could go back and participate in harvesting activities. With this, the famine was officially over although presumably, as in 1943, excess mortality continued far beyond December of 1974, albeit silently.

FAMINE SYNDROME COMPLETED

We have presented here the general profile of the 1974 Bangladesh famine as it developed in the early stages, between February and June, reached its peak during July and October, and finally subsided in late November and December. It is interesting to note that the worst months of the 1974 famine coincided with those of the 1943, 1866, and 1770 famines, although the peak of the latter was spread over a much longer period of time. In order to complete the famine syndrome as depicted in Figure 1.1 (Chapter 1), we have to take a closer look at certain aspects of famine (substates) such as migration, uprooting and separation of families, transfer of assets, crime, breakdown of traditional social bonds, and above all the mortality attributable to the famine. We discuss famine mortality in a separate section.

During 1974, there was considerable population movement in the country. Starving people moved from one place to another in search of food. We do not have hard data to capture the full dimension of such movements in great detail. Our survey of *langarkhana* inmates provided some information on the pattern of migration[68] during the 1974 famine. It should be noted that urban area *langarkhanas* drew migrants from outside the locality, mainly from rural areas, while rural area *langarkhanas* mainly served the population of the same area, although in some cases this meant that people had to walk more than eight or ten miles a day, for two (or one, as the case might be) pieces of bread. Dacca and its *langarkhanas* drew migrants from all over Bangladesh. We therefore selected the data from the Dacca *langarkhana* for more detailed analysis as compared with the data from other *langarkhanas*. Among our sample observations of 788 inmates of eight *langarkhanas* in five districts we find that they originated from fourteen districts, that is, there were people from nine outside districts who moved into one or more of our sample districts (Table 4.8). In terms of thanas, the sample *langarkhanas* attracted people from thirty-six outside thanas. Percentage distribution of inmates by district of origin shows that Mymensingh leads the way, followed by Rangpur, Khulna, and Sylhet. This has, of course, been influenced by our selection of the *langarkhana* locations as well as by the total size of population of the district concerned.

Table 4.8 Origin of All Langarkhana Inmates by District and by Thana

Origin District/Thana	Number of Inmates	Percentage Distribution of Inmates	Origin District/Thana	Number of Inmates	Percentage Distribution of Inmates	Origin District/Thana	Number of Inmates	Percentage Distribution of Inmates
Khulna	179	22.7	*Sylhet*	102	12.9	*Rangpur*	200	25.4
Khulna	81	10.3	Dharampasha	1	0.1			
Kachua	91	11.5				Gaibandha	6	0.8
Others	7	0.9	Chatak	1	0.1	Sundarganj	10	1.3
			Sunamganj	100	12.7	Shaghata	1	0.1
Mymensingh	251	31.9	*Dacca*	2	0.2	Chilmari	131	16.6
Kotwali	97	12.3	Dacca	1	0.1	Ulipur	6	0.8
Dewanganj	114	14.5	Munshiganj	1	0.1	Pirgacha	7	0.9
Islampur	8	0.1				Kurigram	5	0.6
Sribardi	14	1.8	*Noakhali*	1	0.1	Gangchar	4	0.5
Others	18	2.3	Raipura	1	0.1	Palashbari	1	0.1
Comilla	15	1.9	*Jessore*	1	0.1	Mithapukur	4	0.5
Chandpur	15	1.9	Narail	1	0.1	Row Mari	4	0.5
Faridpur	15	1.9	*Pabna*	1	0.1	Sadullapur	1	0.1
Rajoir	4	0.5	Bera	1	0.1	Kotwali	20	2.5
Nasia	2	0.2				Nakeshwar	1	0.1
Ghoshaihat	1	0.1	*Patuakhali*	2	0.2	Sakhata	1	0.1
Pangsha	1	0.1	Patuakhali	2	0.2	Fulbari	1	0.1
Faridpur	7	0.9	*Bogra*	1	0.1	Kaliganj	3	0.4
Barisal	9	1.1	Kohali	1	0.1	Lalmai	3	0.4
Barisal	5	0.6						
Barguna	3	0.4						
Gournadi	1	0.1				Total	788	100

Note: Percentages may not total 100 due to rounding errors.

Distribution of Dacca *langarkhana* inmates by place of origin and average distance travelled, as presented in Table 4.9, reveals some interesting patterns. The majority of the inmates came from Mymensingh district, followed by Comilla, Rangpur, and Faridpur. As many as ten districts were represented in this sample and on average the inmates travelled 124 miles before they finally arrived at the *langarkhana.* Of the total, about 34 percent travelled more than 100 miles. We collected data on the travel time of Dacca *langarkhana* inmates between origin and destination. This actually reflects the period of "wandering" in search of food. For about 20 percent of the inmates, travel time exceeded six weeks, for 35 percent it was between two and six weeks, and for 46 percent it was less than two weeks. Although situations are somewhat different, it is interesting to compare these figures with the findings of a survey by Das[69] of 820 destitutes in Calcutta during the 1943 famine. It was found then that 19 percent of the destitutes abandoned their homes four to twelve weeks back, 24 percent two to four weeks back, 41 percent two weeks back and the rest more than twelve weeks back.

If we consider the movement of all sample *langarkhana* inmates, we find that about 13 percent left their place of origin more than six weeks before the interview. For 11 percent this period varied between two and six weeks while for the rest it was less than two weeks. However, in the last group, those interviewed at rural *langarkhanas* never really left their place of origin. Information collected through our field survey along with newspaper reports, discussion with officials supplemented by data on flood effect suggest that about 50 percent of the *langarkhana* inmates in the country belonged to the group who abandoned their place of origin, at least for some time, in search of food and employment.[70] The total figure on this basis would come to about 2.1 million not counting those who drifted elsewhere without ever showing up at any *langarkhana.* There are also those who died during the period of travel. When asked why they left home the respondents gave us a combination of the following reasons: lack of food, lack of employment, loss of homestead in flood, and loss of land in flood.

Information on the location of other members of the households of *langarkhana* inmates has enabled us to estimate the extent of uprooting (total and partial), and separation of families during famine. Three different locations were identified, *langarkhana* itself, home (that is, place of origin, if different from the location of the *langarkhana*) and others (that is, places not covered by the above two). A household was considered to have been totally uprooted if all members were found to have deserted the original place of residence, and partially uprooted, if some members were reported to have stayed at home.[71] From among total households a hybrid category was identified whose members were

Table 4.9. Distribution of Dacca Langarkhana Inmates by Origin and Distance Travelled

Origin (District)	Distance					Number of Inmates	% Distribution of Total
	10 miles	10 to 30 Miles	30 to 50 Miles	50 to 100 Miles	100 Miles and Above		
Mymensingh	—	—	—	59	—	59	58.41
Comilla	—	—	—	—	15	15	14.85
Rangpur	—	—	—	—	7	7	6.93
Faridpur	—	—	—	—	8	8	7.92
Barisal	—	—	—	6	—	6	5.94
Sylhet	—	—	—	—	2	2	1.98
Dacca	—	1	—	—	—	1	0.99
Jessore	—	—	—	—	1	1	0.99
Pabna	—	—	—	1	—	1	0.99
Noakhali	—	—	—	—	1	1	0.99
Total	—	1	—	66	34	101	100.00

reported to be scattered over all three locations mentioned above. We call this group separated households; they are actually covered under both partially and totally uprooted families. A profile of uprooting and separation of household members of *langarkhana* inmates is presented in Table 4.10. On average, 84 percent of families were totally uprooted; 16 percent partially uprooted, and 6 percent separated. For urban area *langarkhanas* inmates who were both physically and functionally uprooted and/or separated, the corresponding percentages were 84, 16, and 12, respectively. These figures reflect the intensity of disruption of normal family life during the famine period. Besides, there were many cases of desertion. In Rangpur, special homes for deserted children were set up.[72] In Dacca, there were many women who were deserted by their husbands among the inmates of vagrant homes.[73] During our field survey in famine areas we came across many such cases. However, we did not try to enumerate separate cases of desertion of any particular area because that would have involved more time and resources than we were able to spare at that time. Both separation of families and desertion represent a breakdown of the system of security provided by family and kinship ties under traditional social bonds. This is, of course, not unique to the 1974 Bangladesh famine, as reference to erosion of social ties can be found in almost all preceding famines. However, two points should be noted: First, a slow process of disintegration of traditional ties had already set in in Bangladesh rural society and famine only accelerated it. Second, manifestation of breakdown of kinship and family bonds were reversible in the past in the sense that old relationships were restored through the normal process of postfamine societal adjustment. This is no longer true in the Bangladesh scenario today where such processes seem to be irreversible, which is reflected in the rate of permanent destitution.

Sales of assets to obtain wherewithal for purchasing foodgrains is a common phenomenon during all famines. Our survey data indicate that there was considerable sale of different types of assets by *langarkhana* inmates and villagers in 1974. Once people ran out of resources to buy foodgrains, they sold or mortgaged land, sold cattle and agricultural implements, sold household utensils and other valuables (such as ornaments), and, finally, many sold their homesteads. Our field investigators found that a flourishing secondary market for used utensils had developed in the famine areas during the height of the crisis. Bruce Currey says, "During the year after the flood, the sale of household utensils, e.g. *haripatil* (cooking pots), *thala* (brass plates), *chamuch* (brass cooking spoons), *kashar glass* (brass mugs), and *badna* (toilet jugs), was recorded by 36% and 37% respectively of the households in the thanas of Rowmari and Chilmari which were worst affected near the Teesta-Brahmaputra confluence."[74] Households selling their homesteads, naturally had no other alternative but to join the group of

Table 4.10. Uprooting and Separation of Household Members of Langarkhana Inmates

Location of Langarkhana	Total Number of Households	Number of Households Uprooted		Number of Households Separated	Percentage of Households Uprooted		Percentage of Households Separated
		Totally	Partially		Totally	Partially	
Urban Area	400	336	64	49	84.00	16.00	12.29
Mymensingh	97	97	—	—	100.00	—	—
Dacca	101	66	35	11	65.35	34.65	10.89
Khulna	101	90	11	13	89.11	10.89	12.87
Rangpur	101	83	18	25	82.18	17.82	24.75
Rural Area	388	328	60	—	84.53	15.46	—
Bagerhat	91	31	60	—	34.07	65.93	—
Chilmari	102	102	—	—	100.00	—	—
Dewanganj	95	95	—	—	100.00	—	—
Sunamganj	100	100	—	—	100.00	—	—
Total	788	664	124	49	84.26	15.74	6.22

Bangladesh Famine of 1974 / 137

permanent destitutes who drifted toward towns. All sales of land and other assets represented distress sales[75] for *langarkhana* inmates. Among the total inmates, 5 percent sold land, 14 percent sold land and other assets, and 52 percent sold other assets only. The relatively small percentage being involved in land sale actually reflects the fact that the proportion of inmates owning land (including homesteads) was not very large to begin with (68 percent). The corresponding percentages were 3, 5, and 29 for villages surveyed. However, incidence of land sale was much higher in famine areas as compared with nonfamine areas (Table 4.11). According to Akbar,[76] in 1974 107,082 documents of land holding were admitted for (sale) registration in Kurigram subdivision of Rangpur district (a famine area), the figure representing an increase of 6.3 percent over 1973. More revealing are the data on the proportion of owned land sold by different households during the 1974 famine as presented in Table 4.12. It was found that 12 percent of the *langarkhana* inmates owning land sold more than 50 percent of their owned land, the corresponding percentage for villages being slightly above 2 percent. As expected, the proportion is higher in famine areas than in nonfamine areas.

Famine is often associated with an increase in various types of crime. Food rioting and looting have been recorded in all famines of the past. Unlike the 1943 Great Bengal famine, in 1974 newspapers reported many cases of looting of shops and markets and breaking of railway cars.[77] It

Table 4.11. Percentage of Households Selling Different Types of Assets under Distress Condition in 1974 by Regions

Regions		Land	Land and Other Assets	Other Assets	Total
All villages	(1774)	3	5	29	37
Famine area	(869)	6	10	28	44
Ramna	(294)	6	16	41	63
Gaorarang	(235)	10	2	8	20
Kogaria	(179)	1	—	3	4
Dewangamj	(161)	3	20	62	85
Nonfamine area	(905)	1	2	29	32
Nazirpur	(363)	—	2	23	25
Laskarpur	(227)	—	—	9	9
Komorpur	(178)	2	2	39	43
Charbaniari	(137)	2	2	53	57
Langarkhanas	(788)	5	14	52	71

Note: Figures in parentheses represent total number of sample households in different regions. Other assets include livestock, household utensils, ornaments, and so forth.

Table 4.12. Percentage Distribution of Households Owning Land by Proportion of Owned Land Sold in 1974 by Regions

Regions	Proportion of Owned Land Sold			None	Total
	100 Percent	50–99 Percent	Up to 50 Percent		
All villages (1709)	0.18	2.17	6.67	90.99	100.00
Famine area (811)	0.37	4.32	11.47	83.85	100.00
Ramna (262)	0.76	3.44	20.23	15.57	100.00
Gaorarang (228)	0.44	4.82	7.46	87.28	100.00
Kogaria (177)	—	0.56	1.13	98.31	100.00
Dewangarj (144)	—	9.72	14.58	75.69	100.00
Nonfamine area (898)	—	0.22	2.34	97.44	100.00
Nazirpur (362)	—	0.28	2.21	97.51	100.00
Laskarpur (227)	—	—	—	100.00	100.00
Komorpur (178)	—	0.56	3.37	96.07	100.00
Charbaniari (131)	—	—	5.34	94.60	100.00
Langarkhana (539)	5.19	7.05	14.66	73.10	100.00

Note: Figures in parentheses represent total number of sample households owning land in different regions.

was also generally reported that burglary and theft increased significantly in the famine areas during August–November of 1974. Unfortunately, data on famine-related crimes was not collected systematically by any agency. In Table 4.13 we have compiled general data on crime for three years (1972, 1973, and 1974) as recorded by the police directorate of the Bangladesh government. The year following the liberation war was rather unsettled in terms of law and order, consequently the incidence of all types of crime was high compared with preliberation years (not shown here). Except for robbery and burglary, all other types of crime decreased in 1973 but increased sharply the year after. Burglary showed a consistent upward trend, the increase between 1973 and 1974 being much higher than that between 1972 and 1973. In order to isolate the effect of famine conditions, if any, we have presented crime data separately for famine and nonfamine districts and also for the four-month period (August to November) corresponding to the height of famine.

Admittedly, no clear trend emerges from the figures presented in Table 4.13, but two interesting facts come to light. First, an increase in theft and burglary between 1973 and 1974 was sharper for the August–November period than for the rest of the year. Second, theft and burglary taken together in famine districts revealed a slightly higher rate of increase (17.2 percent) than in nonfamine districts (15.5 percent). A final point may be added here. Monthly crime data for different years show that theft and burglary have a seasonal pattern that is inverted U shaped

Table 4.13. Statement of Different Types of Crime in Bangladesh by Region

Region/ Nature of Crime	Number of Cases Reported					
	1972		1973		1974	
	August–November	Annual	August–November	Annual	August–November	Annual
Famine districts						
Dacoity	514	1197	320	1489	408	1246
Robbery	200	613	245	840	226	696
Burglary	1217	3208	1144	3538	1604	4060
Theft	926	3053	818	2543	1128	3068
Murder	254	1652	205	590	293	731
Rioting	796	3037	444	1590	676	1744
Nonfamine districts						
Dacoity	1184	3671	1202	3635	1138	3499
Robbery	1067	2951	1113	3472	1171	3569
Burglary	3228	9495	3500	10288	4134	11981
Theft	4601	15445	4545	13598	6003	15615
Murder	843	4316	687	1981	784	2051
Rioting	2607	8943	1878	5733	2484	6714
All districts						
Dacoity	1698	4868	1522	5124	1546	4745
Robbery	1267	3564	1358	4312	1397	4265
Burglary	4445	12703	4644	13826	5738	16041
Theft	5527	18498	5363	16141	7131	18683
Murder	1097	5968	892	2571	1077	2782
Rioting	3403	11980	2322	7323	3160	8458

Source: Government of Bangladesh, Police Directorate, Dacca.

with the peak period falling in May through July. In 1974, this pattern changed as the number of these crimes revealed an upward trend beginning with March and continuing until October. The importance of this finding lies in the fact that early monitoring of crime data provides an indicator of an oncoming crisis. We have already mentioned earlier that the Bengal Famine Code requires the district officer to carefully observe the trend of crime once it has been determined that a scarcity situation may turn into a famine in the near future.[78]

FAMINE MORTALITY

What was the excess mortality in the 1974 famine of Bangladesh? As in the case of all previous and contemporary famines, perhaps no one will be able to come up with an estimate that will satisfy all. We have noted earlier that different authorities came up with different estimates of excess mortality during the 1943 Great Bengal Famine, the range being between 1.5 million and 3.05 million.[79] The 1974 Bangladesh famine was no exception. There was no systematic attempt to record famine deaths. The Bangladesh government, in fact, discouraged public discussion of excess mortality. With regard to various estimates, Arthur and McNicoll[80] point out such figures as 30,000 being officially acknowledged, 500,000 quoted in Baldwin, and 80,000 in Rangpur district alone mentioned by Wahidul Haque et al. Newspapers reported excess deaths from different parts of Bangladesh and at different times. It is not possible to put these figures together to arrive at an overall estimate of famine mortality. Anjumane Mofidul Islam issued weekly and monthly statements on the number of unclaimed bodies buried by them in Dacca. The total number of such burials came to 2443 between July and December of 1974.

More systematic evidence on excess mortality can be traced in the data on seasonal crude death rates generated by the Cholera Research Laboratory of Dacca and presented here in Table 4.14. The data were collected from a thana (Matlab) in Comilla district, which according to our classification falls into the nonfamine area. Chowdhury and Chen have analyzed the annual findings in a recent paper.[81] Two interesting features of Table 4.14 can be noted. First, mortality during the 1971 civil war reached a higher peak than in the 1974 famine but in 1971 the mortality rate quickly returned to the precrisis level whereas in the case of famine we find that the crude death rate had not fallen to the 1973 level, even in the last quarter of 1975. Second, during 1974, the death rate continued to increase even after the officially acknowledged peak famine period (August–October) was over. Crude death rate reached its peak

Table 4.14. Seasonal Crude Death Rates in Matlab Thana of Bangladesh (1970–1975: Reporting Year, May–April)

Year	May–July	August–October	November–January	February–April
		Crude Death Rate for Quarter (per 1000)		
1970	12.8	15.3	18.1	13.7
1971	17.4	24.2	25.2	18.1
1972	15.3	14.8	18.9	16.5
1973	13.5	17.4	16.3	11.1
1974	13.3	21.1	21.3	24.7
1975	18.5	18.7	18.2	17.3

Source: Data provided by Cholera Research Laboratory, Dacca.

during the November 1974 to January 1975 period. This pattern is, however, quite comparable with that revealed in the 1943 famine. According to Sen, starvation deaths peaked around September and October of 1943, but excess mortality due to cholera, malaria, and smallpox continued up to April 1944. For smallpox, which reached its peak in March and April of 1944, a greater height was reached a year later.[82] Third, the absolute level of crude death rates observed in Matlab during different periods was lower than the available national estimates. A recent estimate put the crude death rate at 19.4 per 1000 for the 1961–1974 period.[83]

In our survey of *langarkhana* inmates and villagers we collected information on deaths in the household during August–October 1974. A question was asked about the cause of each individual death in the household. The answers were not very satisfactory primarily because the respondents, unaided by medical advice were unable to be accurate and unambiguous. In most cases, the respondents were unaware of the medical complexities of the case involved and as an answer promoted his/her best informed prejudices. However, while it is difficult to attribute any particular death specifically to famine starvation or starvation-related diseases, supporting evidence indicates that a good part of the deaths shown in Table 4.15 was the result of the special crisis situation. In any case, the mortality reported during the reference period was much higher than what could be expected under normal circumstances. Furthermore, since for partially uprooted and separated families there was little or no communication between members in different locations, the number of deaths may have been underreported. Some underreporting is also possible due to deliberate suppression of information by the respondents in order to avoid embarrassment.

In total 136 deaths were reported in 1774 households of eight villages and 141 deaths in the households of 788 *langarkhana* inmates. As

Table 4.15.   Statement of Deaths in Survey Households during August–October, 1974

Area	Total Population at Time of Survey	Number of Deaths	Total Population as of Aug. 1, 1974	Deaths as % of Sample Population as of Aug. 1, 1974
All villages	11,366	136	11,502	1.18
Famine area	4,836	74	4,910	1.51
Ramna	1,620	26	1,646	1.58
Gaorarang	1,304	16	1,320	1.21
Kogaria	916	4	920	0.43
Dewanganj	996	28	1,024	2.73
Nonfamine area	6,530	62	6,592	0.94
Nazirpur	2,935	39	2,974	1.31
Laskarpur	1,415	13	1,428	0.91
Komorpur	1,363	5	1,368	0.37
Charbaniari	817	5	822	0.61
Langarkhanas	4,452	141	4,593	3.07
Bagerhat	507	16	523	3.06
Chilmari	453	16	469	3.41
Dewanganj	563	19	582	3.26
Sunamganj	464	22	486	4.53
Khulna	704	8	712	1.12
Rangpur	582	28	610	4.59
Mymensingh	582	14	592	2.35
Dacca	597	18	615	2.93

expected, deaths as a percentage of total sample population was much higher for *langarkhana* inmates than villagers, the same being true of famine areas as compared with nonfamine areas. Converting the death figures into crude death rates (per 1000) for the quarter, we come up with figures of 122.8 for *langarkhana* inmates and 60.4 and 37.6 for villagers in famine and nonfamine areas respectively. In comparison with the estimated normal death rate of 19.4 as quoted above, the excess mortality suggested by the 1974 survey estimates is staggering.

We have ventured to obtain a broad order of magnitude of the total excess mortality due to the 1974 Bangladesh famine, keeping in view the reservation expressed earlier regarding the representative characters of our sample for respective areas. We first calculate the total excess mortality over the period August 1974 to January 1975 by applying the excess mortality rates obtained from our survey data[84] separately to total *langarkhana* population (4,345,277),[85] total rural population in famine area less *langarkhana* population in the same area (160,521,118), and to the total rural population in nonfamine area less *langarkhana* population in that area (497,08786).[86] The estimated excess mortality for this period turns out to be 999,058, almost one million.

We then estimate excess mortality during the next one-year period beginning February 1975 using certain extreme assumptions all of which, if anything, introduced downward bias in our estimate. The assumptions were as follows: (1) There was no excess mortality in Bangladesh attributable to the 1974 famine after January 1976; (2) Beginning February 1975 excess mortality rate for the rural population of famine area except *langarkhana* inmates dropped to the level experienced in nonfamine area during the height of crisis, while in nonfamine area itself excess mortality dropped to zero; (3) *Langarkhana* inmates (returnees to rural areas) in both areas continued to experience excess mortality at the rate of famine area in crisis. Thus we obtain an additional excess mortality to the tune of 459,387 for the period February 1975 to January 1976, which puts the total excess mortality due to the 1974 famine at about 1.5 million, a figure slightly less than that quoted earlier for East Bengal following the 1943 famine. It may be mentioned here that we made no attempt to estimate excess mortality among the urban population not captured within *langarkhana* inmates. There were two reasons for this. First, our survey did not cover urban population. Second, like the 1943 famine, the current famine was essentially a rural phenomenon in the sense that an overwhelming majority of famine victims belonged to rural areas. Nevertheless, to the extent there was excess mortality among the urban population, our estimate of total excess mortality due to the 1974 Bangldesh famine is biased downward. We thus present an estimate of excess mortality attributable to the 1974 famine that, we feel, represents the lower bound to the actual mortality that will probably never be known. Other interested scholars can take this as the starting point and come up with one or more estimates of famine mortality provided they can generate new and more reliable information than was possible for us to do here.[87]

There now remains the question of sex and age distribution of famine mortality. According to authorities on past Indian famines, men succumbed to famine more easily than women, the same being true of children and old persons as compared with middle-age groups.[88] Sen contradicts this finding saying that "it seems possible to argue that from many points of view mortality in the Bengal Famine was essentially a blowing up of normal mortality pattern in Bengal: the famine worked by intensifying the focus of death operating in that poverty-ridden economy."[89] He supports this statement by an analysis of age-sex composition of the excess mortality during the 1943 famine as obtained from death registration data. Unfortunately, we do not have comparative data for the 1974 Bangladesh famine. In order to simplify the task of data collection, we obtained only a three-way breakdown of mortality figures,

Table 4.16. Age and Sex Distribution of Mortality in Survey Households During August–October, 1974

Area	Total (No.)	Men (10 Yrs. and Above)		Women (10 Yrs. and Above)		Children (Below 10 Years)	
		No.	CDR	No.	CDR	No.	CDR
All villages	136	25	25.6	38	42.0	73	74.0
Famine area	74	17	40.4	16	42.0	41	96.8
Nonfamine area	62	8	14.4	22	41.6	32	56.8
Langarkhanas	141	37	125.5	28	89.4	76	186.6
Average CDR (1966–1971)			2.2		8.5		29.0

Note: CDR = Crude Death Rate (per 1000). Average CDR is calculated from George T. Curlin, Lincoln C. Chen, and Sayed Babur Hossain, "Demographic Crisis: The Impact of the Bangladesh Civil War (1971) on Births and Deaths in a Rural Area of Bangladesh." *Population Studies* 30(1):98 (1976); using population weight obtained from Government of Bangladesh, Bureau of Statistics, *Statistical Pocketbook of Bangladesh, 1978*, (Dacca: Bureau of Statistics, December 1977), pp. 72–73.

adult (10 years and above) men, adult women, and children below 10 years. The mortality figures along with the calculated crude death rates are presented in Table 4.16. Taking all villages together, excess death rate among adult women exceeds that among adult men, but this trend is reversed for *langarkhana* inmates. This can be contrasted with the normal average pattern, which reveals that death rate for women is higher than that for men. The adult-children differential in crude death rate became much sharper during the famine as compared with normal times, more so in famine areas. In the absence of more detailed information, we are unable to generalize the overall age-sex pattern of excess mortality during the 1974 Bangladesh famine as revealed by our survey data. However, we can safely assert from the data presented above that children succumbed more easily than adults in this famine.

More detailed information is available for Matlab as presented by Chowdhury and Chen. They showed that "the mortality burdens of the disasters weighted heaviest among the young and the elderly. Infant mortality and the mortality rates among children 1–4 and 5–9 years rose dramatically, as did the death rates of adults over age 45."[90] As for sex differentials, they have the following to say, "During baseline years, female mortality consistently exceeded male mortality in all age groups except infant deaths. The age-specific sex differentials were more pronounced in children 1–4 and 5–9 years and in the childbearing years. Disaster tended to accentuate even further these sex differentials, particularly among children."[91]

NOTES AND REFERENCES

1. More on data and methodology of collection can be obtained from M. Algamir, *Famine 1974: Political Economy of Mass Starvation*, Statistical Annexe, Part I (Dacca: Bangladesh Institute of Development Studies, 1977).
2. A. M. Chowdhury, "Cyclones in Bangladesh," mimeographed, Institute for Space and Atmospheric Research, Bangladesh Atomic Energy Commission, Dacca, January 1974.
3. The secretary to the Ministry was very keen to help us but he was overruled by the Minister-in-charge, apparently on the advice of the joint secretary, who appeared at that stage to wield more power than the secretary. Fortunately, the field-level government officials were unaware of this attitude at the top, and we received excellent cooperation from them. This attitude of the ruling Awami League party government can be contrasted with the attitude of the government of India, which, in spite of its many glaring failings, at least responded by appointing a Famine Commission to look into the 1943 famine and with that of the Bengal government, which partially financed a study of the famine by a team led by Professor P. C. Mahalanobis. In all fairness, the Bangladesh government should probably be credited with the fact that it did not try to stop us from going ahead with the study.
4. See M. R. Khan, "Bangladesh Population During the First Five Year Plan Period (1973–78): An Estimate," *Bangladesh Economic Review* 1(2):186–198 (April 1973).

5. See M. Alamgir, *Bangladesh, A Case of Below Poverty Level Equilibrium Trap* (Dacca: Bangladesh Institute of Development Studies, 1978).
6. See Government of Pakistan, Planning Commission, *Reports of the Advisory Panels for the Fourth Five Year Plan 1970–75*, vol. I, (Karachi: Manager of Publications, 1970), pp. 15–60; A. Rahman, *East and West Pakistan: A Problem in the Political Economy of Regional Planning* (Cambridge, Mass.: Center for International Affairs, Harvard University, 1968), pp. 1–30; Just Faaland and J. R. Parkinson, *Bangladesh, The Test Case for Development* (London: C. Hurst, 1976), pp. 6–8. According to the Advisory Panel of Economists for the Fourth Plan, Bangladesh lost about Rs. 30,000 million to West Pakistan during the 1947–1969 period.
7. M. Alamgir and L. Berlage, *Bangladesh: National Income and Expenditure 1949/50– 1969/70* (Dacca: Bangladesh Institute of Development Studies, 1974), pp. 34–39.
8. M. Alamgir, "Population Growth and Economic Activity of the Population in Bangladesh," a contribution to the country monograph on *Population Situation in Bangladesh*, prepared under the auspices of ESCAP/Bangladesh (forthcoming).
9. M. Alamgir, "Some Analysis of Distribution of Income, Consumption, Saving and Poverty in Bangladesh," *Bangladesh Development Studies* 2(4):740–749 (October 1974).
10. Ibid., pp. 749–760; G. B. S. Mujahid, "Measurement of Poverty in Bangladesh: A Note in Methodology," *Bangladesh Development Studies* 5(4):454 (October 1977).
11. Figures in this paragraph are quoted from Famine Inquiry Commission, 1944, *Report on Bengal* (New Delhi: Manager of Government Publications, 1945), pp. 201–202; M. Alamgir, "Some Aspects of Bangladesh Agriculture: Review of Performance and Evaluation of Policies," *Bangladesh Development Studies* 3(3):269 (July 1975); Alamgir, *Bangladesh*, pp. 101–102.
12. M. Alamgir and L. Berlage, "Foodgrain (Rice and Wheat) Demand, Import and Price Policy for Bangladesh," *Bangladesh Economic Review* 1(1):27–28, 45–46 (January 1973).
13. Famine Inquiry Commission, 1944, *Report on Bengal*, pp. 203–204.
14. Alamgir and Berlage, "Foodgrain Demand," pp. 45–46.
15. Alamgir, *Bangladesh*, p. 20n.
16. Alamgir and Berlage, "Foodgrain Demand," pp. 28–29.
17. Ibid., p. 46.
18. Alamgir, *Famine 1974*, Statistical Annexe, p. 5.
19. Government of Bangladesh, Water Development Board, *Annual Report on Flood in Bangladesh 1974* (Dacca: Water Development Board, 1975).
20. Alamgir and Berlage, "Foodgrain Demand," p. 47.
21. Warren L. Sharp, "A Preliminary Analysis of the 1974 Monsoon in Bangladesh," mimeographed, United States Agency for International Development (USAID), Dacca, September 1974.
22. *Report on Flood*, pp. 6–10.
23. R. C. Majumdar, ed., *The History and Culture of the Indian People*, vol. VIII (Bombay: Bharatya Vidya Bhavan, 1970), p. 735.
24. *Report on Flood*, pp. 10–11; According to Walford, Sylhet, Jessore, and Central Bengal were also affected by flood during 1787. See C. Walford, "The Famines of the World: Past and Present," *Journal of the Statistical Society* 41(3):461 (September 1878).
25. Walford, "Famines of the World," pp. 451–467.
26. M. Azizul Huq, *The Man Behind the Plow* (Calcutta: The Book Company, 1939), pp. 21–26.
27. *Report on Flood*, p. 11.
28. Ibid.
29. Chowdhury, "Cyclones in Bangladesh," p. 7.

30. Detailed data provided by the Storm Warning Centre, Dacca, suggests that Bangladesh suffered from eight cyclonic storms and eleven severe cyclonic storms.
31. *Report on Flood*, pp. 58, 63.
32. Figures provided by Storm Warning Centre, Dacca.
33. Chowdhury, "Cyclones in Bangladesh," p. 7.
34. Alamgir, *Famine 1974*, p. 5. This is consistent with the estimate of crop loss due to flood made by the Department of Agriculture and that due to cyclone made by the World Bank. See S. R. Bose, "Foodgrain Availability and the Possibilities of Famine in Bangla Desh," *Economic and Political Weekly*, Annual Number, February 1972, p. 294.
35. Bose, "Foodgrain Availability," p. 293.
36. *Report on Flood*, p. 89. Since these figures were officially acknowledged after Bangladesh became independent we take it that they are unrelated to the death and destruction that took place during the 1971 war due to army action.
37. Our figure for population decline in 1971 is based on assumed total population of 71 million on January 1, 1971, along with an estimated exodus of 9.5 million people to India and 1 million deaths due to army action. See also Bose, "Foodgrain Availability," p. 299. Immediately after the liberation of Bangladesh, the government claimed that mortality during the war reached 3 million. It is not clear how this figure was arrived at. Other sources put the figure between 600,000 and 1 million. No serious attempt has been made to verify these alternative claims.
38. Ibid., p. 297.
39. Alamgir, *Famine 1974*, pp. 54–55. Bose makes a very important point that in spite of the scare of an impending famine beginning April 1971, the abnormal situation prevailing during the year prevented traders and large farmers from indulging in speculation and hoarding "thereby accentuating grain shortage in the market and pushing up prices," "Foodgrain Availability," p. 303.
40. Alamgir, "Distribution of Income, Consumption, Saving and Poverty in Bangladesh," pp. 754, 758.
41. United Nations Relief Operation in Dacca (UNROD), *A Survey of Damages and Repairs*, Dacca, 1972.
42. For more on these issues, see Alamgir, *Bangladesh*. Soon after liberation, the Bangladesh government nationalized about 85 percent of large-scale industrial assets. See Kholiquzzaman Ahmed, "Aspects of the Management of Nationalised Industries in Bangladesh," *Bangladesh Development Studies* 2(3):675–702 (July 1974).
43. Faaland and Parkinson, *Bangladesh*, pp. 16-20; Gul Afroz and Dilip Kumar Roy, "Capacity Utilization in Selected Manufacturing Industries of Bangladesh," *Bangladesh Development Studies* 4(2):275–288 (April 1976).
44. M. Alamgir and A. Rahman, *Saving in Bangladesh* (Dacca: Bangladesh Institute of Development Studies, 1974).
45. Government of Bangladesh, Planning Commission, *Annual Plan 1973-74* (Dacca: Planning Commission, 1973).
46. Faaland and Parkinson, *Bangladesh*, p. 12; Government of Bangladesh, Bureau of Statistics, *Monthly Statistical Bulletin of Bangladesh* 6(10):106 (October 1977).
47. Sultan Hafeez Rahman, "An Analysis of Terms of Trade of Bangladesh, 1959/60 to 1974/75," *Bangladesh Development Studies* 4(3):375–398 (July 1976).
48. Impact of this cyclone in Patuakhali was brought out clearly during our field survey of village Nazirpur in that district. We found that the economic backbone of the area had been broken by the cyclone. Winter crops (including the *rabi*) were almost entirely destroyed. Damage to houses was severe. More importantly, livestock population was heavily depleted, affecting cultivation of land in the following season. Both middle and small farmers were found to have run into heavy debt.

49. Alamgir, *Bangladesh*, pp. 5–37.
50. Calculated from Government of Bangladesh, Bureau of Statistics, *Statistical Yearbook of Bangladesh, 1975* (Dacca: Bureau of Statistics, 1976), pp. 263, 283.
51. *Daily Ittefaq*, March 29, 1974.
52. *The Bangladesh Observer*, April 4, 1974.
53. Alamgir, *Famine 1974*, p. 47.
54. Government of Bangladesh, Directorate of Procurement, Distribution and Rationing.
55. Alamgir, *Famine 1974*, p. 48.
56. Bruce Currey, "The Famine Syndrome: Its Definition for Preparedness and Prevention in Bangladesh," *Ecology of Food and Nutrition* 7:87–98 (1978).
57. The government responded to this demand on April 24 by deploying the army to stop smuggling and to prevent hoarding and profiteering in foodgrains and other essential commodities.
58. *Daily Ittefaq*, April 13, 1974.
59. *Daily Ittefaq*, April 23, 1974.
60. *Report on Flood*, p. 19. The report pointed out that "in the month of April, 1974, the total rainfall in Sylhet was 24.23 inches against the normal monthly rainfall of 13.37 inches for that month," p. 39.
61. Ibid., p. 79.
62. Ibid., Plates 5, 7, 11, and 12.
63. Flood relief centers represented an apology for relief. These centers were opened in early August and in total there were 138 centers basically providing only accommodation to about 75,000 people. Material help provided was minimal. A spot survey in one such center in Dacca revealed that relief was inadequate and its distribution was mismanaged. Supervision in general was lacking. For example, in one of the centers it was found that no official had been there in the last four days. As the flood water started to recede during the first week in September the relief centers were closed. Government sources (Ministry of Relief and Rehabilitation) indicated that as of August 20, 1974, Taka 1.899 million worth of relief was provided in various forms (cash grants, house grants, test relief works, seed advances, foodgrains, and clothing). If we relate this to the total number of people affected by the flood as shown in Table 4.6, the per capita relief amounts to only Tk. 0.64. Toward the end of August, the government asked all district administrators to step up test relief works but this was not seriously pursued until the end of the year.
64. Md. Ali Akbar, *1974 Famine in Bangladesh*, mimeographed, Department of Social Work, Rajshahi University, October 1975.
65. *Daily Ittefaq*, September 5, 1974.
66. *Daily Ittefaq*, September 7, 1974.
67. *Daily Ittefaq*, October 13, 1974.
68. The term migration is being used somewhat loosely here. In general, most of the movements of people during 1974 represented temporary migration in that the majority of those who left their places of origin came back within the limit of six months. However, there remained a fraction who became permanent migrants.
69. Tarakchandra Das, *Bengal Famine (1943) As Revealed in a Survey of the Destitutes in Calcutta* (Calcutta: University of Calcutta, 1949), p. 63.
70. Currey, "Famine Syndrome," found that in Rowmari thana of Rangpur district, one of the worst flood affected areas, "70% of the households moved outside the thana in search of food and work," p. 94. See also Akbar, *1974 Famine in Bangladesh*. In this context it may be of interest to look at the distribution of Dacca *langarkhana* inmates by the period intervening between arrival in Dacca and in *langarkhana*: 0–2 weeks, 54 inmates; 2–9 weeks, 20 inmates; 4–6 weeks, 13 inmates; 6 weeks and more, 14 inmates.

71. Desertion, and staying back at the place of origin should be understood in a physical and functional sense. In certain cases members of a household did not physically leave home (as in cases of many rural *langarkhana* inmates) but were functionally withdrawn as they became dependent on *langarkhana* for survival. Data for urban *langarkhanas*, however, reflect both physical and functional uprooting and separation.
72. Akbar, *1974 Famine in Bangladesh.*
73. A. Farouk, Rejaul Karim, M. A. Mannan, Abbas Ali Khan, and A. K. Fazlul Huq Shah, *The Vagrants of Dacca City* (Dacca: Bureau of Economic Research, 1976).
74. Currey, "Famine Syndrome," p. 92.
75. Distress sale is defined as that effected for consumption and/or repayment of debt. We include repayment of debt because it represents a reduction in the current purchasing power of the household.
76. Akbar, *1974 Famine in Bangladesh*, Table 12. For Bangladesh as a whole, information gathered by the Bangladesh Bureau of Statistics suggests that, in 1974, about 157 thousand acres went up for sale but how much of it represented distress sale is not known. This was 7 percent more than the figure for 1973. See Government of Bangladesh, Bureau of Statistics, *Statistical Pocketbook of Bangladesh, 1978* (Dacca: Bureau of Statistics, December 1977), p. 125.
77. Concerning the 1943 famine, Aykroyd writes, "The victims made little attempt to loot food shops and stores cornered by prosperous traders; sometimes they died in the street, just outside well-filled and locked storehouses. There was no organized rioting. Coming from different villages, the people lacked any corporate spirit which might have prompted efforts to obtain food by violent means. They belonged to the poorer sections of the population and were accustomed to accept misfortune passively. Moreover, they soon became physically incapable of such purposive action. During the famine, indeed, thefts of rice stores or in transport became very common. But this was largely the work of ordinary thieves, stealing rice because, it had become well worth stealing." W. R. Aykroyd, *The Conquest of Famine* (London: Chatto and Windus, 1974), p. 75.
78. Kali Charon Ghosh, *Famines in Bengal 1770–1943* (Calcutta: India Associated Publishing Co., 1944), p. 3.
79. A. K. Sen, "Famine Mortality: A Study of the Bengal Famine of 1943," mimeographed, London School of Economics, August 1976.
80. W. Brian Arthur and Geoffrey McNicoll, "An Analytical Survey of Population and Development in Bangladesh," *Population and Development Review* 4(1):29 (March 1978); Stephen C. Baldwin, "Catastrophe in Bangladesh: An Examination of Alternative Population Growth Possibilities 1975–2000," *Asian Survey* 17:345–357 (1977); Wahidul Huq, Niranjan Mehta, Anisur Rahman, and Poona Wignaraja, "Towards a Theory of Rural Development," *Development Dialogue* 2:33 (1977).
81. A. K. M. Chowdhury and Lincoln C. Chen, *The Dynamics of Contemporary Famine*, Report No. 47, The Ford Foundation, Dacca, January 1977. For a discussion of the nature of the sample and methodology of collection of data, see George T. Curlin, Lincoln C. Chen, and Sayed Babur Hossain, "Demographic Crisis: The Impact of the Bangladesh Civil War (1971) on Births and Deaths in a Rural Area of Bangladesh," *Population Studies* 30(1):88–90 (1976).
82. Sen, "Famine Mortality," pp. 19–26. On epidemic of infectious diseases during the 1974 Bangladesh famine, see Chowdhury and Chen, *Dynamics of Contemporary Famine.*
83. This estimate comes from the Bangladesh Retrospective Fertility and Mortality Survey carried out by the U.K. Ministry of Overseas Development. According to Arthur and McNicoll, this is the most careful estimate, "Population and Development in Ban-

gladesh," p. 69. For alternative estimates of Crude Death Rate in Bangladesh, see R. H. Choudhury, "Demographic Profile of Bangladesh," typescript, Bangladesh Institute of Development Studies, 1978.

84. As can be seen from figures presented earlier, the excess mortality rates are 103.4, 41.0, and 18.2 for *langarkhana* inmates and villagers in famine and nonfamine areas respectively. These are annual rates; for shorter periods appropriate adjustments have to be made. We use the same rates for both August–October 1974 and November 1974–January 1975 periods. This is supported by the impression gathered by our investigators during field survey and by the evidence from Matlab thana as presented in Table 4.13.

85. *Langarkhana* population refers to the average numbers of persons fed daily during September–November 1974 period as given by the Bangladesh Ministry of Relief and Rehabilitation.

86. Rural populations in famine and nonfamine areas refer to those of August 1, 1974. These figures were arrived at by raising the revised 1974 census figures (for assumed 6 percent underenumeration as mentioned in the *Statistical Yearbook of Bangladesh, 1975*, p. 16) at the rate of 2.86 percent per annum calculated from the data of Retrospective Survey and subtracting the *langarkhana* figures to avoid double counting. Admittedly, *langarkhana* figures include urban *langarkhanas* but this should pose no problem since our survey indicated that the inmates or urban *langarkhanas* were almost entirely composed of rural destitutes.

87. We did consider one alternative methodology for estimating famine mortality in 1974. This was to let our estimated crude death rate follow the patterns of change (same rate of increase or decrease) shown in Matlab data for the period under consideration. As expected, the resulting excess mortality estimate was much higher; it exceeded 2 million. The point we are trying to make is that, by changing underlying assumptions about various parameters, one can produce a wide range of estimates of famine mortality. Given a rather "soft" information base this will only add to the existing confusion over the subject. The best that one can possibly do is to produce a broad order of magnitude and this is precisely what we have tried to do here. Needless to say, we are very sensitive on this issue and accept full responsibility for any inaccuracy.

88. For discussions on age-sex mortality during the famine, see Sen, "Famine Mortality," pp. 25–26.

89. Ibid., pp. 25–26.

90. Chowdhury and Chen, *Dynamics of Contemporary Famine*, p. 9.

91. Ibid., pp. 10–11.

Chapter 5

Famine Victims and
Societal Response

PROFILE OF FAMINE VICTIMS

Famine takes its toll on different groups of people in different ways. It follows from the definition of famine that households affected by famine experience a drastic reduction in foodgrain consumption per capita. Therefore, one way to identify famine victims is to analyze the level of foodgrain consumption of different households during the famine period. A direct consumption survey over a prolonged period of time is a difficult task even under normal circumstances. Therefore, one can look for alternative indications to identify famine victims. Famine substates along with mortality suggest a number of criteria that can be used for this purpose. We used data on migration, mortality, sale of assets, and acceptance of loans under stringent terms to present the socio-economic profile of the victims of the 1974 Bangladesh famine.

The victims of the 1974 famine were forced to physically and/or functionally abandon their homesteads and take refuge at various *langarkhanas*. The household structure of *langarkhana* inmates is presented in Table 5.1. For comparison, we also present the corresponding figures for famine and nonfamine area villages and for Bangladesh as a whole. There is no difference in the adjusted (4.4) and nonadjusted (5.6) household[1] size of *langarkhana* inmates and famine area villagers. But they are both smaller than the household size in the nonfamine area and in Bangladesh as a whole. In the case of *langarkhana*, the small size of household can be explained by the preponderance of members with low average size of landholding. Our survey data confirmed other findings[2] that size of landholding and income are positively correlated with size of household in Bangladesh. Average number of earners and dependency ratio in *langarkhana* inmate households were 1.7 and 2.3 respectively.[3] Both of these figures are comparable with those for all villagers, but, when village data are separated into famine and nonfamine areas, the dependency ratio for *langarkhana* falls between the two. As for the difference between famine and nonfamine areas, a smaller average household size in the famine area can be explained by its vulnerability to natural calamities such as flood. Furthermore, data presented in Table 5.1 suggest that an average *langarkhana* inmate household had fewer men and more children, that is, it was more vulnerable than an average household in other groups. This is clearly brought out by the ratios of adult male to adult female and children to adult.

In terms of landholding, the majority of *langarkhana* inmates belonged to the small-farmer category (Table 5.2). Thirty-two percent of the households did not own any land (including homestead) at all. More than 80 percent belonged to the less-than-one-acre category. These figures are much higher than 1977 "all Bangladesh" figures (11 and 47 percent respectively).[4]

Less than 3 percent of the *langarkhana* inmates belonged to the middle-farmer (2.5 to less than 5.0 acre) group, and most of these households had lost cultivable land and homesteads through river erosion during the flood. The large-farmer group was not represented at all among the *langarkhana* inmates.

Occupational distribution of *langarkhana* inmates is shown in Table 5.3 along with that of 820 destitute units surveyed by Das in Calcutta during the 1943 famine.[5] In both periods, the victims of famine were drawn largely from the laborer class and other petty occupational categories such as petty traders, artisans and craftsman, fishermen, and so forth.[6] There is an important difference between the two periods in that the proportion of farmers in the 1974 sample was much higher (38.7 percent) than that in the 1943 sample (21.2 percent). Reduction in the average size of landholding per household, increase in the average size of household, and the impact of flood in 1974 may explain the shift in occupational distribution of destitutes between the two famine periods as reflected in the above figures.

As for the indebtedness of *langarkhana* inmates, we can see from Table 5.4 that 42 percent of households took out loans during August–October 1974. Considering the crisis situation, this is a low percentage. It only

Table 5.1. Structure of Survey Households

Household Characteristics	Langarkhana	Famine Area	Nonfamine Area	All Villages	Bangladesh
Average size of household					
adjusted	4.4	4.4	5.7	5.1	5.3
unadjusted	5.6	5.6	7.2	6.4	6.0
Average number of earners	1.7	1.8	1.8	1.8	N.A.
Dependency ratio	2.3	2.1	2.9	2.5	N.A.
Ratio of adult male (10 years and over) to adult female	0.93	1.04	1.07	1.09	1.07
Ratio of children (below 10 years) to adult	0.61	0.54	0.51	0.52	0.46

Source: Bangladesh figures were calculated from Government of Bangladesh, Bureau of Statistics, Statistical Pocketbook, 1978 (Dacca: Bureau of Statistics, December 1977), pp. 72–73, 74.

N.A. = not available.

Table 5.2. Landholding of Langarkhana Inmates

Size Group of Landholding (acres)	Ownership Holding[a]			Operational Holding[a]		
	Number of Households	Percentage of Households	Average Landholding (acres)	Number of Households	Percentage of Households	Average Landholding (acres)
0	249	31.6	0.00	631	80.0	0.07
< 0.5	390	49.5	0.03			
0.5– < 1.0	57	7.2	0.74	61	7.7	0.74
1.0– < 2.5	81	10.3	1.60	71	9.0	1.76
2.5– < 5.0	10	1.3	3.77	22	2.8	3.38
5.0 +	1	0.1	5.28	3	0.4	7.56
Total	788	100.0	0.34	788	100.0	0.40

[a]Entire landholding, including homestead, cultivable land, cultivable fallow land, noncultivable waste land, ponds, orchards, forest areas, pasture or any other such area to which the household commands title and use right is defined as ownership holding. This includes mortgaged-in land over which the household has use right for at least one year. Similarly, mortgaged-out land over which the household loses use right for a period of one year and above is excluded from ownership. In other words, owned land over which use right is exercised for part of the year is included in ownership holding. Operational holding refers to the area actually operated. As such it will exclude the amount of owned land rented out and include the amount of land leased (for whole or part of the year). Renting may be on the basis of sharecropping, fixed rental (cash or kind), or any other such arrangement.

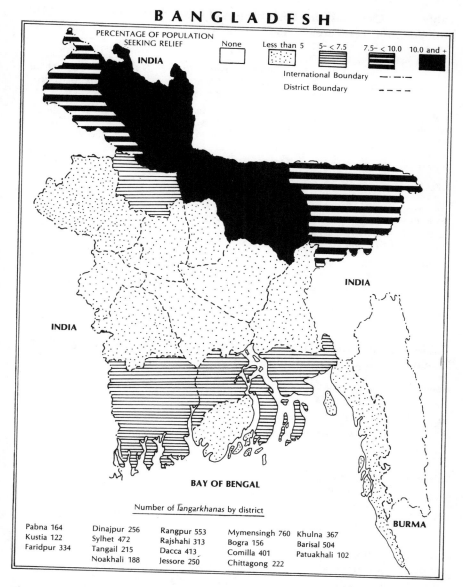

Figure 5.1. Distribution of langarkhanas by districts and percentages of population seeking relief.

Table 5.3. Occupational Distribution of Langarkhana Inmates of 1974 and Calcutta Destitutes of 1943

Type of Occupation	1974		1943	
	Number of Inmates	Percentage of Inmates	Number of Units	Percentage of Units
Farming	305	38.7	174	21.2
Agricultural labor	190	24.1	83	10.1
Nonagricultural labor	161	20.4	251[a]	30.6
Total labor	351	44.5	334	40.7
Others	132	16.8	563	68.7
Total	788	100.0	820	100.0

Source: Data from village and langarkhana survey carried out at the Bangladesh Institute of Development Studies (BIDS) under the direction of the present author; Tarakchandra Das, Bengal Famine (1943), as Revealed in a Survey of Destitutes in Calcutta (University of Calcutta, 1949), p.69.

Note: Occupational distribution of households is determined on the basis of major source of income of the household.

[a]Includes ordinary day laborers and combined farm and ordinary day laborers.

Table 5.4. Amount, Source, and Use of Loans Taken by Langarkhana Inmates during August–October, 1974

Total number of households	788
Number of households taking loan	358
Percentage of households taking loan	45
Amount of loan taken per household (Taka)	325
Source of loan: institutional	4
noninstitutional	96
Use of loan: capital expenditure	1
consumption expenditure	98
other	1

reflects the poor credit worthiness of the *langarkhana* inmates. Limited evidence for normal-period borrowing shows that the percentages of indebted households were 47 and 60 in two areas of Bangladesh.[7] Amount of loan per *langarkhana* household was Tk. 325, which represents a very high level of debt burden when we compare it with the annual per capita income of all *langarkhana* inmate households, which was only Tk. 288. It was also found that 96 percent of loans were obtained from noninstitutional sources (that is, friends and relatives, moneylenders, rich farmers, and so forth). Ninety-eight percent of all loans were used to finance consumption expenditure, which is understandable in view of the crisis situation. It is clear that the famine victims were also those who got heavily indebted during the famine in an attempt to meet their minimum survival needs.[8]

A second criterion used here to identify famine victims was mortality. Using mortality figures for the period August–October, 1974, we calculated crude death rates for different household groups. Households were classified on the basis of size group of operational landholding and occupation. The corresponding crude death rates for different household groups by areas are shown in Table 5.5. As expected, the highest death rate was observed in the lowest landholding group. The relationship between size of landholding and mortality rate does not reveal any particular pattern except for the lowest three groups, where an inverse relationship between the two is observed. However, when we divide the households into below 2.5 acre and above 2.5 acre groups, the inverse relationship between landholding and mortality can clearly be seen. Mortality rates among children (below 10 years) show a similar pattern.

Table 5.5. Mortality by Social Groups during August–October, 1974 (per 1,000)

Household Groups	Famine Area	Nonfamine Area	All Villages	Langarkhanas
Operational landholding (acres)				
< 0.5	100 (148)	62 (98)	83 (123)	
0.5–< 1.0	79 (142)	46 (43)	59 (80)	
1.0–< 2.5	46 (78)	13 (33)	31 (60)	
2.5–< 5.0	9 (12)	36 (38)	27 (29)	
5.0 +	48 (114)	34 (58)	37 (72)	
Less than 2.5	77 (126)	41 (69)	60 (98)	
2.5 and above	23 (44)	35 (47)	31 (46)	
Occupation				
Farming	48 (82)	31 (51)	38 (64)	
Wage labor	129 (201)	56 (72)	88 (128)	
Trade	27 (38)	68 (102)	53 (80)	
Transportation	0 (0)	33 (444)	100 (286)	
Service	26 (28)	8 (0)	16 (12)	
Others	35 (0)	0 (0)	29 (0)	
Total	60 (97)	38 (57)	47 (74)	123 (180)

Note: Figures in parentheses are crude death rates among children under 10 years.

In general, for all groups, the mortality rate in the famine area was higher than that in the nonfamine area, except for the 2.5 to less than 5.0 acre category, where the reverse was true. Support for such an inverse relationship was found in a village study by McCord quoted by Arthur and McNicoll.[9]

Occupational pattern of mortality reveals that, for Bangladesh as a whole, wage laborers suffered the highest mortality among all groups except for transportation workers. Figures for the transportation worker group are somewhat anomalous, which may be attributed to the very small size of this group in the total sample. Traders come next in the mortality scale followed by the "other occupation" group and service workers. A similar ranking holds for mortality among children except that there was no child mortality in the other occupation group. Famine and nonfamine areas show different patterns of mortality by occupation. In the famine area the highest mortality was experienced by wage laborers followed by farmers and traders, whereas in the nonfamine area the mortality ranking was traders, wage laborers, and farmers. All occupational groups experienced mortality during the famine, but, as expected, wage laborers were victimized most. A relatively low mortality rate among service workers is explained by the fact that they had an assured income flow throughout the crisis period, while income earning opportunities of wage laborers and traders were drastically reduced as a result of flood and heavy rains. In addition, traders and other professional workers experienced a decline in income due to a drop in demand, which characterizes any crisis.

Famine victims are usually forced to sell assets to meet consumption needs. In Tables 4.10 and 4.11, we presented some data on the sale of assets by villagers and *langarkhana* inmates under distress conditions. We did not, however, analyze the characteristics of these households. In the case of *langarkhana* inmates, we found that all sale of assets represented distress sale. For villagers, selected characteristics of households selling assets under distress conditions during 1972–1974 are presented in Table 5.6. Here, we have included data for the two years prior to the famine, because there were many families who sold assets during that period to support themselves, and who had little or nothing left to sell in 1974. In the context of our present analysis, we had to take account of such cases. As expected, ranking all villages together, the average landholding and per capita income of households selling assets under distress were lower than the corresponding figures for all households. The same was true separately of famine and nonfamine areas. Again, comparison between famine and nonfamine areas reveals that the averages for landholding and per capita income of asset selling households in the former, are lower than those in the latter. The average size

Table 5.6. Size of Household, Landholding, and Per Capita Income of Households Selling Assets Under Distress Condition During 1972–1974

Area	Number of Households Selling Assets Under Distress Condition	Average Size of Household	Average Landholding per Household (acres)			Per Capita Income (Taka)[b]
			Ownership	Operational	Cultivable[a]	
Households selling assets in distress						
All villages	744	6.1	1.65	1.84	1.35	431
Famine area	421	5.8	1.59	1.62	1.33	547
Nonfamine area	323	6.6	1.74	2.13	1.38	277
All households	Total number of Households					
All villages	1,774	6.4	1.99	2.10	1.65	535
Famine area	869	5.6	1.61	1.61	1.36	536
Nonfamine area	905	7.2	2.35	2.48	1.92	535

[a] Cultivable landholding refers to that portion of owned land that is used for agricultural production or is capable of being used for agricultural production.

[b] Concept of income used here and the methodology of estimation is explained in appendix to Chapter 5. The income figures do not include imputed family labor.

of household shows the expected pattern, that is, a lower average size in lower income and landholding areas or groups of households (not shown in Table 5.6). Summarizing the evidence presented in Table 4.10 and 5.6 together, a larger proportion of households selling different assets under distress conditions come from famine areas, and that, in Bangladesh as a whole, all such households belonged to the low-income and low-landholding categories.

Data on the socio-economic background of households selling assets under distress during the 1974 famine are presented in Table 5.7. Looking at the tenurial status[10] of all village households, we find that the percentage of distress asset selling households was highest among landless laborers, followed by tenant farmers, owner-cum-tenant farmers, and owner farmers. Given the insecurity of tenancy and uncertainty of wage employment in Bangladesh, this is the pattern that one would normally expect to observe in a crisis situation. With slight variation, this tenurial pattern of distress asset sale holds true for both famine and nonfamine areas. The percentages are again higher for famine areas than nonfamine areas. If we analyze the sale of different assets, we find that the highest percentage of households involved in land sale under distress conditions came from among the owner-farmer group. This is explained by the relative importance of this group in terms of area owned. Besides, the structure of asset holding reveals that a major portion of their asset holding was in the form of land. In the sale of other assets, either tenant farmers or landless laborers dominated, reflecting the fact that having no land, members of these groups were forced to sell cattle, household utensils, ornaments, and so forth.

The pattern of distress asset sale by size group of operational land-holding is shown in Table 5.7. Looking at the data for all villages, we find that the percentage of households selling different assets under distress conditions is higher for households belonging to the less than 2.5 acre group, than for those belonging to the 2.5 acre and above group. This relationship, however, does not hold in the case of the famine area except for land sale. This may be due to smaller holdings of other assets among low landholding groups in the famine area as compared with the nonfamine area. In the case of famine area, though, there was no relationship between the size group of landholding and the percentage of households selling assets under distress condition. Sale of assets was uniformly high among all groups although one possible explanation is that in the sample from the famine area there were relatively few observations for the large landholding categories. Taking all villages together, though, land sale under distress conditions was concentrated among small-farmer groups during the 1974 famine. Not only did relatively more small farmers have to sell assets, but they sold a higher

Table 5.7. Percentage of Households Selling Different Assets in 1974 Under Distress Condition by Tenurial Status and Size Group of Landholding (Operational) of Sellers

Household Groups	Famine area					Nonfamine Area					All Villages				
	Number of Households	Percent of Households Selling Assets				Number of Households	Percent of Households Selling Assets				Number of Households	Percent of Households Selling Assets			
		Land Only	Land and Other Assets	Other Assets	Total		Land Only	Land and Other Assets	Other Assets	Total		Land Only	Land and Other Assets	Other Assets	Total
Tenurial status															
Owner farmer	426	5.87	11.97	21.36	39.20	516	0.97	1.55	27.13	29.65	942	3.18	6.26	24.52	33.96
Owner-cum-tenant farmer	154	3.25	11.69	25.97	40.91	220	0.91	1.36	30.91	33.18	374	1.87	5.61	28.88	36.36
Tenant farmer	37	5.41	8.11	27.03	40.55	42	—	—	47.62	47.62	79	2.53	3.80	37.97	44.30
Landless laborer	252	7.14	4.37	40.87	52.38	127	—	2.36	29.92	32.28	379	4.75	3.69	37.20	43.64
Size group of landholding (acres)															
<0.5	357	8.14	5.88	27.73	41.75	275	—	1.45	32.36	33.81	632	4.59	3.96	29.75	38.30
0.9- <1.0	77	7.79	5.19	33.73	46.71	84	1.19	1.19	39.29	41.67	161	4.35	3.11	36.65	44.11
1.0- <2.5	258	3.10	14.73	26.36	44.19	179	2.23	2.23	47.49	51.95	437	2.75	9.61	35.01	47.37
2.5- <5.0	128	4.69	8.59	29.69	42.97	234	0.43	1.71	17.52	19.66	362	1.93	4.14	21.82	27.89
5.0- <7.5	26	3.85	19.23	26.92	50.00	83	1.20	1.20	15.66	18.06	109	1.83	5.50	18.35	25.68
7.5-<12.5	15	—	20.00	33.33	53.33	38	—	—	7.89	7.89	53	—	5.66	15.09	20.75
12.5 +	8	—	12.50	12.50	25.00	12	—	—	16.67	16.67	20	—	5.00	15.00	20.00
<2.5	692	6.22	9.10	27.89	43.21	538	0.93	1.67	38.48	41.08	1,230	3.90	5.86	32.52	42.28
2.5 +	177	3.95	11.30	28.81	44.06	367	0.55	1.36	16.07	17.98	544	1.65	4.59	20.20	26.44
Total	869	5.75	9.55	28.08	43.38	905	0.77	1.55	29.39	31.71	1,774	3.21	5.47	28.75	37.43

Note: Number of households refer to total number of households in the group.

proportion of the holding. This is more evident when we look at Table 5.8, which presents data on the proportion of owned land sold in 1974 by various size groups of landholding of the sellers irrespective of the purpose of sale. There is an inverse relationship between the proportion of owned land sold and the size group of landholding of the sellers. The proportion of owned land sold by the less than one acre holding households is as high as 54 percent. This percentage is almost five times as great as that for households with landholding five acres and above. After land transactions in 1974, the less than one acre group became either landless or near landless.

During a famine, the affected households try to obtain food directly through charity of some kind, or they try to mobilize resources so as to be able to purchase food. In quest of resources, they often contract loans under very unfavorable terms. In Bangladesh, even under normal circumstances, the poor rural households are found to make loans under what is known as the *dadan* arrangement. This arrangement involves short term forward crop sale and purchase that the small farmers, tenants, and other groups enter into in response to their pressing consumption needs.[11] This means is resorted to when all other avenues have been exhausted. Because of the high vulnerability of the households seeking loans under the *dadan* arrangement, the contracting counterparts are able to thrust a very heavy repayment liability on them. We collected data on such loan transactions during July–October 1974 in our field survey.

Table 5.8. Proportion of Owned Land Sold in 1974 by Size Group of Landholding of Sellers in Sample Villages

Size Group of Landholding (acres)	Percent of Owned Land Sold	Average Landholding (acres)
Less than 1	54	0.41
1–< 2	24	1.45
2–< 2.5	12	3.18
5 +	11	6.88

Note: Average landholding refers to current status after the sale was effected.

Data on *dadan* transactions are presented in Table 5.9. This information was provided by the acceptors of *dadan*. For famine area we could cover only two villages, because data were not collected for Dawanganj and, for Kogaria, the relevant figures turned out to be internally inconsistent. Thirty-seven percent of the households of the six remaining

Table 5.9. Loan Contracted by Dadan Acceptors by Regions and Selected Household Characteristics, July–October, 1974

Household Groups	Famine Area				Nonfamine Area				All Villages			
	Number of Households Accepting Dadan	% of Total House-holds	Amount Taken per Household (Taka)	Implicit Annual Interest Rate	Number of Households Accepting Dadan	% of Total House-holds	Amount Taken per Household (Taka)	Implicit Annual Interest Rate	Number of Households Accepting Dadan	% of Total House-holds	Amount Taken per Household (Taka)	Implicit Annual Interest Rate
Tenurial status												
Owner farmer	103	35	312	411	200	39	418	456	303	37	382	444
Owner-cum-tenant farmer	23	36	272	351	103	47	619	441	126	44	555	432
Tenant farmer	3	30	72	201	23	55	755	258	26	50	676	258
Landless laborers	33	21	152	450	42	33	266	393	75	26	216	411
Size group of landholding (acres) (operational)												
<0.5	61	26	168	429	107	39	242	516	168	33	215	492
0.9– <1.0	30	51	208	411	37	44	381	357	67	47	304	375
0.9– <2.5	54	34	295	423	79	44	540	327	133	40	441	354
0.9– <5.0	14	24	395	369	102	44	627	405	116	40	599	402
0.9– <7.5	2	29	2188	405	39	47	660	615	41	46	719	585
0.9– <12.5	1	20	1300	177	5	13	818	315	6	14	898	282
12.5 +	—	—	—	—	—	—	—	—	—	—	—	—
<2.5	145	21	224	422	223	41	371	391	368	30	313	401
2.5 +	17	10	659	361	146	40	642	459	163	30	640	448
Size of Household												
5 members	93	31	201	414	107	37	316	339	200	34	263	366
6–8 members	51	32	380	198	168	45	472	456	219	41	451	405
9 +	18	27	603	405	93	38	672	435	111	36	661	432
Total	162	31	269	406	368	41	478	426	530	37	414	422

Note: Here famine area covers only two villages, Ramna and Rangpur district and Gaorarang in Sylhet district.

163

villages contracted loans under *dadan* arrangements during July–October 1974. The average amount of loan taken per household was Tk. 414, the implicit annual interest rate being 422 percent. The interest rate was uniformly high in all villages except in Nazirpur, where it was much higher than others. Nazirpur, as we explained earlier, was not particularly hard-hit by flood but the situation had reached a crisis point because of the devastating cyclone of December 1973. If we leave out Nazirpur, then the implicit annual interest rate turns out to be higher for the famine area than for the nonfamine area. But both the proportion of households taking loans under *dadan* arrangements and the amount of loan taken per household were higher in the nonfamine area than in the famine area. Since the famine area was relatively harder hit by flood, there was less scope for negotiating loans on the basis of future transactions in crop because of the uncertainty of the harvest outcome. In other words, although demand for loans was presumably high in famine area, supply dried up and the market was rationed—the higher demand causing higher interest rates, the unsatisfied demand forcing more asset sales in the famine area than otherwise would have been the case.

Analyzing the data for different social groups, it was found that households in all tenurial and landholding groups contracted loans under *dadan* arrangements in 1974.[12] Landless laborers paid a relatively higher implied annual interest rate when compared to other tenurial groups, except in nonfamine areas where owner farmers paid the highest rate of interest followed by owner-cum-tenant farmers.[13] This is explained by the weak bargaining position of all farmer groups in Nazirpur in the famine area who had been severely hit by a cyclone in the previous year. Many households were actually seeking a second round of short-term crisis loans without having repaid the first. Loan amounts and implicit interest rates do not reveal any systematic pattern by size group of landholding, possibly because of opposing need and collateral patterns. However, both the proportion of households taking loans and the implicit annual interest rates were higher for households in the below 2.5 acre category than those in above 2.5 acre category. By classifying households by size, it was found that when all villages were taken together the amount of loan per household and the implicit annual interest rate increased with the size of household. Other things remaining the same, needs of the household increase with its size but its ability to repay increases because the number of earners increases with the size of the household, and also the value of the collateral (landholding) increases, which follows from the observed positive relationship between size of household and landholding. Proportions of households accepting *dadan* differed little between different size groups, the proportion for the middle-size households being slightly above the other two.

From the above it is clear that during the 1974 Bangladesh famine the intensity of suffering was different for different socio-economic groups. Landless laborers, small farmers, petty traders and other professionals suffered most during the famine. Among all social groups, suffering was more intense in the famine area as compared with the nonfamine area, although there were some exceptions.

The field survey clearly revealed that all areas of Bangladesh were affected by famine to a certain extent during 1974. However, given the basic difference between famine and nonfamine areas, it will be helpful to analyze some general characteristics of these areas.

It was noted earlier that the famine districts were more vulnerable to flood than nonfamine districts. In 1974 the former suffered much heavier flood damage than the latter. The situation was particularly serious in the single *boro* crop area of Sylhet district, which was hit by an early flash flood. Areas between the rivers Teesta and Jamuna in Rangpur district were also affected severely due to repeated floods in 1974. Poor households in both of these areas of Sylhet and Rangpur districts are highly vulnerable to famine even in an otherwise normal year. The vulnerability of the famine area to flood should also be considered in light of the fact that our survey data (Table 5.10) showed that the average size of cultivable landholding in the famine area was 30 percent lower than that in the nonfamine area, although data for 1973–1974 did not show any difference in the per capita income of the two areas (Table 5.6). For all tenurial groups, the average landholding was lower in the

Table 5.10. Average Landholding of Survey Households by Regions and Tenurial Status

Tenurial Status	Number of Households	% of Households	Average Landholding per Household (acres)		
			Ownership	Operational	Cultivable
Famine area					
Owner-farmer	426	49.0	2.33	1.95	2.26
Owner-cum-tenant	154	17.7	2.46	3.19	2.11
Tenant farmer	37	4.3	0.13	1.41	—
Landless laborer	252	29.0	0.09	0.09	—
Nonfamine area					
Owner farmer	516	57.0	3.01	2.31	2.50
Owner-cum-tenant	220	25.3	2.47	4.47	2.06
Tenant farmer	42	4.6	0.36	3.24	—
Landless larborer	127	14.0	0.14	0.14	—

famine area than in the nonfamine area. Table 5.11 contains data on the size distribution of landholding (ownership) in the two areas. The Gini coefficient of land distribution shows a higher degree of inequality in ownership in the famine area (0.62) as compared with the nonfamine area (0.59). The difference in the degree of inequality of land distribution between the two areas narrows down when one considers operational landholding.[14]

The pattern of holding of other types of assets such as cattle, plough and transport equipment (cart, boat, rickshaw) in the two areas is shown in Table 5.12. The percentage of households not owning any cattle or plough was much higher in the famine area as compared with the nonfamine area. Similarly, for all levels of ownership (in terms of number owned) the percentage is higher in the nonfamine area than in the famine area except in one cattle owning category. There was no significant difference between the two areas in the ownership of transport equipment.

A similar relationship holds if we classify households by tenurial status or size group of operational landholding (not shown in Table 5.12). In the famine area, the percentages of tenant households owning no cattle or plough were 43 and 46, the corresponding figures for the nonfamine area being only 5 and 10 respectively. The importance of this finding lies in the fact that tenants were much more vulnerable to pressure from landowners in the famine area than in the nonfamine area since in addition to land they had to rent draft power and plough from middle and large landowners.

Data on total and nonland asset holding are presented in Tables 5.13 and 5.14. The pattern of ownership of total assets [15] is similar to that of landholding. We, therefore, restrict our comments to nonland asset

Table 5.11. Size Distribution of Landholding (Ownership) of Survey Households

Household Groups	Famine Area		Nonfamine Area	
	% of Households	% of Area	% of Households	% of Area
< 0.5	41.7	3.7	24.1	2.1
0.5– < 1.0	10.6	4.6	15.6	4.8
1.0– < 2.5	30.5	30.6	27.2	19.9
2.5– < 5.0	11.2	23.8	22.1	33.1
5.0– < 7.5	13.5	12.8	6.5	17.1
7.5– < 12.5	1.3	7.6	2.9	11.5
12.5 +	1.4	17.1	1.7	11.5

Table 5.12. Percentage Distribution of Households in Survey Villages Owning Cattle, Plough, and Transport Equipment

Type of Asset	Famine Area	Nonfamine Area	All Villages
Number of cattle			
0	54	33	43
1	14	12	13
2	16	21	19
3 and above	16	33	25
Total	100	100	100
Number of ploughs			
0	62	44	53
1	31	43	37
2	6	12	9
3 and above	1	1	1
Total	100	100	100
Transport equipment	16	17	16

Table 5.13. Total Asset Holding Per Household by Tenurial Status and Size Group of Landholding (Operational)

	Asset Holding per Household (Taka)	
Household Groups	Famine Area	Nonfamine Area
Tenurial status		
Owner farmers	12,839 (828)	21,669 (1,149)
Owner-cum—tenant farmers	13,636 (1,346)	18,384 (1,984)
Tenant farmers	1,758 (599)	5,181 (1,329)
Landless laborers	886 (76)	1,634 (113)
Size Group of Landholding (acres)		
< 0.5	1,869 (96)	5,183 (215)
0.5 – < 1.0	3,948 (240)	12,032 (471)
1.0 – < 2.5	8,750 (777)	12,924 (1,097)
2.5 – < 5.0	15,380 (1,404)	19,673 (1,688)
5.0 – < 7.5	43,700 (1,892)	30,948 (2,112)
7.5 – < 12.5	62,212 (4,719)	63,082 (2,858)
12.5 +	73,872 (6,029)	110,999 (10,474)
Total	9,042 (692)	17,294 (1,215)

Note: Figures in parentheses are nonland asset holding.

Table 5.14. Size Distribution of Total Assets by Regions

Size Group of Total Assets (Taka)	Famine Area		Nonfamine Area	
	% of Households	% of Total Assets	% of Households	% of Total Assets
0	6.33	0.00	0.55	0.00
0– < 2,000	27.50	3.02	10.83	0.71
2,000– < 5,000	16.80	6.11	16.80	3.33
5,000– < 10,000	20.71	17.14	20.77	8.99
10,000– < 15,000	14.04	18.98	13.15	9.31
15,000– < 25,000	7.59	16.40	15.80	17.99
25,000– < 35,000	3.57	11.35	10.50	17.80
35,000– < 50,000	1.27	5.51	6.08	14.76
50,000– < 75,000	1.04	7.17	2.65	9.11
75,000 and above	1.15	14.32	2.87	18.01

holding of village households. The value of nonland assets per household in the nonfamine area is almost double that of the famine area. In both areas, owner-cum-tenants have the highest value of nonland assets per household, which is consistent with the fact that they lead also in average size of landholding (owned and operational) among different tenurial groups and that ownership of draft animal and implements is essential for qualifying to lease land. The positive relationship between operational landholding and nonland asset holding is clearly brought out in Table 5.13. Looking at Table 5.14 one can see that, like the distribution of landholding, the distribution of total assets was more unequal in the famine area (Gini coefficient = 0.61) than in the nonfamine area (Gini coefficient = 0.53).

We discussed earlier the socio-economic background of the famine victims and some of the characteristics of famine and nonfamine areas to indicate which factors explain differential famine intensity among social groups and regions. This was, however, not intended to be a complete causal analysis of the 1974 famine, a task that will be taken up in Chapters 6 through 8. It was interesting to note the similarity between the socio-economic background of the 1974 famine victims and that of the victims of earlier famines in the Indian subcontinent. Such an outcome can be attributed to the working of social processes through different historic epochs that left a large number of people vulnerable to famine. As we noted in Chapter 3, the famine syndrome itself had been triggered off by one or a combination of factors at different times in the past. Besides, the government's reaction to crisis played an important part in either aggravating or reducing the suffering of the famine-affected people. Following the famine, societal adjustment processes bring the economy back to its prefamine low-income–low-foodgrain intake equilibrium. We shall discuss governments' reaction and societal adjustment processes following the 1974 Bangladesh famine in the next section.

SOCIETAL RESPONSE

Free Food Relief

As early as in Pathan and Moghul rule in India, free food distribution was undertaken by the government to relieve the distress of the famine-affected population. However, available evidence indicates that such relief efforts were limited to major urban centers and did not cover a significant proportion of the affected population. The British famine relief policy moved away from the concept of free dole except under extreme circumstances. The famine codes were developed around the central theme of relief works. The famine-affected population was expected to receive wages against manual work with which they could perchase necessary food. The major argument against free dole was that, on the one hand, it undermined human dignity and on the other, it encouraged more people to seek relief than was warranted. Be that as it may, during the late nineteenth- and early twentieth-century famines in British India, free food distribution in *langarkhanas* constituted only a minor part of the famine relief effort of the government.[16]

In 1974, when the famine broke out, Bangladesh did not have a Famine Code of its own. The government could have invoked the old Bengal Famine Code, but this was not done.[17] The government of Bangladesh officially declared famine in late September although it had adopted some relief measures following the devastating flood. Beginning in September, the government's relief effort was concentrated primarily on free food distribution to the famine-affected people through *langarkhanas*. A summary statement of food relief during September–November 1974 is presented in Table 5.15. Some *langarkhanas* were opened in early September, a few even before. Most of these were operating under private initiative with occasional assistance from the government. Government-sponsored *langarkhanas* were not in operation in full swing before the first week of October, and they were closed down by the end of November. Both the total number of *langarkhanas* and the average number of persons fed daily fluctuated during this three-month period. Figures presented in Table 5.15 actually reflect the maximum level of operation that was reached in October 1974. At one point 5792 *langarkhanas* were providing food to about 4.35 million people or 6.08 percent of the total population of the country. In terms of both the number and proportion seeking relief, the figures were indeed quite high.[18]

Table 5.15. Statement of Cooked Food Relief in Langarkhana by Regions, September–November, 1974

Area Division/District	No. of Langar-khanas	No. of Persons Fed Daily	Per Capita Daily Distr. of Wheat (seers = 2.05725 lbs.)			Calorie Equivalent of Daily Wheat Ration			No. of Persons Fed Daily as % of Total Population	Average No. of Persons Fed per Langar-khana
			Sept.	Oct.	Nov.	Sept.	Oct.	Nov.		
Dacca	1,722	1,273,460	—	—	—	—	—	—	5.97	740
Dacca	413	155,745	0.15	0.32	0.03	565	1,204	113	2.05	377
Mymensingh	760	898,982	0.04	0.12	0.05	151	452	188	11.88	2,177
Tangail	215	70,510	0.09	0.29	0.04	339	1,091	151	3.39	328
Faridpur	334	148,223	0.13	0.31	0.00	489	1,167	0	3.65	444
Chittagong	1,283	800,908	—	—	—	—	—	—	4.30	624
Chittagong	222	54,736	0.17	0.12	0.00	640	452	0	1.27	247
Comilla	401	205,066	0.08	0.32	0.10	301	1,204	376	3.52	511
Sylhet	472	362,728	0.07	0.16	0.06	263	602	226	7.62	768
Noakhali	188	178,378	0.06	0.19	0.06	226	715	226	5.50	949
Chittagong Hill Tr	0	0	0.00	0.00	0.00	0	0	0	0.00	0
Khulna	1,345	785,849	—	—	—	—	—	—	5.54	555
Khulna	367	245,700	0.04	0.15	0.03	151	565	113	6.91	669
Kushtia	122	64,900	0.09	0.21	0.00	339	790	0	3.45	532
Jessore	250	128,500	0.07	0.16	0.00	263	602	0	3.86	514
Barisal	504	280,985	0.07	0.22	0.05	263	828	188	7.15	558
Patuakhali	102	65,764	0.10	0.28	0.07	376	1,054	263	4.39	645
Rajshahi	1,442	1,485,060	—	—	—	—	—	—	8.57	1,030
Rajshahi	313	147,520	0.14	0.38	0.05	527	1,430	188	3.46	468
Pabna	164	57,900	0.22	0.55	0.12	828	2,069	452	2.06	353
Dinajpur	256	221,000	0.07	0.17	0.03	263	640	113	8.60	863

Table 5.15 (continued)

Bogra	156	123,000	0.08	0.17	0.03	301	640	113	5.51	788
Rangpur	553	935,640	0.03	0.12	0.08	113	452	301	17.18	1,692
Total	5,792	4,345,277	0.06	0.18	0.05	226	677	188	6.08	750

Source: Number of *langarkhanas*, number of persons fed daily, and amount of wheat distributed from Government of Bangladesh, Ministry of Relief and Rehabilitation. Carlorie equivalent is calculated from data presented in Government of Bangladesh, Bureau of Statistics, *Statistical Yearbook of Bangladesh, 1975* (Dacca: Bureau of Statistics, 1976), p. 261. Total population (unadjusted 1974 figures) from *Statistical Yearbook of Bangladesh, 1975*, p. 16.

Like the 1899–1900 famine, there was considerable interregional variation in the proportion of the population seeking relief in *langarkhanas* during 1974 (Figure 5.1). The percentage was highest in Rangpur (17), followed by Mymensingh (12), Dinajpur (9), and Sylhet (8). The Dinajpur figure is somewhat misleading since a considerable proportion of *langarkhanas* inmates in this district came from the adjoining district of Rangpur. To a certain extent this is true of *langarkhanas* in major urban centers such as Dacca. What is important to note is that the amount of food distributed per capita was very small. Except in some areas during the month of October, the calorie equivalent of food per capita was far short of the minimum requirement, considering the fact that *langarkhana* inmates had little or no other support available. The data presented in Table 5.15 and the information collected during our field survey reveal that a reasonable level of food distribution was maintained only during one month, from the end of the first week of October to that of November. Besides, it is somewhat disconcerting to note that the famine victims in the relatively harder hit districts received less food per capita as compared with other areas. For example, in October, Rangpur, Mymensingh, and Sylhet were among the bottom three districts measured by per capita daily distribution of wheat. Clearly, the relevant government machinery failed to ensure food relief distribution according to needs of different areas in 1974. On the whole, the relief came too late, it was too little, and it was stopped too soon.[19]

There were some serious problems associated with the management of food relief distribution through the *langarkhanas*. First, it was alleged that the officials managing *langarkhanas* misappropriated a considerable amount of the food resources that were meant for distribution among the famine-affected people. Second, the rural *langarkhanas* often did not receive supplies of wheat in time. These *langarkhanas* were primarily nonresidential, so that many people had to walk long distances to get their daily ration of bread. Naturally when the wheat supply was interrupted, their suffering was further intensified. Third, sometimes, instead of properly prepared bread, flour paste (flour mixed with water), which was very difficult to digest, was distributed. It contributed to the increase of gastro-intestinal diseases among *langarkhana* inmates. Sanitation in residential *langarkhanas* was very poor. In some places no arrangement was made for supplying drinking water. Therefore, it was not surprising that mortality inside *langarkhana* limits was quite high. The situation prevailing in *langarkhanas* came out sharply in the course of our field investigation, summarized in the following paragraphs.

Rangpur town had one of the first *langarkhanas* in the country. It was initially opened by the local business community and later received support from the government. The daily ration for the inmates was either bread or *khitchuri*. Most of the inmates of this *langarkhana* were professional beggars and ordinary laborers. Some were migrants from rural areas. Many took odd jobs during the day and came to the *langarkhana* at the time of food distribution. It was found that some people wanted to conceal their identity. They came mostly from among the low, fixed-income earning groups. The *langarkhana* management appreciated their position and saved some food for them (their ration) every day. Such instances indicated how deep the impact of the 1974 famine was in certain areas. The inmates appeared unhappy with the management of the *langarkhana*. They complained that the relief officer, in collusion with the management personnel, misappropriated a fair portion of the relief articles.

Another *langarkhana* visited by our field investigator was located outside Rangpur town. It was the largest in the country with 10,500 registered inmates. A sample of 101 inmates was selected from this *langarkhana* for our survey. The *langarkhana* was spread over three acres of land. The majority of inmates lived in the open because only a few shelters had been constructed. Like the other *langarkhana* already described, this one was started by the local community but at the time of our survey it was under government management. According to the records of the *langarkhana*, almost all the inmates came from the flood affected areas of Rangpur district. The *langarkhana* presented a famine scenario at its worst. The inmates were nothing more than human skeletons; they all appeared to be at the last stage of physical survival. As one looked around, one found many groaning from hunger pain, diseases, and physical exhaustion—others dying. There was little companionship and sympathy among the inmates for fellow inmates. Members of the same family were found quarreling over a piece of bread. A child died in front of the parent, or a parent in front of helpless children, who appeared completely dazed by what was going on around them. It was clear that the worst victims among the inmates were children one to four years of age. Many in this group were so emaciated that it was hard to believe that they were still alive. In the *langarkhana*, the majority among the dead were children and the elderly. The following quote from the diary of our field investigator, Mr. Nabiul Islam, succinctly described the situation that prevailed in the *langarkhana*.

Every day there were many deaths in the *langarkhana*. As the management prepared for their burial, the owners (relatives) of the dead bodies waited by their side—some were weeping while others appeared to have turned into stone out of grief. The place gave the appearance of a market for dead bodies. In the eyes of the survivors one could see expressions of desparation combined with hatred and resentment towards the rest of the world.

The management board of the *langarkhana* distributed two pieces of uncooked bread per person every day. The inmates had to collect their own fuel and cook their bread. Sanitary conditions in and around the *langarkhana* were very poor. The management was so unwilling to accept criticism that they withdrew relief privileges from inmates who complained to visitors about the condition of the *langarkhana*. As winter approached, a sufficient quantity of warm clothes, *sarees* and *lungis*, arrived for distribution among the inmates. They were entered in the relief registry book and stored in the godown. Our field investigator reported that these items were smuggled out at night for sale in the open market instead of being distributed among the inmates. The district administration did nothing to curb such leakage of relief resources.

The situation prevailing in the *langarkhanas* of Mymensingh and Dewanganj area included in our survey was no different. The Dewanganj *langarkhana* was opened on September 30, 1974, and it was closed on November 30, 1974. During this period, a total of 42,420 pounds of wheat flour was distributed to about two to three thousand people per day. The calorie equivalent of per capita ration varied between 640 and 414. In addition, beginning the third week of October, 450 kg. of milk powder was also distributed. The *langarkhana* of Kotwali thana in Mymensingh was opened on October 11, 1974 and it was closed on November 12, 1974. In order to present a detailed picture of the relief afforded through a *langarkhana*, we present the daily amount of the Mymensingh *langarkhana* in Table 5.16. The total number of inmates fluctuated between 1900 and 3100. The per capita calorie equivalent of food relief distributed in this *langarkhana* fluctuated between 212 and 324. Clearly, the relief was far below the minimum requirement per capita. Therefore, *langarkhana* assistance by itself could not possibly have saved many lives during the 1974 Bangladesh famine.

The fourth *langarkhana* we surveyed was located in Sunamganj, a subdivision of Sylhet district. It was found that only forty-one pounds of wheat flour was allotted each day for the 500 inmates. The management of relief distribution was very poor. At the time of survey, our field investigator found that a number of godowns in the subdivisional headquarters were packed with relief items, but no arrangement was made to distribute them to the famine-affected people. On enquiry, the subdivisional relief and rehabilitation officer confided that he was waiting for instructions from the Ministry of Relief and Rehabilitation about the distribution procedure. The union council officials responsible for the managment of the *langarkhana* complained that they had to stop operation because of the discontinuation of relief supply from the subdivisional headquarters. As a matter of fact, the *langarkhana* was closed long before the famine-affected people were in a position to take

Table 5.16. Daily Account of Relief Distribution in Kotwali Thana Langarkhana in Mymensingh

Date 1974		No. of Persons Relieved	Per Capita Daily Relief Distribution		
			Wheat Flour (grams)	Milk Powder (grams)	Calorie Equivalent of Daily Ration
October	11	—	—	—	—
	12	—	—	—	—
	13	2,100	71.1	17.6	259
	14	2,300	64.9	21.7	241
	15	2,500	59.7	20.0	221
	16	2,600	57.4	19.2	213
	17	2,600	57.4	19.2	213
	18	3,100	96.3	16.1	346
	19	2,000	56.0	25.0	212
	20	2,400	62.2	20.8	230
	21	2,400	62.2	20.8	230
	22	2,000	74.7	19.0	272
	23	2,000	74.7	19.0	272
	24	2,000	74.7	25.0	276
	25	1,900	78.6	26.3	291
	26	2,000	74.7	19.0	272
	27	2,500	59.7	20.0	221
	28	2,500	89.6	20.0	324
	29	2,600	86.1	19.2	312
	30	2,500	89.6	15.0	321
	31	2,600	86.1	14.4	309
November	1	2,660	84.2	18.8	306
	2	2,720	82.3	18.4	298
	3	2,680	83.6	18.7	303
	4	2,740	81.7	18.2	296
	5	2,790	80.3	17.9	291
	6	2,770	80.9	18.1	293
	7	2,760	81.1	18.1	294
	8	2,800	80.0	17.9	290
	9	2,720	82.3	18.4	298
	10	2,740	81.7	18.2	296
	11	2,740	81.7	18.2	296
	12	2,690	83.3	18.6	301

care of themselves. It was clear that the subdivisional and district relief authorities did not fully appreciate the extent of damage suffered by the people in the outlying areas.

Field investigators visiting other areas brought back similar impressions of *langarkhanas*, except in Satkhira town of Khulna district, where a *langarkhana* was opened by the local authority as soon as the first sign of an abnormal price rise of essential commodities was visible.

Apparently, this *langarkhana* was successful in relieving the distress of the affected people who sought help there. Its success was attributed to the honest and efficient management by the subdivisional officer concerned. The general condition prevailing in *langarkhanas* during 1974 famine can be summarized with the following quote from a report on famine by Anisur Rahman.

> The typical picture of a langarkhana is one where utterly inadequate quantities of eatables or semi-eatables are distributed to hundreds of men, women and children by persons with lathis (sticks) in their hands. The city langarkhanas have relatively more to give than the country ones for various reasons: the former got priority in the distribution of official supplies because of nearness to headquarters, and also because foreign visitors, journalists and television photographers are taken to these centers for overseas publicity, private contributions are also greater in the city centers than in the country ones. The supply situation progressively worsens as you go deeper in the country. In the unions of Rangpur, I have seen langarkhanas where hundreds of starving people came from four, five, six miles afar and wait all day, finally to get only *one* chapati (hand made bread) the weight of which varies according to daily relative supply of Ata (wheat flour). These are not residential kitchens, and the journey to and from the langarkhanas back to the village may cost more calories than the langarkhana supplies. The starving people naturally expect and want more. Indiscipline results, and I have seen the management literally beating them until these once-human beings sob and weep into submission and discipline is restored.[20]

International Aid

International response to the flood and famine of 1974 in Bangladesh was only lukewarm in comparison with that following the liberation war of 1971. Bangladesh had received about one billion dollars worth of grants and loans up to fiscal year 1974–1975. Although in 1974–1975 disbursement of aid was almost double (U.S. $918 million) that of the year before (U.S. $481 million), there was no significant shipment of emergency relief materials from abroad during the first half of the year, which was when the flood and famine struck the country. Food imports picked up later that year and at the end of 1974–1975 total food aid amounted to U.S. $375 million as against U.S. $233 million in 1973–1974.[21] A better indicator of international concern for the crisis facing Bangladesh could be the disbursement of U.S. food aid (the United States has been the largest donor since liberation) under PL–480 Title II grants (for disaster relief and humanitarian purposes). In 1973–1974 this amounted to only

U.S. $2.7 million, down from $59.4 million in 1972–1973. The figure increased to U.S. $4.5 million in 1974–1975. Assuming that the entire amount of food aid under Title II grants came in calendar year 1974, the domestic food supply had been augmented by only 32,475 tons at the prevailing import prices. One of the first responses to Bangladesh's appeal for international relief came on July 28, 1974 from the Red Cross, which assured all possible help. However, we do not know how much aid was actually received from this source. On August 13, 1974, the World Food Programme sanctioned U.S. $1 million for food aid to the flood-affected population of Bangladesh.

Between the second week of August and the end of December, aid in different forms was received for flood and famine victims from different countries of the world and various international organizations. A separate account for such aid inflow was not available, but the press releases of the Ministry of Relief and Rehabilitation during the period under consideration indicated only a modest inflow. Three forms of aid were most important, food grains, cash, and medical relief. Food aid was received from such countries and organizations as the United States, the European Economic Community, Thailand, Pakistan, Sweden, India, Indonesia, and Australia. The United States committed over 200,000 tons of wheat on an emergency basis. Cash aid of over U.S. $34 million was received for the flood victims from Saudi Arabia, United Kingdom, Algeria, Qatar, Canada, Iran, and East Germany. Medical relief came from Vietnam, the Soviet Union, and the Red Cross. In addition, the Red Cross, through its local chapter, organized special feeding programs; the same was done by UNICEF for children. Admittedly, this account of international aid during the flood and famine of 1974 is somewhat sketchy, but in the absence of comprehensive data we could not present a better picture.

Other Forms of Relief

The famine-affected population received gifts in cash and kind (other than food relief through *langarkhana*) from the government and private sources during 1974. In our survey, we collected data on gifts received by households in various forms from different sources. The relevant figures are presented in Table 5.17. On the whole, among the villagers 19.4 percent of the households received gifts during 1974, the figures being 34.2 and 5.2 for the famine and nonfamine areas respectively. The percentage turned out to be much higher among *langarkhana* inmates (60.0). Of the households receiving gifts, an overwhelming majority received them from the government. Gifts from the government were in the form of cash grant, house grant, seed grant, wheat, wheat flour,

Table 5.17. Statement of Gift Received by Survey Households in Cash and Kind by Regions, Source, and Household Groups

Household Groups	Famine Area						Nonfamine Area					
	Proportion of Households Receiving Gift			Amount of Gift Received per Household (Taka)			Proportion of Households Receiving Gift			Amount of Gift Received per Household (Taka)		
	Total	Govt.	Others	Total	Govt.	Others	Total	Govt.	Others	Total	Govt.	Others
Tenurial status												
Owner farmer	29.8	29.8	0.5	60	59	50	34.9	2.7	0.8	161	125	288
Owner-cum-tenant farmer	27.3	27.3	0.7	108	103	180	68.2	6.4	0.5	209	217	100
Tenant farmer	32.4	32.4	—	30	30	—	21.4	19.1	2.4	43	47	10
Landless laborer	46.0	44.8	1.9	71	63	231	3.9	3.9	—	44	44	—
Size group of operational landholding (acres)												
< 0.5	35.0	34.3	1.9	66	57	180	3.6	3.3	0.4	112	91	300
0.5- <1.0	31.2	31.2	—	66	66	—	7.1	6.0	1.2	49	38	100
1.0- <2.5	28.7	28.7	—	82	82	—	6.7	5.6	1.1	161	118	375
2.5- <5.0	28.1	28.1	—	56	56	—	5.6	4.7	0.9	222	252	55
5.0- <7.5	26.9	26.9	—	107	107	—	6.0	6.0	—	44	44	—
7.5-<12.5	26.7	26.7	—	40	40	—	2.6	2.6	—	185	185	—
12.5 +	12.5	12.5	—	260	260	—	—	—	—	—	—	—
Total	34.2	33.8	0.9	70	66	180	5.2	4.5	0.7	141	131	180

sarees, lungis, children's clothing and other miscellaneous cash grants. The average value of gift received per household was higher in nonfamine areas than in famine areas, and higher from other sources than from the government. It is clear that the value of gift per household was very small irrespective of the region concerned. Although the average value of gift received per household was higher from nongovernment sources, they accounted for only a small proportion of total gifts. This is not surprising because, during a crisis situation such as famine, village charity tends to dry up quickly. The few families receiving gifts from other sources during crisis periods are usually tied to the donors through a patron-client relationship, and therefore the average value of gifts was found to be larger than that from the government.

Analyzing the gift data by household groups, we found that in the famine area, the proportion of households receiving gifts was highest among the landless laborers, followed by tenant farmers, owner farmers, and owner-cum-tenant farmers. The ranking for the nonfamine areas was, owner-cum-tenant farmer, owner farmer, tenant farmer, and, finally, the landless laborers. The opposing ranking between famine and nonfamine areas can be attributed to the fact that in the former, gift distribution was more need-determined than in the latter. This is also confirmed by the fact that the proportion of households receiving gifts was inversely related to the size group of the operational landholding in the famine area, but no such pattern emerged in the case of the nonfamine area. The value of gift received per household does not reveal any regular pattern. Nevertheless, on the whole, it emerges from Table 5.17 that the government was by far the most important source of gifts, that the value of gift per household was small for all household groups, that middle and large farmers had an edge over small farmers in terms of access to government relief (measured by gifts per household), and that the distribution of gifts from the government was more balanced (meaning need-determined) in the famine area as compared with the non-famine area.

Provincial famine codes formulated during British rule emphasized the role of relief works and agricultural credit during a famine. The government of Bangladesh did not allocate any funds for relief works in 1974. Test relief works were not undertaken until January 1975. On the other hand, the total amount of *Taccavi* loans, which are hardship loans, declined from Tk. 14.7 million in 1973–1974 to Tk. 10 million in 1974–1975.[22] The government, however, provided some seed grants but the amount was very small in comparison with the area and the number of households affected by the flood. According to the Ministry of Relief and Rehabilitation, a sum of only Tk. 418 million was given as seed grants up to August 20, 1974.[23] Of this, the famine district received Tk.

2.1 million. As a matter of fact, it was revealed during our survey that among the flood-affected households not replanting *aman* (winter crop), a majority (92 percent) cited lack of money/seedlings as the reason for not replanting.

SOCIETAL ADJUSTMENT

The famine syndrome triggers off societal response in various forms as discussed in the last section, and it initiates processes of societal adjustment that, in a country such as Bangladesh, work toward restoring the original low-income–low-foodgrain intake equilibrium. Following the 1974 famine, a number of changes were observed in the rural labor market. First, areas severely affected by famine experienced a shortage of labor supply due to migration, death, and ill-health of the laborers.[24] However, many middle and small farmers who normally hired laborers during peak activity periods were unable to do so to the same extent because they had also been adversely affected by the flood and famine. Second, to the extent to which farmers were unable to replant *aman* crops following the flood, there was a reduction in harvest employment. Our survey data revealed that replanting of the winter crop was not done on 12 percent of the cultivable area in 1974, the percentages for the famine and the nonfamine areas being 29 and 1 percent, respectively. Third, during the course of 1975, the loss of the rural labor force was perhaps overcompensated through reverse migration from urban areas, increase in landlessness, and deterioraton in the economic status of the middle and small farmers, who were forced into the labor market to prevent their standard of living from falling below an acceptable level. Fourth, the famine forced changes in the mode of wage payment in many areas. Wages in kind and contract wage gave way to money wages to the disadvantage of the laborers.[25]

For the reasons cited above, there was no significant improvement in the bargaining power of the rural laborers in spite of considerable famine mortality. The postfamine situation in the labor market can be seen in Figure 5.2. Real wage indexes fluctuated between July 1974 and December 1975. There was some improvement in real wages in both famine and nonfamine areas beginning in September of 1975 as compared with the base (July 1974), but data for 1976 (not shown here) did not reveal any sustained upward trend. The real wage rate has tended to fluctuate around the prefamine level. The situation in the labor market improved with the introduction of works programs, particularly the Food-for-Work program, beginning in January of 1975.[26] As can be seen in Figure 5.2, the pattern of real wage movement during the postfamine period in famine and nonfamine areas was similar.

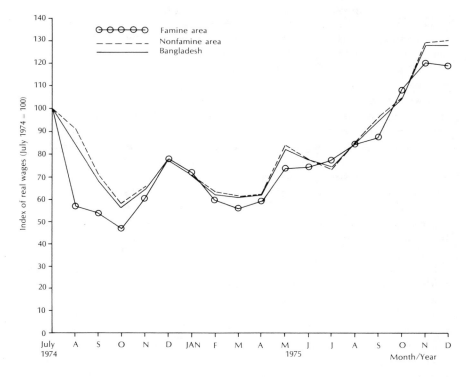

Figure 5.2. Movement of real wages of agricultural laborers, July 1974 to December 1975.

Famine often results in a permanent influx of migrant population into urban areas. In 1974, however, the movement of population from rural to urban areas, particularly to Dacca, was only of temporary duration because of two policies adopted by the government. First, the *langarkhanas* were closed down after only a short period of operation, which left the famine immigrants without any support. Second, at the end of December 1974, the ruling party declared an emergency in Bangladesh, and assumed special powers under which strong measures were taken against all forms of urban squatting. Both the temporary and semipermanent squatter settlements were levelled to the ground and the inhabitants were forced to leave the cities and towns. It is difficult to estimate the magnitude of reverse migration during this period. The returnees to the rural areas consisted primarily of the survivors of urban *langarkhanas* and the squatter population of major urban areas who had migrated in the late 1960s.[27]

The 1974 Bangladesh famine accelerated the process of pauperization in the rural society. The proportion of households owning less than 0.5 acres (including homestead) increased from 31.8 percent in January 1974 to 32.8 percent in November 1974 (Table 5.18). In other words, within less than one year, landlessness increased by about 3 percent, which represented a very high rate of destitution. Our survey data reveals that the increase in landlessness came entirely from the famine area, while in the nonfamine area there was a slight decline in the proportion of landless households. In general, the incidence of landlessness was already higher in the famine area as compared with the nonfamine area. This process of increasing landlessness has continued beyond 1974. A recent survey carried out by the Bangladesh Bureau of Statistics placed the proportion of landless households at 34.3 percent in 1974.[28]

Changes in the pattern of landownership, through purchase and sale of land during January–November 1974, are shown in Table 5.19. A number of interesting features can be noted from this table. On the whole, new recruits to the landless category came from both small-farmer and middle-farmer groups. Gains in landholding were made by both middle and large farmers. During the period under consideration, both famine and the nonfamine areas lost land through net sale to outsiders. In total, all villages lost about 1 percent of landholding. This land has possibly gone to the government (through land acquisition for public construction) and/or to people from urban areas. Although it is difficult to assess the total impact of such transfer on the rural economy, there is no doubt that this represents an enhancement of the power base of the urban elite. The shift in the relative strength of the different social groups can be

Table 5.18. Landlessness Among Survey Households

Area	January 1974	November 1974
All villages	31.8	32.8
Famine area	39.2	41.7
Ramna	38.8	40.5
Gaorarang	42.1	46.0
Kogaria	34.6	34.6
Dewanganj	41.0	45.3
Nonfamine area	24.6	24.3
Nazirpur	27.0	27.0
Laskarpur	27.8	27.8
Komorpur	19.1	18.0
Charbaniari	20.4	19.7

Note: Landless households are defined here as those with less than 0.5 acres of landholding (ownership).

Table 5.19.   Changes in the Pattern of Landownership Between January 1974 and November 1974

Landholding Groups	Famine Area				Nonfamine Area				All Villages			
	No. of Households		Land Owned (acres)		No. of Households		Land Owned (acres)		No. of Households		Land Owned (acres)	
	Jan. 1974	Nov. 1974	Jan. 1974	Nov. 1974	Jan. 1974	Nov. 1974	Jan. 1974	Nov. 1974	Jan. 1974	Nov. 1974	Jan. 1974	Nov. 1974
< 0.5	341	362	50.06	51.20	223	220	38.79	38.01	564	582	88.85	89.21
0.5– < 1.0	106	92	74.20	64.42	140	139	102.98	101.30	246	231	177.18	165.72
1.0– < 2.5	265	265	426.70	427.43	239	245	395.53	402.00	504	410	822.23	829.43
2.5– < 5.0	104	97	351.06	323.76	201	201	707.98	711.25	305	298	1,059.04	1,035.01
5.0– < 7.5	29	30	173.00	178.46	61	60	373.66	371.36	90	90	546.66	549.82
7.5–< 12.5	13	11	123.91	105.61	26	25	247.21	238.90	39	36	371.12	344.51
12.5 +	11	12	223.54	239.28	15	15	264.29	264.52	26	27	487.83	503.80
Total	869	869	1,422.47	1,390.16	905	905	2,130.44	2,127.34	1,774	1,774	3,552.91	3,517.50

assessed more clearly from the land transaction matrixes. The present author has analyzed this data in a separate study, therefore, only the major findings will be noted here.[29] We first make a few observations on the changes in the economic status of households between January 1974 and November 1974.

During famine some households gained in status through net purchase of land while others lost through net sale. In Table 5.20 we have identified households in different landholding (ownership) groups according to whether their net position improved or deteriorated. Figures are also presented separately by region. Among all households, 9 percent experienced a decline and 4 percent an improvement in their economic status (measured by changes in landholding) between January 1974 and November 1974. Therefore, a net 5 percent of households faced economic deterioration during the famine period. As expected, this figure is much higher for the famine area (9 percent) than for the nonfamine area (0.33 percent). It is interesting to note that in both the famine and the nonfamine areas, the net percentage of households suffering economic deterioration varied inversely with the size group of landholding. However, looking at the figures for decrease in landholding, one can see that all household groups except the largest size group (12.5 acreas and above) had experienced status decline during the period under consideration.

On land transaction we have two sets of data. The first set was obtained from the sellers of land, who told us about the amount of land sold, sale price, and the identity of the buyer classified broadly as large farmer, middle farmer, small farmer, businessman, and others. The second set was collected from the buyers of land, who informed us of the amount of land purchased, purchase price, and the identity of the seller, classified broadly as mentioned above. The land market was dominated basically by the large-farmer group. From the seller's data it was found that 38 percent of the buyers were large farmers, followed by medium farmers (20 percent), and others (19 percent). Although land sales were made by households in different landholding categories, almost three-quarters of the sales were made by the less than 5 acre group. The share of the less than 2 acre households was above 50 percent. From the purchasers data it was also found that the large farmers and small farmers led the category of purchasers and sellers respectively. In 1974, the small farmers constituted 47 percent of the sellers. On the basis of land transacted during 1972–1974, we found that the 5 acre and above category of households purchased slightly above one-third of the land transacted, while small farmers were responsible for over 40 percent of the land sold. In terms of transactions between groups, small farmers sold primarily to large farmers and businessmen. It is clear that the famine-induced land transactions strengthened the position of the rural elite.

Table 5.20. Changes in Economic Status of Households Between January 1974 and November 1974 by Regions

Landholding (Ownership) Groups (acres)	Famine Area				Nonfamine Area				All Villages			
	Increase		Decrease		Increase		Decrease		Increase		Decrease	
	No. of House-holds	% of House-holds	No. of House-holds	% of House-holds	No. of House-holds	% of House-holds	No. of House-holds	% of House-holds	No. of House-holds	% of House-holds	No. of House-holds	% of House-holds
< 0.5	5	1.38	47	12.98	2	0.92	5	2.29	7	1.21	52	8.97
0.5- <1.0	1	1.08	14	15.22	1	0.71	3	2.13	2	0.86	17	7.30
1.0- <2.5	18	6.79	44	16.60	8	3.25	10	4.07	26	5.09	54	10.57
2.5- <5.0	12	12.37	16	16.49	4	2.00	4	2.00	16	5.39	20	6.73
5.0- <7.5	6	20.00	5	16.67	5	8.47	1	1.69	11	12.39	6	6.74
7.5-<12.5	6	54.55	2	18.18	1	3.85	1	3.85	7	18.92	3	8.11
12.5 +	4	26.67	—	—	—	—	—	—	4	14.81	—	—
Total	52	5.98	128	14.73	21	2.32	24	2.65	73	4.11	152	8.57

Note: Percentages are calculated on the basis of total households each landholding (ownership) group.

In addition to land, households lost other assets including draft animals, milch animals, plough, and transport equipment during the flood and famine.[30] Loss of farm assets seriously affected the productivity of households and in many cases it resulted in permanent changes in the economic and social status of the household in terms of tenurial status and occupation status. Tenant households and also owner-cum-tenant households that lost farm assets were unable to lease as much land as they did before, and were forced to enter the labor market to supplement their income. A similar situation was faced by fishermen, independent transport workers, and petty professionals who lost their income earning assets through sale or flood damage. On the other hand, the demand for land under sharecropping increased, because many middle and small farmers, having lost their own land through sale, looked for land to lease. But the supply of land in the market declined for the following reasons. First, the very small owners who used to rent out their land because it was uneconomic for them to operate it themselves were now dispossessed of the ownership through sale. Second, other households who used to rent out land had their ownership holding reduced through sale so that they reverted to owner management farming. Third, in the year following the famine there was a move by the government to declare all land sales of 1974 void. This was not, however, seriously followed up. In any case, the large landowners who had acquired land during the famine became cautious and were unwilling to rent out land to either original owners or old tenants. Fourth, the previous reason along with the overall deterioration of the economic status of a large number of farm households resulted in land being rented out in smaller parcels.

The consequence of the interplay of abovementioned forces on land relations in rural areas can be seen by analyzing the changes in tenurial status between 1974 and 1977—the two periods for which survey data were available. The figures are presented in Table 5.21. The percentage of farm households renting in land increased from 33 in 1974 to 39 in 1977, but the area operated under tenancy declined from 25 percent to 23 percent. Therefore, the vulnerability of tenant households increased in the face of unfavorable changes in the land market as mentioned earlier. Clearly, the 1974 famine had contributed to the strengthening of the semifeudal production relations in Bangladesh agriculture. In other words, the position of the rich farmers, moneylenders, and businessmen became stronger in relation to that of the small farmers, landless laborers, and petty professionals. As the size of the landless laborer group increased, its members became even more tied to agriculture since the scope for subsidiary employment in nonagricultural activities was further reduced.

In addition to enhancing their command over productive resources, the large farmers and businessmen also made gains during the crisis period

Table 5.21. Changes in Land Tenancy Between 1974 and 1977

Tenurial Status	1974	1977
	Percentage of farms	
Owner farms	67	61
Owner-cum-tenant farms	27	32
Tenant farms	6	7
Total	100	100
	Percentage of farm area	
Owner operated	75	77
Tenant operated	25	23
Total	100	100

Source: The 1974 percentages from BIDS Survey of villages and *langarkhanas* carried out under the direction of the present author. The 1977 percentages from *Statistical Pocketbook of Bangladesh, 1978* (Dacca: Bureau of Statistics, December 1977), p. 120.

through their control over the market for short-term survival loans (*dadan*). It was found from our survey data that, in both famine and nonfamine areas, large farmers were the most important source of loans under *dadan* arrangement in terms of number and amount of loan contracted. The respective figures for all villages were 59 percent and 62 percent in 1974 (Table 5.22). This relationship holds irrespective of the size group of landholding (ownership) and tenurial status of households contracting loans under the *dadan* arrangement. Next in importance to large farmers as suppliers of loans were businessmen and medium farmers, followed by relatives and others, and money lenders. It is interesting to note that money lenders are not as important in this market as they are on the overall rural credit market. That is because money lenders prefer to have some physical asset as security against loans, which is not admissable under *dadan* contracts. The importance of businessmen is explained by the fact that they are mostly traders in the local market dealing primarily in rice.

The postfamine societal adjustment processes are no less complex than the prefamine causal sequence that triggered off the famine syndrome. We have so far discussed the approach of the 1974 famine, the consequences of the famine as reflected in different substates, and excess mortality, and the societal reaction and adjustment processes that followed the famine. It will now be interesting to examine carefully the causal sequence that led to the 1974 famine. We have shown earlier that the famine syndrome is initiated by a sharp decline in foodgrain intake per capita. Factors causing a fall in foodgrain intake are foodgrain availability decline, foodgrain price increase, fall in real income, absenᵣ of social security, and inadequate institutional arrangement to tacᵏᶦ

Table 5.22. Distribution of Households Accepting Dadan and Amounts of Loan Contracted by Source and Regions

Source of Dadan	Famine Area				Nonfamine Area				All Villages			
	No. of Hseholds	% of Hseholds	Amount of Loans (Taka)	% of Loans	No. of Hseholds	% of Hseholds	Amount of Loans (Taka)	% of Loans	No. of Hseholds	% of Hseholds	Amount of Loans (Taka)	% of Loans
Small farmer	31	13.48	8,864	9.05	1	0.27	220	0.13	32	5.35	9,084	3.32
Medium farmer	31	13.48	10,990	11.22	29	7.88	14,220	8.09	60	10.03	25,210	9.21
Large farmer	122	53.04	62,139	63.44	231	62.77	108,078	61.50	353	59.03	170,217	62.19
Relatives and others	23	10.00	8,594	8.77	24	6.52	8,590	4.89	47	7.86	17,184	6.28
Money lenders	6	2.61	1,840	1.88	40	10.87	22,070	12.56	46	7.69	23,910	8.74
Businessmen	17	7.39	5,529	5.64	43	11.68	22,550	12.83	60	10.03	28,079	10.26
Total	230	100.00	97,956	100.00	368	100.00	175,728	100.00	598	100.00	273,684	100.00

situation arising from foodgrain shortage. In the next three chapters we shall investigate how important each of these factors was in causing 1974 famine, or in aggravating the suffering of the famine affected population.

Appendix to Chapter 5:
Rural Household Income

Rural household income was estimated as the sum of the net flow of receipts from different sources (types of economic activities) during the accounting period 1973–1974. Theoretically, income is a net concept, because from the gross receipts all current production expenses are deducted. The current expenses of production do not include depreciation allowance, but do include the cost of repairs and maintenance. The following steps were involved in estimating rural household income in this study. Income from farming was estimated by subtracting from the value (producer's price multiplied by the quantity of output) of agricultural produce (for example, rice, jute, sugarcane, tobacco, pulses, potato, chillis, other crops, vegetables, and fruits), the current expenses of production incurred by the household. The current expenses are hired labor, fertilizer, seed, feed, and wastage. Separate estimates were obtained directly from the respondents for the first two items. For others, 10 percent for rice and 5 percent for other items were deducted from the gross value of produce. Net income from other sources was obtained directly from the respondents. These include livestock, poultry, forestry, fishery, share/rent received, wage income, income from transport equipment, such as rickshaw, cart, boat, and so forth, income from trade and business, salary income, and other income.

Admittedly, since village households do not maintain detailed accounts, the responses on some of the nonfarm sources of income may be subject to a margin of error. We did not make any attempt to estimate the extent of such error, although in certain cases unusually high or low figures were reverified. Similarly, in stating crop production figures, the respondents may have made mistakes because of memory lapses or they may have deliberately suppressed facts. To the extent to which it was possible, we cross checked those figures with statements on landholdings by the respondent. In gross receipts from farming, we did not include the value of fodder crops, both products and by-products. It was assumed that this item would cancel out with the current expenses for livestock, which were not deducted when arriving at gross income. A similar approach is followed in national income accounting in many countries, including Bangladesh.

Apart from what is described above, two different estimates of total income were arrived at depending on whether imputed value of family labor was included or not. The value of family labor was estimated by multiplying the total number of days of household work by all working members of the family by the average value of per capita rice consumption in each family and then inflating the resulting amount by 20 percent to account for expenditure on other items. Rice comsumption of the household was estimated indirectly by adding its net purchase (purchase minus sale) of paddy to net output defined as gross output plus amount received as share/rent, gifts, and loans less the part allowed for seed, feed, and wastage (10 percent of gross output), payment of share/rent, and payment to labor in kind. Rice consumption was valued at producer's prices. The rationale for using "average consumption" as the basis for the valuation of family labor is that it reflects the actual cost incurred to sustain family labor during the period over which the activity is carried out. Another basis of valuation could have been the "minimum subsistence cost," but for individual families it would have been an intractable concept. Data on employment of family labor on the farm was not collected by our field investigators in Dewanganj. Therefore, income with imputed family labor could not be calculated for this area.

NOTES AND REFERENCES

1. Size of household was estimated in unadjusted adult units. Unadjusted unit refers to simple head count measure. Adjusted adult unit was arrived at by weighting the adult male, adult female, and children by 1.0, 0.9, and 0.5, respectively. Admittedly, one could use different sets of weights but this was not attempted here.
2. M. Alamgir, "Some Analysis of Distribution of Income, Consumption, Saving and

Poverty in Bangladesh," *Bangladesh Development Studies* 2(4):805–806 (October 1974); Nuimuddin Chowdhury and A. Latif, "Land Ownership and Fertility in Two Areas of Bangladesh," *Bangladesh Development Studies* 5(2):239–246 (April 1977).

3. Dependency ratio is defined as the ratio of nonearning members of the household to earning members. The concept used here is different from the way it is usually defined in the demographic literature.

4. See F. Tomasson Jannuzi and James T. Peach, *Report on the Hierarchy of Interests in Land in Bangladesh*, United States Agency for International Development, Washington, D.C., September 1972, Table D-1 in appendix.

5. Tarakchandra Das, *Bengal Famine (1943), as Revealed in a Survey of the Destitutes in Calcutta* (Calcutta: University of Calcutta, 1949), pp. 67–69. It may be pointed out that because of the difference in the sample and distribution of occupational groups, the two surveys are not strictly comparable. However, comparison of general pattern is still of some interest.

6. Das included professional beggars in his sample but we did not.

7. M. Hossain, "Farm Size and Productivity in Bangladesh," *Bangladesh Economic Review*, 2(1):310 (January 1974).

8. Available data for a "normal" period suggest that noninstitutional sources supply about 85 percent of the credit requirement of agricultural households and that about 50 percent of the total borrowing is used for family expenditure (other than capital expenditure). See M. Alamgir, "Some Aspects of Bangladesh Agriculture: Review of Performance and Evaluation of Policies," *Bangladesh Development Studies* 3(3):272–273 (July 1975). A lower share of institutional sources in total borrowing of *langarkhana* inmates is another indication of their poor credit worthiness.

9. W. Brian Arthur and Geoffrey McNicoll, "An Analytical Survey of Population and Development in Bangladesh," *Population and Development Review*, 4(1):51 (March 1978). Crude death rates by family landholding were found to be the following in 1974 in a village of Noakhali, a nonfamine district according to our classification.

Size of Landholding (Acres)	Crude Death Rate	Death Rate of Children Ages 1–4
0	35.8	86.5
less than 0.5	28.4	48.2
0.5–3.0	21.4	49.1
3.0+	12.2	17.5

10. Tenurial status is defined on the basis of the relation of the operator to the land. Accordingly, households are classified into four groups, (that is, owner farmers, owner-cum-tenant farmers, tenant farmers, and landless laborers). Owner farmers are those who own and operate cultivable land other than homestead. Such households may rent out a portion of their owned land but do not lease any land. In some extreme cases, they may rent out the entire amount of owned cultivable land. Owner-cum-tenant farmers operate both owned and rented land other than homestead. They may also rent out a portion of their owned land. Tenant farmers operate only rented land. They do not own any cultivable land although they may own a homestead. Landless laborers are defined as those who do not own or rent any cultivable land but they may own a homestead. The number of landless laborer households is lower than the number of wage laborer households as defined under occupational classification because the latter includes landowning and tenant households whose major portion of income comes from wage labor.

11. Various types of transactions are effected under *dadan* arrangements. In our field survey, we came across the following instances: (1) Crop against crop. Under this

arrangement, the *dadan* acceptor takes a crop loan against the promise of paying back to the owner of *dadan* (creditor) a higher amount of crop after harvest. The difference between loan and repayment liability depends on the mutually agreed price at which the crop at two different times is evaluated. When the crop loans are taken, prices are usually much higher than at the postharvest period when a lower price prevails. The result being that the *dadan* acceptor may end up returning two maunds of rice for a loan of one maund of rice after a period of three or four months. (2) Cash against crop. The *dadan* acceptor takes a cash loan against the promise of selling crop to the *dadan* owner after harvest at a precontracted price to realize the loan equivalent. (3) Crop against cash. Here the crop loan is contracted against cash repayment liability. The amount of cash liability is determined by the imputed value of the crop loan. (4) Sometimes cash loan against cash payment was also presented to us as a *dadan* transaction by the respondent. (5) Similarly, there were instances of a mixed *dadan* transaction, which involved both cash and crop on either both or one part of the transaction. For convenience of analysis, all kinds of transactions were converted into cash equivalents by using relevant market prices.

12. Admittedly, data presented in Table 5.9 reveals no systematic pattern in the relative importance of different social groups as acceptors of *dadan*. On the contrary, the data provided by those who offered *dadan* showed that small farmers dominated as acceptors in terms of number and amount of loan taken.

13. Tenant farmers were found to be paying the lowest interest rate in all areas. This is due to the patron-client relationship between large farmers and their tenants, who are also tied through the creditor/debtor relationship, particularly with respect to crisis loans.

14. On the basis of operational landholding, the Gini coefficient for the famine area was 0.59 and that for the nonfamine area 0.54. These coefficients were calculated by applying linear approximations to the underlying Lorenz curve.

15. Total assets include the value of owned landholding (as defined in Note 4), livestock (bullock, cow, and goat), plough, mechanical agricultural implements, rickshaw, cart, and boat. Consumer durables, cash holding, saving certificates, shares, ornaments, and so forth have been left out of consideration. The respondents were asked to give the amount/number and the present value of each item. For landholding, average normal price prevailing during the period of survey was used. The figures quoted by respondents for each item was cross-checked by independent inquiry by the field investigator in the relevant area. Homestead was evaluated at twice the normal price for landholding. Forest, cultivable waste area, and so forth, were evaluated at the same price as cultivable landholding and therefore the total value of assets may have been slightly overestimated.

16. A departure from this policy was made during the 1943 Great Bengal Famine, when, according to the 1944 Famine Inquiry Commission, "The provision of cooked food to starving people was the most important relief measure during the acute stages of the famine. In November 1943 the total number of food kitchens reached 6,625. Of these, 551 were financed and run by private relief organizations, 4,469 by government, while the remainder were subsidized by government but run by other agencies. Most of the kitchens were opened after the issue in August of the circulars giving instructions about relief measures. From December 1943 onwards the food kitchens were gradually closed down and homeless and indigent people were housed and fed in work houses, destitute homes, and orphanages." See Famine Inquiry Commission, 1944, *Report on Bengal* (New Delhi: Manager of Government Publications, 1945), p. 70.

17. The government actually had four different codes available for handling disaster conditions: The *Famine Code of 1913*, the *Famine Manual of 1941*, the Emergency Standing Order for Relief, and the *Cyclone Code of 1970*.

18. For comparison we present the following table that shows the proportion of the population seeking relief at different periods during the 1899–1900 famine.

Province	End Dec. 1899	End Mar. 1900	End May 1900	Beginning May 1900
Central Prov.	14.50	18.70	22.12	17.89
Berar	8.8	13.4	15.7	6.5
Bombay	5.24	13.08	12.28	12.6
Ajmer	20.8	18.3	26.7	10.1
Punjab	7.27	13.2	10.5	2.4

See *Report of the Indian Famine Commission 1901* (Calcutta: Office of the Superintendent of Government Printing, India, 1901), p. 4.

19. During the three-month period under consideration, the Bangladesh government distributed a total of 36,056 tons of wheat through *langarkhanas*. This quantity represented less than 5 percent of the total available government stock of wheat.
20. Anisur Rahman, "The Famine," mimeographed, University of Dacca, November 7, 1974.
21. Figures on grants and loans are quoted from Government of Bangladesh, Ministry of Finance, *Bangladesh Economic Survey 1975-1976* (Dacca: Superintendent Bangladesh Government Press, 1976), pp. 182–183.
22. Government of Bangladesh, Ministry of Agriculture, *Bangladesh Agriculture in Statistics, 1973* and addendum (Dacca: Ministry of Agriculture, 1974).
23. After this period seed grants would have been of little use for the winter crop.
24. In the Chilmari thana of Rangpur district our field investigator found many young people who had become so weak from nutritional deficiency that they were unable to perform a normal day's work.
25. Edward J. Clay, "Institutional Changes and Agricultural Wages in Bangladesh," *Bangladesh Development Studies* 4(4):423–440 (October 1976). Wages in kind and contract wages expressed as a percentage of output during harvest implied higher monetary equivalent than the money wages offered.
26. See M. Alamgir, "The Experience of Rural Works Programme in Bangladesh," in *Planning for Effective Public Rural Works Programmes: Case Studies from Bangladesh, India and Pakistan* (Bangkok: United Nations Economic and Social Commission for Asia and the Pacific, 1979), pp. 11–68.
27. In 1972 an estimated 400,000 people lived in squatter settlements in Dacca alone. See M. Alamgir, "Approaches Towards Research Methodology on Problems of Urbanization in Bangladesh," Research Report No. 15 (New Series), Bangladesh Institute of Development Studies, Dacca, 1973. See also A. Farouk, Rezaalkarim, M. A. Mannan, Abbas Alikhan, and A. K. Fazlul Huq Shah, *The Vagrants of Dacca City* (Dacca: Bureau of Economic Research, 1976).
28. Government of Bangladesh, Bureau of Statistics, *Statistical Pocketbook of Bangladesh, 1978* (Dacca: Bureau of Statistics, December 1977) p. 118. We have used the same definition of landlessness as above. However, the landholding classification of the Bureau of Statistics provided figures separately for the zero landholding group and the 0.01 to 1.0 acre landholding group. From the latter, we calculated the proportion of households in the 0.01 to 0.49 acre category by linear interpolation and added it to that in the zero landholding group to obtain the estimate for the less than 0.5 acre group.
29. M. Alamgir, *Bangladesh, A Case of Below Poverty Level Equilibrium Trap* (Dacca: Bangladesh Institute of Development Studies, 1978), pp. 102–112.
30. Considerable cattle mortality due to flood was reported by some *langarkhana* inmates and village households. This was confirmed by the reports of our field investigators.

Twenty-two percent of the total cattle owned by villagers was lost, the percentages were 24 and 20 for famine and nonfamine areas, respectively. In Sylhet, our survey households lost 44 percent of their cattle. The field investigator in the area reported that one could see dead cattle on the roadside even as late as November 1974.

Chapter 6

Foodgrain Availability

Famine is intimately related to the availability of foodgrain. For the analysis of famine a broad definition of foodgrain availability was presented in Chapter 2. It was emphasized that foodgrain availability, narrowly defined, may or may not have any bearing on a famine. The geographical, interclass, and seasonal distribution of foodgrains have important implications for foodgrain intake per capita and hence for famine. Relationships (2.1) through (2.11) of Chapter 2 suggest that the important elements of foodgrain stock and availability are production, import, government procurement and offtake, marketed surplus, private trade in foodgrain, export, leakage through smuggling and destruction due to natural disaster, mode of wage payment, and population. While analyzing foodgrain stock and availability at the national, regional, and household level, at the beginning of and during 1974, we shall separately take up the components mentioned above.

NATIONAL STOCK AND AVAILABILITY

Stock

The availability of foodgrains during any period depends, among other things, on the stock at the beginning of the period. In Bangladesh foodgrains include three different types of rice (*aman, aus,* and *boro*) and wheat. We shall use the calendar year as the reference period in our analysis. According to relationship (2.1) of Chapter 2, stock at the beginning of any period consists of government stock, trading stock, and private stock. The government stock at the beginning of the period t equals carryover of stock from period t-2, imports during period t-1, internal procurement during t-1 less exports, offtake through the rationing system, and loss in shipment and storage. Data on the government stock of foodgrains at the beginning of the year are presented in Table 6.1. It may be noted that over the years the relative importance of wheat in total stock increased. For comparison, we also present data on the foodgrain requirement calculated on the basis of 14.4 ounces per capita/day and population figures presented in Table 6.23. It is difficult to quote a figure that is a safe limit (lower) for beginning of the year stock of foodgrains. One can, however, look at the data for the 1960s to get some ideas on this issue. During this period, the foodgrain stock held by the government at the beginning of each year varied between 4 and 6 percent of annual requirements, except in 1963 and 1967, when the level went below 3 percent. In both of these years mild scarcity of foodgrains was experienced. In 1974, the beginning of the year stock was again very

Table 6.1. Government Stock of Foodgrains on 1st January and Annual Requirement in Bangladesh 1961–1976 (000 tons)

Year	Rice	Wheat	Total	Requirement	Stock as % of Requirement
1961	259	61	320	7,997	4.00
1962	315	55	370	8,207	4.51
1963	99	135	236	8,423	2.80
1964	145	313	458	8,644	5.30
1965	339	125	464	8,871	5.23
1966	155	274	429	9,104	4.71
1967	125	124	249	9,344	2.66
1968	126	279	405	9,589	4.22
1969	88	479	567	9,841	5.76
1970	141	174	275	10,100	2.75
1971	183	411	594	10,365	5.73
1972	235	240	475	10,637	4.47
1973	14	123	137	10,917	1.25
1974	44	223	267	11,204	2.38
1975	30	151	181	11,498	1.57
1976	345	548	893	11,800	7.57

Source: Stock figures were obtained from Government of Bangladesh, Directorate of Procurement, Distribution and Rationing.

low, only 2.38 percent of the annual requirement though the figure was considerably higher than that of 1973. Therefore, in an aggregate sense, the government was inadequately prepared to tackle a food crisis in 1974.

The government stock of foodgrains is important from the point of view of meeting a crisis, because the amount of private and trading stock carryover between years is nil or negligible. There was a controversy over the estimate of the private (including trading) stock carryover by the Famine Inquiry Commission of 1944. The majority of the members of the commission held the view that "the carry-over at the beginning of 1943 was probably sufficient for about 6 weeks requirements."[2] Mr. Afzal Hossain, a member of the commission, disagreed maintaining that there was no such carryover of rice into 1944. According to Faruk, who studied the rice marketing system of East Pakistan (Bangladesh), traders do not carry stocks into the next crop year for a number of reasons.

> The primitive way of storing rice in East Pakistan discourages a storage period of more than 8 to 10 months. Quality then diminishes because facilities are damp, lacking in proper aeration and fumigation, and are located in a warm, humid climate. This is further accentuated by the high moisture content of the grain caused by poor drying facilities. . . . The traders in East Pakistan, though unsophisticated, are fully aware of this potential source of the qualitative and quantitative loss of stored grain, and most of them said that they unload their stocks after no more than 8 or 9 months' storage. Finally, from past experiences the traders anticipate that the prices in post-harvest months will be significantly lower than in September, October, and November.[3]

The above is also applicable to private stock. On the one hand, the farmers do not have much staying power and on the other, they have poor storage facilities. In our survey, it was revealed that very few of the village households had rice in storage at the time of the *aman* harvest in December 1973, and in each case the amount involved was very small.[4] Therefore, for all practical purposes, the figures in Table 6.1 represented the stock of foodgrains in Bangladesh at the beginning of different calendar years. As for 1974, we have contended earlier that the government stock level was lower than what could be considered as normal. However, in order to assess the capability of the government to tackle the situation arising from foodgrain shortage or sharp increase in foodgrain prices, it is also important to analyze the stock position at different points of time within the year. Table 6.2 presents data on the end of the month stock of foodgrains in government storages (central storage depot, local storage depot, and silos) during July 1972 to June 1975.

The stock figures quoted here should be treated as only an upper limit because there is significant (10 percent) storage loss, which is not

Table 6.2. Government Stock of Foodgrains at the End of the Month, July 1972–June 1975 (000 tons)

Month	1972	1973	1974	1975
January		193	161	319
February		245	139	224
March		498	163	244
April		495	172	282
May		412	219	438
June		309	184	728
July	450	204	320	
August	419	209	347	
September	349	263	219	
October	248	348	137	
November	218	278	130	
December	160	238	181	

Source: Government of Bangladesh, Directorate of Procurement, Distribution and Rationing.

Note: The figures for the end of December 1972 and 1973 given in this table could not be reconciled with those for the first of January 1973 and 1974 in Table 6.1.

generally recorded. Furthermore, the stock figure include foodgrain in ships and in transit within the country. In other words, the amount of foodgrains that could actually be released from government stock was well below what is shown in Table 6.2.

The end of the month stock was lower for each month in 1974 than for the corresponding month in 1973, except for July and August. The stock apparently declined beginning in July 1973 as compared with earlier months. There was some recovery during September and October of 1973, but it did not last long. Throughout 1974, the end of the month stock was roughly equivalent to what was normally distributed under the government rationing system. A substantial stock buildup did not take place until January 1975 when the worst period of famine was over. It is clear that, in 1974, the ability of the government to influence the supply and price of foodgrain through open market operation was severely limited by the availability of food resources within its command. Furthermore, as we shall see later, the government had only a relatively small amount of foodgrain available at its disposal to distribute in the rural areas, after it had met the demand of the urban population covered by statutory and modified rationing.

Relationships (2.4), (2.5), and (2.6) in Chapter 2 define total and per capita availability of foodgrains at the national level. The availability of foodgrains during any period is given by domestic production, imports, offtake from government stock, net changes in private and trading stock, internal procurement by the government, exports and leakages. As mentioned before, we shall analyze the different components of the availability of foodgrains in Bangladesh on a calendar year basis. Although we are more specifically interested in the situation prevailing in 1974, we shall also analyze the trend over the 1960s and early 1970s so that the background of the famine is more clearly understood.

Production

Trend over time. Bangladesh produces both rice and wheat. Wheat accounts for a very small proportion of net output of foodgrains in the country. According to data presented in Table 6.23, the share of wheat in total net output of foodgrains increased from 0.3 percent in 1961 to 1.7 percent in 1976 (the figure for 1974 was 1 percent). Acreage under wheat increased from 140 thousand acres in 1961 to 311 thousand acres in 1975, but the yield rate showed only a modest increase, from 8.7 maund (716 pounds) per acre to 10 maunds (828 pounds) during the same period. The yield rate compares unfavourably with the same elsewhere in the world and more importantly the per acre yield of wheat in quantity is lower than that of *boro*, the spring rice that competes with wheat for land.[5] In comparison with earlier years, wheat production in 1974 was normal, the absolute level of output being slightly above the average for the previous five years.

The relative importance of the different rice varieties in the total rice output is shown in Table 6.3. *Aman* is the most important rice crop in all areas. However, between the 1960s and 1970s, the share of *aman* in total rice output declined from 69 percent during the 1961–1965 period to 56 percent during the 1971–1976 period. On the other hand, the *boro* crop increased its share from 5 percent to 19 percent over the same period. The

Table 6.3. Relative Share of Aman, Boro and Aus in Total Rice Output

Period	Aman			Boro			Aus		
	F[a]	NF[b]	ALL[c]	F[a]	NF[b]	ALL[c]	F[a]	NF[b]	ALL[c]
1961–1965	61.8	72.1	69.1	11.0	2.7	5.1	27.2	25.2	25.8
1966–1970	58.7	63.5	62.1	15.4	9.7	11.3	25.9	26.8	26.5
1971–1976	57.4	55.2	55.8	17.9	19.8	19.3	24.8	25.0	24.9
1974	60.5	55.5	56.9	14.4	20.5	18.8	25.1	24.0	24.3

Source: Table 6.4.
[a]Famine districts
[b]Nonfamine districts
[c]Bangladesh

share of *aus* crop also declined but only by a small margin. The importance of *boro* increased more sharply in the nonfamine districts (from about 3 percent to 20 percent) as compared with the famine districts where, beginning in the mid-1960s *boro* accounted for about one-sixth of the total rice crop output. For famine districts, such continued importance of *boro* has meant a higher degree of vulnerability to food shortage due to the fact that the area is susceptible to early flash floods. Farmers producing *boro* crop in the low lying areas during the winter and spring have no alternative crop possibility; therefore, their fight against nature continues. In 1974, an early flash flood severely damaged the *boro* crop in certain areas of the Sylhet district. In the famine districts as a whole, during this year the share of *boro* in the total rice output was lower than the average for 1971–1976 period.

The total output of rice increased from an average of 9.8 million tons during the 1961–1965 period to 11.0 million tons during the 1971–1976 period (Table 6.4) The total rice output increased at the rate of only 1.44 per annum (Table 6.5). The bulk of this growth came from expansion of acreage, increase in yield being very small. Among individual rice crops, *boro* showed the highest rate of growth per annum between 1961 and 1976 in all areas. This can be attributed to the introduction of HYV seeds in the mid-1960s, and also to substantial area expansion in nonfamine districts. Prior to the introduction of HYV, the *boro* cultivation was concentrated more in the low lying areas of famine districts where some stagnant water was available. The new seed along with the expansion of dry season irrigation through low-lift pumps allowed *boro* area expansion in other districts. Consequently, in the nonfamine districts, acreage increase was twice as important as yield increase. As for the other two rice crops, the *aman* output declined in Bangladesh as a whole, as well as in the nonfamine districts. The decline was due to a decline in both the yield and the acreage. On the other hand, in the famine districts, there was only a very low rate of growth that came entirely from yield increase. The small growth in the output of *aus* came entirely from acreage expansion since, over the period under consideration, there was a declining trend in yield rate in all areas. This is explained by the greater susceptibility of *aus* crop to variations in weather conditions as compared with other crops.

We shall then analyze the 1974 rice output level in relation to the trend over time (Table 6.5). While the total output of rice in 1974 was above the trend, looking at different crops separately, it is found that the *boro* and *aus* output were below the trend. In the famine districts, the *boro* output was 18 percent below the trend. The shortfall in the *boro* output can be attributed to the early flash floods in the Sylhet district, an important *boro* producing area. The 1974 *aus* output was slightly below the trend for

Table 6.4. Production of Rice in Bangladesh, 1961–1976 (000 tons)

	Aman[a]			Boro			Aus			Total			Per Capita Total Output (net) of Rice (tons)
	F[b]	N[c]	ALL[d]	F[b]	N[c]	ALL[d]	F[b]	N[c]	ALL[d]	F[b]	N[c]	ALL[d]	ALL[d]
1961	1,771	4,803	6,574	340	108	448	819	1,510	2,329	2,930	6,421	9,351	0.154
1962	1,723	4,929	6,652	395	90	485	706	1,496	2,202	2,824	6,515	9,339	0.150
1963	1,424	4,622	6,046	251	231	482	822	1,835	2,657	2,497	6,688	9,185	0.144
1964	1,720	5,570	7,290	250	259	509	581	1,920	2,501	2,551	7,749	10,300	0.157
1965	1,947	5,315	7,262	301	269	570	853	2,065	2,918	3,101	7,649	10,750	0.160
Average 1961–1965	1,717	5,048	6,765	307	192	499	756	1,765	2,521	2,780	7,005	9,785	0.153
1966	1,794	5,005	6,799	303	315	618	689	1,985	2,674	2,786	7,305	10,091	0.146
1967	1,485	4,434	5,919	370	461	831	864	2,205	2,069	2,719	7,100	9,819	0.139
1968	1,829	4,983	6,812	446	668	1,114	819	1,864	2,683	3,094	7,515	10,609	0.146
1969	1,919	4,951	6,870	614	998	1,612	816	2,147	2,963	3,349	8,096	11,445	0.154
1970	1,939	5,011	6,950	617	1,286	1,903	763	2,100	2,863	3,319	8,397	11,716	0.153
Average 1966–1970	1,793	4,877	6,670	470	746	1,216	790	2,060	2,850	3,053	7,683	10,736	0.148
1971	1,829	4,083	5,912	672	1,520	2,192	630	1,711	2,341	3,131	7,314	10,445	0.133
1972	1,779	3,916	5,695	482	1,256	1,738	787	1,486	2,273	3,048	6,658	9,706	0.120
1973	1,524	4,063	5,587	557	1,513	2,070	716	2,086	2,802	2,797	7,662	10,459	0.126
1974	1,970	4,729	6,699	469	1,751	2,220	816	2,043	2,859	3,255	8,523	11,778	0.139
1975	1,679	4,321	6,000	562	1,688	2,250	910	2,320	3,230	3,151	8,329	11,480	0.132
1976	1,869	5,176	7,045	573	1,713	2,286	734	2,277	3,011	3,176	9,166	12,342	0.138
Average 1971–1976	1,775	4,381	6,156	553	1,574	2,126	766	1,987	2,753	3,093	7,942	11,035	0.132

Source: M. Alamgir, *Famine 1974: Political Economy of Mass Starvation in Bangladesh*, Statistical Annexe, Part II (Dacca: Bangladesh Institute of Development Studies), pp. 7-26; *Monthly Statistical Bulletin* 6(10):26–29 (October 1977).
[a]Refers to previous December output
[b]Famine districts
[c]Nonfamine districts
[d]Bangladesh

Table 6.5. Growth of Rice Output in Bangladesh, 1961–1976

Rice Variety	Output	Area	Yield	% Deviation of 1974 from Trend		
				Output	Area	Yield
Aman						
Famine districts	+0.48	−0.75	+1.22	+9.3	+0.3	+9.0
Nonfamine districts	−0.88	−0.18	−0.70	+5.1	+0.7	+4.4
Bangladesh	−0.51	−0.32	−0.18	+6.8	+0.6	+5.7
Boro						
Famine districts	+5.24	+2.32	+2.92	−18.0	−12.0	−6.9
Nonfamine districts	+20.57	+14.34	+6.23	−5.9	−2.9	−3.1
Bangladesh	+13.55	+8.36	+4.99	−3.5	−1.6	−1.8
Aus						
Famine districts	+0.22	+0.64	−0.42	+5.1	+2.8	+2.2
Nonfamine districts	+1.62	+2.22	−0.59	−2.7	−5.3	+2.8
Bangladesh	+1.20	+1.77	−0.57	−0.6	−3.2	+2.8
Total						
Famine districts	+1.08	+0.04	+1.05	+3.6	−0.6	+3.2
Nonfamine districts	+1.58	+1.32	+0.27	+3.8	−0.8	+4.6
Bangladesh	+1.44	+0.96	+0.47	+3.5	−0.7	+4.3

Note: Growth rates are calculated from exponential trend.

Bangladesh as a whole, but in the case of the famine districts the *aus* output exceeded the trend by 5 percent. On the other hand, the 1974 *aman* output in the famine and nonfamine districts exceeded the trend value by 9.33 and 5.12 percent respectively.

Another way of looking at output data would be to integrate the effect of population growth. Analyzing the figures for per capita net output of rice[6] (Table 6.4), we find that there was a sharp decline in the years following the liberation of Bangladesh, as compared with the earlier years (that is, population growth outstripped output increase). The average per capita net output of rice declined from 0.153 tons during the 1961–1965 period to 0.148 tons during the 1966–1970 period to 0.132 tons during the 1971–1976 period, the figure for 1974 being 0.139 tons. It may be pointed out that for all years in the 1970s, the per capita net output of rice was lower than the minimum requirement (0.147 tons). It is interesting to note that the per capita net output of rice was actually higher in 1974 as compared with all other years of the 1970s although it was well below the level realized in the 1960s. Therefore, analyzing the rice and wheat output figures (total and per capita), it appears that the 1974 famine could not be attributed to a drastic shortfall in the aggregate foodgrain output. But as the trend analysis by individual crops suggests, there was uneven distribution of changes in output during different cropping seasons, which may have had contributed to a tight market availability situation in the second half of 1974. However, seasonal variation in the domestic output alone could not explain the intensity of suffering of the people in 1974, especially when one considers the fact that, in absolute terms, the level of output of all types of crops was higher in 1974 as compared with the year before.

The impact of the 1974 flood was reflected in the shortfall of output of *aus* and *boro* from the trend rather than in an absolute decline in output over the previous year. In this context, the above-trend output level of the *aus* crop in 1974 in the famine districts that were particularly hard hit by the flood needs to be explained. Data presented in Table 6.5end output level of the *aus* crop in 1974 in the famine districts that were particularly hard hit by the flood needs to be explained. Data presented in Table 6.5 show that both acreage and the yield rate were above the trend value. The yield rate was also above the trend value in the nonfamine districts. Therefore, it seems that there was a very high potential yield increase in 1974 for *aus* that outweighed the damage caused by flood. The other explanation for the level of the *aus* output in the famine districts could be that, while the flooding was extensive in this region, the actual damage to the *aus* crop was concentrated in limited areas. We know that this was true of the *boro* crop, which was hit hard mostly in Sylhet district. For *aus*, evidence on the area specific crop damage due to the 1974 flood can be found from our survey data presented in Table 6.6. Heavy loss of the *aus* output in the flood was reported from four villages, two in the famine area and two in the nonfamine area. In contrast, there was almost no damage to *aus* crop in the remaining four villages. The percentage loss of output was higher in

Table 6.6. Extent of Crop Damage Due to Flood as Reported by the Survey Villagers

Area	Loss of 1974 Aus Paddy as % of 1973 Net Output	
	of All Households	of Families Affected
All villages	16.74	35.49
Famine area	22.14	47.72
Ramna	43.32	44.94
Gaorarang	—	—
Kogaria	—	—
Dewanganj	50.91	51.91
Nonfamine area	13.70	28.79
Nazirpur	30.69	31.41
Laskarpur	0.42	1.75
Komorpur	—	—
Charbaniari	56.90	61.49

the famine area than in the nonfamine area, but the difference between the two areas was smaller in terms of percentages of families affected. The evidence on the area of specific flood damage corroborates other reports that suggest that, even within the famine districts, there was considerable variation between localities in the intensity of suffering (see Table 6.6).

Causal Analysis of Output Changes. The production of foodgrains in Bangladesh has lagged behind requirement. The government has adopted new programs from time to time to promote foodgrain production but to no avail. The problems associated with food production are those that emanate from the basic characteristics of the agricultural sector itself. In what follows, we discuss the factors affecting foodgrain output. More specifically, we focus attention on (a) physical contraints, (b) the technological and organizational parameters, and (c) sources and uses of agricultural credit.

Physical Constraints and Productivity. Bangladesh agriculture is characterized by low productivity, which can be attributed to the dominance of traditional technology. This is a historic phenomenon and very little attempt was made in the past by the government to improve the situation. We have already noted that the *Zemindars* took little interest in improving the productivity of agriculture. On the other hand, the government itself did little to promote new agricultural technology although it was recommended by various famine commissions and the Royal Commission on Agriculture of 1928. There were some improvements of seeds and in gravity irrigation in the desert areas of Punjab and Sind (but not in Bengal), but no encouragement was given to extension work, fertilizer use, or livestock improvement. The situation did not change significantly even in the recent past except that since the mid-1960s the new HYV technology (seed, fertilizer, pesticide, and water) was introduced along with institutionalization of the extension service and popularization of cooperatives. But despite all these measures, figures for the early 1970s suggest that Bangladesh ranks very low on the productivity scale as compared with other developing countries in Asia and Africa.[7]

The land:man ratio is quite unfavourable in Bangladesh. Per capita agricultural land (cultivable) has declined over time, the figure for 1975–1976 being only 0.29 acres.[8] In addition to the productivity of land being very low, the intensity of land use is also low as the figure for 1975–1976 indicates (148.48).[9] The problem of the agricultural sector has been further aggravated by the subdivision and fragmentation of landholdings.[10] These developments are the direct result of three forces: (1)

stagnant net cultivable area; (2) high rate of population growth; and (3) operation of the traditional law of inheritance. There is no hard data on the effect of declining average farm size and the increasing incidence of fragmentation on productivity. It can be said a priori that increasing fragmentation acts as an obstacle to the diffusion of HYV technology and also to the introduction of selective nonlabor displacing mechanization, and thus it probably hinders yield increase. Fragmentation may reduce output by increasing waste of land resources through land demarcation and also through reducing the flexibility of farming operation and involving considerable loss of time and energy. While there is some cross-section evidence that smaller farms are relatively more productive than larger ones, it is not clear what happens during a period of continuous and relatively fast decline in the size of holding combined with increased fragmentation.

We have already discussed the problem of floods and heavy rainfall, a situation becoming worse every year due to the inflow of about 1.7 billion tons of sediment that is raising the river beds all over Bangladesh. An equally serious problem exists in the form of uneven distribution of rainfall during the year, with the result that during the dry months of winter, most of the cultivable land remains unutilized except where irrigation facilities are available. Irrigation in Bangladesh was almost exclusively carried out by indigenous methods (for example *doons,* swing baskets, and others)[11] until the introduction of the new HYV technology, which brought along with it irrigation by power pumps and tubewells. Canal irrigation has always been of minor importance.

Technology and Organization of Agriculture. In Bangladesh, the new seed-fertilizer-irrigation technology of rice was introduced in different phases. During the early years it was confined to fertilizer distribution and irrigation with a small number of pumps and tubewells. The first HYV seed of rice, called IR–8 (improved *boro*) was introduced in 1966. An *aman* season variety called IR–20 was introduced in 1970. This was followed by the import and indigenous development of a number of other HYV seeds (for example IR–5, IR–442, *Chandina, Mala, Mukti,* and *Biplab*). Data on the net land area irrigated, fertilizer distributed, and planted under HYV are presented in Table 6.7.

It appears that only a very small proportion of the area under cultivation benefits from supplementary irrigation. However, the official figures seem to be inflated. A number of studies, including those carried out at the Bangladesh Institute of Development Studies, reveal that both low-lift pumps and deep tubewells operate at about a 25 percent level of efficiency in terms of normal capacity utilization.[12] The underutilization of irrigation capacity has been attributed to a number of factors, such as

Table 6.7. Irrigation, Fertilizer Distribution, and Area under HYV in Bangladesh, 1967–1968 to 1975–1976

Year	Net Land Area Irrigated (million acres)	Net Land Area Irrigated as % of Total Net Cropped Area	Fertilizer Distributed (000 tons)	Area Under HYV (million acres)	Area Under HYV as % of Total Gross Cropped Area Under Rice
1967–1968	0.43	1.98	227		
1968–1969	0.47	2.64	237		
1969–1970	0.84	3.86	277	0.65	2.55
1970–1971	1.18	5.52	306	1.14	4.66
1971–1972	0.98	4.81	24	1.54	6.70
1972–1973	1.38	6.62	384	2.63	11.05
1973–1974	1.51	7.20	380	3.83	15.69
1974–1975	1.55	7.54	282	3.57	14.75
1975–1976	1.85	8.82	448	3.84	15.02

Source: Adapted from M. Alamgir, "Agriculture Sector in Bangladesh," mimeographed, Bangladesh Institute of Development Studies, Dacca, March 1977.

Note: Area irrigated includes mechanical and canal (gravity) irrigation only. Indigenous methods are omitted.

lack of availability of fuel in sufficient quantity and time, lack of proper repair and maintenance facilities, lack of incentive for pump group managers,[13] domination of pump groups by large farmers, inadequate government supervision, and lack of adequate and timely supply of credit.

In 1974 it was reported that the *boro* crop was adversely affected in certain areas because of nonavailability of low-lift pumps for supplementary irrigation. In Thakurgaon 55,000 acres were affected because of inadequate water supply due to inactive deep tubewells. This was attributed to the scarcity of fuel and spare parts. Ironically enough this occurred at a time (April–May) when other parts of the country started to go under flood water.[14]

For canal irrigation, the Ganges-Kobodak project is the only significant project in operation. Unfortunately, since its inception in 1954, the project has been suffering from a number of structural and management problems, the most important being annual siltation of the intake channel. During a visit to the project area in 1974 as a member of the Evaluation Team set up by the Bangladesh Planning Commission, I found that the official figures grossly exaggerated the area irrigated by the project. On critical scrutiny, the officials at the project site were unable to account for even 10,000 acres of dry season irrigation while published figures claimed 61,292 acres[15] as the net irrigated area.

Furthermore, the figures quoted by officials included a substantial portion that was not directly irrigated, but benefited from residual moisture. In recent years the project has been having difficulties in providing irrigation because of the withdrawal of water by India at Farakka (upper reach of the Ganges, just outside Bangladesh) during dry months. Although a short-term agreement has been reached between India and Bangladesh over the sharing of the Ganges water, the situation remains very uncertain for the Ganges-Kobodak project. It was reported in May of 1974 that about 10,000 acres of land was adversely affected in Jessore district because the Ganges-Kobodak project failed to supply irrigation water.[16]

Reliable data on the actual use of fertilizer and its distribution among different crops are not available. Official data refer to distribution only. There is always a gap between distribution and application of fertilizer due to wastage in the process of distribution and leakage through smuggling into India. According to the information provided by the Bangladesh Rifles (border security force), fertilizer has been one of the major items smuggled across the border. However, the total amount of fertilizer lost this way is unknown. The official distribution figures reveal that between the early and late 1960s the amount of fertilizer distributed increased fourfold, but there has been some fluctuation in the distribution since the early 1970s (Table 6.7). The following facts are important in understanding the relationship between fertilizer use and agricultural productivity increase in Bangladesh. First, the supply of chemical fertilizer falls far short of demand (supply is about 10 percent of the estimated demand). Second, the use of fertilizer, like that of mechanised irrigation, is dominated by the large-farmer group, who use it less efficiently than the small farmer group. Third, fertilizer use has increased more slowly than area under HYV. If we assume that fertilizer is used primarily in the area under HYV, then the above would imply that the dosage per acre has gone down over time (Table 6.7). This should be considered along with the findings of Ahmed, who estimated that in Bangladesh the fertilizer use was only 3 percent of the recommended dose in *aus*, 2 percent of the recommended dose in *aman*, and 16 percent of the recommended dose in *boro*.[17] These are only crude estimates based on a number of assumptions, but they confirm the view that fertilizer application in Bangladesh is low compared with many other countries of the world.[18] There is the additional problem that farmers do not use balanced doses of different types of fertilizer. The use pattern reveals predominance of nitrogenous fertilizers.

The low level of fertilizer application to rice is unfortunate in view of the chronic food shortage in the country. Analysis of production data revealed a high to moderate degree of response of different varieties of rice to the application of fertilizer.[19] However, it is difficult to interpret the estimated response coefficients because they depend on the level and time of distribution of irrigation water and management efficiency. It is, therefore, more desirable to study each agricultural technology only as a package. For example, it has been found in many countries, including Bangladesh, that there are problems associated with both the supply and demand aspects of fertilizer use. These problems are associated with the organization and structure of agriculture, the status of other inputs included in the technology package, and the government procurement, distribution, and pricing policies regarding fertilizer. The rice price also plays an important role, as we shall discuss in the next chapter.

Agriculture in Bangladesh is organized on a household farm basis, with the average size being rather small. We indicated earlier that for all farms taken together, the average farm size declined between 1960 and 1974. The distribution of land ownership is highly skewed and the situation has apparently worsened between the 1960s and the 1970s.[20] Our survey data showed that the average size of landholding (operational) of the large-farmer group (7.5 acres and above) was about 10 times that of the small-farmer group (less than 2.5 acres). The middle and large farmers are increasing control over land while the small farmers are losing ground. To the extent to which available evidence suggests a negative relationship between farm size and land productivity,[21] increasing polarization of landholding will have an adverse affect on agricultural output including foodgrains. On the whole, most of the agricultural units are organized with small amounts of land and capital per head of agricultural working force, which accounts for low productivity in agriculture, as mentioned earlier. Very little surplus is generated on most of the farms to promote new technology, which includes application of chemical fertilizer.

The effect of the small average size of landholding on productivity has to be analyzed along with the effect of the prevailing tenurial system. As for sharecropping, it is sometimes claimed that such arrangements may be more socially desirable than owner operation with hired labor, because the sharecropper using family labor only will tend to increase labor input until its marginal value product is zero. Against this, one may argue that insecurity of tenancy may take initiative from the operator to introduce innovation in farming practices. It is difficult to say a priori what the outcome of the interaction between these two opposing forces will be.

The outcome will depend on the extent to which the following reservations on the two opposing viewpoints hold. First, the sharecropper may withdraw labor long before marginal value product reaches zero if he has alternative use of his labor at a positive value product. Second, sharecropping need not affect adoption of new technology if the landlord agrees to share costs and risk. Analysing farm level data, Hossain found no relationship between tenurial status and productivity.[22]

As for fertilizer use, Hossain found limited evidence of a higher level of application on large farms as compared with small farms, but according to him, "It could not offset the large negative effect of labour use on productivity."[23] Using regression analysis, he found that at the farm level "the coefficient of tenancy on fertilizer use is neither systematic nor significant."[24] Hossain defined tenancy as the proportion of landholding rented. On the other hand, the analysis of interdistrict fertilizer use data revealed a highly significant effect of the tenancy variable measured by the proportion of owner operated farms in the district.[25] Asaduzzaman correctly pointed out that the present level of fertilizer is low primarily because of supply constraints.[26] Supply constraints refer to the total availability of fertilizer as well as its distribution. Ahmed's analysis showed a significant effect of district storage capacity of fertilizer on the absorption of fertilizer. The coefficient of storage capacity was greater than 1, and it was statistically significant.[27] According to the Bangladesh Agricultural Development Corporation, which has the monopoly on the internal and external procurement of fertilizer, in 1975–1976 the domestic supply of fertilizer amounted to 49 percent of the total supply of fertilizer in the country. Bangladesh produces two types of nitrogenous fertilizer—urea, which is very widely used (70 percent of total amount applied) and ammonium sulphate (AS)—and one type of phosphatic fertilizer—triple superphosphate (TSP) (Table 6.8). It imports urea, AS, TSP, and also muriate of potash (MP), hyperphosphate (HP), and NPK. As of 1975–1976, dependence on imports for these different types of fertilizers was 20 percent for urea, 85 percent for TSP, and 100 percent for MP and NPK. There was no import of HP that year, but Bangladesh depends entirely on external sources of supply for this item also. Capacity utilization of both urea and TSP plants has been low. In 1975–1976, utilization as a percentage of the rated capacity was 63 percent for urea and 26 percent for TSP. In 1974–1975, domestic production was even lower because of a major accident at the Ghorasal factory, which accounts for 76 percent of the rated capacity of urea. The production of TSP is entirely dependent on importing rock phosphate from abroad. Bangladesh has been unable to secure a stable source of supply of raw materials for TSP. In 1973–1974, TSP could not be produced due to the unavailability of rock phosphate.

It is apparent that the new HYV technology remains highly import-intensive, as reflected in the country's dependence on the foreign supply of fertilizer and irrigation equipment and also of pesticides and fungicides. Fertilizer has been very tight in the international market

Table 6.8. Production of Fertilizer in Bangladesh, 1969–1970 to 1976–1977 (Ton)

Year	Urea	TSP	Ammonium Sulphate
1969–1970	96,705	—	—
1970–1971	93,092	—	—
1971–1972	55,959	—	—
1972–1973	186,701	—	5,006
1973–1974	269,324	—	10,129
1974–1975	82,244	26,068	4,856
1975–1976	280,510	48,190	5,710
1976–1977	281,343	47,222	9,114

Source: Government of Bangladesh, Bureau of Statistics, *Statistical Pocketbook of Bangladesh, 1978* (Dacca: Bureau of Statistics, December 1977), p. 183.

since the early 1970s. This was evident in the significant rise in the world price of fertilizer as well as the shortage of world supply. During this period Bangladesh suffered because of the high cost of importing fertilizer and also because the developed countries, who usually export fertilizer, gave preference to their own farmers in the allocation of fertilizer. Procurement price and the amount of imports of different types of fertilizer are shown in Table 6.9. It can be seen that the sharp increase in import price occurred in 1973–1974 and resulted in a drastic shortage of imports. This, combined with a fall in domestic procurement (production), resulted in a sharp decline in the amount of fertilizer distributed in 1974–1975, as shown in Table 6.7. However, total fertilizer distribution in 1973–1974 was comparable with that of 1972–1973, although per-acre application was much lower. One should further consider the fact that available evidence indicates fertilizer was not available when it was needed for the *boro* crop and that there was considerable leakage through

Table 6.9. Amount of Imports and Price of Imports of Fertilizer, 1970–1971 to 1975–1976

Year	Import Price (TK./ton)			Imports (1000 tons)		
	Urea	TSP	MP	Urea	TSP	MP
1970–1971	476	476	350	105	149	2
1971–1972	476	476	350	108	3	—
1972–1973	476	476	350	129	116	—
1973–1974	828	1134	766	—	96	—
1974–1975	3496	3382	1244	140	47	7
1975–1976	2776	2776	2179	71	219	37

Source: Data provided by Bangladesh Agricultural Development Corporation (BADC).

smuggling. Therefore, on the whole, the year 1974 witnessed a drastic fall in the actual use of fertilizer in Bangladesh. This has shown up at least partly in the below-trend acreage and yield of *boro*. The anomalies with respect to fertilizer distribution in 1974 are confirmed by the reported high fertilizer price in the open market and supply shortages in various parts of the country.[28] The point made here is that good crop would have been realized with normal fertilizer input, conceivably reducing shortages in many areas.

The problems with respect to fertilizer distribution in Bangladesh need to be elaborated further. As mentioned earlier, the Bangladesh Agricultural Development Corporation has complete monopoly over internal and external procurement of fertilizer. This is a public sector body that is also responsible for input supply and small irrigation schemes such as low-lift pumps and deep tubewells. The fertilizer is distributed from thana level stores to a set of licenced dealers and thana central cooperatives, who in turn sell it to the farmers at controlled prices. This system of procurement and distribution of a very important agricultural input does not always work smoothly, with the result that the farmers do not get fertilizer when needed. Data from a survey undertaken in Pakistan in 1969–1970 and quoted by Ahmed reveal that 76 percent of the respondents were unable to get fertilizer in time.[29] Asaduzzaman mentions that the seasonal procurement pattern is not always consistent with the seasonal demand pattern.[30]

A transportation bottleneck and inadequate storage facilities complicate matters further. In this context, Ahmed's finding of a significant positive coefficient for district storage capacity in the regression explaining interdistrict variation in fertilizer distribution has two important implications. First, it suggests that under the existing circumstances, farmers are supply constrained in their use of fertilizer. Second, an increase in the district storage capacity will facilitate timely distribution of fertilizer so that it will have a demand augmenting effect. As of now, it is found that there is considerable variation in the district level storage capacity per unit of cultivated area.[31] However, it is not only the capacity, but the quality of capacity that is extremely important. It is alleged that old stock of fertilizer carried over is often spoiled because of lack of adequate protection. There is need for improving the thana level storage capacity and the efficiency of the distribution system.

The cornerstone of the foodgrain production policy of Bangladesh is subsidization of the use of modern agricultural inputs (for example, seed, fertilizer, water, and pesticides). The rates of subsidy vary widely among different types of inputs. Table 6.10 presents figures for rates of fertilizer subsidy in recent years. The rates of fertilizer and irrigation water subsidy in 1975–1976 are presented separately in Table 6.11. It is

Table 6.10. Rates of Subsidy on Different Types of Fertilizer, 1971–1972 to 1974–1975 (percent of cost)

Year	Urea	TSP	MP	Average
1971–1972	57	61	67	65
1972–1973	41	64	47	48
1973–1974	18	58	55	26
1974–1975	11	60	34	27

Source: Mujibur Rahman, "Procurement, Distribution and Pricing Policies for Agricultural Inputs and Outputs in Bangladesh—A Critical Review," *Political Economy*, Journal of the Bangladesh Economic Association, Conference Volume, 1976, p. 325.

apparent that rates of subsidy, although declining, are quite high. In view of the sharp increase in the procurement price of fertilizer, government raised the subsidy in 1975–1976. In addition, a sizeable subsidy is given for seeds. According to planning commission estimates, in 1973–1974 the rates of subsidy on transplanted *aman* seed and *boro* seed were 43 percent and 32 percent respectively.[32] Notwithstanding the subsidy, the seed distribution program suffers from a credibility gap mostly because of the poor quality of the seeds. The germination rate is low, and there is no quality control to ensure purity of seed variety. The result is that, unlike other inputs, offtake is lower than availability from the government seed stores.

The subsidy on various inputs was designed to encourage their use among the farmers. But it has resulted in inefficient use of the resources by large and middle farmers who have been able to preempt the limited supply. The small farmers hardly benefit from the subsidy program, since they always have to pay a premium to gain access to modern

Table 6.11. Rates of Subsidy on Fertilizer and Irrigation Water in 1975–1976 (percent of cost)

Item	Subsidy
Fertilizer	53
Pump irrigation	46
Low-lift pump	44
Shallow tubewells	34
Deep tubewells	67
Hand pumps	29
Gravity irrigation	100

Source: Government of Bangladesh, FAO/UNDP Mission, "Selected Policy Issues in Agriculture," Food Policy Working Paper II, Dacca, April 15, 1977, pp. 11-12.

inputs. Table 6.11 clearly shows the perverse subsidy structure for pump irrigation which was observed by the FAO/UNDP mission. Pumps, the use of which is dominated by large farmers (for example, deep tubewells and low-lift pumps), are more heavily subsidized than those frequently used by small farmers (for example, handpumps). Authorities agree that the food situation of Bangladesh would have been quite different had the utilization of low-lift pumps been more efficient. In certain cases, raising the cost of an input has improved use efficiency. For example, pesticides, which were at one time fully subsidized, were largely wasted, and farmers often did not receive supplies when they needed them most, thus raising the risk associated with the adoption of HYV. Recently, with the reduction of subsidy, the use and distribution patterns of pesticides have become more rational.

Modern inputs and anomalies with respect to their pricing and distribution apart, foodgrain production has been seriously constrained by the availability of draft power. In 1970, Bangladesh had 2.45 cattle per household, which included bulls, bullock, cows, and young stock. Applying the 1972–1973 bullocks to cattle ratio, the draft power works out to be only 0.79 per household, the figure increasing to 1.63 if we include all cows. The corresponding figures were 0.69 and 1.42 in 1973–1974.[33] From our survey data we found that the average number of cattle per household was 0.96 in all villages, 0.80 in famine villages, and 1.05 in nonfamine villages. Forty-three percent of all village households and 60 percent of small farmers (less than 2.5 acres) had no draft power.[34] The FAO/UNDP mission writes, "The present position is, indeed, a depressing one. Existing cattle are undernourished and emaciated, a pair (of 500 lbs. each) being able to plough only 4 acres."[35] The government in the past paid little or no attention to the precarious livestock situation. The growth of livestock population has been adversely affected by the feedgrain shortage and natural disasters. No systematic attempt has ever been made to improve either feed supplies or the quality of cattle breeding. Famine prevention policies in Bangladesh cannot overlook the status of the cattle population.

Agricultural Credit: The FAO/UNDP mission correctly pointed out that

Agricultural credit is one of the major obstacles to the faster adoption of the high cost new technology—on which the entire production strategy depends. Field surveys indicate that it is largely the shortage of capital and credit that prevent the small farmer from using these inputs. The high levels of risk and indebtedness, in turn, make more difficult the economic working of an efficient agricultural credit system in the country.[36]

The credit market, as discussed earlier, is characterized by shortfall in supply, taking both institutional and noninstitutional sources together. Village survey data (Table 6.12) show that in terms of both the percentage of households reporting debt and the average amount of loan per household, the landowning families (owner farmers and owner-cum-tenant farmers) are ahead of nonlandowning households (tenant farmers and landless laborers). Other things being equal, this reflects the importance of land as collateral in the credit market. The same is reflected in the figures presented for different size group of landholding.

Institutional sources provided only about 9 percent of the total credit supply (Table 6.13). In general, owner farmers had greater access to institutional credit. Similarly, access to institutional credit was positively related to the size of landholding. This was only to be expected, since marketable collateral is an important basis for the distribution of credit. Among noninstitutional sources, money lender was the most important source, accounting for about 35 percent of the total credit, followed by friends and relatives (32 percent), businessmen (18 percent), and other (5 percent). There are four major institutional sources providing credit to the agricultural sector. These are the commercial banks, the Bangladesh Krishi Bank, *Taccavi,* and the cooperative societies. The magnitude of their operation in terms of loans provided is shown in Table 6.14. The operation of commercial banks in the agricultural sector is only a recent phenomenon but they have emerged as an important source of credit.

Table 6.12.   Average Size of Debt per Household in Survey Areas

Household Group	% of Household Reporting Debt			Average Amount of Loan per Household (Taka)		
	Fa	NFb	AllC	Fa	NFb	AllC
Tenurial status						
Owner farmer	42.5	63.9	54.2	478	908	759
Owner-cum-tenant farmer	46.1	70.5	60.4	681	1,082	956
Tenant farmer	43.2	69.0	57.0	250	588	468
Landless laborers	36.5	75.6	49.6	277	412	346
Size group of landholding (operational) (acres)						
Small	39.7	69.1	52.6	377	635	525
Medium	46.8	68.1	61.1	710	1,233	1102
Large	56.5	44.0	47.9	865	972	932
Total	41.4	67.4	54.7	461	859	711

aFamine area
bNonfamine area
cAll villages

Table 6.13. Percentage Distribution of Credit by Source and Household Groups

Household Group	Famine Area		Nonfamine Area		All Villages	
	I[a]	NI[b]	I[a]	NI[b]	I[a]	NI[b]
Tenurial status						
Owner farmer	5.38	94.62	13.35	86.65	11.53	88.47
Owner-cum-tenant farmer	6.72	93.28	9.21	90.79	8.65	91.35
Tenant farmer	—	100.00	1.71	98.83	0.95	99.05
Landless laborers	—	100.00	1.64	98.36	1.00	99.00
Size group of landholding (operational) (acres)						
Small	2.89	97.11	6.10	95.90	5.12	94.88
Medium	8.80	91.20	13.31	86.69	12.59	87.41
Large	4.44	95.56	29.93	71.07	21.14	78.86
Total	4.82	95.18	10.74	89.26	9.32	90.68

[a]Institutional source
[b]Noninstitutional source

The Bangladesh Krishi Bank provides medium- and long-term loans. The available evidence suggests that its loans are concentrated among the medium and large farmers. The cooperative societies have also been dominated by the rural elite.[37]

Data from various surveys, including our own, reveal that farm households require short-, medium-, and long-term credit, which are normally put to the following uses: family expenditure; farm expenditure, current and capital; nonfarm business expenditure; repayment of old debt; and so forth. Table 6.15 shows that 24 percent of the total loan in all villages was devoted to capital expenditure, 10 percent for the famine area and 28 percent for the nonfamine area. There was a positive relationship between the size of landholding and the share of capital expenditure, as was to be expected. It is interesting to note that both the owner-cum-tenant farmers and the tenant farmers devoted a higher proportion of loans to capital expenditure than the owner farmers. If we look at the expenditure on agricultural inputs alone (not shown here) the relationships of Table 6.15 hold. On this basis, it can be argued that sharecroppers and tenants use credit more efficiently than other groups. This behavioral pattern may sometimes be imposed in the sense that landowners impose certain types of capital expenditure on sharecroppers and tenants. However, the expenditure on agricultural inputs accounted for only 10 percent of the total loans. Hossain[38] found that input purchase for cultivators is financed mostly from internal resources that, however,

Table 6.14. Agricultural Credit from Institutional Sources in Bangladesh, 1969–1970 to 1975–1976 (Taka million)

Year	Commercial Banks		Bangladesh Krishi Bank		Taccavi		Cooperative Societies		Total	
1969–1970	—	—	100.7	(41.8)	7.8	(3.2)	132.2	(54.9)	240.7	(100.0)
1970–1971	—	—	69.7	(48.3)	1.7	(1.2)	73.0	(50.6)	144.4	(100.0)
1971–1972	—	—	96.4	(29.9)	115.0	(35.7)	110.9	(34.4)	322.3	(100.0)
1972–1973	N.A.	—	179.0	(48.2)	60.0	(16.2)	132.0	(35.6)	371.0	(100.0)
1973–1974	116.9	(33.9)	135.7	(39.3)	14.7	(4.3)	78.0	(22.6)	345.3	(100.0)
1974–1975	152.7	(35.9)	176.3	(41.4)	10.0	(2.3)	86.7	(20.4)	425.7	(100.0)
1975–1976	206.1	(42.7)	185.1	(38.3)	N.A.	—	91.7	(19.0)	482.9	(100.0)

Source: Government of Bangladesh, Ministry of Agriculture, *Bangladesh Agriculture in Statistics, 1973* (Dacca: Ministry of Agriculture, 1974), p. 89, Addenda, Corrigenda, p. 7; Government of Bangladesh, Ministry of Finance, *Bangladesh Economic Survey 1973–1974* (Dacca: Superintendent Bangladesh Government Press, 1974), pp. 52–54; *Bangladesh Economic Survey 1974–1975* (Dacca: Superintendent Bangladesh Government Press, 1975), pp. 105–109; *Bangladesh Economic Survey 1976–1977* (Dacca: Superintendent Bangladesh Government Press, 1977), p. 40.

Table 6.15. Use of Credit by Village Households (percentage distribution)

Household Group	Famine Area Current	Famine Area Capital	Nonfamine Area Current	Nonfamine Area Capital	All Villages Current	All Villages Capital
Tenurial status						
Owner farmer	91.3	8.7	76.3	23.7	79.7	20.3
Owner-cum-tenant farmer	90.6	9.4	59.6	40.4	66.5	33.5
Tenant farmer	52.4	47.6	16.3	38.7	59.6	40.4
Landless laborers	90.2	9.8	91.0	9.0	90.7	9.3
Size group of landholding (operational) (acres)						
Small	89.8	10.2	81.3	18.7	83.9	16.1
Medium	94.0	6.0	65.2	34.8	69.1	30.9
Large	100.0	0.0	43.9	56.1	63.3	36.7
Total	90.0	10.0	71.5	28.4	76.0	24.0

are not very large in absolute terms. Therefore, on the whole, the farmers were able to devote only a small amount of resources (borrowed or internally generated) for input purchase. In the context of raising agricultural productivity, the important question remains whether the credit used for consumption expenditure should be considered as nonproductive. The consensus among many experts seems to be that in a country where the majority of farm families operate below the poverty level, at least a part of the consumption expenditure should be included under working capital. This argument, however, would not apply to large farmers who tend to consume a greater proportion of credit, implying resource misallocation.

The analysis presented here suggests that the available resources have not been efficiently utilized in the agricultural sector so as to bring about a sustained rate of growth of productivity, particularly in rice production. Total amount of surplus available for adopting productivity raising measures was very limited, but what really affected the prospect of output growth most is the lack of an institutional framework for assisting the cultivators in drawing up a well-coordinated production plan and in implementing it accordingly, thus ensuring the optimum utilization of inputs currently available. This would have required coordination in the supply of inputs by the relevant government agencies. So far, the experience of Bangladesh has been that in aggregative terms, the supply of modern inputs has increased over time without commensurate rise in output. This point is demonstrated clearly when we compare the trends of HYV rice yield in Table 6.16 with those of input use as presented in Table 6.7. There has been a declining yield trend for all types of HYV. The modern inputs have been spread thin over a wider area, and a major

Table 6.16. Yield of HYV Rice in Bangladesh, 1969–1970 to 1976–1977 (tons per acre)

Year	Aman	Aus	Boro	Total
1969–1970	1.28	0.58	1.48	1.41
1970–1971	1.06	1.33	1.39	1.32
1971–1972	1.11	1.07	1.22	1.16
1972–1973	0.71	1.02	1.23	0.95
1973–1974	0.96	1.16	1.11	1.03
1974–1975	0.86	0.99	1.00	0.95
1975–1976	0.88	0.98	1.03	0.96
1976–1977	0.86	0.92	0.98	0.92

portion was preempted by the large and middle farmers, who apparently utilized them less efficiently.

Imports

We discussed earlier that beginning in the late 1930s, Bengal turned from a net exporter of foodgrains to a net importer of foodgrains. East Bengal as a whole, however, remained a rice-surplus area throughout the 1940s, except for the years around the Great Bengal Famine. After the partition of India, East Pakistan (Bangladesh) did not make any substantial import of foodgrains until about 1956–1957, when a total of 592 thousand tons of foodgrains (rice, 532 thousand tons, and wheat, 59 thousand tons) were imported. Since then, with some fluctuations, the total imports of foodgrains have increased over the years. The composition of imports changed as the share of wheat increased beginning in 1962–1963 (Table 6.17). Imports of foodgrains as a percentage of total requirement increased from 8.7 percent in 1960–1961 to 25.9 percent in 1972–1973 and then declined to 12.5 percent in 1975–1976. According to Islam, "Starting in the mid-1950s there had been a continuous rise in the imports of foodgrains as a result of the rapid growth of population coupled with a stagnant or slowly rising output."[39] While the observation on the population and output growth is correct, data presented in Table 6.17 show that in a macro accounting sense, chronic food gap of a substantial margin emerged only in the 1970s. There were only two years (1962–1963 and 1966–1967) in the 1960s when net domestic output of Bangladesh fell short of the requirement, estimated on the basis of 14.4 ounces per capita/day.

Admittedly, one can disagree with the assumption made here about the per capita foodgrain requirement. Many authors have also questioned the accuracy of the official output data.[40] But the fact remains

Table 6.17. Import of Foodgrains into Bangladesh, 1960–1961 to 1975–1976

Year	Rice	Wheat	Total	Import as % of Requirement	Food Gap (000 tons)
1960–1961	464	234	698	8.7	−448
1961–1962	206	202	408	5.0	−233
1962–1963	542	894	1436	17.0	+116
1963–1964	346	656	1002	11.6	−657
1964–1965	95	250	345	3.9	−835
1965–1966	380	543	923	10.1	−10
1966–1967	432	568	1100	11.8	+455
1967–1968	307	712	1019	10.6	−11
1968–1969	236	833	1069	10.9	−543
1969–1970	502	1045	1547	15.3	−537
1970–1971	342	804	1146	11.1	+865
1971–1972	670	1018	1688	15.9	+1800
1972–1973	390	2435	2825	25.9	+1423
1973–1974	82	1584	1667	14.9	+506
1974–1975	260	2030	2290	19.9	+1062
1975–1976	395	1075	1470	12.5	+498

Source: Government of Bangladesh, Bureau of Statistics, *Statistical Yearbook of Bangladesh, 1975,* p. 259; Government of Bangladesh, Planning Commission, *Arthanaitik Shamikhya,* p. 193; Tables 6.1 and 6.23.

Note: Food gap equals requirement less net output. Calendar year requirement figures of Table 6.1 were related to fiscal year (for example, 1961 to 1960–1961) import figures. Similarly, calendar year food gap figures are shown against corresponding fiscal year.

that the annual imports of foodgrain in the 1960s were unrelated to the aggregate food gap of Bangladesh, although officials found one means or another to justify imports. Two factors have influenced the volume of foodgrain imports over the years. First, for political reasons the government subsidized price to the major urban areas and to some special interest groups. Second, beginning in the early 1960s, a large amount of surplus U.S. wheat was made available to the government under PL–480 Title I and II, which provided substantial budgetary support. It strengthened the position of the government, since under the provisions of the agreement, it was able to initiate a works program in the rural areas of East Pakistan (Bangladesh). The rural works program soon turned into a powerful instrument for mobilizing political support.[41] The government was naturally very enthusiastic about importing foodgrains under this program. Besides, it has been argued that availability of foodgrains under PL–480 had a dampening effect on the government and private efforts to promote domestic production.

There is little doubt that a considerable food gap existed in the country beginning in 1970–1971 despite a small surplus shown in 1973–1974. Between 1972–1973 and 1975–1976, Bangladesh imported about 8.3 million tons of foodgrains from abroad. During the first two years after liberation, just about all of the imports were financed by food aid. But later Bangladesh also purchased foodgrains in the commercial market. A number of factors adversely affected Bangladesh's ability to maintain a smooth import flow during the early years after liberation. First, import planning by the government was done on a very short term basis and without adequate information, which reduces its effectiveness to face an emergency situation. This was primarily because, unlike the early 1960s, the donors (particularly the United States) were unwilling to make long-term commitments regarding food supply. Second, donors insisted that Bangladesh use their vessels for the shipment of foodgrains, a practice that often delayed arrival of imports.[42] Third, as the international prices of foodgrains increased sharply and availability declined, Bangladesh's ability to make emergency purchases in commercial markets was severely curtailed. At a very critical moment in 1974, Bangladesh could not obtain U.S. government credit to purchase foodgrain. Furthermore, shipment of foodgrain under PL–480 was delayed because, presumably Bangladesh had disqualified itself by selling jute to Cuba. McHenry and Bird observe, "The U.S. government employed its food aid leverage in Bangladesh for the most trifling of political purposes."[43]

According to Islam, the import planning for 1974–1975 was based on a highly optimistic projection of domestic output of 13 million tons,[44] whereas the actual output turned out to be 11.2 million tons. What the import planners always overlooked is the extent of leakage of foodgrains through smuggling. The factors mentioned above, along with anomalies in import planning, resulted in the monthly import flow as given in Table 6.18. In 1974, during the two most difficult months (September and October), imports were among the lowest. Even earlier in the year, the import levels of January–April were much lower than those of 1973. These figures, as we noted earlier, were reflected in the end of the month stock figures (Table 6.2). It has been alleged that during this period the Bangladesh government did not take advantage of the possibility of diverting some foodgrains from India's import schedule, which the latter was favourably inclined to comply with. According to the suggested terms, the diverted foodgrains would have to be given back to India once Bangladesh's own foodgrain import came through. Apparently, the planning commission, for reasons best known to it, objected to this deal. One reason was, of course, that the commission had not anticipated any problem with the prospective inflow of aid-financed foodgrain imports.

Table 6.18. Monthly Import of Foodgrains into Bangladesh, July 1972–December 1975 (000 tons)

Month	1972	1973	1974	1975
January		228	38	195
February		194	90	77
March		467	99	173
April		212	147	177
May		179	224	291
June		126	135	424
July	355	83	291	176
August	295	159	225	197
September	272	263	29	93
October	161	287	76	214
November	227	59	190	108
December	109	83	149	247

Source: M. Alamgir, *Famine 1974: Political Economy of Mass Starvation in Bangladesh*, Statistical Annexe, Part I (Dacca: Bangladesh Institute of Development Studies, 1977), p. 48.

Internal Procurement

Procurement of foodgrains at the domestic market presented an alternative to importing foodgrains from abroad. In the past, the government had intervened in the market through internal procurement with the avowed purpose of stabilizing domestic prices (more so to provide price support to farmers), discouraging producers from consuming more than the requirement per capita, stopping smuggling from the border belt, augmenting emergency food stock and reducing speculative hoarding by farmers and traders. Despite the highly desirable objectives associated with the internal procurement of foodgrains, it has never been pursued vigorously by the government. McHenry and Bird observed, "Since it is much easier to order a shipment of food through the embassy in Washington than to spend time and money on a domestic procurement program, a definite complacency has settled over the bureaucracy."[45]

Up to 1975–1976 only rice was procured internally, but later wheat was also added to the list. The procurement operation is usually concentrated in the November–March period when the *aman* crop is harvested and marketed by farmers. A combination of voluntary and compulsory procurement methods were applied in different periods. It can be seen from the figures presented in Table 6.23, that the amount of internal procurement was rather small in all years except 1975 and 1976. In the 1960s, the highest amount procured was in 1964 (1.3 percent of net production). In the early 1970s internal foodgrain procurement was almost nil. Beginning in 1974, the government decided to take internal procurement more seriously than before. In that year, out of a target of 400,000 tons the actual amount procured was only 71,000 tons. A number of factors contributed to the failure of the procurement program in 1974 and its modest success in the following two years.

At no point in the 1950s and 1960s, was the government confronted with a real threat of famine. Therefore, it was never under pressure to build up an emergency food stock. In any case, as we mentioned earlier, beginning in the early 1960s, the government had relatively easy access to the U.S. surplus wheat supply. Until very recently, the procurement price was always lower than the market price; actually it was also lower than the harvest price. The latter comparison is important because it is during this period that the government procurement agents competed with traders to buy up the supply. Table 6.19 presents data on the harvest price and the internal procurement price of rice (aman) in the postliberation of Bangladesh.

When the internal procurement price was lower than the market price and the government attempted to procure foodgrain on a compulsory basis, it had a depressing effect on domestic production irrespective of the actual level of procurement. On the other hand, a procurement price higher than the harvest/market price creates certain problems. First, if the internal price is maintained at a much higher level than what it would otherwise have been, it produces an adverse effect on the well-being of deficit families. Second, it provides an incentive for the government purchasing agents to collude with the local traders in depriving the farmer of his due price.

In 1974, it was alleged that the government agents were not available to purchase foodgrains from farmers at the specified time. The farmers,

Table 6.19. Harvest Price and Internal Procurement Price of Aman Rice in Bangladesh, 1972–1973 to 1976–1977 (Tk./maund)

Year	Harvest Price	Internal Procurement Price
1972–1973	63	54
1973–1974	100	72
1974–1975	212	120
1975–1976	112	120
1976–1977	112	120

Source: Procurement price from M. Alamgir, Famine 1974: Political Economy of Mass Starvation in Bangladesh, Statistical Annexe, Part I (Dacca: Bangladesh Institute of Development Studies, 1977), p. 53. Harvest price from Government of Bangladesh, Bureau of Statistics, Statistical Yearbook of Bangladesh, 1979, p. 368.

Note: 1 maund = 82.29 pounds.

who brought their produce from a long distance, were then forced to sell to the local traders at a price lower than the procurement price. At times the government agents refused to purchase paddy/rice from the farmers, saying that the produce did not conform to the quality requirement. Again the farmers had no other alternative but to turn to the traders. Some agents did not aggressively pursue their task of procurement in the month of November and December of 1973 when the 1974 *aman* was harvested. By the time they became active, the market price had gone above the procurement price. In many cases, the agents were procuring 45 seers (92.58 pounds), instead of the standard 40 seers (82.29 pounds), for a maund (a unit of weight = 40 seers or 82.29 pounds) under different pretexts. Furthermore, they refused to give proper receipts of sale so that ultimately a significant proportion of the procured paddy/rice found its way to the private trading stock. On the whole, the 1974 procurement operation resulted in the farmers losing confidence in the program and the traders obtaining a greater control over food resources. In addition to the failure of the internal procurement effort in 1974, the government created an additional problem by restricting interdistrict movement of foodgrains through a normal trading channel, with an adverse effect on regional availability and prices. The result of the 1974 procurement drive was very poor despite the fact that the basis of procurement was compulsory and an attempt had been made to identify surplus farmers in each area through the local levy committees. This is because the levy committees were composed of the members of the ruling party and they reportedly allowed their sympathizers (who came largely from among the surplus farmers) to escape compulsory levy. The government thus lost an important opportunity to build up some emergency stock and discourage speculative hoarding, both of which would have contributed toward reducing suffering of the people in the later months of the year when famine visited the country.

The government had not developed appropriate procurement machinery in the past and, therefore, when it attempted to undertake a substantial procurement operation without adequate preparation, it failed completely to achieve its objective. Major institutional problems with respect to the procurement operation were: (1) identification of surplus farmers; (2) mobilization of adequate resources to finance the procurement operation; (3) making the procurement agents functionally more efficient and job conscious; (4) providing suitable storage facilities at the procurement centers; and (5) policing of the procured foodgrain in storage so as to avoid pilferage and other storage losses. In early 1977, the government, in an attempt to overcome some of the problems mentioned here, decided to extend credit to the private traders/purchasers to lift paddy/rice from the market on its behalf. It produced the perverse result of strengthening the speculative activities of traders, and the open market prices were pushed above the normal level. After a brief period of trial the government decided correctly to abandon this method of procurement.[46]

Government Distribution (Offtake) of Foodgrains

The imported and internally procured foodgrains are distributed by the government at a subsidized price through a system of rationing. The annual trend of government foodgrain distribution followed closely that of imports. Total distribution of both rice and wheat increased in the 1970s as compared with the 1960s (Table 6.23), the importance of wheat increasing over time. Government offtake as a percentage of requirement increased from 6.1 percent in 1961 to 19.3 percent in 1973, the figure for 1974 was 15.3 percent. In absolute terms, the total amount of foodgrain distributed by the government in 1974 was the lowest since liberation, except for 1976. There is a seasonal pattern in government offtake of foodgrains that is counter to the availability from internal production. Nineteen seventy-four was unusual in that there was little fluctuation by month, and the level was about the same as the 1973 average (Table 6.20), which meant a lower per capita offtake given the population growth.

Public distribution of foodgrains mostly benefits selected groups of population in the country. The distribution takes place under four major categories. The first is statutory rationing, covering six cities, and all

Table 6.20. Monthly Distribution of Foodgrains by Government in Bangladesh, 1973 and 1974 (000 tons)

Month	1973	1974
January	143	127
February	157	121
March	175	131
April	206	137
May	253	130
June	214	162
July	151	152
August	153	182
September	170	177
October	187	151
November	145	148
December	123	109

Source: M. Alamgir, *Famine 1974: Political Economy of Mass Starvation in Bangladesh,* Statistical Annexe, Part I (Dacca: Bangladesh Institute of Development Studies, 1977), pp. 49–50.

families within the city limits irrespective of income level are eligible to draw a weekly ration. The cities covered are Dacca, Narayanganj, Khulna, Rajshahi, Chittagong and Rangamati. The second system of rationing is called modified rationing. Only the low-income groups such as the day laborers in both rural and urban areas are covered under this system. The third system of distribution is relief and is earmarked for the people affected by natural calamities. The final category is termed "other" and it includes distribution to select groups such as the government employees, teachers and student dormitories, large-scale industrial enterprises having at least fifty employees, and priority groups (hospitals, jails, ansar, police, the Bangladesh Rifles and the Armed Forces). The distribution of foodgrains under statutory rationing and "others" is regular, but in other systems continuous supply is not assured. The per capita allotment is much higher under statutory rationing and for "other" groups than under modified rationing and relief. It is only under modified rationing and relief that the rural poor get any assistance, and an analysis of foodgrain distribution under different heads clearly reveals the bias in favor of large urban counties and the special select groups included under "others." In postliberation Bangladesh, the share of the three largest cities in total government offtake fluctuated between 18 and 45 percent (Table 6.21). According to the 1974 population census, these cities accounted for only 4.6 percent of the total population of the country. The total foodgrains distributed through statutory rationing and to the select "other" groups, was 41 percent and 58 percent of the total government offtake in 1973 and 1974 respectively. What these figures also suggest is that even under extremely difficult situations such as those prevailing in 1974, the government did not change the pattern of distribution in favor of the poor—in fact, modified ration and relief were a lower proportion of total ration in 1974 than 1973, implying that the rural poor received even less during the famine. The supply of subsidized foodgrains to the large urban centers and special interest groups was

Table 6.21. Distribution of Cereals through Statutory Rationing System in Bangladesh, 1972–1973 to 1976–1977 (000 tons)

Year	Dacca		Chittagong		Khulna		Distribution in 3 Cities as % of Total
	Rice	Wheat	Rice	Wheat	Rice	Wheat	
1972–1973	129	142	35	97	22	53	18.3
1973–1974	71	208	92	40	10	92	29.7
1974–1975	75	563	20	54	14	71	45.4
1975–1976	117	75	38	18	34	25	18.4
1976–1977	145	63	43	13	42	18	22.0

Source: *Monthly Statisical Bulletin* 6(10):40–41 (October 1977).

maintained at all cost. The large urban centers also claim the major share of the preferred cereal, that is, rice distributed through the rationing system. In 1973, statutory rationing areas and other select groups received 99.8 percent of the total rice offtake.

The monthly pattern of distribution of cereals through the modified rationing system and relief in 1973 and 1974 is shown in Table 6.22. It is apparent that in comparison with the total population involved, the amount of foodgrain distributed was very small.

Table 6.22. Distribution of Cereal Through Modified Rationing and Relief (000 tons)

Months	1973			1974		
	Modified Rationing	Relief	Total	Modified Rationing	Relief	Total
January	62,377 (43.5)	10,595 (7.4)	72,972 (50.9)	43,474 (34.2)	2,862 (2.3)	46,336 (36.5)
February	76,849 (49.0)	6,002 (3.8)	82,846 (52.8)	45,254 (37.5)	2,736 (2.3)	47,990 (39.7)
March	91,622 (52.2)	10,553 (6.0)	102,175 (58.2)	53,386 (40.7)	2,886 (2.2)	56,272 (42.9)
April	136,005 (65.9)	5,930 (2.9)	141,935 (68.8)	48,130 (35.1)	2,518 (1.8)	50,648 (36.9)
May	168,267 (66.5)	12,111 (4.8)	180,378 (71.3)	56,198 (43.4)	1,458 (1.1)	57,656 (44.5)
June	131,440 (61.5)	10,028 (4.7)	141,468 (66.1)	58,514 (36.2)	3,861 (2.4)	62,375 (38.6)
July	63,785 (42.2)	9,144 (6.0)	72,929 (48.2)	62,266 (40.8)	1,621 (1.1)	63,887 (41.9)
August	78,041 (51.0)	7,372 (4.8)	85,413 (55.8)	77,079 (42.3)	10,215 (5.6)	87,284 (47.9)
September	98,761 (58.0)	5,615 (3.3)	104,376 (61.3)	67,432 (38.0)	14,666 (8.3)	82,098 (46.3)
October	112,965 (60.5)	5,595 (3.0)	118,560 (63.5)	34,823 (23.0)	32,456 (21.4)	67,279 (44.5)
November	70,463 (48.5)	4,044 (2.8)	74,507 (51.3)	35,388 (23.8)	31,700 (21.4)	67,088 (45.3)
December	47,738 (38.8)	4,318 (3.5)	52,056 (42.4)	26,488 (24.3)	9,412 (8.7)	35,900 (33.0)
Total	1,138,308 (54.8)	91,307 (4.4)	1,229,615 (59.2)	608,492 (35.2)	116,391 (6.7)	724,883 (41.9)

Source: M. Alamgir, *Famine 1974: Political Economy of Mass Starvation in Bangladesh,* Statistical Annexe, Part I (Dacca: Bangladesh Institute of Development Studies, 1977), pp. 49–50.

Note: Numbers in parentheses show percentage of total offtake.

Foodgrain Availability—Total and Per Capita

From the components discussed above, we can calculate the foodgrain availability so that a causal analysis of famine based on these figures may be misleading. First, the annual aggregate data do not reveal the total availability of foodgrains shows a consistent upward trend except in a few years, but given the population growth, per capita availability shows considerable fluctuation. As the figures suggest, in all years under consideration, the per capita availability of foodgrains was higher than the minimum requirement of 14.4 ounces/day. However, availability per capita was lower in the 1970s as compared with the 1960s. In 1974, the famine year, per capita availability was higher than all other years in the 1970s, it was actually 14 percent above the level of 1973. One could hardly anticipate a famine in 1974 from the availability figures shown in Table 6.23.

There are a number of problems with the figures of per capita availability so that a casual analysis of famine based on these figures may be misleading. First, the annual aggregate data do not reveal the seasonal and regional and by income pattern of foodgrain availability. Second, questions have been raised with respect to the reliability of the basic data used to estimate foodgrain availability. Third, figures presented in Table 6.23 do not take account of the annual private and trading stock build up and leakage of foodgrains through smuggling and destruction by natural hazards (fire, flood, cyclone, and so forth). Let us consider the second point first.

Problem with Production Estimate. Production data for the 1960s and 1970s have an upward bias. The bias in the data for the 1960s resulted from the fact that the official estimates did not rely entirely on the sample crop cutting method of estimation (objective). Instead, there was considerable emphasis on the subjective or eye estimation method. In the 1960s, the extent of the upward bias was found to have had fluctuated between 2.3 percent in 1966–1967 and 14.4 percent in 1959–1960 of the official production data.[47] The official figures of the 1970s were based on the objective estimation method but an upward bias was introduced in the final figures released by the government in order to indicate to the aid donors that Bangladesh was able to make progress in her effort to increase production of foodgrains.[48] It is interesting to note that the donors were willing to go along with the request of the Bangladesh government for food aid irrespective of the domestic performance, but on record they insisted on some evidence that appropriate measures were being taken to increase food production. The Bangladesh

Table 6.23. Per Capita Availability of Foodgrains in Bangladesh, 1961–1976

Year	Net Output (000 ton)			Government Offtake			Internal Procurement (000 ton)	Total Available for Consumption (000 ton)	Population (000)	Per Capita Availability (Oz/day)	Index of Per Capita Availability
	Rice	Wheat	Total	Rice	Wheat	Total					
1961	8,416	29	8,445	317	174	491	26	8,910	54,531	16.0	100.00
1962	8,405	35	8,440	449	429	878	10	9,308	55,964	16.3	101.88
1963	8,267	40	8,307	496	653	1,149	4	9,452	57,434	16.2	101.25
1964	9,270	31	9,301	138	374	512	125	9,688	58,944	16.1	100.63
1965	9,675	31	9,706	364	573	937	12	10,631	60,492	17.3	108.13
1966	9,082	32	9,114	512	522	1,034	92	10,056	62,082	15.9	100.00
1967	8,837	52	8,889	346	536	882	7	9,764	63,713	15.0	93.75
1968	9,548	52	9,600	318	574	892	22	10,470	65,388	15.7	98.13
1969	10,301	83	10,384	328	667	995	9	11,370	67,106	16.6	103.75
1970	10,544	93	10,637	393	955	1,348	6	11,979	68,869	17.1	106.88
1971	9,401	99	9,500	495	751	1,246	6	10,740	70,679	14.9	93.13
1972	8,735	102	8,837	673	1,771	2,444	10	11,271	72,535	15.3	95.63
1973	9,413	81	9,494	153	1,925	2,078	—	11,572	74,441	15.3	95.63
1974	10,600	98	10,698	131	1,597	1,728	71	12,355	76,398	15.9	99.38
1975	10,332	104	10,436	386	1,404	1,790	204	12,022	78,405	14.9	93.13
1976	11,108	194	11,302	553	754	1,310	395	12,217	80,466	14.8	92.50

Source: M. Alamgir, *Famine 1974: Political Economy of Mass Starvation in Bangladesh*, Statistical Annexe, Part I (Dacca: Bangladesh Institute of Development Studies, 1977), pp. 5–48; Government of Bangladesh, Bureau of Statistics, *Statistical Pocketbook of Bangladesh, 1978*, p. 69.

Note: Total availability for consumption equals net output plus government offtake less internal procurement.

officials are, however, confident about the effectiveness of their own political counter leverage against the donors (prospect of famine, internal chaos, left-wing take over, and regional instability) so that they continue to plan for large food imports while doing little on the domestic production front except perhaps manipulating production estimates. Besides, even with an inflated production series, the government can claim a substantial "food gap" by using a high level of per capita foodgrain requirement (15.5 ounces/day),[49] knowing full well that this is never achieved in reality. There is yet another dimension to the foodgrain production estimates in Bangladesh that has something to do with the need for striking an administrative balance between the Ministry of Agriculture and the Food Ministry.

Islam puts it in the following way

> The Ministry of Agriculture tended to lean towards high estimates, since as a ministry in charge of increasing agricultural production, a high output appeared to reflect favourably on its performance; the Food Ministry had bias towards a lower estimate, because if there was a shortfall in output, there would be pressure to distribute more food through the public distribution system, which it would not be able to meet.[50]

Seasonality in Foodgrain Availability. Since the upward bias in the production estimate was common to all years, it is difficult to comment on its implication separately for 1974 unless one can obtain a reliable estimate of the absolute level of bias in different years. While this bias was estimated for the 1960s, no such estimate exists for the 1970s. This is mainly because the official adjustments to the production figures in the 1970s were essentially of an ad hoc nature. However, it is well known that this bias is mostly concentrated in the estimation of *aman* output and therefore, in a year when the later crops such as *boro* and *aus* do not perform as well as one had expected, the difficulty faced by the people in the lean period (July–October) is further aggravated. In 1974, the total output of both *boro* and *aus* was below the trend although in per capita terms the *boro* output was higher in 1974 than in 1973. However, the per capita *aus* output was lower. This implies that in 1974, the seasonal pattern of foodgrain availability was more uneven than in normal years. The seasonal fluctuation in the availability of foodgrains was further contributed to by the pattern of monthly foodgrain distribution by the government under the rationing system. The normal counter-seasonal pattern with respect to domestic crop production was not maintained in the government distribution of foodgrains in 1974. Although we do not have firm data on the seasonal availability of foodgrain in 1974, we can tentatively suggest that the availability during the

July–October 1974 period was lower than what is suggested by the annual aggregate figure in Table 6.23.

Yet another factor that may have had some influence on the seasonal availability of foodgrains is the time pattern of market arrivals (sale) of various types of paddy. Related data are presented in Table 6.24. Two patterns emerge clearly from these figures. Immediate postharvest sales either increased or remained unchanged for all rice crops except *aus* in the nonfamine area in 1974 as compared with 1973, which could, for our purpose here, be considered as a normal year. One reason for such increased sale of paddy at this time was perhaps the increased cash flow requirement of households due to the overall price increase. A second but not so important reason was the attempted compulsory procurement of paddy. The major victims of both were the small farmers who were forced to come back to the market earlier than usual to purchase foodgrains presumably at a much higher price, a point that will be analyzed in the next chapter. As we shall explain later, a large part of this early sale in 1974 had been pre-empted by speculators and smugglers. A second pattern that emerges is that the later sales of paddy were prolonged and a substantially higher proportion of all crops in all areas was sold after 8 weeks in 1974 as compared with 1973. It suggests that surplus farmers were withholding paddy sales in the hope of benefitting from price rise. This is reflected more sharply in the sale pattern of *aus* than in that of other crops. In the nonfamine areas, the proportion of immediate postharvest *aus* sale actually declined from 29 percent in 1973 to 23 percent in 1974, and the compensatory increase in sales took place in the post eight-week period. This has been partly contributed to by the fact

Table 6.24. Time Pattern of Sale of Paddy by Survey Villagers

Area and Time Pattern	1973			1974		
	Aman	Boro	Aus	Aman	Boro	Aus
All villages						
Within 2 weeks	18	27	28	21	27	24
2 to 8 weeks	42	25	34	40	23	33
8 weeks and above	40	48	39	40	50	43
Famine areas						
Within 2 weeks	7	28	23	7	27	26
2 to 8 weeks	35	25	37	33	23	30
8 weeks and above	58	47	40	60	50	44
Nonfamine areas						
Within 2 weeks	24	—	29	28	—	23
2 to 8 weeks	47	17	33	42	—	33
8 weeks and above	29	83	38	30	—	43
Total	100	100	100	100	100	100

that difficulties with *aman* sowing due to flood had given rise to speculation about a poor output in winter. In other words, unlike other years, the surplus farmers and traders could consider carrying rice stocks into the next *aman* season. As it turned out, the 1975 *aman* output was 10.4 percent lower than the 1974 output, and the rice price after going down slightly in the months of November and December 1974, increased again continuously up to April of 1975.

Leakages Through Smuggling and Storage Loss. Two other factors figure importantly in the total availability (annual and seasonal) of foodgrains—leakages through smuggling and storage loss and destruction. Storage loss is significant even in normal years (3 to 5 percent). In 1974, it was probably higher because of heavy rains and flood. The official reports on the 1974 flood mention storage loss but do not give separate figures. From our field survey we obtained some data on the storage loss due to flood from the *langarkhana* inmates. But the village households did not report any storage loss. We, therefore, do not suggest any figure for total storage loss since it would be highly speculative. But if we are bold enough to apply a 5 percent loss in storage in 1974, the per capita daily availability turns out to be 15.1 ounces which is still higher than the minimum requirement (14.4 ounces/day).

Even more difficult than the above, is to estimate the volume of rice smuggled across the border into neighboring India. Some observers believe that the amount involved is substantial and claim that food aid encourages smuggling.[51]

There is no direct estimate of smuggling except the figures generated by the Bangladesh Rifles on the value of incoming and outgoing smuggled items seized at the border posts throughout Bangladesh. From the list of main items smuggled in/out, we find that a wide variety of goods are involved and that, between 1972 and 1974, there was some change in the composition of illegal trade. The important outgoing items were, Bangladesh currency, gold/silver, fish, jute, rice/paddy, medicine, gunny bags, fertilizer, and so forth, and the incoming items were birri and leaves (indigenous cigarettes), cattle, betel nuts/leaves, cloth, machinery/spares, cotton, thread, car/truck, metals, tobacco, and so forth. If seizure can be taken as an indicator of the actual volume involved then according to the data provided to us by the Bangladesh Rifles, the magnitude of smuggling more than doubled between 1972 and 1974, growth was higher for inflow than outflow. The total amount involved in smuggling could be estimated if one had prior knowledge of the probability of seizure at the border. Rahim obtained a crude estimate of this probability and used it to estimate the total value of smuggling outflow in 1972–1973.[52] He did not make a separate estimate for foodgrains. The ranks of seized items according to value are presented in Table 6.25. The rank of rice/paddy was rather low. If the popular belief regarding the volume of rice/paddy smuggling was correct then the above ranking means that the actual outflow of rice takes place largely through unguarded or difficult-to-guard routes.

It should be noted that Bangladesh has about fourteen hundred miles of land border and a little less of open sea coast, any portion of which could be used for smuggling. It is almost impossible for any official force to police such a vast area. The job of guarding the border areas is made even more difficult because historically a natural trade relationship existed between many areas on either side of the border. Organized smugglers often take advantage of such soft spots. Finally, border policing cannot be very effective if smuggling operations are carried out

Table 6.25. Ranks of Smuggled (Outgoing and Incoming) Items Seized at Border Posts of Bangladesh, 1972–1973 and 1973–1974

Items	Outgoing		Items	Incoming	
	1972–1973	1973–1974		1972–1973	1973–1974
Currency	1	3	Birri and leaves	1	1
Gold/silver	8	1	Cattle	3	7
Fish	3	2	Betelnuts/leaves	4	3
Jute	2	10	Cloth	2	2
Rice/paddy	12	7	Spices	10	17
Gunny bags	5	6	Machinery/spares	8	6
Fertilizers	14	13	Cotton	9	11
Medicine	9	4	Catchu	11	17
Cycle	6	15	Thread	6	4
Flour	17		Timber	12	17
Eggs & milk powder	17	5	Pen	15	17
Skins	15	9	Orange	15	12
Boat	4	12	Car/truck	5	5
Dal	11	22	Elastic	13	14
Chilly	10	22	Scent	14	9
Wrist watch	16	14	Plastic articles	15	17
Turmeric	11	16	Launch/Engine	7	17
Playing cards	7	22	boats		
Blades	13	22	Soyabin oil	10	16
Bangles	17	19	Chemicals	16	15
Flour	17	8	Cloves	16	16
Molasses	17	21	Metals	16	8
Sugar	17	20	Tobacco	16	10
Salt	17	17	Opium	16	13
Washing powder		18			
Cumin seeds	10	11			

Source: Bangladesh Rifles.
Note: Ranks are based on the value of items seized.

with administrative and political support of the ruling elite, as hinted by McHenry and Bird.[53] We mentioned in Chapter 4 that government did not admit that smuggling was an important factor affecting the foodgrain availability in early 1974 but this attitude later changed and the government felt obligated to deploy the army to stop smuggling across the border. In the last quarter of the year all statements on the existing food situation by leaders of the ruling party mentioned smuggling as an important cause of the crisis.

Notwithstanding this admission about continued foodgrain smuggling, there was no basis for making even a rough estimate of the magnitude involved. Reddaway and Rahman carried out an exercise to estimate the scale of smuggling out of Bangladesh. For rice, they used two different approaches:[54] the first involved comparison of the rice price in the border belt with that in a neighboring town, with the view that, in the case of large scale smuggling, the border belt price would be higher than the neighboring town price, the reverse finding implying that smuggling was not significant. Comparing prices of eight pairs of places, they concluded that the volume of rice smuggling was not significant. If all movements of rice in Bangladesh followed exactly the routes selected by Reddaway and Rahman then perhaps their conclusion could have been accepted, even though the quality of the data used could still be questioned. They considered only a very small sample of places and these were selected somewhat arbitrarily and as such could not reflect the overall situation. More importantly, they ruled out the possibility that smuggling was done by the big operators who collected rice at places inland and moved it across the border by boats, barges, trucks, and so forth. Our field investigators from almost all areas reported use of these means for smuggling.[55] In Bangladesh, the process of foodgrain price formation and the pattern of foodgrain movement is much more complex than what is suggested by Reddaway and Rahman.

The second approach used by Reddaway and Rahman was "based on a direct comparison of rice prices on either side of the border, using the black market rate of exchange."[56] Using data for only two places, Comilla in Bangladesh and Agartala in India, they concluded that the "figures, which ran from August 1974 to November 1974, consistently showed that the Indian price was substantially lower than the Bangladesh price, even when converted at the black-market rate of exchange; there was, in consequence no apparent incentive to smuggle rice from Comilla to Agartala."[57]

This approach has a number of shortcomings. First a sample of only one pair of places cannot be very reliable. Second, Comilla is not a usual surplus area, but draws its own supply from other places. Third, the period considered is different from that used in the first approach and the authors do not explain the use of a different reference period. The rice that was smuggled out in 1974 was lifted from the market soon after the *aman* harvest. In the months of August to November 1974 there was no harvest and all markets in the country reported absolute shortage, which could be attributed to the withdrawal by hoarders and smugglers in earlier months (Reddaway and Rahman chose a period after the main smuggling had taken place). Finally, to the extent to which illegal trade obtained its supply from imported foodgrain, the effective cost of purchase (for the smuggler) was much lower than was reflected in the market price. The relative profitability calculation of the type carried out by Reddaway and Rahman should have taken this into account. We should make it clear, though, that while we have some reservations about the methodology adopted by Reddaway and Rahman to estimate the scale of foodgrain smuggling, their pioneering effort should be appreciated.

We take a straightforward approach to the problem of smuggling. We feel that given the length of the border with India, the difficulty of policing it, and a historic trade relationship between markets on either side of the border, movement of a certain amount of foodgrains and other items across the border is unavoidable and could actually be considered a normal feature. The food system of Bangladesh should be studied taking this factor as a given datum. Our interest here is only to find out whether the scale of smuggling was excessive, such that the domestic food system was unable to absorb it without giving way to a significant increase in prices.

We have used an indirect method to answer this question. We start by estimating a foodgrain absorption function applying the method of least squares to the time series data for the period 1956–1957 to 1970–1971. The official availability figures presented in Table 6.23 are taken as domestic absorption. It includes actual consumption, normal storage loss, and normal leakage through smuggling. The absorption function is specified as follows:

$$F = f(DP, y) \tag{6.1}$$

where F = foodgrain absorption per capita measured in pound/year
    DP = domestic price of rice per maund in Taka
and y = per capita income in Taka at 1959–1960 factor cost.

The function (6.1) is specified as linear.[58] In regression analysis DP has been deflated by PF the nonrice foodgrain price index (1959–1960 = 100) to eliminate the effect of general inflation in other food items. Three separate functions are fitted to retail price of medium rice ($DPMR$), wholesale price of medium rice ($DPMW$), and wholesale price of coarse rice (*DPCW*). The equations apparently give good fit as measured by corrected R^2 (Table 6.26). Coefficients of both price and income variables are highly significant. Moreover, the Durbin-Watson statistic does not indicate presence of autocorrelation in these estimated equations.

We then proceed to test if the additional observations for the post-1971 period (1971–1972, 1972–1973, 1973–1974, and 1974–1975) belong to the same population or not. Applying Chow-test,[59] we reject the null hypothesis that the additional observations obey the same relation as the first. Furthermore, Table 6.27 shows that the predicted values of foodgrain absorption in the post-1971 period are systematically lower than the observed values by a wide margin. Before we jump to any conclusions, we must point out that in certain cases the predicted values turn out to be very low, actually lower than what one would expect even under extremely distressing circumstances. We had some problems in estimating comparable per capita income figures for prediction due to noncomparable GDP series between pre- and post-1971 periods, absence of a consistent GDP deflator series, and some doubts about the underlying population estimates. However, while low predicted value could be due partly to an underestimation of the per capita income, this is unlikely to be sufficient to explain away the difference between the observed and the predicted values.

Since the homogeneity hypothesis has been rejected, one could argue that there has been a significant shift in the underlying structural relationship in the post-1971 period. We do not have a sufficient number of observations to run a separate regression analysis that would be meaningful. In any case, looking separately at the prediction for

Table 6.26.   Regression Results: Domestic Absorption Functions

Dependent Variable	Constant	Independent Variables		$\bar{R}^2$	SEE	DW
		DP	Y			
1956–1957 to 1970–1971						
(a) F	−29.77	−436.6[a]	1.843[a]	0.8062	14.05	1.41
	(0.4829)	(4.222)	(7.639)			
(b) F	0.9806	−424.0[a]	1.699[a]	0.8024	14.19	1.51
	(0.01549)	(4.154)	(7.303)			
(c) F	−40.17	−540.6[a]	1.912[a]	0.8090	13.95	1.32
	(0.6581)	(4.272)	(7.770)			

Note: Figures in parentheses are *t*-statistic. The specification of the domestic price variable (*DP*) was as follows: Equation (a) = Domestic retail price of medium quality rice (*DPMR*); Equation (b) = Domestic wholesale price of medium quality rice (*DPMW*); Equation (c) = Domestic wholesale price of coarse quality rice (*DPCW*).

[a]Significant at 1 percent level.

Table 6.27. Predicted and Observed Values of Foodgrain Absorption in Bangladesh During 1972–1973, 1973–1974, and 1974–1975

Year/Equation	Domestic Foodgrain Absorption Per Capita (F) (pound/yr.)	
	Predicted	Observed
1972–1973		
(a)	255	352
(b)	257	352
(c)	229	352
1973–1974		
(a)	217	363
(b)	230	363
(c)	211	363
1974–1975		
(a)	271	340
(b)	281	340
(c)	259	340

Note: (a), (b), and (c) refer to corresponding equations in Table 6.26.

1975–1976, we see that the observed value falls within 1 percent confidence interval of the predicted value, which makes us reconsider the question of a permanent shift in the underlying structural relationship. It seems plausible, therefore, that the official observed absorption figures for 1972–1973, 1973–1974, and 1974–1975 do not represent normal absorption as defined above. The large positive residual can be attributed to storage loss over and above the normal allowance, excessive leakage through smuggling, and annual stock buildup by traders and households. Actually, a part could also be attributed to the systematic upward bias in the estimation of domestic availability of foodgrains.[60]

On the basis of the analysis presented, we can suggest a number of conclusions, although they may embody a certain amount of speculation. First, during the first few years after liberation, actual availability of foodgrain in Bangladesh was significantly lower than the observed (official) figures. Second, in the three years considered in Table 6.27, foodgrain availability probably fell short of a minimum requirement level. Third, although a precise figure cannot be quoted, excessive smuggling was a feature of the food system of Bangladesh during the period under consideration. Once the border with India was virtually closed following the political change in 1975, such leakage was drastically reduced. This shows up, as we mentioned before, in the fact that for at least 1975–1976 the official absorption figure was found to fall within an acceptable distance of the predicted value. One may question our methodology, but one cannot altogether reject the hypothesis that the 1974 famine in Bangladesh was partly caused by foodgrain availability decline.

REGIONAL STOCK AND AVAILABILITY

Stock

Data are available on the stock of foodgrain held by the government in different local storage depots (LSD) throughout the country. Comparable data for private and trading stock are not easy to come by. However, if we are considering only the beginning of the year stock, then we can ignore the private and trading stock carryover since the amount is small. Here we attempt to present a picture prevailing at mid-1974 because the famine symptoms became more apparent then. For a complete assessment of the situation, it would be important to estimate stocks with households and traders but unfortunately we do not have any basis to carry out this exercise. We therefore look at the government stock alone, which, as we mentioned earlier, is a good indicator of the preparedness of the authority to meet a food crisis. The reason we consider foodgrain stock only at the local storage depots (as opposed to central storage depots and silos) is that the allotment to the ration shops for distribution among households is made from these points.

There was considerable variation in the total and per capita stock of foodgrains among different centers. In almost all centers the stock level was much lower than that of 1973. During our survey, many district and local level officials admitted that on a number of occasions during 1974, the foodgrain stock at local storage depots was seriously depleted, and they were forced to temporatily suspend normal distribution. The regional stock situation should be considered with the fact that, in 1974, movement of foodgrains within the country became difficult because of disruptions of the transportation system due to floods. We have already mentioned that movement of private stocks was seriously curtailed because of the interdistrict cordoning that was imposed in early 1974. The ability of the government to move foodgrains from the ports to central storage depots and then to local storage depots was adversely affected by the depletion of the rolling stock of the Bangladesh Railway following the 1971 liberation war. Inland water transport and road transport (trucks) carried a higher proportion of foodgrains in the 1970s than before. Bangladesh received a large fleet of trucks through the United Nations soon after liberation but by 1974 it was almost all scrapped due to poor maintenance. In any case, there have been competing demands for carrying space on all types of transport in recent years and consequently the distribution of foodgrains (like the distribution of other essentials) to different regions has suffered delays.

Availability

From relations (2.7), (2.8), and (2.9) of Chapter 2 we know that foodgrain availability (total and per capita) at the regional level is determined by output, government offtake, private stock, changes in private and trading stock, net interregional imports, internal procurement, and leakages. Unfortunately, for Bangladesh we only have reliable data by district on output and government offtake. For annual availability, we can ignore private and trading stock changes. Internal procurement of foodgrains was small in all years, and, at the district level the figures do not make much difference. Interdistrict movement of foodgrains through a private trading channel is important, but, as we mentioned before, in 1974 it was restricted. Districtwide data on leakages are almost impossible to obtain. We therefore use the production and offtake data to obtain a broad order of magnitude of the foodgrain availability per capita in different districts of Bangladesh in 1973 and 1974. Domestic production of wheat is not considered here since the amount is very small. First we look at the district level rice production data as shown in Table 6.28. The *aman* output of 1974 was higher than that of 1973 in all districts except three—Pabna, Barisal, and Patuakhali. For Patuakhali the decline was sharp, (41.9 per cent). This can be attributed to the severe cyclonic storm of December 1973. Similarly, the *boro* and *aus* output registered an increase in most districts with a few exceptions (for example, Tangail, Sylhet, Khulna, and Patuakhali for *boro*, and Chittagong, Noakhali, Comilla, Barisal, and Patuakhali for *aus*). In terms of total rice output only Barisal (9.6 percent) and Patuakhali (33.0 percent) experienced a decline in 1974 as compared with 1973. For the average region, the per capita net output is a good indicator of availability since the benefit of the government offtake is largely limited to specific groups and areas. Using this criterion it is found that in 1973, per capita net output of ten districts was lower than the minimum requirement (0.147 tons) whereas in 1974 such districts were only five (that is population rise did not outstrip production rise). Adding government offtake (Table 6.30) to net output one finds that per capita availability of foodgrains in 1974 was below the minimum requirement in Dacca, Faridpur, Pabna, and Kushtia only (that is, government transfers had evened out availability slightly [Table 6.29]). The per capita availability of foodgrains in 1974 was higher in thirteen districts, and lower in the remaining six districts than in 1973. It is interesting to note that among the districts experiencing a decline in per capita availability, only the Dacca district had per capita availability of foodgrains below the minimum requirement (that is, distribution between districts was more equitable) partly due to government offtake. In the absence of data on other components of availability at the district level, it is difficult to link the annual aggregate data to the 1974 famine. In particular, the interdistrict variation in availability as shown in Table 6.29, does not seem to be correlated with other indexes of famine that we examined earlier. However, it is evident that foodgrain availability in many districts in 1974 would fall below the minimum requirement level, once adjustment is made for storage loss, leakage through smuggling, and interdistrict movement.

We made an attempt to capture the seasonal dimension of regional availability by making a separate estimate for the period July–October 1974 for each district. From our survey data we found that about 18 percent of the *boro* output is marketed by the farmers, out of which about 9 percent is marketed two months after the harvest, that is, after July. We assumed that the *aman* output and the rest of *boro* output is largely consumed by the end of June. Thus, we calculated the foodgrain availability during July–October as (0.9 (*aus* output) + 0.09 (*boro* output) + government offtake). It should be noted that some amount of output is carried over beyond June, but it is assumed here that this amount cancels out with what is carried over beyond October from the availability figure estimated above. The resulting figures for July–October 1974 in per capita terms are presented in Table 6.29. It is found that as many as eleven districts experienced availability shortfall measured against a requirement level of 14.4 ounces/day/per capita. Some of the districts show a much higher level of per capita availability, which could probably be due to our inability to capture the interregional movement of foodgrains. Two of the famine districts, Rangpur and Mymensingh, were included among the above minimum level availability districts.

The distribution of famine intensity in 1974 could not be explained entirely by the district level availability figures as estimated above. In addition to making allowance for storage loss, smuggling and interdistrict movement, there is need for an analysis of the intradistrict distribution of food resources among various localities as well as among various classes of people. Both are somewhat affected by the pattern of government offtake of foodgrains under different rationing schemes within each district. Data presented in Table 6.30 suggest that on the whole, districts with statutory rationing received much more in per capita terms than other districts, but the primary beneficiaries were the residents of the major urban centers located in those districts. Concentrating our attention on the critical four-month period from July to

Table 6.28. Production of Rice by Districts, 1973 and 1974

Districts		Aman	1973 Boro	Aus	Total	Per Capita Total Net Output (ton)	Aman	1974 Boro	Aus	Total	Per Capita Total Net Output (ton)	Aman	% Change over 1973 Boro	Aus	Total
Dacca		276	211	138	625	0.079	305	216	154	675	0.082	+10.5	+2.4	+11.6	+8.0
	%	44	34	22	100		45	32	23	100					
Kishoreganj		224	315	99	638 ⎫		291	318	96	705 ⎫		+29.9	+1.0	−3.0	+10.5
	%	35	49	16	100 ⎬ 0.196		41	45	14	100 ⎬ 0.221					
Mymensingh		478	116	277	871 ⎭		621	125	319	1,065 ⎭		+29.9	+7.8	+15.2	+22.3
	%	55	13	32	100		58	12	30	100					
Tangail		141	58	65	264	0.125	166	55	101	322	0.146	+17.7	−5.2	+55.4	+22.0
	%	53	22	25	100		52	17	31	100					
Faridpur		198	67	138	403	0.098	237	71	176	484	0.112	+19.7	+6.0	+27.5	+20.1
	%	49	17	34	100		49	15	36	100					
Chittagong		299	183	162	644	0.144	372	194	159	725	0.155	+24.4	+6.0	−1.9	+12.6
	%	47	28	25	100		51	27	22	100					
Chittagong Hill Tracts		14	15	38	67	0.130	38	17	38	93	0.173	+171.4	+13.3	0.0	+38.8
	%	21	22	57	100		41	18	41	100					
Noakhali		277	78	150	505	0.154	297	147	94	538	0.157	+7.2	+88.5	−37.3	+6.5
	%	55	15	30	100		55	27	18	100					
Comilla		408	151	246	805	0.136	515	227	94	836	0.136	+26.2	+50.3	−61.8	+3.9
	%	51	19	30	100		62	27	11	100					
Sylhet		415	408	145	968	0.200	574	293	201	1,068	0.212	+38.3	−28.2	+38.6	+10.3
	%	43	42	15	100		54	27	19	100					
Rajshahi		405	82	151	638	0.147	405	120	154	679	0.150	0.0	+46.3	+2.0	+6.4
	%	63	13	24	100		60	17	23	100					
Dinajpur		327	14	163	504	0.193	485	14	167	666	0.244	+48.3	0.0	+2.5	+3.21
	%	65	3	32	100		72	3	25	100					

Table 6.28 (continued)

Rangpur	631	33	294	958	0.173	775	51	296	1,122	0.194	+22.8	+54.5	+0.7	+17.1
%	66	3	31	100		69	5	26	100					
Bogra	266	34	80	380	0.168	326	40	112	478	0.202	+22.6	+17.6	+40.0	+25.8
%	70	9	21	100		68	8	24	100					
Pabna	143	41	67	251	0.088	135	60	87	282	0.095	−5.6	+46.3	+29.9	+12.4
%	57	16	27	100		48	21	31	100					
Khulna	248	38	39	325	0.089	377	32	53	462	0.121	+52.0	−15.8	+35.9	+42.2
%	76	12	12	100		82	7	11	100					
Barisal	360	130	174	664	0.166	334	147	119	600	0.144	−7.2	+13.1	−31.6	−9.6
%	54	20	26	100		55	25	20	100					
Patuakhali	234	69	39	342	0.225	136	64	29	229	0.144	−41.9	−7.2	−25.6	−33.0
%	68	20	12	100		59	28	13	100					
Jessore	192	21	213	426	0.126	241	26	264	531	0.151	+25.5	+23.8	+23.9	+24.6
%	45	5	50	100		45	5	50	100					
Kushtia	51	5	124	180	0.094	69	5	147	221	0.111	+35.3	0.0	+18.5	+22.8
%	28	3	69	100		31	2	67	100					
Total	5,587	2,070	2,802	10,459	0.128	6,699	2,220	2,859	11,778	0.139	+19.9	+7.2	+1.8	+12.6
%	53	20	27	100		57	19	24	100					

Source: M. Alamgir, *Famine 1974: Political Economy of Mass Starvation in Bangladesh*, Statistical Annexe, Part I (Dacca: Bangladesh Institute of Development Studies, 1977.

243

Table 6.29. Per Capita Availability of Foodgrains by District (ounce/day)

Districts	1973	1974	% Change	July–October 1974
Dacca	14.5	13.8	−4.58	11.1
Mymensingh	20.6	22.8	+10.68	16.4
Tangail	14.7	15.3	+4.08	13.7
Faridpur	12.0	13.5	+12.50	13.5
Chittagong	18.4	19.7	+7.07	15.8
Chittagong Hill Tract	14.8	14.4	−2.70	21.8
Noakhali	17.8	16.7	−6.18	10.4
Comilla	16.1	14.9	−7.45	6.8
Sylhet	21.4	22.1	+3.27	13.9
Rajshahi	15.6	15.8	+1.28	11.2
Dinajpur	20.4	25.1	+23.04	18.1
Rangpur	18.3	20.1	+9.84	15.2
Bogra	19.3	20.8	+7.77	14.3
Pabna	10.4	10.8	+3.85	9.9
Khulna	13.8	16.2	+17.39	8.6
Barisal	18.6	16.0	−13.98	11.1
Patuakhali	24.1	15.7	−34.85	8.1
Jessore	14.6	16.3	+11.64	22.1
Kushtia	12.0	12.8	+6.67	22.2

Source: Government of Bangladesh, Directorate of Procurement, Distribution and Rationing, and author's own calculation.

October, we find that in 1974 the government offtake was lower than in 1973 in twelve districts, which included Rangpur and Mymensingh, two of the worst famine-affected areas. Interestingly enough, this list also includes Dacca and Khulna, which have statutory rationing areas. That Rangpur and Mymensingh revealed a higher than minimum average availability of foodgrains per capita during July–October 1974 (Table 6.29) despite a significant shortfall in the government offtake over the previous year (11 percent and 42 percent respectively; see Table 6.30), reaffirms the point made earlier that estimates of physical availability of foodgrains at the national and regional levels may be misleading indicators of famine, particularly in a situation where information on storage loss, smuggling, and interdistrict movement and distribution by income class is missing. Similarly, the fact that government offtake was lower in Dacca and Khulna in July–October 1974 as compared with 1973 does not tell us the entire story unless we also note that the burden of offtake decline was borne solely by areas other than those under statutory rationing, that is, outside Dacca and Khulna.

Table 6.30. Government Offtake of Foodgrains by District (quantity in maunds)

Districts	1974				1973				% Change Between July/Oct. 1973–1974
	Jan./June	July/Oct.	July/Dec.	Jan./Dec.	Jan./June	July/Oct.	July/Dec.	Jan./Dec.	
Dinajpur	396,008	368,145	478,641	874,649	602,259	322,248	477,068	1,049,327	+14.24
Rangpur	738,082	615,363	1,039,986	1,778,068	1,055,793	693,191	907,412	1,963,205	−11.23
Bogra	289,520	263,649	362,936	652,456	1,402,710	309,296	390,371	1,793,081	−14.76
Rajshahi	614,548	546,480	786,847	1,401,395	691,001	516,676	748,717	1,439,718	+ 5.77
Pabna	593,578	411,260	622,606	1,216,184	675,502	490,485	700,329	1,375,831	−16.15
Kushtia	471,759	406,750	556,895	1,028,654	854,664	407,905	584,942	1,439,606	− 0.28
Jessore	649,063	542,996	811,272	1,460,335	1,118,378	724,793	987,912	2,106,290	−25.08
Khulna	2,310,976	1,631,271	2,218,228	4,529,204	2,819,962	1,645,401	2,361,408	5,181,370	− 0.86
Barisal	815,623	952,544	1,316,271	2,131,894	1,404,083	863,769	1,118,243	2,522,326	+10.28
Patuakhali	291,274	305,841	405,925	697,199	497,688	293,330	337,048	834,736	+ 4.27
Faridpur	844,842	843,475	2,138,161	2,983,003	1,536,046	867,131	1,178,927	2,714,973	− 2.73
Dacca	6,936,238	4,043,102	6,337,011	13,273,249	7,782,349	4,620,597	7,030,593	14,812,943	−12.50
Mymensingh	988,677	744,335	1,412,720	2,401,397	1,618,606	1,286,827	1,454,171	3,072,777	−42.16
Tangail	341,751	150,688	247,943	589,694	826,519	465,729	630,455	1,456,974	−67.64
Sylhet	732,733	749,108	1,011,463	1,744,196	1,423,987	678,340	95,108	2,375,068	+10.43
Comilla	1,181,559	934,067	1,494,072	2,675,631	2,727,172	1,320,447	1,811,590	4,538,762	−29.26
Noakhali	48,471	572,298	732,870	1,219,341	1,493,674	735,847	954,496	2,448,170	−22.23
Chittagong	2,635,348	2,353,242	3,231,412	5,866,760	3,223,878	1,392,209	2,045,881	5,269,759	+69.03
Chittagong H.T.	115,907	94,258	139,987	255,894	210,814	59,085	81,275	292,089	+59.53

Note: 1 maund = 82.29 pounds.

Source: Government of Bangladesh, Directorate of Procurement, Distribution and Rationing.

245

It will now be worthwhile to summarize our major findings on the stock and availability of foodgrains at the national and regional level in Bangladesh during 1974.

1. In 1974, the beginning of the year stock of foodgrains with the government was lower than what could be considered as normal, indicating a low level of preparedness on the part of the government for meeting a crisis.

2. Throughout 1974, the end of the month stock at government storage facilities was barely sufficient to meet the monthly normal requirement for distribution under various types of rationing. In other words, there was no margin in excess of the previously committed reserve that could be utilized to intervene in the market for providing adequate relief to the distressed population.

3. The total output of rice in 1974 was above the trend, but separately both *aus* and *boro* crops were below the trend. In particular, the *boro* crop was severely damaged by early flash floods and consequently the total output in that year was 18 percent below the trend in the famine districts. Despite these, we found that the per capita net output of rice in Bangladesh in 1974 was actually higher than that in other years of the 1970s, although it was well below the level realized during some years of the 1960s. However, seasonal variation in the expected output probably affected seasonal availability adversely.

4. The foodgrain import plan for 1974 was prepared on the basis of an optimistic assumption about domestic production. The output target was not realized and, in addition, the government was unable to ensure timely import flow of the required amount due to a number of unfavorable economic and political factors.

5. Due to inadequate preparation, the government failed to take full advantage of the compulsory procurement (of foodgrain) drive initiated in early 1974 in order to build up an emergency reserve.

6. The 1974 government offtake of foodgrains was unusual in the sense that there was little monthly fluctuation to match the variation in availability from domestic output and the per capita offtake was lower than that in 1973. In addition, the poor of the rural and small urban areas received less through the government distribution system during this year than in a normal year. In any case, the amount distributed outside the statutory rationing areas has always been a very small fraction of the total amount distributed.

7. The official data suggest that in 1974 per capita availability of foodgrains at the national level was higher than all other years in the 1970s, but was slightly lower than the levels attained in the

1960s, except for 1967. We found that there are some problems with these figures, particularly those relating to the postliberation years when smuggling of foodgrains into neighboring India emerged as an important source of leakage from the food system. The official figures also need to be corrected for abnormal storage loss and private and trading stock buildup. We acknowledge that a part of this unaccounted supply could be explained by ad hoc adjustments made by the Ministry of Agriculture to the original production estimates of the local level officials based on crop-cutting method. Our analysis tentatively suggests that if we allow for leakages as mentioned above, the estimated per capita food-grain availability for Bangladesh in 1974 would fall short of a minimum requirement level by a significant margin.

8. It seems that the normal pattern of seasonal availability of foodgrains had been adversely affected in 1974 by the destruction of the *boro* crop by early flash floods, by prolonged retention of marketable foodgrains by the surplus farmers, and by the absence of a counter-seasonal pattern in the government offtake through the rationing system. Our best guess-estimate is that the per capita availability of foodgrains during July–October 1974 was considerably lower than the average for the year, which would easily explain the critical situation prevailing during that period.

9. Evidence on the regional stock and availability of foodgrain is rather weak. Looking at the foodgrain stocks held only at the local storage depots of the government, it is found that there was considerable variation in the total and per capita stock among different centers and that in almost all centers the stock level was much lower in 1974 than in 1973. On the basis of our analysis of foodgrain availability at the regional level, we could only say that in 1974 per capita availability of foodgrains in many districts of Bangladesh was probably below the minimum requirement level, once appropriate adjustments were made for storage loss, leakage through smuggling, and interdistrict movement. However, in the absence of necessary data on the above and also on district level income distribution, the estimated availability figures could not explain interdistrict variation in famine intensity in 1974 as measured by other indicators (Chapter 4). This remains true also when we concentrate our attention on the July–October 1974 period even though we find that eleven districts experienced availability shortfall in this period in terms of the minimum requirement level.

We may, on the basis of (1) through (9) above, repeat what we said before in this chapter that the available evidence suggests that we cannot reject the hypothesis that the 1974 Bangladesh famine was caused partially by a fall in the per capita foodgrain availability as conventionally defined. The decline in availability was very pronounced during July–October 1974. The decline in the annual availability per capita was apparently caused by shortfall (in relation to actual requirement) in imports, shortfall in relation to normal commitment level in government offtake, and leakages due to abnormal storage loss and smuggling.

Certain districts/regions presumably suffered from availability decline more than others due to a shortfall (in relation to the anticipated level) in production on account of natural disaster, shortfall in government offtake, breakdown of the internal distribution system, breakdown of the transportation and communications system, interference by the government with the internal movement of foodgrains, and leakages due to abnormal storage loss and smuggling.

The decline in foodgrain availability per capita was more pronounced during certain months of 1974 (July–October) than other months. This can be attributed to shortfall in the production of *boro*, shortfall in imports, shortfall in government offtake, leakages due to abnormal storage loss and smuggling, speculative hoarding by traders and surplus farmers, breakdown in the internal distribution system, and breakdown in the transportation and communications system.

One factor that we have not elaborated on, but that remains true throughout the analysis of this book, is that the consequences of adverse forces in 1974 would have been more moderate had the rate of population growth been lower in Bangladesh. Since no significant changes in this parameter can be anticipated over the short run, this should be taken as given.

It should be emphasized here that the availability decline was measured in relation to other years in the 1960s and 1970s, and also in relation to a minimum requirement level of 14.4 ounces per capita/day. Although it is difficult to identify a precise cutoff point, the existing knowledge seems to indicate that for widespread excess deaths to occur, as they did in 1974, the actual foodgrain intake of individuals must have fallen well below the 14.4 ounces limit. This information cannot be captured unless one looks at the intra- and interhousehold distribution of foodgrain intake and availability. We have little knowledge of actual intake, particularly of its intrahousehold distribution.[61] In the remainder of this chapter we carry out only a limited analysis of the foodgrain intake and availability at the household level.

HOUSEHOLD STOCK AND AVAILABILITY

While relationship (2.3) in Chapter 2 identifies the determinants of household stock of foodgrains at the beginning of any time period, for annual accounting this is only of academic interest because farm households in Bangladesh are said to carry very little stock from one year into another. As for the status of household stock at various points of time within the year, we can say very little because in our own survey we did not make any attempt to collect this data except for a point of time just prior to 1973–1974 *aman* harvest. The reported amounts were negligible. We felt that response to such a question would be subject to a large margin of error. We do not know of any other survey that attempted to collect this information. However, from the pattern of sale of paddy we concluded earlier that in 1974 the staying power of the small and marginal farmers were substantially reduced under the pressure of the general unfavorable socio-economic environment. In particular, the unprecedented rate of inflation had increased their demand for cash. On the contrary, the surplus farmers were found to carry stock of foodgrain for periods longer than usual. The most important implication of the above finding is that the small and marginal farmers along with the landless laborers became more vulnerable to market forces in 1974 as compared with other years.

An analysis of the market forces (in land, labor, capital, and product markets) is extremely important for understanding the entire dimension of foodgrain availability at the household level. This is clearly brought out by relationships (2.10) and (2.11) in Chapter 2. As these relationships show, for a typical household, foodgrain availability can be defined as the potential flow within the command of the household. This flow is a function of net output, stock at the beginning of the period, share/rent received/paid in kind, amount sold to the government procurement agent, and other gifts and credit received (net) in kind, wages received/paid in kind, leakages, government distribution, transfer to other households, nonfoodgrain income, wage employment (in rural and non-rural activities), sale prices of foodgrain in the market, government distributed foodgrain, and capital assets, purchase price of foodgrain, and money wages in the rural and nonrural activities. In other words, actual foodgrain intake by individual members of the community will be affected by a variation in the values of any one of the variables identified.

Our analysis of the situation faced by individual households in 1974 is carried out at several levels. First, on the basis of our survey data, we examine the distribution of foodgrain available for consumption among households (classified according to different criteria) during the period 1973–1974. This will be done in this section. Second, we analyze the behavior of foodgrain prices in both historic and current context in order to identify the abnormalities in the annual or seasonal pattern during the postliberation period, particularly 1974. This will be the subject matter of Chapter 7, which will also take a look at the normal and transacted value of capital assets, mainly of land in 1974 in relation to 1972 and 1973. Third, the time trend and seasonal pattern of nominal and real wages is examined in Chapter 8. We also analyze the level and structure of rural household income. Furthermore, an indepth analysis is carried out on what happened to employment and total wage income during July–October 1974 as compared with the same period in 1973.

In general, the amount of foodgrain available for consumption of the survey households was estimated indirectly from data on production, receipt and payment of share/rent in kind, and gross sale and purchase of paddy. For paddy producing households an estimate was made of the net output available, defined as gross output plus the amount received as share/rent, gifts, and loans less the part allowed for seed, feed, and wastage (assumed to be 10 percent of gross produce), payment of share/rent, and payment to labor in kind. The household consumption figure was arrived at by adding net purchase (purchase minus sale) of paddy to net output. To obtain per capita consumption, the total household consumption figure was divided by the size of household. For nonproducer households, foodgrain consumption level was estimated directly from the information provided by the respondents on their average daily household rice consumption.

Clearly, the household foodgrain consmption level estimated by following the procedure described in the previous paragraph can provide us with only an order of magnitude of the actual intakes of the individual members of the household. For one thing, we do not know the intrafamily distribution of foodgrain consumption. Secondly, we could not capture the seasonal pattern of foodgrain consumption at the household level. Thirdly, we have figures only for July 1973 to June 1974 and, therefore, are unable to say anything about the levels of household foodgrain consumption during the critical July–October 1974 period. However, we can say that during this period the 4.2 million inmates of *langarkhanas* relied entirely on free distribution of foodgrains from private and government sources. In Table 5.15 we have shown that the amount of foodrelief provided by the government was far below the minimum requirement.

We have presented some data on the state of deprivation of survey households measured in relation to the minimum requirement of 14.4 ounces per capita/day (328.5 pounds per year). Households have been classified according to different criteria. Severely deprived households are those with a per capita foodgrain consumption level less than 50 percent of the minimum requirement level. Most of the famine victims probably came from this group. Others falling between this level and the minimum requirement level are called moderately deprived. Unfortunately, we do not have data for any other year for comparison but it is clear from the figures in Table 6.31 that the situation was desperate even in the first half of 1974 (which is subsumed under 1973–1974.) On the whole, as high as 24 percent of households were found to be severely

Table 6.31. Levels of Foodgrain Consumption Deprivation of Survey Households in Eight Villages of Bangladesh in 1973–1974 (Percentages of households falling in given per capita consumption groups)

	Moderately Deprived (164.2 pounds to 328.5 pounds)	Severely Deprived (less than 164.2 pounds)
All groups	12.2	23.8
Landholding groups (operational holding)		
less than 0.5 acres	21.5	26.7
0.5– < 1.0 acres	13.9	35.0
1.0– < 2.5 acres	8.6	24.7
2.5– < 5.0 acres	4.0	14.1
5.0– < 7.5 acres	3.3	12.2
7.5–< 12.5 acres	—	8.3
12.5+ acres	—	11.1
Tenurial groups		
Owner farmers	12.1	21.5
Owner-cum-tenant farmers	8.3	23.7
Tenant farmers	19.0	38.0
Landless laborers	14.8	26.6
Occupational groups		
Farmers	6.3	18.9
Wage earners	25.5	31.3
Traders and businessmen	15.2	34.8
Transportation workers	12.5	25.0
Salary earners	12.8	29.6
Others	15.6	18.8

deprived. They came from all size group of landownership (operational). This is slightly misleading because those in the above 2.5 acre category are drawn almost entirely from Nazirpur village, which, as we noted earlier, had suffered severely from a cyclone in October 1973. It is somewhat difficult to explain why the percentage of severely deprived households was higher in the 0.5 to less than 1.0 acre category as compared with the less than 0.5 acre category.

Among different tenurial groups, the tenant farmers appear to be the most deprived, even more so than the landless laborers. This may suggest that the tenants are subjected to a higher degree of exploitation than other groups. On the one hand, they face unfavorable terms of cost and produce sharing and, on the other, in certain situations their own labor time is pre-empted by landlords as forced free-labor. It is not surprising that among ocupational groups the wage earners rank high under both moderately deprived and severely deprived categories. The high percentage of traders and businessmen can only be explained by the fact that the distribution of total income is more skewed for this group as compared with all other groups.

Figures in Table 6.31 also point to a very important fact. Households depending on the market for purchase of foodgrains and/or for sale of labor power appear to be more vulnerable as measured by their status of foodgrain consumption deprivation. Therefore, terms of purchase of foodgrains (price) and sale of labor power (wage) should constitute an important component of analysis of famine. These dimensions are analyzed in Chapters 7 and 8.

The above findings however, should, be qualified by the fact that in an extreme scarcity situation households are likely to consume seeds, a fact we have not explicitly taken into account. But given the fact that the deprived households belong mostly (above 80 percent) to the small-farmer (less than 2.5 acres) group accounting for only about 22 percent of total output, the amount of support available from seed crop would be minimal and furthermore the consumption of seed puts them in a vulnerable position the next year.

NOTES AND REFERENCES

1. This figure represents the minimum required consumption per capita in a balanced diet (consumption bundle) supplying 2100 calories. See M. Alamgir, "Analysis of Distribution of Income, Consumption, Saving and Poverty in Bangladesh," *Bangladesh Development Studies* 2(4):815 (October 1974).
2. Famine Inquiry Commission, 1944, *Report on Bengal* (New Delhi: Manager of Government Publications, 1945), p. 15.
3. Muhammad Osman Faruk, *Structure and Performance of the Rice Marketing System in East Pakistan,* Cornell International Agricultural Development Bulletin 23, Cornell University, Ithaca, May 1972, pp. 76–77.
4. See also S. R. Bose, "Foodgrain Availability and the Possibilities of Famine in Bangla Desh," *Economic and Political Weekly,* Annual Number, February 1972, p. 294.
5. The yield figures are quoted from Government of Bangladesh, Ministry of Agriculture, *Bangladesh Agriculture in Statistics, 1973* (Dacca: Ministry of Agriculture, 1974), p. 27; and Government of Bangladesh, Bureau of Statistics, *Statistical Pocketbook of Bangladesh, 1978,* (Dacca: Bureau of Statistics, December 1977), pp. 152–153. The increase in wheat output came mostly through increase in the area under wheat.
6. Net output is estimated by deducting 10 percent for seed, feed, and wastage from gross output.
7. See M. Alamgir, "Some Aspects of Bangladesh Agriculture: Review of Performance and Evaluation of Policies," *Bangladesh Development Studies* 3(3):262 (July 1975).
8. Calculated on the basis of the population figure in Table 6.23 and the cultivable area obtained from *Statistical Pocketbook, 1978,* pp. 112–113.
9. Ibid., p. 117. Present level of cropping intensity is considered low because in many areas of Bangladesh triple cropping is possible.
10. Available data indicate that the index of fragmentation increased from 194 in 1960 to 297 in 1973. The index is calculated as the ratio of the number of separate plots to the

area of operational holding expressed in percentage terms. See M. Alamgir, *Bangladesh, A Case of Below Poverty Level Equilibrium Trap* (Dacca: Bangladesh Institute of Development Studies, 1978), p. 52.

11. In 1975–1976, 1.6 million acres were irrigated by these methods. *Statistical Pocketbook, 1978*, p. 133.

12. Mahmudul Alam, "Capacity Utilization of Low-Lift Pumps Irrigation in Bangladesh," Research Report No. 17 (New Series), Bangladesh Institute of Development Studies, 1974; Mahmudul Alam, "Capacity Utilization of Deep Tubewell Irrigation in Bangladesh: A Time Series Analysis of Comilla Thana," *Bangladesh Development Studies*, 3(3):495–504 (October 1975).

13. Because of the small size of landholding per household, low-lift pumps and tubewells are operated in groups that are managed by either a member of the group or a salaried manager.

14. *Daily Ittefaq*, January 20, 1974; January 23, 1974; February 2, 1974; February 6, 1974; March 15, 1974; April 30, 1974; and May 21, 1974; *Bangladesh Observer*, June 7, 1974; June 18, 1974.

15. *Bangladesh Agriculture in Statistics*, Addenda and Corrigenda, p. 6.

16. *Daily Ittefaq*, May 8, 1974.

17. Raisuddin Ahmed, *Foodgrain Production in Bangladesh: An Analysis of Growth, Its Sources and Related Policies*, International Food Policy Research Institute, Washington, D.C., May 1976, p. 37.

18. *Bangladesh Agriculture in Statistics*, p. 85.

19. According to Ahmed, the elasticity of output of *boro* with respect to fertilizer varies between 0.1015 and 0.1317, the corresponding figures for *aman* being 0.0046 and 0.0422. See Ahmed, *Foodgrain Production in Bangladesh*, pp. 42, 125.

20. Alamgir, "Aspects of Bangladesh Agriculture," p. 268.

21. Mahbub Hossain, "Farm Size and Productivity in Bangladesh," *Bangladesh Economic Review*, 3(1):478 (January 1974); Mahbub Hossain, "Farm Size, Tenancy and Land Productivity: An Analysis of Farm Level Data in Bangladesh Agriculture," *Bangladesh Development Studies*, 5(3):315 (July 1977). This result is due to higher labor use per unit of land on small farms as compared with large farms.

22. Hossain, "Farm Size, Tenancy and Land Productivity," pp. 315–316. Variation in resource position of different households blurs the relationship. In the same household, Hossain found that sharecropped land was cultivated less intensively than owned land, indicating that sharecropping is an inefficient arrangement.

23. Ibid., p. 331.

24. Ibid., p. 337.

25. Ahmed, *Foodgrain Production in Bangladesh*, pp. 61–62. Ahmed found the coefficient of tenancy to be positive and statistically significant. This is somewhat misleading because such a relationship may have been imposed by an underlying positive correlation between fertilizer use and tenancy structure by area.

26. Md. Asaduzzaman, "A Report on Bangladesh Fertilizer, Demand, Supply and Marketing," mimeographed, Bangladesh Institute of Development Studies, August 1975, pp. 1–23.

27. Ahmed, *Foodgrain Production in Bangladesh*, pp. 60–61.

28. *Daily Ittefaq*, April 13, 1974; October 21, 1974; October 30, 1974; December 1, 1974; December 6, 1974; December 11, 1974.

29. Ahmed, *Foodgrain Production in Bangladesh*, p. 56.

30. Asaduzzaman suggests a required lag of two months between procurement and distribution of fertilizer, "A Report on Bangladesh Fertilizer," p. 22.

31. Ahmed, *Foodgrain Production in Bangladesh*, p. 148.

32. The rate of seed subsidy would be on the order of 50 percent if account is taken of unsold stocks and sale at less than official price. See Mujibur Rahman, "Procurement, Distribution and Pricing Policies for Agricultural Inputs and Outputs in Bangladesh—A Critical Review," *Political Economy*, Journal of the Bangladesh Economic Association, Conference Volume, 1976, pp. 324–325.

33. These figures are calculated on the basis of data given in *Statistical Pocketbook, 1978*, pp. 164–165; Government of Bangladesh, Bureau of Statistics, *Statistical Yearbook of Bangladesh 1979* (Dacca: Bureau of Statistics, 1979), p. 105.

34. These figures refer to only those households that reported no ownership of bullock and cow. As such, they do not include households owning bullock and cow but no draft power.

35. Government of Bangladesh, FAO/UNDP Mission, "Selected Policy Issues in Agriculture," Dacca, April 15, 1977, p. 48.

36. Ibid., p. 40.

37. Alamgir, "Aspects of Bangladesh Agriculture," pp. 290–291; 293.

38. Hossain, "Farm Size, Tenancy and Land Productivity," p. 311.

39. Nurul Islam, *Development Planning in Bangladesh, A Study in Political Economy* (London: C. Hurst, 1977), p. 113.

40. See M. Alamgir and L. Berlage, *Bangladesh: National Income and Expenditure*, (Dacca: Bangladesh Institute of Development Studies, 1974), pp. 17–21.

41. M. Alamgir, "The Experience of Rural Works Programme in Bangladesh," in *Planning for Effective Public Rural Works Programmes: Case Studies from Bangladesh, India and Pakistan* (Bangkok: United Nations Economic and Social Commission for Asia and the Pacific, 1979), pp. 11–68.

42. Islam, *Development Planning in Bangladesh*, p. 114.

43. Donald F. McHenry and Kai Bird, "Food Bungle in Bangladesh," *Foreign Policy* 27:82 (Summer 1977).

44. Islam, *Development Planning in Bangladesh*, p. 133.

45. McHenry and Bird, "Food Bungle in Bangladesh," p. 79.

46. Government of Bangladesh, Ministry of Finance, *Bangladesh Economic Survey 1976–77* (Dacca: Superintendent Bangladesh Government Press, 1977), p. 17.

47. Alamgir and Berlage, *Bangladesh*, p. 183.

48. Islam, *Development Planning in Bangladesh*, p. 116.

49. Ibid., p. 117.

50. Ibid., p. 116.

51. See McHenry and Bird, "Food Bungle in Bangladesh," pp. 76–77; Just Faaland and J. R. Parkinson, *Bangladesh, The Test Case for Development* (London: C. Hurst, 1976), p. 127.

52. A. M. A. Rahim, "An Analysis of Smuggling in Bangladesh," *Bangladesh Bank Bulletin*, 14:4–5 (August 1974).

53. McHenry and Bird, "Food Bungle in Bangladesh," pp. 76–77.

54. See W. B. Reddaway and Mizanur Rahman, "The Scale of Smuggling Out of Bangladesh," Research Report No. 21 (New Series), Bangladesh Institute of Development Studies, Dacca, 1975, pp. 1–22.

55. Reports from Patuakhali said that large boats filled with rice moved at night into the Bay of Bengal to Calcutta and Howrah in India. From Gobindaganj, Rangpur, the field investigator reported that he saw truckloads of rice/paddy moving in the direction of the border belt where traders maintained large storage facilities in a nearby market place. Interestingly enough, all these movements took place with the explicit knowledge of the local officials.

56. Reddaway and Rahman, "Scale of Smuggling Out of Bangladesh," p. 12.

57. Ibid., p. 12.

58. We consider it likely that the function identified is a demand one. Supply is exogenous and does not vary much with relative price, and shifts in supply could also be considered exogenous, for example, food aid or weather-induced good harvest. The absorption function is fairly stable over a short period for a near-subsistence economy.
59. J. Johnston, *Econometric Methods* (New York: McGraw-Hill, 1971), 2nd ed., p. 207.
60. Such a bias could originate from the fact that at no stage was the government willing to acknowledge the severity of foodgrain deprivation on the part of the general masses. A lower availability figure would have contradicted this position.
61. In a normal period children and women probably suffer from a higher level of calorie-protein gap as compared with adult male members of the family. The status of children apparently deteriorates further during a period of food shortage. Limited data available from the 1976 Nutrition Survey of Bangladesh tend to support this hypothesis although not fully. See *The Situation of Children in Bangladesh*, The Foundation for Research on Educational Planning and Development, Dacca, July 1977, p. 113; Kamaluddin Ahmad (ed.), *Nutrition Survey of Rural Bangladesh* (Dacca: Institute of Nutrition and Food Science, December 1977), pp. 54–69.

Chapter 7

Prices

INTRODUCTION

In Chapter 4 references were made to the movement of rice prices during 1974. We present here a more systematic treatment of rice prices with a historic perspective. Both temporal and seasonal changes in prices of foodgrain, mainly rice, are discussed with a view to throwing light on the role played by this factor in aggravating the famine situation nationally, regionally or, for that matter, at the household level through differential impact on the well-being of different households. The analysis is organized in the following way. First, we discuss the annual trend of wholesale prices at the national level over the period 1956–1957 to 1975–1976. Both medium and coarse quality rice is included in the discussion although there is not much difference between the two in the underlying trend. This analysis is combined with an analysis of the movement of rice prices relative to prices of other important commodities, for example, jute and manufactures. In addition, a more in-depth analysis of the rice price movement by months in 1973 and 1974 is presented.

Second, regional differences in price movements are analyzed. This includes analysis of the movement of the wholesale price of coarse quality rice in various districts between October 1972 and the corresponding month in 1973 and 1974. The month of October was chosen because, from the point of view of famine, this has historically turned out to be the most difficult month. We also present a comparative picture of the prices of essential commodities (rice, wheat, pulses and edible oil), as reported by our sample villagers. An attempt is made to correlate the rate of price increase between October 1973 and 1974 in different districts with indexes of famine intensity (as measured by the proportion of population served in the *langarkhana* and the depth and duration of flood). Furthermore, price spread between districts and the coefficient of variation of interdistrict prices by month is calculated in order to see if the revealed patterns for 1974 are significantly different from those of 1973. Such findings could be related to the regional variation in the famine intensity.

Third, a causal analysis of price changes is presented. This is composed of temporal, seasonal, and spatial analysis in order to capture the influence of the different factors in the determination of rice prices. To keep the discussion manageable, we look at the wholesale price of coarse quality rice only. In the temporal analysis we have developed a model of price determination using time series data for the period 1956–1957 to 1972–1973. The seasonal analysis is carried out by estimating the trend adjusted seasonal factors. The idea is to identify the underlying seasonal pattern, if any, and examine whether it has gone through changes over time; we are particularly interested in seeing if 1974 presents a markedly different picture as compared with other years and why. The spatial analysis of rice prices is carried out with a view to examine the intermarket relationships and to find out the factors that may have caused regional variation in the magnitude of rice price increase during 1974 over the previous year.

TREND IN RICE PRICE OVER TIME

Annual Trend in Rice Prices (Undeflated)

Before analyzing the data on rice prices, we must point out a number of characteristics of the available data set. First, there is no *one* price of rice. Data are collected by the Bureau of Statistics for three rice varieties: fine, medium, and coarse. These grades are not standardized and properly specified, with the result that price data collected from different markets often refer to different specifications and at no stage are such differences sorted out to ensure consistency. This problem has been noted for Bangladesh by Faruk[1] and for Indonesia by Goldman.[2] The prices referred to here are wholesale and retail market prices. We concentrate our attention on medium and coarse quality rice since they constitute the bulk of the total amount of rice entering the market. Longtime series data are available on wholesale prices of both these varieties of rice. Similar data on retail prices are available for medium quality rice, while for coarse quality rice, retail price data are available for the postliberation period (1972–) only.

Second, there are a number of other prices of rice that are also relevant for our analysis here. These are controlled price, internal procurement price, and import price. Controlled price is the price at which foodgrains distributed through the government rationing system are sold. It is presumed by the authority that the rice sold in ration shops is of medium quality. However, in an earlier paper I have argued that rationed rice and medium quality rice are not perfect substitutes from the point of view of consumers.[3] In fact, the government distributed rice is considered inferior to local rice. Internal procurement price is the price at which government agents buy rice in internal markets during the harvest period. While the government provides some specification of the rice to be procured, it is not clear if the agents follow the specifications (defined by maximum moisture content and percentage of broken rice and foreign element) strictly and uniformly across markets. Finally, import price refers to the price of imported rice. Qualitatively, of course, this is the same rice as that distributed through the rationing system (except for a little amount that comes out of the internally procured rice), but the unit prices of the two differ because of the subsidy element in the case of rationed rice. It may be pointed out here that the difference between the market price (retail) of local rice, adjusted for marginal rate of substituton between local rice and imported rice, and the price of rationed rice represents the amount by which the purchaser of one unit of rationed rice is better off in terms of disposable income.[4] Therefore, as suggested in Chapter 6, from the point of view of consumer welfare, it is important to analyze who benefits from the system of rationing during a normal period as well as during a period of scarcity.

Making the above points, we can turn to an analysis of the trend in rice price over time. Let us first take up the movement of nominal prices as shown in Table 7.1 and Figure 7.1.[5] Movement of nominal rice price has important implications for the general price stability in the country and thereby for the welfare of the average consumer, for whom rice is an important item in the daily budget. Also rice price is important in determining disposable income of producers, hence, it can create demand-pull inflationary pressures.

Data presented in Table 7.1 show that the annual price movements are similar for medium and coarse quality rice except that the level of the former is higher. The same is true of the comparison between wholesale

Table 7.1. Trend in Prices of Rice in Bangladesh, 1956–1957 to 1975–1976

Year	Medium Quality Rice Wholesale Price	Retail Price	Controlled Price	Internal Procurement Price	Import Price	Coarse Quality Rice Wholesale Price	Nonrice Food Price Index (1959–1960 = 100)
1956–1957	27.83	28.61	20.00	18.06	23.29	22.51	85.47
1957–1958	28.02	28.67	21.46	18.69	23.22	24.92	100.17
1958–1959	29.81	30.19	22.50	19.69	21.64	25.82	96.66
1959–1960	31.60	31.91	22.90	19.60	18.48	26.25	100.00
1960–1961	28.84	29.30	23.33	19.69	17.45	24.23	107.35
1961–1962	29.39	30.21	23.75	19.69	18.55	26.93	113.93
1962–1963	31.34	32.28	23.75	19.69	17.85	29.12	116.75
1963–1964	26.99	28.93	23.75	19.69	18.52	25.17	118.46
1964–1965	28.61	30.07	25.60	21.71	19.76	26.81	128.21
1965–1966	34.05	36.00	25.60	21.71	19.51	31.91	118.12
1966–1967	43.63	45.90	25.60	26.63	22.74	41.23	129.15
1967–1968	39.57	44.32	30.80	28.21	25.24	36.18	129.74
1968–1969	44.70	46.23	30.80	28.21	25.09	40.60	134.70
1969–1970	43.12	45.60	30.80	29.79	42.25	39.50	138.47
1970–1971	41.48	45.30	30.00	29.79	24.39	38.73	180.56
1971–1972	54.53	57.20	30.00	37.85	24.17	47.38	212.77
1972–1973	83.63	89.60	30.00	54.00	38.43	79.16	313.26
1973–1974	113.31	120.50	41.86	72.63	62.29	104.82	433.28
1974–1975	228.03	244.40	60.00	120.00	123.70	223.30	773.61
1975–1976	141.16	153.90	73.28	120.00	205.08	129.06	739.50

Source: M. Alamgir, *Farmine 1974: Political Economy of Mass Starvation in Bangladesh*, Statistical Annexe, Part I (Dacca: Bangladesh Institute of Development Studies, 1977), p. 53. Nonrice Food Price Index is author's own calculation.

Note: Taka per maund = 82.29 pounds.

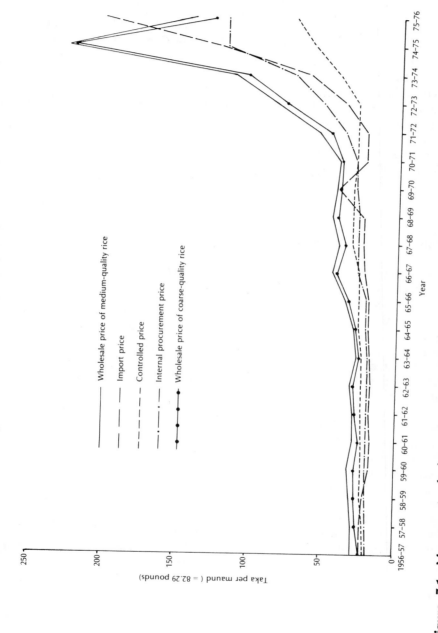

Figure 7.1. Movement of rice prices (undeflated) in Bangladesh, 1956–1957 to 1975–1976.

261

and retail prices, and in this case the level of the latter is higher. These observations are confirmed by Figure 7.1. On the whole, there is a significant upward trend in all rice prices. Visual examination suggested that a linear trend would fit well up to the period 1971–1972. This was confirmed by a linear trend regression where the coefficient of determination was found to be very high (0.85).[6] The rice price rise accelerated over the period between 1970–1972 and 1974–1975 before a decline in the absolute level took place. Without going back very far, between 1969–1970 and 1974–1975 the price of rice increased by more than fivefold. It is not difficult to see that poor consumers would be seriously affected by such movement in rice price.

Although a linear trend fitted data quite well, it is important to note that on a different occasion, prior to 1971–1972, the consumers had to adjust to an irreversible upward movement in the base price of rice. This occurred in two steps over two years, 1965–1966 and 1966–1967. Thus, we get the following distinct periods. The first extends between 1956–1957 and 1964–1965 when the average wholesale price of medium quality rice mildly fluctuated around Taka 29 per maund (82.29 pounds). A wide range of factors affecting both the supply and the demand for rice account for the relative stability of rice prices from 1956–1957 to 1964–1965. While there was some year-to-year fluctuations, average output of rice increased from slightly above seven million tons over the 1955–1960 period to about ten million tons in the 1960–1965 period.[7] This period coincided with the beginning of substantial imports of foodgrains. Systematic channels were developed to import foodgrains, particularly following an agreement with the U. S. government in 1961 for the supply of wheat under PL–480. In addition, the national food administration was streamlined in 1955–1956. The subsequent period was characterized by an increase in the government offtake of foodgrains. In addition, the government was able to effect a more timely release of foodgrains, that is, a counter-seasonal (keeping in view the availability from domestic production) pattern of foodgrain distribution was set up. All of these were aided by an augmentation and fortification of the foodgrain storage facilities of the government. Controls over prices and interregional movement of rice were removed in 1960. Also, the practice of internal foodgrain procurement with zonal cordoning and acquisition of surplus stock of *Jotdars* (large farmers) residing within five miles of the border belt was abandoned in 1960. The factors mentioned so far affected the market availability of foodgrains. On the demand side, it can be said that the population growth rate was lower than what it turned out to be in the late 1960s and 1970s. Equally important was the fact that the large-scale injection of wheat in the food system took the pressure off rice somewhat, although, according to consumers' perception, wheat was never accorded the status of a perfect substitute for rice.

Second, the above period of stability was followed by two years of transition to a higher price level of rice. During this period the country had fought a war with India during which government expenditure on defense, financed through inflationary means, increased sharply. There was also a decline in the total output of rice and the shortfall was not made up by increased imports. This, combined with natural population growth, resulted in a decline in per capita availability of foodgrains (Table 6.23). Thus, we find that rice (medium quality) price (wholesale) increased by 17 percent in 1965–1966 and another 29 percent in 1966–1967 over the average level of 1956–1957 to 1964–1965. Beginning in 1966–1967, the rice price found a higher base level. This is indicated by the fact that over the next four years, the annual average wholesale price of medium quality rice fluctuated around Taka 43 per maund, that is, 52 percent higher than the average of the previous period discussed above. To get a relative measure of events it may be noted that the wholesale price index (1959–1960 = 100) increased by 37 percent between these two periods. A number of other factors that apparently played a role in sustaining the higher base level of rice price and not allowing it to come down to the pre-1965 level were acceleration in the populaion growth rate, virtual abandonment of the internal procurement of rice, reimposition of restrictions on foodgrain movement from the five-mile border belt, and political unrest, which from time to time seriously interferred with the internal movement of foodgrains.

After 1972, there was a sustained upward movement in rice prices. This continued until 1974–1975 (Figure 7.1). Between 1971–1972 and 1974–1975 annual rates of increase in rice price (wholesale/medium quality) were 55, 35, and 101 percent respectively. Clearly, the rice price level had shifted upward irreversibly. It is not, however, yet clear what that level is going to be although there is no doubt that the percentage shift between 1967–1971 and post-1972 periods in the base rice price level would be much larger than that which occurred between the first two periods as identified here. For our purpose, the most interesting observation is that famine occurred during a period of violent upswing in market (wholesale and retail) prices of rice (Figure 7.1). Extrapolating from our earlier analysis we find that the kink in the temporal rice price curve was associated with war (1971), natural calamaties (1972, 1973, 1974), smuggling, deficit spending by the government, decline in foodgrain availability as compared with earlier periods, and continued population pressure. The vulnerable groups in the society had been subjected to the severe price pressure in 1972 and 1973, but the "big push" in 1974 literally crushed them. The 1974 "big push" in rice prices came in the wake of flood, shortfall in imports, shortfall in government offtake, leakages due to abnormal storage loss and smuggling, breakdown in the internal distribution system, breakdown of the transportation and communication system, interference by the government with the internal movement of foodgrains, and speculative hoarding by traders and surplus farmers.

Monthly Trend in Rice Prices (Undeflated)

Movement of annual average prices of rice does not adequately reflect the full magnitude of price increase during the 1974 famine as compared with previous years. To get a complete picture of what really happened with prices we must look at the monthly trend in prices beginning in July 1971. This is shown in Figure 7.2. Considering October as the reference month, we find that the rate of rice (medium quality) price (wholesale) increase between 1971 and 1972, 1972 and 1973, and 1973 and 1974 were 70, 24, and 170 percent respectively. The corresponding figures for coarse quality rice were 77, 22, and 180 percent respectively. While there was a substantial price increase between July 1971 and December 1973 (95 and 105 percent for wholesale price of medium and coarse quality rice respectively), between month variations show both positive and negative rates of increase. However, beginning in January 1974, consumers were subjected to continuous price increase until October 1974. During this period the wholesale price of medium quality rice increased by 207 percent and that of coarse quality rice by 216 percent. Monthly average rate of price increase works out to be about 21 percent in both cases.

Controlled Price, Internal Procurement Price, and Import Price

Table 7.1 and Figure 7.1 also show the movement of controlled price, internal procurement price of rice over the period 1956–1957 to 1975–1976. As compared with the internal market prices, both controlled price and internal procurement price show only moderate increase over the period under consideration. But import prices experienced sharp increases between 1972–1973 and 1975–1976,[8] after a period of relative stability over the 1960s. The levels and movement of these three prices have important welfare implications for different population groups in the country, particularly during a distress period.

To the extent that the controlled price was kept below the market price, it provided a cushion of safety to those among the poor who

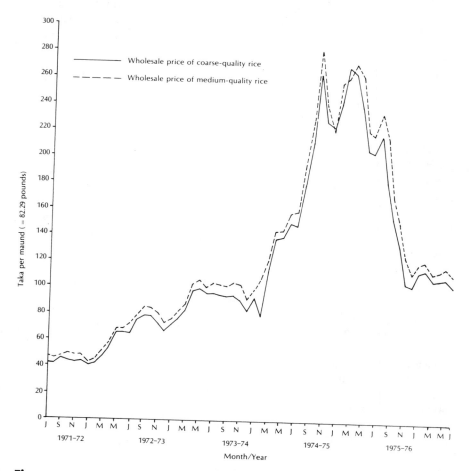

Figure 7.2. Movement of rice prices (undeflated) in Bangladesh by Month, 1971–1972 to 1975–1976. *Source:* M. Alamgir, *Famine 1974: Political Economy of Mass Starvation in Bangladesh,* Statistical Annexe, Part I (Dacca: Bangladesh Institute of Development Studies, 1977), pp. 54–55.

benefited from it. But we pointed out in Chapter 6 that this number was not very large. However, there is no denying the fact that the poor residing in the areas covered by the statutory and modified rationing system are partially protected from the onslaught of a famine assuming of course, that the offtake is not reduced drastically. We saw that this did not happen in Bangladesh in 1974. Therefore, the incidence of excess death during famine in these areas fell mainly on the temporary migrant population who converged there in the hope of obtaining food relief.

On the other hand, sale of rice through the rationing system at prices below cost involves a large transfer payment from the rest of the economy to the section of the population covered by it. Now, there is an important element of perverse resource transfer here because the system, as we noted before, covers not only the poor, but also others who could well afford to pay the market price. It is difficult to separate out this component. But data presented in Table 7.2 clearly indicate that the amount of food subsidy has been quite large in the postliberation period. A target group oriented distribution of the benefit from food subsidy could have saved many more lives in 1974. A larger question involved here is the relative merit of diverting the resources from food subsidy to direct investment for raising the productivity and income of the target group over the longer period.

The government has, in recent years, raised controlled prices to reduce subsidy burden, and it has also started to limit the benefit of subsidized foodgrain distribution to relatively low-income groups. In view of the rising import cost (Table 7.1) the former has not really reduced the overall budgetary burden by as much as one would like and the latter measure is yet to go far enough to restrict the benefit of food subsidy to the vulnerable groups only.

In the above context the relevance of import prices of rice and wheat is obvious. On the one hand, they indicate the degree of pressure exerted on the otherwise precarious balance of payments of the country, and on the other, they determine how much subsidy would have to be paid to the consumers. Although we are specifically showing data related to rice only, the same is true of wheat. As mentioned before, wheat constitutes the dominant share of foodgrain imports. Movement of wheat import prices, along with the data on total cost of foodgrain (rice and wheat) imports, is also presented in Table 7.2. From the point of view of the analysis of famine the important point is that the Bangladesh government has been spending a considerable amount of resources on food subsidy and foodgrain imports without necessarily enhancing the food security of the vulnerable groups of the society. On the contrary, one can reasonably speculate that the present pattern of resource allocation

Table 7.2. Food Subsidy and Cost of Foodgrain Imports

Year	Food Subsidy[a] (Tk./million)	Food Subsidy as % of Current Revenue Expenditure of the Government	Import Price of Wheat (Tk./m. ton)	Cost of Foodgrain Imports (Tk./million)	Cost of Foodgrain Imports as % of Total Merchandise Imports
1972–1973	783	26.9	900	953	NA
1973–1974	963	21.8	1889.81	3209	44
1974–1975	916	16.2	1836.06	4300	40
1975–1976	1006	14.7	2194.45	3913	27
1976–1977	760	9.3	2205.00	1344	10
1977–1978	1060	10.3	2100.00	3563	17

Source: Government of Bangladesh, Ministry of Finance, and Bangladesh Bureau of Statistics.

[a]This is nominal subsidy and does not include costs of procurement, handling, and distribution.

reduces the capability of the government to either provide a larger amount of emergency assistance to the distressed population when required or to augment the income earning capacity of this group.

Internal procurement price has similar implications for food subsidy as import price since internally procured rice is normally distributed through the rationing system. But it is important from a different consideration also. We noted earlier that the amount procured internally has not been very large and, in general, the surplus farmer has been able to avoid the "net" of the government procurement agent. We have also brought out the fact that internal procurement price does not compare favorably with the ruling market price at the time of procurement when the price in any case is lower than at other times of the year. Therefore, to the extent that small farmers are forced to sell foodgrains to either the government procurement agent or the trader at harvest time and then buy back their required amount later in the open market at a higher price, there are perverse transfers involved, first from the rural poor to the urban rich covered by the rationing system, and second from the rural poor to the traders and surplus farmers with more staying power. Our survey data revealed that in 1974 during the worst period of famine (July–October), buyers had to pay 268 percent higher than the prevailing procurement price in the December 1973–January 1974 period. The differential in the rate of price increase between the famine and the non-famine areas was relatively small (32 percent). The lesson to be learned from this is that in a period when a difficult food situation is anticipated, the government should tighten the foodgrain procurement operation by way of offering an incentive purchase price, increasing surveillance to capture the marketable foodgrains of the surplus farmers, and pre-empting excess purchase by traders. As for the small farmers, who are in any case forced to sell a part of their crop to meet immediate pressing cash needs, government procurement agents can hold their stock until such time as they re-enter the market to buy back foodgrains.

Movement of Deflated Rice Price

We discussed earlier the movement of nominal prices, which has a real component and a monetary component. Real supply and demand factors influence real prices of rice. In order to eliminate the influence of inflation, we deflate nominal rice prices by the nonrice food price index. (The index is presented in Table 7.1.) Movement of the deflated prices (wholesale) of medium and coarse quality rice is shown in Figure 7.3. As expected, the movement of the two reveals almost an identical pattern. Unlike nominal prices there is no systematic trend in deflated prices. If anything, deflated price shows a downward trend over the years. However, given the nature of fluctuations in the price (deflated) curves (Figure 7.3), it would help to look at different segments separately.

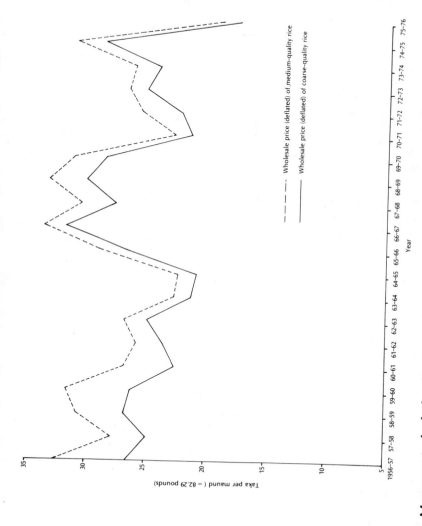

Figure 7.3. Movement of wholesale prices (deflated by non-rice food price index) of rice in Bangladesh, 1956–1957 to 1975–1976.

The deflated price of rice reveals a declining trend between 1956–1957 and 1964–1965, and then it increases over the course of the next two years. With some fluctuations a downward trend sets in between 1965–1966 and 1970–1971. This is followed by an upswing that continues up to 1974–1975. The final year in the graph shows a sharp fall in the deflated price of rice. While movements in the deflated price of rice are surrogates for movements in the factors underlying supply and demand for foodgrains, they have a different meaning of their own.

The deflated rice price also represents the terms of trade (relative price) between the main calorie and protein source (rice = 62 percent of total calorie requirement and 45 percent of protein requirement according to the 1975–1976 Bangladesh Nutrition Survey) and other sources of calorie and protein. In a period of declining relative prices of rice both the producers and nonproducers would reduce consumption of other sources of calorie and protein (due to income and substitution effect). This will have the effect of reducing the protein intake (particularly of animal protein, not to speak of other nutrient elements) of many individuals who are now on the margin. If the declining relative price is accompanied by an increase in rice price, then without a compensating change in income, the marginal (both producer and nonproducer) consuming units will probably experience shortfall in both calorie and protein. Over a period of rising relative price of rice, the marginal families would tend to reduce rice consumption in favor of lesser sources of calorie and protein. In particular, as a source of energy they will first move to starchy staples and ultimately to "famine foods." The situation becomes even more difficult if, as happened between 1973 and 1974, prices of all sources of calorie and protein rise sharply. The viability of the consuming units would then depend on their income earning opportunities, a subject we take up for discussion in the Chapter 8. It may be noted here that the precise impact of the relative price change on calorie and protein intake of consuming units will depend on the level of income, and income and price (own and cross) elasticities of demand. However, the vulnerability of the marginal families in postliberation Bangladesh (with the climax reached in 1974) should be evident from the movement of retail price of medium quality rice and the nonrice food price index as shown in Table 7.1.

It is equally important to analyze the movement of rice/jute and rice/manufactures price relatives. These indicators will reflect the well-being of the consuming units relying on the sale proceeds of jute and manufactured items to purchase foodgrains. In the case of manufactures, our focus is primarily on the owners of family-based enterprises with or without hired labor. Since we did not have separate data, we have used the price index for the entire manufacturing sector. Figure 7.4 shows the movement of the price relatives discussed here.

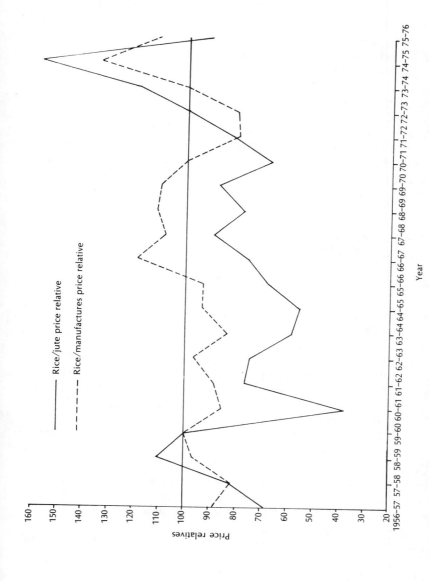

Figure 7.4. Rice/jute and rice/manufactures price relatives, 1956–1957 to 1975–1976. *Source:* Government of East Pakistan, Bureau of Statistics, *Statistical Digest of East Pakistan 1965 and 1968;* Government of Bangladesh, Bureau of Statistics, *Statistical Digest of Bangladesh, 1972, Statistical Yearbook, 1975 and Monthly Bulletin of Statistics,* various issues.

It is clear from Figure 7.4 that there was considerable fluctuation in the movement of both the price relatives. However, beginning in the mid-1960s, the rice/jute price relative shows an upward trend that becomes even sharper between 1970–1975 with considerable welfare loss for the jute growers. Traditionally, it has been claimed that jute growers never received a just price for their product because of the operation of the middleman. The movement of the price relative against jute resulted in reduction of jute acreage in favor of *aus* rice.[9] Jute being a relatively more labor-intensive crop a shift from jute to *aus* was naturally followed by a considerable loss in employment of the agricultural laborers in 1974. We shall come back to this point again in Chapter 8. Similarly, the small producers of manufactured items also suffered drastic terms of trade loss vis-à-vis rice producers over the period 1972–1975. Therefore, the preceding analysis leaves no doubt in our minds that a wide range of people suffered in terms of trade loss during the immediate postliberation years, and that the lowest point was reached in 1974.

REGIONAL VARIATION IN PRICE MOVEMENTS

Movement of Rice Prices by District

Movement of the annual average prices of rice by district is similar to the movement of national average prices as discussed earlier. There are, however, some differences in the rate of price increase between districts. This is more true of the postliberation period than the preceding years. Table 7.3 shows the movement of average retail price of coarse quality rice for the month of October in different postliberation years. In the famine districts the rice price increased by 254 percent between October 1972 and October 1974, the figure for nonfamine districts was slightly lower (246 percent). Apparently, in both areas, there was a sharp acceleration in rice prices in the second year. The rate of acceleration was considerably higher in the famine districts. As shown in Table 7.3 the rate of price increase in individual districts during the first year varied between 17 and 46 percent, and in the second year, between 122 and 226 percent. The famine districts were among the lowest ranking districts in the first year in terms of rate of price increase, the opposite was true of the second year although Mymensingh and Rangpur did not make the top three.

We have analyzed the monthly movements in the average retail prices of coarse quality rice in the three famine districts separately over the period January 1973 to June 1975 (Figure 7.5). For comparison we also

Table 7.3. Movement of Retail Price of Rice (Coarse Quality) by District

Districts	Oct. 1972	Oct. 1973	Oct. 1974	% Change between Oct. 1972 and Oct. 1973	% Change between Oct. 1973 and Oct. 1974	% Change between Oct. 1972 and Oct. 1974
Dacca	74.36	97.86	263.92	31.60	169.69	254.92
Mymensingh	78.83	93.87	276.44	19.08	194.49	250.68
Tangail	77.79	101.42	273.33	30.38	169.50	251.37
Pabna	75.47	101.63	249.18	34.66	145.18	230.17
Bogra	74.66	93.75	227.25	25.57	142.40	204.38
Rangpur	86.08	103.13	274.78	19.81	166.44	219.21
Dinajpur	75.00	99.00	254.45	32.00	157.02	239.27
Rajshahi	75.55	101.42	230.96	34.24	127.73	205.70
Kushtia	72.50	96.42	232.94	32.99	141.59	221.30
Jessore	75.00	95.26	236.89	27.01	148.68	215.05
Khulnia	71.82	92.75	233.43	29.14	151.68	225.02
Barisal	66.75	90.88	268.53	36.15	195.48	302.29
Patuakhali	64.59	94.21	269.56	45.86	186.13	317.34
Faridpur	72.09	95.41	248.93	32.35	160.90	245.30
Comilla	72.16	84.47	265.53	17.06	214.34	267.97
Sylhet	68.12	84.20	274.72	23.61	226.28	303.29
Noakhali	70.20	86.94	283.75	23.85	226.37	304.20
Chittagong	68.47	97.00	215.55	41.67	122.22	214.81
Chittagong Hill Tracts	62.45	78.69	203.61	26.00	158.75	226.04
Famine districts	77.68	95.73	275.31	23.24	187.59	254.42
Nonfamine districts	71.80	99.46	247.36	38.52	148.70	244.52
Average Bangladesh	72.73	94.11	251.78	29.40	167.54	246.18

Source: M. Alamgir, *Famine 1974: Political Economy of Mass Starvation in Bangladesh,* Statistical Annexe, Part I (Dacca: Bangladesh Institute of Development Studies, 1977), pp. 56–58.

Note: Tk./maund = 82.29 pounds

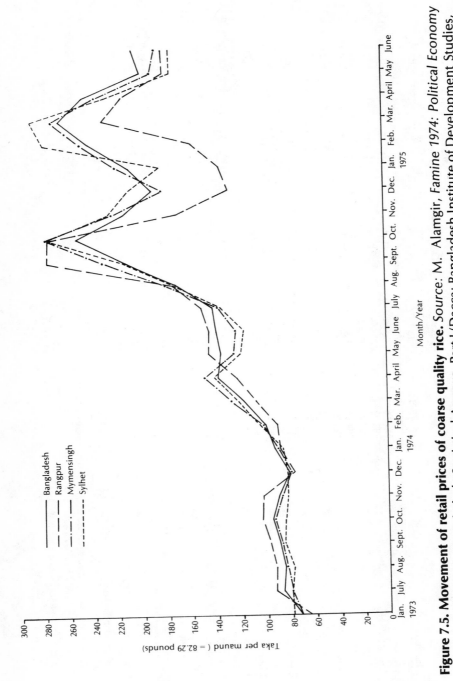

Figure 7.5. Movement of retail prices of coarse quality rice. *Source*: M. Alamgir, *Famine 1974: Political Economy of Mass Starvation in Bangladesh*, Statistical Annexe, Part I (Dacca: Bangladesh Institute of Development Studies, 1977), pp. 56–58.

show the overall Bangladesh picture. What stand out clearly are some features of the price movement in the Rangpur district. Rangpur started the period at the lowest level among these three districts (it was also the lowest among all districts) but prices increased sharply between January and July 1973. The price level continued to rise after July and at the same time it remained above most of the other districts until November 1973. The December *aman* harvest brought some relief and the rice price level came down significantly (it was again among the lowest in the country, although not the lowest.) But from that point onward rice prices increased continuously without any fluctuation whatsoever until September–October 1974. This was completely at variance with the experience of other districts where a downswing in prices was observed between April and June 1974. Throughout this period the Rangpur prices were above other famine districts, except in August. What is rather interesting to note is that the peak in rice price was reached in all famine districts at about the same level (Tk. 275/maund = 82.29 pounds) and at the same time (October 1974). But more importantly, a very high peak price prevailed in Rangpur for two successive months. Following October 1974, prices dropped in all famine districts but more sharply in Rangpur. And again when an upsurge in rice prices came in February–March 1975, Rangpur prices held below the level of other districts.

It is not very difficult to look for an explanation of the rice price movement in Rangpur during the period under consideration. In the earlier part of 1974 prices had probably been influenced by an actual decline in foodgrain supply (particularly on account of abnormal storage and smuggling loss), although observed figures showed differently. Besides, recurrent flood in that year seriously handicapped the government's ability to distribute foodgrains to the severely affected areas. The normal marketing channels were also disrupted due to the flood damages sustained by the transportation and communication system. In the isolated local markets of the district, rice traders were observed (by our field investigators) to have been pre-empting all supplies. Consequently, on certain occasions, prices were found to increase by the hour. In the post-October period the price trend seems to have been influenced by both the demand (lower purchasing power of the famine victims) and supply (1975 *aman* output despite difficulties with planting due to flood was higher than the year before) factors. On balance, prices were substantially pulled down.

Sylhet district presents an interesting case in its rice price movement during the period prior to the 1974 famine. There was very little fluctuation in prices over the period January 1973 to January 1974. During this period price increase was small (7 percent), but the first sign of trouble was evident in the fact that unlike other districts rice price did not decline following that year's *aman* harvest. On the contrary, price of rice continued to increase, a process that received a further boost from the flash flood that hit the *boro* crop. The rice price jumped by 66 percent in the course of the next three months in anticipation of a poor *boro* harvest. However, despite an apparent loss of a part of the *boro* crop, rice price declined in May and June, but thereafter it followed the pattern of other districts. The rice price increase over the critical months had hurt this district more than others because many households were dependent on a single crop (*boro*) and alternative employment opportunities were very limited, so a high price of rice led to a severe foodgrain deprivation for many families. And compared with other districts, the adverse effect of rice price increase was relatively more evenly distributed, if that is any consolation.

The price trend shown for Mymensingh is slightly misleading because this is a very large district and the flood intensity was different in different parts of the district. Our own survey village was located in one of the worst affected areas of the district, close to the river Brahmaputra (Figure 4.1). Nevertheless, during the critical months of 1974, the district average price level was significantly higher than the national average. Between June and October 1974, the rate of rice price increase in Mymensingh was 126 percent as compared with 81 percent for Bangladesh as a whole.

Districtwide movement of rice prices reveal some differences in the underlying pattern during prefamine, and famine, and postfamine periods. While either visually or in a statistical accounting sense such differences may sometimes appear to be of minor significance; in reality, under the threat of an extreme foodgrain deprivation of marginal households, they may actually indicate the difference between life and death for the individuals on the threshold of death. For example, prevalence of a very high peak price over two consecutive months in Rangpur had possibly been translated into a large number of excess deaths as compared with districts that were similar in all other respects, but had a shorter duration of high peak price. No less important was the fact that compared with other districts, Rangpur had already experienced a higher level of rice price in 1973. As we shall explain later, such evidence on the deviation of district level price from the national average has important implications for a famine forewarning system.

Price Spread Between Districts

In order to fully capture the regional dimension of famine, it is important to analyze interregional variation in rice prices. We again use district level prices for this purpose. Since districts differ in the underlying supply and demand factors, prices are likely to differ accordingly. Our purpose here is to find out if 1974 presented a pattern different from what one would normally expect.

Interdistrict variation in rice prices was relatively small in the 1950s and 1960s. In 1970, the range (measured in taka) of district level average price (retail) of rice (coarse) was only seven. In 1972–1973, it was reduced to even five and then it moved up to nineteen in 1973–1974, fifty-one in 1974–1975, and seventeen in 1975–1976. Clearly, the interdistrict variation in rice prices during the famine period was out of line with other years. It is difficult to interpret every increase in the range of district level rice prices, but a large jump should be a matter of concern. From the point of view of expost analysis of famine, it makes sense to look at the interdistrict spread of annual average rice prices, but if one were interested in monitoring the likelihood of famine occurrence, then it would be necessary to take a look periodically, within the same year, at such price spreads. The range of district level prices of rice is obviously a crude indicator either to detect the imminence of famine or its likely intensity (particularly regional variation of intensity), but it would certainly tell one that something may be wrong. For example, prior to the 1974 famine, the rice price range increased from nineteen in October 1973 to thirty-two in January 1974, and sixty in June 1974. This clearly tells us that there was a problem with interdistrict flow of foodgrains. We have already talked about the restriction imposed by the government on interdistrict foodgrain movement in 1974.

The observations made above are also borne out by the estimated coefficient of variation of monthly and annual district level rice prices. Our calculation based on wholesale price of coarse quality rice shows that the coefficient of variation of the annual average district level prices was higher for 1974 than for 1973. Estimates for monthly observations reveal the influence of seasonal pattern of rice production in the sense that the coefficient of variation is higher for harvesting months than others. Also, the coefficient of variation seems to be positively correlated with the magnitude of marketed surplus of each crop. However, comparing 1973 and 1974, it was found that the estimates of monthly coefficients of variation of district level rice prices were higher by month in 1974 than corresponding months of 1973 except for March, April, and May when the opposite was true. These months in 1974 were characterized by general market expectations of a difficult period ahead. This, along with an indifferent *boro* crop, reduced market supply all around so that the normal interdistrict variability in rice prices due to natural factors could not be observed.

We tried to correlate the ranks of districts in terms of absolute rice (coarse quality) price (retail) in different years to see if 1974 showed a weaker relationship with any of the other years as compared with other pairs of years. The respective rank correlations were all positive, but low and statistically not significant (at any conventional level). What this really means is that market and nonmarket forces could significantly alter the relative position (measured by the level of rice price) of different districts from year to year. Therefore, it seems that although a certain degree of inherent difference between districts will remain in terms of vulnerability to famine, the government should not be too narrowly focused in its famine prevention activities. The experience of 1974 is very vivid in that people in all districts of Bangladesh found themselves in the grip of a famine.

It is evident that the interdistrict spread in the rate of rice price increase could be used as a surrogate for famine intensity. We found a statistically significant (at 5 percent level) rank correlation (0.42) between rate of rice price increase at the district level between October 1973 and October 1974 and the percentage of population in *langarkhanas*. In this context, it may be noted that the association between ranks of districts according to flood intensity (product of maximum depth of innundation and the period of innundation) and according to rice price increase, as mentioned above, turned out to be positive but low (0.19) and statistically not significant. A similar result was obtained when we related flood intensity and the percentage of population in *langarkhanas* (rank correlation = 0.0149). This does not necessarily rule out the flood of 1974 as having aggravated the suffering of the people, but it points to the fact that the famine could not be attributed to flood alone.

Comparison of Prices of Essential Items as Reported by Survey Villagers

We conclude this section by making brief comments on the reported price levels of essential items of consumption and of land in our survey villages. The relevant data are presented in Tables 7.4 and 7.5. For rice and wheat flour the levels of price increase are clearly within the range shown earlier. Famine villages apparently experienced a higher rate of price increase of these two items than nonfamine villages. Prices of other sources of calorie and protein (pulses and edible oils in this instance) also increased sharply, but their average weighted rate of increase was lower than that of cereals. It is not surprising that we found many among our survey villagers who had been deprived of the required minimum of both calorie and protein in 1974.

It is equally important to examine what happened to land prices during this period. Land price represents the terms at which vulnerable

Table 7.4. Comparison of Prices of Essential Commodities as Reported in Village Survey (price in Taka, per seer)

Area	Rice			Wheat Flour			Pulses (Masur)			Edible Oil (Mustard)		
	1973	1974	% Change	1973	1974	% Change	1973	1974	% Change	1973	1974	% Change
Total villages	2.88	6.69	132.29	1.92	4.71	145.31	2.64	5.18	96.21	13.72	34.81	153.72
Famine villages	2.53	6.97	175.49	1.59	4.64	191.82	2.62	5.49	109.54	14.44	33.50	131.99
Nonfamine villages	3.23	6.40	98.14	2.25	4.78	112.44	2.67	4.87	82.40	12.99	36.11	177.98
Famine area												
Ramna	2.52	8.03	218.65	1.23	5.25	326.83	2.26	5.77	155.81	16.08	39.86	197.89
Gaorarang	2.74	5.78	110.65	1.53	3.50	128.76	2.75	5.21	89.45	11.90	28.78	141.85
Kogaria	2.72	8.06	196.32	1.94	5.04	159.79	3.34	5.96	78.44	16.77	37.37	122.84
Dewangonj	2.14	6.00	180.37	1.64	4.75	189.63	2.12	5.00	135.85	13.00	28.00	115.38
Nonfamine area												
Nazirpur	2.83	7.12	151.59	1.85	4.57	147.03	2.06	4.26	106.80	10.37	40.00	285.73
Laskarpur	2.61	6.23	138.70	1.97	5.04	155.84	2.36	5.41	108.08	12.41	34.28	176.23
Komorpur	3.69	5.86	58.81	2.54	4.73	86.22	3.05	4.95	62.56	16.56	34.04	105.49
Charbaniari	N.A.	N.A.	—	N.A.	N.A.	—	—	N.A.	—	N.A.	N.A.	—

Note: Price data refer to the July–October period. 1 seer = 2.06 lbs.

279

Table 7.5. Sale Price of Land per Acre as Reported in the Village Survey (Taka)

Area/Farmer Group	1972	1973	1974
Bangladesh	3695	3241	3458
Small farmer	3052	2691	3154
Medium farmer	3019	3253	3713
Large farmer	6190	5500	5386
Famine area	3311	2749	3385
Small farmer	2745	3273	3153
Medium farmer	3348	1515	4200
Large farmer	4570	2749	4078
Nonfamine area	4196	4325	3656
Small farmer	3426	2938	3157
Medium farmer	2557	2983	3037
Large farmer	8450	5765	8291

families with some landholding can buy time before facing ultimate destruction. Data presented in Table 7.5 suggest that in the postliberation period land prices did not rise commensurate with either the general wholesale price index or specifically the food price index. On the contrary, the average land price declined between 1972 and 1974. Clearly, the land market was no sellers' market. However, there is no systematic pattern between the famine and nonfamine areas nor is there any systematic pattern in the land price received by different size groups of farmers. It is very difficult to make any conjecture on the basis of this evidence since we are dealing with average figures without making allowance for differences in land quality or in the specific circumstances under which land transaction had taken place. We had shown earlier that a large part of land transactions in postliberation Bangladesh had taken place under extreme distress situations.

CAUSAL ANALYSIS OF PRICE CHANGES

Temporal Analysis

In this section we shall present a formal analysis of rice price changes. We use annual time series data to explain the variation in average wholesale and retail prices of rice. This is followed by seasonal and spatial analysis. For the formulation of famine prevention policies we need to identify the causal factors underlying rice price variations between different time periods. An analysis of annual data, although deficient in many ways, will reveal the fundamental factors determining the price of rice.

Our first approximation of the world is that fluctuations in annual average prices of rice can be explained primarily by the interaction of supply and demand forces. This was the essence of our presentation in Figure 2.7 of Chapter 2. We further noted there that in the situation prevailing in Bangladesh, the rationing system in principle does not influence the level of prices in the market for nonrationed foodgrain. This implicitly assumed that variation in controlled prices did not affect the supply and demand curves for local foodgrain. Since there is very little carryover of foodgrain from one year to another under private account, the cost of storage and storage loss do not enter into the formation of annual average prices. The cost of government stock carryover is not relevant because it is covered by the rationing system. A question nevertheless remains whether the controlled price or, for that matter, the import price affects expectations, which according to Working[10] influence the process of price formation. Working, however, was concerned with the role of expectations on the pattern of seasonal inventory buildup and releases that influence the observed seasonal prices. To the extent that annual averages carry these seasonal influences, the expectation element remains relevant for annual time series analysis.

Import prices are indicators of the prevailing supply and demand situation in the international market. In periods of rising import prices, a country such as Bangladesh suffers because it cannot import as much as it would like due to foreign exchange constraint. It also suffers because during such periods supply of concessionary food imports seems to dry up. The effect of these two facts on the domestic market shows up in a steeper slope (the kink appearing at a higher price level) of the rising part of the supply curve of foodgrain (Figure 2.7 of Chapter 2). With no change in the position of the demand curve of foodgrain the above (change in the slope of the supply curve) will have the effect of raising annual average prices. A period of declining import prices will tend to make this curve flatter and, therefore, create a lower market equilibrium price. We are assuming here that import prices do not affect consumer expectations in a manner that will have any perceptible impact on the formation of demand.

Controlled price of rice may have a direct impact on the demand formation under the assumption that rationed foodgrain and local foodgrain are imperfect substitutes. It is also assumed that the controlled price is below the market price. A rise in the controlled price will lead to a shift to the right in the demand curve for local foodgrains given the fact that consumers prefer local foodgrain to imported foodgrain. This is likely to happen even if the price of rationed foodgrain does not increase enough to equal the previous market price. The result of the shift in the demand curve will be a new equilibrium (higher) price for local food-grain. A fall in the controlled price will have the opposite effect. Since the rationing system does not cover much of the total population of the country, it is unlikely that either the import price or the controlled price will have a large effect on the local market price; in other words, the relevant elasticities of response are likely to be low, although a priori one could say that it will be higher for controlled price than for import price.

The government procurement price of rice enters in an important way into supply responses and demand formation via expectations. The procurement price affects primarily the main rice crop, *aman*. A relative-ly high procurement price may induce farmers to sell a part of their postharvest marketed crop to government agents with the result that normal supply into the open market is reduced. Now this will not affect the price level as such if the domestically procured foodgrain is pumped back into the food system to meet part of the demand without com-pensating reduction in the amount of imports. On the other hand, a high procurement price may be taken as an indicator of a possible difficult supply situation (so that the market reads it as an attempt by the government to pre-empt supply); this will feed into expectations of a higher return from prolonged retention on the part of traders and surplus farmers. In the end, the average picture for the year may be reflected by a shift to the left in the market supply curve of local foodgrain, with no change in the position of the demand curve; this will mean a higher price. However, there is a possibility that at least a section of the consumers (primarily the poor) will respond to the situation by curbing demand, that is, voluntary belt-tightening in terms of reduced foodgrain con-sumption. This will shift the demand curve to the left, except that this move will probably be counterbalanced (or more than counterbalanced) by panic purchases by other consumers. The result of the combined shifts in the two curves may, therefore, be a still higher market price of rice if one accepts that, in an environment such as that of Bangladesh (with a large fraction of the population being on the margin of subsistence), the extent of a leftward shift in the demand curve is likely to be small. Again, given the supply and demand situation, procurement price will still have a positive influence on the market along the lines suggested above, even if it is designed only as a support price for the farmer. Now, considering the fact that some of the reactions to government procure-ment prices noted here work in opposite directions, the final outcome will depend on the relative strength of different expectations, and it will largely remain an empirical issue. However, coming back to our region of concern, it may be safely speculated that a positive relationship between procurement price and market price of rice will characterize the situation. In any case, both controlled price and procurement price are policy instruments within the control of the government. It would be worthwhile to examine empirically what effect, if any, they have on the annual average price of rice.

Let us now specify the model explaining variation in the annual average prices (wholesale and retail) of medium and coarse quality rice in Bangladesh over the period 1956–1957 to 1972–1973. This is the longest stretch prior to the 1974 famine for which reliable price data are available to carry out econometric investigation. As mentioned earlier, for coarse quality rice we only have information on wholesale prices. Therefore, our dependent variables are *DPMR, DPMW,* and *DPCW* (see note to Table 7.6 for definition). Explanatory variables considered here include import price (*PI*), controlled price (*PC*), procurement price (*PR*), per capita income (*y*) to reflect demand influences and per capita availability of foodgrains (*F*) to capture supply influences. A generalized structure of the model is as follows:

$$P = f(F, y, PI, PC, PR) \qquad (7.1)$$

where *P* is rice price.

We specify linear relationships between variables. Parameters were estimated by least squares regression. In order to isolate the effect of different variables on rice prices we introduce them in stages. Our starting point was the truncated relationship where only supply (*F*) and demand (*y*) factors were noted. Then, other variables were introduced separately, one at a time, so that the total number of explanatory variables never exceeded three. We do this for two reasons. First, the price variables were found to be highly correlated, which made it difficult to introduce them together in regression estimates because of undesirable consequences of multicollinearity. Second, we wanted to save adequate degrees of freedom for a meaningful hypothesis testing. This is why, although *PI* and *PC* were only moderately correlated (0.62), we did not introduce them together. As for specification of variables, domestic market prices were deflated by the nonrice food price index, but the other price variables were not. *PC* and *PR* are government instruments and the relevant authority uses them in nominal terms. Consideration of the movement of the underlying real part hardly enters into the process of decision-making. Import price (*PI*) could not be deflated because of a lack of a suitable price index.

A word should be added on the definition of *F*, which includes here both rice and wheat, imported and local. This actually contradicts our contention that local and imported foodgrain, and also rice and wheat

Table 7.6. Price Model: Regression Results

Dependent Variable	Independent Variables					Constant	$\bar{R}^2$	SEE	D-W
	F	y	PC	PI	PR				
1. DPMR	−0.00064[c] (1.934)	0.00107[b] (2.554)				0.2286[b] (2.249)	0.23	0.0329	1.06
2. DPMR	−0.00110[b] (3.009)	0.00135[a] (3.403)	0.00527[c] (2.136)			0.1768 (1.803)	0.39	0.0294	1.67
3. DPMR	−0.00091[a] (3.103)	0.00130[a] (3.612)		0.00284[b] (2.681)		0.1943[b] (2.171)	0.47	0.0274	1.62
4. DPMR	−0.00138[a] (4.892)	0.00226[a] (5.692)			0.00367[a] (4.248)	0.0726 (0.903)	0.65	0.221	2.04
5. DPMW	−0.00077[b] (2.460)	0.00106[b] (2.665)				0.2642[b] (2.626)	0.29	0.0311	1.37
6. DPMW	−0.00109[b] (2.957)	0.00125[a] (3.119)	0.00376 (1.499)			0.2272[b] (2.284)	0.35	0.0298	1.81
7. DPMW	−0.00100[a] (3.449)	0.00125[a] (3.518)		0.00244[b] (2.326)		0.2347[b] (2.647)	0.46	0.0271	1.88
8. DPMW	−0.00136[a] (4.346)	0.00201[a] (4.558)			0.00295[a] (3.071)	0.1386 (1.551)	0.56	0.0246	2.05
9. DPCW	−0.00048 (1.701)	0.00091[b] (2.565)				0.1736 (1.922)	0.23	0.0279	1.25
10. DPCW	−0.00089[b] (2.933)	0.00116[a] (3.529)	0.00474[b] (2.308)			0.1270 (1.559)	0.41	0.0244	1.94
11. DPCW	−0.00071[b] (2.850)	0.00111[a] (3.634)		0.00242[b] (2.695)		0.1443 (1.903)	0.47	0.0232	1.69
12. DPCW	−0.00115[a] (5.353)	0.00199[a] (6.590)			0.00333[a] (5.062)	0.0320 (0.524)	0.72	0.0168	2.32

Table 7.6 *(continued)*

Note: The following symbols have been used here:

DPMR = Domestic retail price of medium quality rice per maund in Taka;
DPMW = Domestic wholesale price of medium quality rice per maund in Taka;
DPCW = Domestic wholesale price of coarse quality rice per maund in Taka;
F = Foodgrain availability per capita (pound/year);
y = Per capita income in Taka at 1959–1960 factor cost;
PI = Price of imported rice per maund in Taka;
PR = Domestic procurement price per maund in Taka;
PC = Controlled price per maund in Taka.

In regression equations DPMR, DPMW, and DPCW are expressed as actual price deflated by the nonrice foodgrain price index. Figures in parentheses are t-statistics.

[a]0.01 level of significance
[b]0.05 level of significance
[c]0.10 level of significance

may not be perfect substitutes. They should all have been explicit arguments in the price model (7.1). As a matter of convenience and also keeping in view the limitation of the number of observations, we specified only one supply variable. However, the effect of possible substitution is picked up by PC in some of the specifications of the model (Table 7.6).

It should be noted that we are dealing here with what may be considered as a reduced form equation of a complete supply-demand model of the rice market, but we do not go so far as to specify the underlying supply and demand functions. All of these simplifications in terms of the model and variable specifications do not worry us much because at this stage of our analysis what we are really interested in is to see which variables matter in rice price formation, and not so much in the precision of specific coefficient estimates and/or in the estimation of a more complete set of parameters.

The results of our exercise are presented in Table 7.6. While dealing with the time series data, one is always worried about autocorrelation, but fortunately in this case only equations (7) and (9) appear to have some problem. The Durbin-Watson test on the null hypothesis of positive autocorrelation is inconclusive at 1 percent level of significance. Other equations are free from positive autocorrelation. It is interesting to note that all coefficients have the expected sign. The basic supply and demand variables by themselves explain little although the coefficients are statistically significant at conventional levels as shown by results of equation (5). We, of course, ignored results of equations (1) and (9) because of an inconclusive D-W test. In any case, the corrected R^2 for both is lower than equation (5)($\overline{R}^2 = 0.29$).

Introduction of other price policy variables and import price improves results in all cases. $\overline{R}^2$ increases and all coefficients are found to be highly significant except the coefficient of PC in equation (6). As can be seen from Table 7.6 there is a systematic pattern in the improvement of regression results judged by both $\overline{R}^2$ and the level of significance of the estimated coefficients. The introduction of PR as an explanatory variable in the model along with F and y (equations [4], [8], and [12]) produces the best results followed by other specifications including PI and PC (in this order). Among three different dependent variables, equations with $DPCW$ perform better than others. The point that emerges clearly from this analysis is that the explanatory variables identified here explain a large part of the variation in domestic market prices of rice. In particular, the influence of procurement price appears to be highly significant in the determination of the level of annual average prices of rice in Bangladesh. A better showing of PR as compared with PI and PC is not surprising in view of the fact that PR is declared at the beginning of the most important harvest of the year and it has almost the whole of the year to work its influence out. There is no such time pattern in changes of *PC* and *PI*. As for *PI*, it takes a while for the information to be communicated to various agents in the local markets. It is very revealing that despite a rather low level of actual procurement, the procurement price set by the government played a crucial role in the determination of market prices of rice. This has something to do with our earlier observation in Chapter 6 that low procurement prices combined with occasional attempts at compulsory levy had the effect of discouraging domestic production of rice, but this probably worked with one year lag. Otherwise it would be difficult to reconcile the findings of regression analysis here with our earlier statement. To sum up, the lesson that we learn from Table 7.6 is that, while there may be perfectly good reasons for tampering with *PR* and *PC* by the government, it should not be done in a manner so that it can feed into adverse speculations by traders and surplus farmers to the detriment of vulnerable consumers.

Seasonal Analysis

When discontinuous production is confronted with continuous consumption, price fluctuations related primarily to production cycles is an inevitable outcome. Admittedly, this is a very simplistic explanation of seasonal fluctuations in rice prices. In reality, a wide range of factors seem to influence seasonal fluctuations in prices, for example, changes in seasonal production levels, cost of storage (including loss in storage) and marketing, rate of increase of general price level, availability of storage facilities, resistance of rice variety to deterioration in quality over time, political stability, natural calamity, expectations about substitute crops, purchase patterns of consumers, retention pattern of surplus farmers and traders, imports, and government intervention. It is clear that expectations play an important role in the determination of seasonal prices. Needless to say, there is a high degree of interdependence among many of the factors identified above. An understanding of the relative importance of each of these factors is essential for formulating stabilization policies with respect to the rice market; thus protecting the interests of both producers and consumers, as the case may be, while at the same time meeting the requirements of macro-economic stability.

The seasonal fluctuations in the wholesale price of coarse quality rice are analyzed here with a view to ascertain if there is an underlying stable seasonal pattern in rice prices. Assuming that the answer to this question is positive, we proceed to look at the seasonal pattern of the 1974 rice price and compare it with the normal pattern. Finally, we test the hypothesis that there is exploitation of consumers through the rice market by traders and surplus farmers. In our analysis the unit of time is the crop year spreading from November to October of the following year, covering *aman, boro* and *aus* varieties of rice, in that order.

The crop year starts with the anticipation of *aman* harvest during November, December, and January[11] leading to a decline in rice prices that continues until early February, immediately after the *aman* harvest is completed. After this period, rice prices increase through June despite the *boro* harvest during April, May, and June. The role of price increase during this period depends on how the market expectations regarding future supply and demand are modified on the basis of government procurement price, import plans, controlled price, import price, and above all the latest market intelligence regarding the approximate amount of *aman* rice harvested.

The reason why the *boro* harvest does not appear to affect rice prices is that its arrival in the market is generally matched by appearance of deficit producing families as buyers since their stocks have run out by then. The *aus* harvest of July and August has some influence in lowering prices, although not very perceptible in most years. The marginal effect of *aus* crop is probably explained by the fact there is considerable uncertainty regarding the realized level of output due to natural factors (flood) and that there is consumer resistance to this quality of rice. While commenting on the influence of *aus* harvest on the seasonal prices of rice, Asaduzzaman maintained that "uncertainty in production and consumer's resistance combine to stabilize the price somewhat."[12]

What is said in the previous paragraph can be matched against the production-consumption balance by month worked out by Faruk[13] for the period 1959-1960 to 1967-1968 under certain assumptions about the monthly distribution of production, average consumption per capita, conversion factor for consumption units from total population, and the proportion of nonhuman consumption. His findings were: (1) October is the month of largest deficit and December of highest net surplus; (2) positive balance is obtained in the months of December, January, February, March, and April, therefore, this is the time for traders to buy; (3) *aus* has some effect on seasonal variation in the price of rice but not *boro*; and (4) July–October is the optimum period for government operation of buffer stock. Faruk found that seasonal price increases could not be explained by cost of storage, but he was not inclined to accept it as evidence of excess profit of traders. He feels that,

"in the absence of more detailed business and transaction data and, more importantly, a proper valuation of the skill and time of the trader, computation of profits in this manner may be a grossly imperfect method of measuring market imperfections."[14]

Asaduzzaman analyzed data on medium and coarse quality rice for the period 1950–1972. He applied the method of moving averages (roughly similar to what Goldman did for Indonesia) to find stable seasonal factors. Furthermore, an *F*-test for stability of seasonal factors turned out to be significant at the 5 percent level. His analysis showed that seasonal patterns were similar for the two types of rice and that December and January were trough months for coarse and medium quality respectively. He compared seasonal factors for five yearly periods between 1955 and 1970 and concluded that "the fluctuation during 1960–1965 are dampened compared to those in other two sub-periods."[15] His most important observation was that "the curves of de-seasonalized averages are almost horizontal and look like straight lines signifying that seasonal fluctuations alone are responsible for the ups and downs in the prices in a given year. . . . seasonality of production, apparently, is the sole reason behind price fluctuation."[16] Government offtake, he feels, had some dampening effect on price fluctuations but not much. Asaduzzaman essentially agreed with Faruk in downplaying the exploitative role of rice traders. In our analysis, we extend the period of coverage of both Faruk and Asaduzzaman, and re-examine some of the observations made by them particularly with a view to explaining the abnormal behavior of rice prices during 1974, the famine year.

In order to identify the underlying seasonal pattern in rice prices (coarse quality wholesale) we follow a relatively simple-minded approach. We eliminate trend influences (including general inflation) by drawing linear segments between July to July of successive years (actually the points taken fall halfway between June and July) and then calculating the seasonal price relatives as the ratio of observed prices to the corresponding trend price. What we get is trend adjusted seasonal price indexes. Variation in seasonal price indexes is explained by variation in underlying supply and demand forces that incorporate, among others, seasonal production and expectation variables. We take periodic averages of monthly price relatives to obtain a periodic seasonal pattern.

For consistency of analysis we use here the same periods for aggregation as was done in the case of temporal analysis. Results of our exercise are presented in Figure 7.6. Apparently, there is a stable seasonal pattern with slight variation from period to period. Using the average absolute monthly deviation of price relatives from one as the index of average seasonal amplitude we find the following average amplitudes:

Period I:	0.0615
Period II:	0.0042
Period III:	0.0455

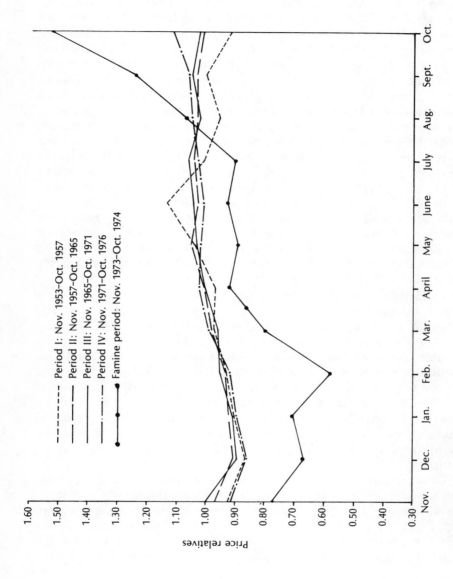

Figure 7.6. Seasonal price relatives.

Period IV:	0.0616
1974:	0.2211

These results indicate that Periods II and III were more stable than the other two. This essentially confirms the earlier findings of Asaduzzaman. The abnormally high level of average seasonal price increase in 1974 is clearly indicated by the average seasonal amplitude as shown above. In Figure 7.6, 1974 stands out as showing a significantly different seasonal pattern than other periods that basically conform to the pattern we hinted at at the beginning of this discussion on seasonal price variation. The curve for Period IV and more specifically that for 1974 bring forth the critical nature of the July–October period mentioned earlier by Faruk.

In order to understand the implications of seasonal variation in rice prices for the welfare of different groups in the society, especially the consumers, we need to examine carefully the information presented in Table 7.7. Looking at the periodic results it is found that December is the month of lowest price relative in all cases while the month of highest price relative varied between periods. In general, the month of highest price relative got pushed back in years/periods of supply difficulties. Thus, in years of known supply difficulties including, of course, 1974, October turned out to be the month of highest price relative. Both relative supply difficulty and the resulting percentage change in seasonal price relative appear to be positively associated with the number of months between highest and lowest price relatives. In this context, the negative changes in price relatives imply that the previous year had been a very difficult year so that rice price had risen relatively very high just prior to the beginning of the current crop year during which a downward adjustment took place. This happened once in 1955–1956 and a second time in 1974–1975, neither of which come as a surprise to us.

We now examine the increases in seasonal price relatives to see if traders (or more generally market agents since surplus farmers also enter in the market) earn supernormal profits. At the outset we should point out that there are a number of problems in such an analysis. First, we do not have firm data on cost of storage. Second, price data used here were presumably collected from secondary and terminal markets. But traders often purchase paddy/rice at farm yard and/or primary markets. Similarly, surplus farms sell at farm yard, primary market, and also at secondary market depending on the distance and means of transport. Third, Faruk pointed out that the Bangladesh rice market is operated by agents who conduct business at various levels. Actual costs and returns for an agent depend on the nature of his operation. Therefore, if one finds seasonal price increase in excess of the cost of storage, one can not easily say who gets it.

Table 7.7. Seasonal Price Increases in Bangladesh, 1953–1976

Year (November–October)	Month of Lowest Price Relative	Month of Highest Price Relative	Number of Months Between Lowest and Highest Price Relative	Absolute Increase (+) Decrease (−) in Seasonal Price Relative	Percentage Change in Price Relative
1953–1954	December	September	9	0.2421	30
1954–1955	November	September	10	0.3580	47
1955–1956	October	November	11	−0.1349	−13
1956–1957	February	June	4	0.5582	66
1957–1958	November	May	6	0.2919	35
1958–1959	January	May	4	0.2706	33
1959–1960	November	May	6	0.1912	20
1960–1961	November	July	8	0.1759	27
1961–1962	December	June	6	0.1934	22
1962–1963	January	August	7	0.1018	10
1963–1964	April	October	6	0.2362	28
1964–1965	December	July	7	0.1616	18
1965–1966	January	September	8	0.3475	42
1966–1967	December	May	5	0.3077	31
1967–1968	March	September	6	0.2937	36
1968–1969	December	July	7	0.1421	13
1969–1970	December	May	5	0.1983	23
1970–1971	January	May	4	0.2095	24
1971–1972	January	September	8	0.3935	52
1972–1973	December	April	4	0.2752	31
1973–1974	February	October	8	0.9457	163
1974–1975	October	February	8	−0.6980	−89
1975–1976	November	October	11	0.6810	105

Table 7.7 *(continued)*

Period I (1953–1957)	December	June	6	0.2682	31
Period II (1957–1965)	December	May	5	0.1427	16
Period III (1965–1971)	December	July	7	0.1660	19
Period IV (1971–1976)	December	September	9	0.3305	45

We are primarily concerned with the welfare of consumers vis-à-vis surplus farmers and traders. One may consider any one of the following three measures to reflect loss of consumer welfare, through seasonal price increases:

1. Difference between seasonal price increase and storage cost assuming that the consumers themselves stored rice/paddy.
2. Difference between seasonal price increase and cost of procurement and storage by the government assuming that it undertook the entire task of holding grains for consumers thoughout the year.
3. Difference between seasonal price increase and storage cost of traders and surplus farmers. Note, however, that in a normal year the bulk of grain holding is probably done by traders.

From data provided by Faruk[17] for 1967–1968, the storage cost for a trader appear to run in the neighborhood of little over 1 percent per month. On the other hand, data from a different survey for the year 1964–1965[18] tells us that the price spread between farm yard price and primary market on one hand and secondary market on the other, can not be explained by transportation and handling costs alone. This implies that for traders purchasing paddy/rice at farm yard or at primary markets, the real gain will be higher than is indicated by figures in the last column of Table 7.7. In any case, to obtain an order to magnitude for measure (3) above, we compare the cost of storage with the monthly rates of return implicit in percentage change in seasonal price relatives. As expected, the traders appear to have gained most in Period IV. If one considers years such as 1973–1974 and 1975–1976, there is little doubt that the rice traders earned supernormal profits at the expense of consumers. The figure for 1975–1976 should, however, be considered along with that of 1974–1975 when traders may have suffered losses since the month of lowest price relative (October) followed the month of highest price relative (November).

However, the question remains as to what explains the existence of excess mark up for traders even in a normal year.[19] One could resort to arguments presented by Faruk that we mentioned earlier; but we feel that there is an element of excess profit in the earnings of rice traders. This points towards the fact that intertemporal arbitrage does not eliminate excess profit because of market imperfection. Although other analysts did not focus this, the rice market of Bangladesh is characterized by an oligopolistic market structure with barriers to entry. There are no formal barriers to entry but informally there are many. These barriers are the need to acquire a specialized skill; education; access to capital and storage facilities; government regulations in the form of licensing, antihoarding, and designation of selling areas; and the need to meet the challenge of the arduous task of collecting rice from scattered points and putting it up for sale in the terminal markets.

For famine prevention three policy conclusions emerge from the above discussion. First, the implicit barriers to entry into the rice trade should be removed so as to improve its efficiency in intertemporal allocation of supply. Second, government should probably play a more active role by expanding its procurement, open market, and rationing operations so as to avoid a situation such as that of 1974. Clearly, traders are normally not in a position to expropriate too high a margin of excess profit, but they wield enormous power in a difficult year. We have already discussed the operation of the forward sale and purchase (*dadan*) markets and the terms associated with them. It is neither necessary nor practical in a country like Bangladesh to nationalize rice trade (the failure of the Indian experiment is well known), but the government should maintain the capability of intervening in the market effectively whenever necessary. The government offtake of foodgrains apparently smoothed the price fluctuations in Period II, the improvement over Period I being very marked, but it soon lost grip over the situation. We have seen in Chapter 6 that the normal distribution machinery of the government is totally inadequate to cope with an emergency. As a matter of fact, all studies of public distribution systems indicate that in years of foodgrain scarcity (reflected in unusually high mark up for traders) these systems do not function very well in that available stocks dwindle to very low levels. Thus, many needy families are forced to go without rations, which seriously affects their nutritional status as was the case in 1974. High market prices also increase the propensity of leakage from the rationing system. A third policy conclusion relates to credit. Since access to capital is an important barrier to entry into rice trade, the government must be very careful not to allow the rice traders to take advantage of liberal credit policy as happened in 1977 when, with government money, traders cornered the rice market.

Spatial Analysis

It is useful to know the geographical pattern of rice flow so that in periods of crisis one may easily identify the relatively weak spots in market links. This knowledge is important for two other considerations as well. First, the government can monitor spatial flow of foodgrains; any sign of abnormal movement will provide impetus for the formulation of counter measures. Second, if for some reason government itself intervenes in the normal trade flow across regions, it can do so by taking account of the needs of different regions and making provisions for additional supply under its direct supervision.[20]

One can apply "transfer cost test" and "correlation test" to get at the spatial structure of the rice market and evaluate its operational efficiency. Faruk found that for most of the markets he studied, the sale price in the terminal market exceeded the sale price in primary or secondary markets by more than the transfer cost (packing, transport, handling, and normal traders' commission). He comes out with a number of arguments explaining positive price spread between markets.[21] As in his intertemporal analysis, he falls short of characterizing instances of positive price spread as indicative of market imperfections. Even with our very limited data we found evidence of positive price spread between markets after making allowance for transfer cost. But, unlike Faruk, we essentially explain this in similar terms as we did in the case of seasonal price variation.

As for market integration, Faruk used his 1967–1968 survey data to calculate intermarket correlations for prices of medium quality rice from which he drew the following broad conclusions.

> Although in the aggregate all the markets show significantly high correlation among their prices, certain important variations with respect to the individual markets are interesting and noteworthy.
>
> a. correlation among 3 terminal markets is relatively lower than between them and other intermediate and primary markets.
>
> b. The secondary distribution markets have high correlation among themselves.
>
> c. The terminal markets generally show lower correlation with the larger secondary markets than with the smaller ones.[22]

We have used data on monthly retail prices of coarse quality rice for 1973 and 1974 to examine intermarket relationship. Complete data sets were available for twenty-seven marketing centers in 1973 and thirty-five in 1974. For our purpose here, we consider 1973 as a normal year and present correlation between six terminal markets in central Bangladesh and other intermediate markets for that year in Table 7.8. It may be pointed out that all markets, even though some may be predominantly intermediate, make sales for terminal use. In contrast to the finding of Faruk, we found that correlation among terminal markets is high and actually higher than between them and other markets as shown in Table 7.8 with very few exceptions. A high degree of association (measured by correlation coefficients) between the two markets reflect a degree of market integration due either to the fact that one draws supplies from the other or that they draw supplies (whole or a part) from a common third source.

A further examination of Table 7.8 reveals that there is a systematic spatial pattern in the degree of association between the six terminal markets and other markets. This is brought out clearly for Narayanganj in Figure 7.7, which shows that contours of lower correlation spread out.

Table 7.8. Intermarket Correlation Coefficients for Monthly Retail Prices of Coarse Quality Rice, 1973 (between central terminal markets and other markets)

Market Centers	Dacca	Narayanganj	Mirkadim	Manikganj	Narsingdi	Bhairabbazar
Dacca	1.00					
Narayanganj	0.94	1.00				
Mirkadim	0.88	0.95	1.00			
Manikganj	0.89	0.93	0.90	1.00		
Narsingdi	0.86	0.93	0.93	0.91	1.00	
Bhairabbazar	0.87	0.92	0.85	0.93	0.88	1.00
Kishoreganj	0.75	0.76	0.76	0.78	0.72	0.74
Netrokona	0.74	0.70	0.65	0.64	0.63	0.59
Mymensingh	0.84	0.74	0.71	0.73	0.68	0.69
Jamalpur	0.76	0.72	0.71	0.67	0.69	0.64
Tangail	0.89	0.79	0.81	0.72	0.70	0.67
Sirajgonj	0.78	0.70	0.75	0.76	0.64	0.61
Bogra	0.81	0.78	0.79	0.87	0.79	0.74
Rangpur	0.78	0.64	0.67	0.65	0.59	0.52
Dinajpur	0.71	0.62	0.65	0.66	0.67	0.54
Rajshahi	0.84	0.74	0.77	0.77	0.75	0.65
Pabna	0.87	0.79	0.82	0.81	0.77	0.65
Kushtia	0.89	0.86	0.87	0.92	0.92	0.81
Jessore	0.79	0.75	0.79	0.73	0.81	0.67
Khulna	0.87	0.88	0.90	0.89	0.93	0.82
Barisal	0.90	0.87	0.88	0.87	0.85	0.83
Patuakhali	0.82	0.85	0.87	0.81	0.87	0.80
Faridpur	0.83	0.87	0.82	0.85	0.88	0.85
Comilla	0.33	0.53	0.54	0.51	0.69	0.63
Sylhet	0.51	0.68	0.73	0.66	0.78	0.71
Chowmohani	0.57	0.73	0.74	0.70	0.81	0.80
Chittagong	0.74	0.80	0.82	0.70	0.86	0.72

Source: Price data obtained from the Department of Agricultural Marketing and Intelligence, Government of Bangladesh.

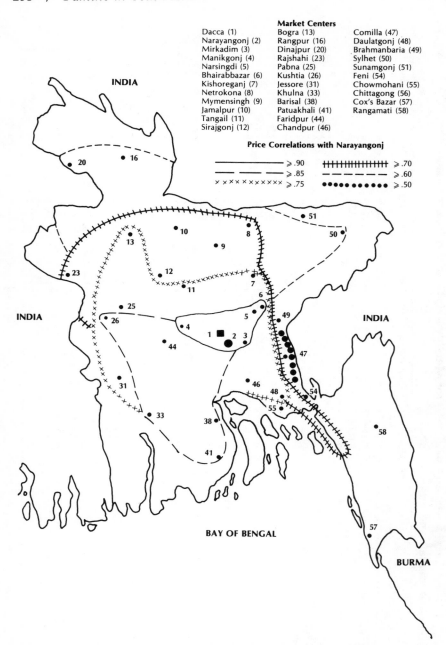

Figure 7.7. Pattern of market relationships between Narayangonj and other centers of Bangladesh, 1973.

The terminal markets have a closer relationship with southern market centers (except those located in southeastern region) than northern market centers, a finding similar to that of Faruk.[23]

One can also use an intermarket correlation matrix to delineate marketing zones.[24] Using a coefficient of 0.80 as the cutoff point we were able to clearly identify two marketing zones: the central-southern and the western. The intermarket correlation coefficients for these two zones are presented in Tables 7.9 and 7.10. Markets of the east are not totally delinked with one another or with the other two zones but the association is relatively weak.

The famine of 1974 had marked influence on the observed association among rice markets. In a real sense the spatial structure of rice markets probably became more disintegrated in 1974 as compared with 1973. Flood had destroyed communication and transportation in many areas, and the government had imposed restrictions on the interdistrict movement of foodgrains. But when we look at the correlation coefficients, we find a much higher level of intermarket association in 1974 than in 1973. This is clear from Figure 7.8. Taking Narayangonj as the point of reference again, we find that its correlation with virtually all other markets exceeded 0.90. This does not reflect a higher level of market integration in 1974, but rather is a result of supply difficulty induced expectations, panic purchases by consumers, hoarding by traders including prolonged retention by surplus farmers, and an overall environment of uncertainty. Goldman made a similar observation about a high correlation among prices in Java in 1957.[25]

There was, however, no change in the basic spatial structure of rice markets in 1974 except that a very low correlation between Narayangonj and Patuakhali, on the one hand, and Rangpur and other markets, on the other, needs an explanation. We saw in Table 7.9 that Patuakhali belonged to the central-southern market zone. In 1974, it was alleged that this market became integrated with markets outside the country since smuggling by boat through the Bay of Bengal route thrived during that year. Therefore, it is not surprising that correlation of prices between Patuakhali and terminal markets was lower in 1974 than in 1973. Rangpur stands out as another example of low correlation with almost all other markets, including those within the western market zone. It is clear that this market had little interaction with other markets in 1974 and the whole district, particularly the border belt, became a haven for smugglers. Actually, monthly rice prices in Rangpur had behaved somewhat differently from other districts beginning July 1973 (See Figure 7.5).

To sum up, we can only say that the uniformly high correlation among rice markets of Bangladesh in 1974 provides an excellent proof of how a

Table 7.9. Central-Southern Market Zone (intermarket correlation coefficients, 1973)

Centers	Dacca	Narayangonj	Mirkadim	Manikgonj	Narsingdi	Bhairabbazar	Barisal	Patuakhali	Faridpur
Dacca	1.00	0.94	0.88	0.89	0.86	0.87	0.90	0.82	0.83
Narayangonj		1.00	0.95	0.93	0.93	0.92	0.87	0.85	0.87
Mirkadim			1.00	0.90	0.93	0.85	0.88	0.87	0.82
Manikgonj				1.00	0.91	0.93	0.87	0.81	0.85
Narsingdi					1.00	0.93	0.87	0.87	0.88
Bhairabbazar						1.00	0.88	0.85	0.85
Barisal							1.00	0.80	0.83
Patuakhali								1.00	0.87
Faridpur									1.00

Note: Intermarket correlation coefficients are calculated on the basis of monthly wholesale prices of coarse quality rice obtained from the Department of Agricultural Marketing and Intelligence, Government of Bangladesh.

Table 7.10. Western Market Zone (intermarket correlation coefficients, 1973)

Centers	Bogra	Rangpur	Dinajpur	Rajshahi	Pabna	Kushtia	Jessore	Khulna
Bogra	1.00	0.84	0.89	0.91	0.94	0.92	0.84	0.90
Rangpur		1.00	0.92	0.96	0.92	0.76	0.86	0.80
Dinajpur			1.00	0.95	0.88	0.83	0.93	0.87
Rajshahi				1.00	0.95	0.88	0.93	0.91
Pabna					1.00	0.90	0.85	0.89
Kushtia						1.00	0.88	0.96
Jessore							1.00	0.95
Khulna								1.00

Note: Intermarket correlation coefficients are calculated on the basis of monthly wholesale prices of coarse quality rice obtained from the Department of Agricultural Marketing and Intelligence, Government of Bangladesh.

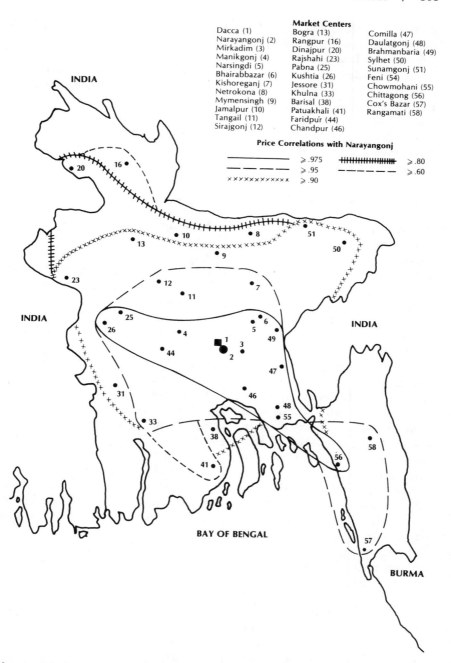

Market Centers

Dacca (1)
Narayangonj (2)
Mirkadim (3)
Manikgonj (4)
Narsingdi (5)
Bhairabbazar (6)
Kishoreganj (7)
Netrokona (8)
Mymensingh (9)
Jamalpur (10)
Tangail (11)
Sirajgonj (12)

Bogra (13)
Rangpur (16)
Dinajpur (20)
Rajshahi (23)
Pabna (25)
Kushtia (26)
Jessore (31)
Khulna (33)
Barisal (38)
Patuakhali (41)
Faridpur (44)
Chandpur (46)

Comilla (47)
Daulatgonj (48)
Brahmanbaria (49)
Sylhet (50)
Sunamgonj (51)
Feni (54)
Chowmohani (55)
Chittagong (56)
Cox's Bazar (57)
Rangamati (58)

Price Correlations with Narayangonj

⩾ .975   ⩾ .80
⩾ .95   ⩾ .60
× × × × × ×   ⩾ .90

Figure 7.8. Pattern of market relationships between Narayangonj and other centers of Bangladesh, 1974.

panicky situation can get further aggravated by actions of the government. The basic problem is that in a period of sharp uniform rise in prices, price loses its effectiveness as an indicator of relative intensity of suffering (other things being equal). Thus, as the critical months (July–October) of 1974 approached, one could not tell from looking at the price trend or level alone whether or not Rangpur district was suffering more than Noakhali district. In a difficult year, to the extent to which it is feasible, the government should assist in maintaining normal intermarket linkages; if necessary by generating supplementary flows should a normal artery be disrupted.

Analysis of General Price level

The movement of nominal price of rice during postliberation Bangladesh should be understood within the context of an unprecedented inflationary pressure that had been plaguing the country. According to the data compiled by the Bangladesh Bureau of Statistics, the wholesale price index (1969–1970 = 100) stood at 240 in 1972–1973, then it increased to 304 in 1973–1974, and 454 in 1974–1975. On the other hand, the cost of living index (1969–1970 = 100) of government employees in Dacca increased from 178 in 1972–1973 to 237 in 1973–1974 and 345 in 1974–1975.[26]

We do not have a long enough series to econometrically estimate parameters of a model of inflation. Without going into an elaborate discussion of the contemporary theories of inflation and their applicability to Bangladesh, we can safely hypothesize that the following factors contributed to the overall price increase during this period: a decline in output and availability of goods and services, a very large increase in money supply, an increase in velocity of money, an increase in wage rate, and an increase in price of imports and devaluation.

Bose showed that total availability of goods declined by 19 percent in 1972 as compared with 1969–1970.[27] In per capita terms, the decline in availability was even higher. According to my own calculation, per capita availability of goods declined further through 1973 and 1974.

As for money supply, M_1 (currency and demand deposits) increased by 50 percent from Tk. 3875 million to Tk. 5795 million between December 1971 and December 1972. It further increased by 39 percent to Tk. 8079 million over 1973 and by another 16 percent to Tk. 9378 million over 1974.[28] The major expansionary forces were government fiscal operations (deficit financing) and net borrowing by the nationalized sector.[29]

While velocity (income) of circulation declined in 1972–1973 as compared to 1969–1970, thus holding off price increase to less than the maximum possible limit, inflationary expectations of the following year raised velocity significantly. This trend further accelerated in

1974–1975.[30] Both money wage rate and import prices increased sharply[31] but the former was basically responding to the general increase in price level. Further, on the cost front, the cost of production of important industrial goods increased significantly as it is reflected in the prices of these goods at the factory gate.[32] Finally, the devaluation of January 1972 had the effect of raising the prices of importables and exportables in domestic currency.

We can summarize the general price situation in Bangladesh during 1972–1975 with the following quote from the Two Year Plan:

> Runaway inflation characterized post-independence Bangladesh economy; the price level that was increasing at an alarming rate took a critical turn towards the end of 1974 leading to fast deterioration in the purchasing power of the people, affecting adversely the savings and investment capabilities and export trade. Floods and droughts caused extensive damage to foodgrain and other agricultural crops and their production fell short of normal level. On the other hand, scarcity of essential industrial raw materials and spares, labour unrest and limited size of the market (contributed by inflation) all combined to restrict industrial output. In a situation of short supply of essential commodities, deficit financing by the government exerted further pressure on the price level. At the same time, inflation in the western economies triggered by fuel and food crisis had its impact on the price level of Bangladesh. Besides, various imperfections in the internal trade and distribution channels created artificial scarcities which aggravated the inflationary situation further.[33]

We have carried out a rather exhaustive survey of rice price and general price movements and their causative factors within a historic perspective. Now the obvious question is, do prices matter? It is claimed that average price elasticity of demand for foodgrain is rather high; it is higher for low-income as compared with upper-income groups. Unfortunately, we do not have separate estimates of price elasticity of demand by income group in the case of Bangladesh. Currently available estimates of overall elasticity vary depending on the methodology of estimation.[34] Research on Indonesia has brought out estimates of high price responsiveness of rice intake of the poor.[35] Therefore, we can perhaps safely conclude that for Bangladesh price is an important variable that should be considered in the context of formulating famine prevention and famine relief policies.

NOTES AND REFERENCES

1. Muhammad Osman Faruk, *Structure and Performance of the Rice Marketing System in East Pakistan*, Cornell International Agricultural Development Bulletin 23, Cornell

University, Ithaca, May 1972, pp. 54–55.

2. Richard Goldman, "Seasonal Rice Prices in Indonesia, 1953–1969: An Anticipatory Price Analysis," *Food Research Institute Studies* 13(2):117 (1974).

3. M. Alamgir and L. Berlage, "Foodgrain (Rice and Wheat) Demand, Import and Price Policy for Bangladesh," *Bangladesh Economic Review* 1(1):34 (January 1973).

4. Ibid., p. 35. We are considering here only medium quality rice.

5. For an earlier analysis of yearly movement of rice (medium quality) prices over the period 1951–1952 to 1967–1968, see Raquibuz M. Zaman and M. Asaduzzaman, *An Analysis of Rice Prices in Bangladesh*, Research Report No. 2 (New Series), Bangladesh Insitute of Development Studies, Dacca, July 1972, pp. 12–19.

6. Introduction of observations for later years reduced R^2 significantly. The time trend (linear) was fitted to the data on the wholesale price of coarse quality rice over the period 1953–1971.

7. Figures quoted from Government of Bangladesh, Ministry of Agriculture, *Bangladesh Agriculture in Statistics, 1973* (Dacca: Ministry of Agriculture, 1974), p. 6.

8. These prices are quoted in domestic currency. Therefore, the price increases observed here represent the combined effect of international price rise and devaluation of the Bangladesh Taka in May of 1975.

9. Jute acreage figures for different years in postliberation Bangladesh are as follows: 1972–1973, 2,215,000 acres; 1973–1974, 2,196,000 acres; 1974–1975, 1,417,000 acres; 1975–1976, 1,277,000 acres; 1976–1977, 1,603,000 acres.

10. Holbrook Working, "A Theory of Anticipatory Prices," *American Economic Review* 8(2):188–199 (May 1958). For an application to Indonesia, see Goldman, "Seasonal Rice Prices in Indonesia," pp. 129–138.

11. It is not clear how harvest is distributed over different months. The following figures are only suggestive. *Aman*: 30 percent in November, 60 percent in December, and 10 percent in January. *Boro*: 60 percent in April, 30 percent in May, and 10 percent in June. *Aus*: 10 percent in June, 20 percent in July, and 70 percent in August.

12. M. Asaduzzaman, "The Seasonal Variation in Price of Rice: Bangladesh 1950–1972," *Bangladesh Economic Review* 1(2):213 (1973).

13. Faruk, *Rice Marketing System in East Pakistan*, pp. 77–78. Note that our suggested distribution of monthly production in Note 11 is different from Faruk's on p. 77 of the reference cited here.

14. Ibid., p. 91. Faruk compared the actual price of stored rice with expected price under alternative assumptions about the storage period to arrive at the net seasonal increase in price. In estimating the expected price he took account of godown rent, interest on capital, quantity lost over time, and depreciation of sacks. See ibid., p. 80.

15. Asaduzzaman, "Seasonal Variation in Price of Rice," p. 215.

16. Ibid., pp. 218–219.

17. Faruk, *Rice Marketing System in East Pakistan*, p. 80.

18. Government of East Pakistan, Bureau of Statistics, *Master Survey of Agriculture in East Pakistan* (6th Round) (Dacca: Bureau of Statistics, 1966).

19. The Bangladesh result differs somewhat from the Indonesian one as obtained by Goldman. He concluded that "on the average, supplies are allocated efficiently over time in Javanese rice markets," Goldman, "*Seasonal Rice Prices in Indonesia*," p. 123.

20. This is unfortunately not realized in practice. In periods of foodgrain shortage governments in Bangladesh too often resorted to imposing barriers on interdistrict movement of foodgrains, ostensibly for the purpose of checking speculative movements by traders and also for checking smuggling. This causes further difficulty in deficit regions because the government almost invariably fails to ensure supply from alternative sources.

21. To mention a few: "non-standardized grading system," "price data used for intermarket comparisons represent an average of all transactions and have no reference to any particular consignment," and "value and remuneration of traders' skill and expertise." See Faruk, *Rice Marketing System in East Pakistan*, pp. 73–75.

22. Ibid., pp. 57, 61.

23. Ibid., p. 60.

24. Foodgrains produced in each zone are primarily absorbed within it. In other words terminal markets within each zone receive supplies from other markets of the same zone. However, this does not necessarily rule out interzonal movement of foodgrains completely.

25. Goldman, "Seasonal Rice Prices in Indonesia," p. 122.

26. Government of Bangladesh, Bureau of Statistics, *Statistical Yearbook of Bangladesh, 1979* (Dacca: Bureau of Statistics, 1979), p. 379.

27. S. R. Bose, "The Price Situation in Bangladesh—A Preliminary Analysis," *Bangladesh Economic Review* 1(3):255 (July 1973).

28. *Statistical Yearbook, 1979*, p. 315.

29. Government of Bangladesh, Ministry of Finance, *Bangladesh Economic Survey, 1972–1973* (Dacca: Superintendent Bangladesh Government Press, 1973); *Bangladesh Economic Survey 1973–1974* (Dacca: Superintendent Bangladesh Government Press, 1974); *Bangladesh Economic Survey 1974–1975* (Dacca: Superintendent Bangladesh Government Press, 1975); *Bangladesh Economic Survey 1975–1976* (Dacca: Superintendent Bangladesh Government Press, 1976).

30. A. K. M. Siddique, "Money and Inflation in Bangladesh," *Bangladesh Development Studies* 3(1):30–31 (January 1975); Sadiq Ahmad, "The Problem of Inflation in Bangladesh," mimeographed, Bangladesh Institute of Development Studies, 1978, pp. 1–29.

31. *Statistical Yearbook 1979*, pp. 291, 386.

32. Ibid., p. 375.

33. Government of Bangladesh, Planning Commission *Two Year Plan 1978–80*, (Dacca: Planning Commission, March 1978) p. 66.

34. Alamgir and Berlage, "Foodgrain Demand."

35. Peter C. Timmer, "Food Prices as Nutrition Policy Instrument," Paper presented at MIT/INP conference on Interface Problems Between Nutrition Policy and Its Implementation," Cambridge, November 5–8, 1979.

Chapter 8

Wages, Employment, and Real Income

INTRODUCTION

The 1974 famine of Bangladesh was associated with a drastic decline in real wages, employment of casual labor, and in the real income of the vulnerable groups in the society. However, such a decline was not an isolated phenomenon. It was a continuation of the past trend of deterioration of the living conditions of the rural and urban poor in Bangladesh. As indicated earlier, the unusual events of 1974, including the devastating flood, had aggravated the situation to a point where widespread excess death due to a sharp decline in foodgrain intake became a natural outcome. In order to appreciate what happened in 1974, we need to develop an understanding of how wage, employment, and income of households are determined in Bangladesh. These elements, along with overall foodgrain availability and prices, ultimately determine the command of households over food resources. Since the famine in question was primarily a rural phenomenon, we shall concentrate our attention more on the structure of the rural labor market and on the structure of the village economy, in general.

The level and trend of real wages of agricultural and industrial laborers being a crucial parameter in determining the well-being of these groups, we begin our analysis in this chapter by looking at what happened to real wages over the past two decades or so.[1] Employment and income of rural households is analyzed separately. A detailed picture of the interdistrict variation in wages and seasonality in both wages and employment is also presented here. A causal analysis of wage determination is presented in order to indicate the variables that may have had significant influence on the temporal, spatial, and seasonal variations in real wages of laborers. Furthermore, an in-depth analysis of the structure of employment, income, and poverty in rural Bangladesh is carried out. The purpose of this is to capture the structural/institutional factors that are responsible for making certain groups more vulnerable to famine than others. This will hopefully provide additional pertinent information that the policy-makers can use in the formulation of antifamine/antipoverty measures. Some data are presented on the extent of loss of employment and income of the rural poor during 1974 as compared with 1973 due to flood. The chapter concludes with a discussion of a suggested model of income and employment determination of rural households in Bangladesh.

REAL WAGES OF RURAL AND URBAN LABORERS

Trend in Real Wages

It is desirable to study the trend in real wages of laborers within the perspective of the movement of real income per capita of the total, agricultural, rural, and urban populations as thrown up by national accounts data. A declining trend in the real income per capita of both the agricultural and rural populations between the early 1950s and the late 1960s was noted in Chapter 4. Five yearly averages of agricultural value added per capita during the 1960s were far below the level observed for the early 1950s.[2] The movement of rural income per capita is somewhat involved. There was a declining trend between 1949–1950 and 1959–1960. The early 1960s experienced a recovery and the upswing was maintained through the late 1960s, but at no point did the absolute level reach that of the early 1950s. The causal factors explaining fluctuations in real income per capita of the agricultural and rural populations have been discussed earlier by Bose[3] and Alamgir and Berlage.[4]

The real income per capita of the urban population reveals considerable fluctuations (coefficient of variation was higher for urban [0.10] than for either agricultural [0.07] or rural [0.05] income per capita), although over the longer run a declining trend dominates. According to one estimate, the average figure for 1965–1970 was 5 percent lower than that of 1949–1955. Five yearly averages show that real income per capita of the urban population declined between 1949–1955 and 1955–1960.

There was a strong recovery in the following period (1960–1965) when the average figure exceeded that of the previous period by 22 percent. This was followed by a decline of 19 percent during 1965–1970. As expected, urban income per capita was always higher than rural income per capita. Looking at the relative movement of the two series, one can conclude that rural-urban income disparity widened during the 1950s and early 1960s, but the trend was slightly reversed in the late 1960s. The trend of the first period can be explained by a transfer of income from rural to urban areas through fiscal and price mechanisms. On the other hand, the recovery of the second period may be attributed to a growth in non-agricultural activities in rural areas, mainly in the form of rural works programs and also to the introduction of HYV technology in agriculture.

Even though the data base is limited, the period following the liberation of Bangladesh in December 1971 experienced a sharp decline in total per capita income. This trend continued up to 1974–1975, and there was only a slight recovery in 1975–1976.[5] With 1969–1970 as the base year, the index of real income (total) per capita stood at 86 in 1974–1975 and 90 in 1975–1976. It seems reasonable to assume that both the rural and urban populations shared in the decline in real income per capita. To sum up, there was no improvement in the real income per capita of the agricultural, rural, and urban populations during the 1950s and 1960s over the late 1940s; an appreciable decline in all of the above took place in the early 1970s.

The evidence presented here does tell us something about the movement in the well-being of the bottom strata of the population. Since the average trend is likely to underestimate the extent of change in the condition of the poor, it is desirable that the status of the poor be studied separately. Famine victims come mainly from among the poor. By all accounts, the agricultural laborers are the poorest of the poor in rural areas while their counterparts in urban areas are the unskilled workers. Other groups of interest are the industrial workers, the construction workers, and the fisheries workers. These also happen to be the groups for which consistent wage data are collected on a regular basis, thus enabling one to analyze the intertemporal changes in their well-being.[6]

Movement of the index of real wages of the different groups of workers identified here are shown in Figures 8.1 and 8.2. Nominal wages were deflated by appropriate price indexes to arrive at real wages.[7] Clearly, there is no long-term trend in the movement of real wages of agricultural laborers. This is confirmed by trend regression analysis.[8] From Figure 8.1, one can make a number of observations. First, one can discern a two-and-a-half cycle in temporal movement of real wages. The first extends between 1949 and 1964, with a downswing phase (1949–1953) and an upswing phase (1956–1964). Nineteen fifty four and 1955 could be considered as local aberrations. The second one is a shorter cycle

Figure 8.1. Movement of real wage indexes of agricultural and urban unskilled workers, 1949–1975. *Sources:* M. Alamgir, "Some Analysis of Distribution of Income, Consumption, Saving and Poverty in Bangladesh," *Bangladesh Development Studies* 2(4):754, 758 (October 1974); M. Alamgir, *Bangladesh, A Case of Below Poverty Level Equilibrium Trap* (Dacca: Bangladesh Institute of Development Studies, 1978), p. 12. The author has made some revisions on the basis of latest available data.

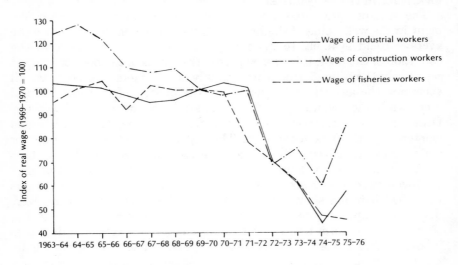

Figure 8.2. Movement of real wage indexes of industrial, fisheries and construction workers in Bangladesh, 1963–1964 to 1975–1976. *Source:* Government of Bangladesh, Bureau of Statistics, *Monthly Statistical Bulletin* 6(10):58 (October 1977).

covering the following five years (1964–1969). The first two years represent the downswing of the cycle and the last three, the upswing. Finally, we observe a downswing in real wages of agricultural laborers beginning in 1969.

Second, considering the annual figures, it is found that the index of real wage was lower than 1949 in twenty out of the total of twenty-seven years for wich data are shown here. In other words, there was no question of any sustained improvement in the well-being of the agricultural laborer households over what they enjoyed in late 1940s. In Chapter 3 it was speculated that the level of living of the rural poor had deteriorated between the 1930s and 1940s, particularly as a consequence of the 1943 Great Bengal Famine, which brought in its wake tremendous social dislocation.[9]

Third, from the point of view of the analysis of the 1974 Bangladesh famine, the post-1969 trend of real wages of agricultural laborers is of particular importance since it represents a prolonged period of rather sharp decline in calorie intake of the members of agricultural laborer households. As will be shown later, actual intake of calories probably declined to an unacceptable minimum level throughout the year 1974. To be more precise, between 1969 and 1974 the real wage earnings[10] of agricultural laborers declined by 40 percent. The decline was of the order of 10 percent between 1973 and 1974. At this point two other pieces of evidence on the movement of the real wage of agricultural laborers can be seen. The first is that wage in rice equivalent declined by 60 percent between 1969 and 1974. The extent of decline in rice wage in 1974 was 11 percent over 1973, a figure close to that quoted above for Bangladesh as a whole.[11] The second piece of evidence comes from the village survey data of this study (Table 8.30a). It was found that in all areas the real wage rate of agricultural laborers declined by 43 percent between July–October 1973 and July–October 1974. By concentrating on the critical months alone, the village survey data has put the problem of a sharp decline in real wages in proper perspective. The annual average data somewhat blurred the extent of decline in real wages between 1973 and 1974. It is interesting to note that the rate of decline in real wages of agricultural laborers was actually higher in the nonfamine area (47 percent) as compared with the famine area (33 percent).

Fourth, while a large number of factors interacted to determine the level of real wages of agricultural laborers, at the aggregate level it is possible to isolate a few. During the early 1950s the growth rate of the agricultural labor force exceeded that of agricultural value added. Furthermore, there was no move toward increasing crop intensity or adopting more labor using technology. This period actually coincided with an era of post-Korean war boom that led to near collapse of the jute trade, as a result of which the government introduced jute acreage licensing in order to restrict output of jute. This naturally resulted in considerable loss of agricultural employment and a consequent drop in both normal and real wages of agricultural laborers. The rise in real wages in the 1956–1964 period can be explained in terms of a rise in value added per agricultural worker as well as the introduction of the Rural Works Program in 1961, which generated off-season employment for poor households. Furthermore, the early 1960s also witnessed the beginning of the use of fertilizers and small-pump irrigation in rice cultivation, which helped raise the crop intensity somewhat. The sharp fall in real wages during 1964–1966 was accompanied by a fall in agricultural value added per capita. Total value added stagnated during this period; public investment expenditure in agriculture was drastically cut back as a result of the cash crunch that came in the wake of the Indo-Pakistan war in 1965. In the years since 1966, the real wage rate increased over the first few years up to 1969 with the introduction of HYV which increased labor absorption. But this trend could not be sustained as the agricultural labor force continuted to grow at a rate far in excess of agricultural output and income (there was a decline in the postliberation period), and also, as will be explained later, the early optimism about the possible extent of employment expansion due to introduction of HYV did not quite materialize.[12]

As for the movement of real wages of other groups of workers (primarily urban), it is found that during the 1960s the more organized of these groups (for example, industrial workers) was able to effect a more spontaneous wage price adjustment than all other groups of laborers (including, of course, the agricultural laborers) considered here. However, since liberation a very sharply declining trend, even more so than that of the agricultural laborers, set in. This happened despite the fact that in the first few years after liberation Bangladesh witnessed a very high level of militant trade union activities among industrial laborers that often forced money wages up, but apparently never enough to forestall a decline in real wages. There is little doubt that by 1974 the condition of these groups of laborers had indeed become very vulnerable; they probably had little resistance power left to withstand a prolonged period of foodgrain intake decline. To a certain extent the urban laborers were protected in 1974 since the urban *Langarkhanas* were apparently better supplied with foodstuff. But their rural counterparts in non-agricultural occupations had no such luck; they suffered more than the agricultural laborers since their purchasing power declined further than the rest of the population. A similar situation was noted in the Great Bengal Famine of 1943.

In order to provide a more detailed picture of the movement of the living conditions of the poor households in Bangladesh from liberation through the famine period, the monthly real wage indexes are presented in Figure 8.3 for Bangladesh as a whole and also for the three famine

Figure 8.3. Movement of real wage indexes of agricultural laborers by month, July 1972 to December 1975.

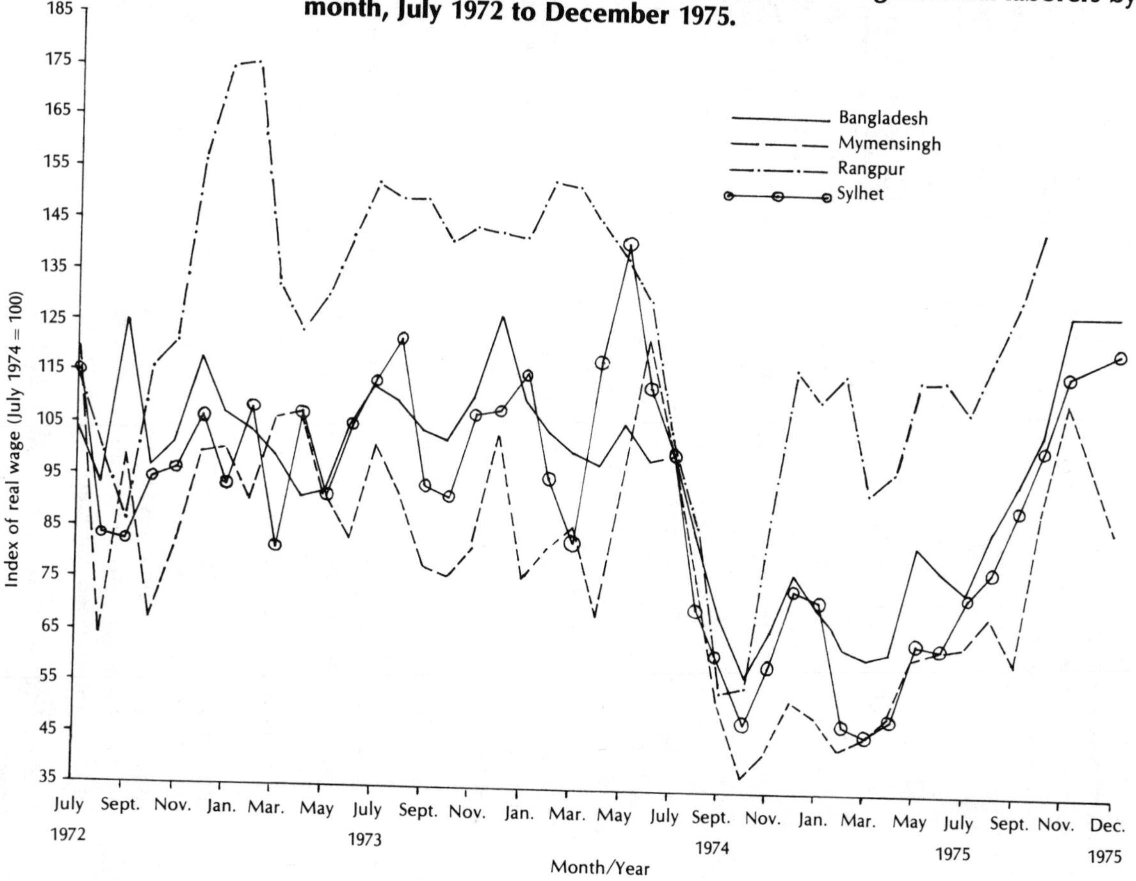

Bangladesh
Mymensingh
Rangpur
Sylhet
Index of real wage (July 1974 = 100)
185
175
165
155
145
135
125
115
105
95
85
75
65
55
45
35
July 1972
Sept.
Nov.
Jan.
Mar.
May
July 1973
Sept.
Nov.
Jan.
Mar.
May
July
Sept. 1974
Nov.
Jan.
Mar.
May
July 1975
Sept.
Nov.
Dec. 1975
Month/Year

districts separately. These indexes were constructed by deflating the nominal wages by the price index of coarse quality rice. As expected, there was considerable month-to-month fluctuations in the real wage index, which, as will be explained later, have a lot to do with the seasonal nature of crop production activities and availability of agricultural employment opportunities. What is important to date here is the fact that in all areas, real wages went through a phase of sharp decline over the period May–October 1974. They recovered a little after October 1974, although, except for Rangpur, the reversal in the trend of real wages was not significiant until July 1975. The adjustments of real wages of agricultural laborers in the postfamine period were discussed earlier in Chapter 5.

The condition of the agricultural laborers in 1974 is reflected much better in the monthly calorie wage per capita by district as shown in Table 8.1. For further analysis, one should contrast the calorie wage levels with the FAO/WHO recommended minimum requirement level of 1890 calories.[13] Clearly, even in the early part of the year, the majority of the districts were calorie deficient. The situation apparently deteriorated as the year advanced. From Table 8.1 it appears that August–November was the most difficult period, since during these months no district reached the minimum required level of calorie wage per capita. This information should not let one forget that the problem is further aggravated due to intradistrict and intrafamily inequality in the calorie intake distribution. Some comments were made on intrafamily distribution of calorie and protein intake in Chapter 6. Further information is available in the study by Arens and Beurden who write:

> If a laborer comes home with his meagre earnings, he has to share them with the family members who are dependent on him. After he himself has eaten, not much is left for the others. Therefore, his wife, who might have been husking paddy with the *dheki* for half a day, or who might be pregnant, is in even greater trouble, as she gets only what is left over after her husband and children have eaten.[14]

Intradistrict variation in calorie wages comes out from figures in Table 8.1, which suggest that Sylhet district on the average enjoyed an above minimum requirement level of wages of agricultural laborers until July, but our own field investigators found that in many areas calorie wage remained depressed throught the year.

Interdistrict Variation in Real Wages of Agricultural Laborers

Available data permit one to carry out an analysis of the interdistrict variation in real wages. Starting with Table 8.1, one finds that in 1974

Table 8.1. Calorie Wage per Capita of Agricultural Laborer Households in Bangladesh by Month during 1974 (number of kilocalories)

Districts	January	February	March	April	May	June	July	August	September	October	November	December
Mymensingh	1497	1610	1681	1360	2156	2414	1959	1502	1045	738	846	1042
Rangpur	1499	1612	1606	1602	1458	1370	1055	906	574	576	932	1237
Sylhet	2757	2269	1973	1845	2214	2720	2399	1675	1349	1153	1408	1771
Dacca	2044	1874	1713	1649	2176	1770	2241	1683	1441	1093	1149	1144
Tangail	1567	1557	1319	1429	1553	1454	1404	1238	986	731	855	951
Faridpur	1311	1219	1177	1104	1163	1011	1217	1035	843	973	744	877
Chittagong	2351	2326	2375	2101	2560	2420	2353	1684	1605	1419	1438	1454
Chittagong Hill Tracts	2430	2282	2392	2246	2710	2608	2464	1916	1668	1296	1457	1498
Noakhali	2164	1976	1918	1893	2170	2039	1987	1623	1323	972	1022	1438
Comilla	1786	1199	1416	1317	1434	1354	1510	1456	1143	897	1053	1079
Rajshahi	1535	1366	1323	1219	1182	1122	1110	1159	975	883	1089	1107
Dinajpur	1851	1596	1547	1799	1663	1372	1557	1322	1214	876	1105	1533
Bogra	1521	1400	1414	1174	1181	1142	1187	1161	1007	722	831	951
Pabna	1340	1430	1314	1132	1057	991	963	807	681	575	549	618
Khulna	1598	1442	1377	1306	1277	1131	1195	1040	831	706	840	1224
Barisal	1723	1981	1591	1725	1993	1785	1831	1451	1224	875	1081	1398
Patuakhali	2017	2061	1618	1437	1707	1533	1709	1331	1125	913	1150	2036
Jessore	1004	978	974	862	1009	922	945	912	695	645	722	854
Kushtia	1116	1120	1048	856	1041	970	976	997	738	717	716	807

Source: Nominal wage and rice price from M. Alamgir, *Famine 1974: Political Economy of Mass Starvation in Bangladesh*, Statistical Annexe, Part I (Dacca: Bangladesh Institute of Development Studies, 1977), pp. 57–58, 92; size of household from Government of Bangladesh, Bureau of Statistics, *Statistical Yearbook of Bangladesh, 1979*, p. 108.

Note: Nominal wage was converted into rice wage by applying the retail price of coarse quality rice. Rice wage was then converted into kilocalorie by using conversion factor as explained in note to Table 5.15. Finally, this figure was divided by the average size of household as obtained from 1973 household census assuming that household size remained the same in 1974.

there was considerable variation in the level of calorie wage per capita in various districts. The range was as high as 1426 calories in January 1974, but as the situation deteriorated in all districts, it was reduced and by November 1974 the range of calorie wage among districts was found to be 904. This also indicates that in 1974 the position of the districts varied widely in terms of "calorie gap" (difference between required minimum and actual intake). For example, during October 1974 the calorie gap (in percentage terms) varied between 70 percent in Rangpur and Pabna and 25 percent in Chittagong. It may be pointed out that ranking districts according to calorie gap does not necessarily put the famine districts among the top three.

Further, information on the interdistrict variation in real wage rice equivalent is presented in Table 8.2, which covers the years 1972-1973 to 1975-1976. It can be seen that the range of the annual average wage was stable in the first two years; it declined in 1974-1975 as expected and

Table 8.2. District Level Wage (Rice Equivalent) of Agricultural Laborers in Bangladesh (in seers)

District	1972–1973	1973–1974	1974–1975	1975–1976
Mymensingh	2.69	2.63	1.57	2.51
Rangpur	2.08	2.37	1.46	2.31
Sylhet	3.34	3.60	2.17	3.67
Dacca	2.83	3.24	1.95	2.70
Tangail	2.47	2.37	1.53	2.25
Faridpur	2.13	2.07	1.44	2.19
Chittagong	3.13	3.52	2.20	3.31
Chittagong H. Tracts	2.60	3.61	2.15	3.44
Noakhali	2.92	3.36	2.13	3.22
Comilla	2.69	2.57	1.79	2.90
Rajshahi	2.24	2.11	1.55	2.50
Dinajpur	2.34	2.23	1.69	2.75
Bogra	2.16	2.07	1.62	2.83
Pabna	2.42	2.07	1.41	2.64
Khulna	1.71	2.09	1.41	2.70
Barisal	2.66	3.27	2.10	3.06
Patuakhali	2.88	2.64	2.12	2.67
Jessore	1.72	1.84	1.27	2.16
Kushtia	1.53	1.79	1.36	2.16
Mean	2.45	2.60	1.73	2.74
Range	1.81	1.81	0.93	1.51
Coefficient of variation (CV)	0.19	0.24	0.18	0.16

Source: Nominal wage and rice price from M. Alamgir, Famine 1974: Political Economy of Mass Starvation in Bangladesh, Statistical Annexe, Part I (Dacca: Bangladesh Institute of Development Studies, 1977), pp. 56–59, 90–94.

Note: 1 seer = 2.05725 kilogram

increased again in 1975–1976. The coefficient of variation shows a declining trend beginning in 1973–1974. This may be an indication that the labor market is becoming more integrated. One should, however, be cautious in pushing this point too far because micro level studies on wages of agricultural laborers suggest that a wide variation in the level of wages actually operates even within a small locality. Wages of agricultural laborers appear to be determined by, among others, the structure of the labor market as characterized by the mode of wage payment (traditional share payments, daily wages with prepared food, fixed contract payments in cash, with or without food, and so forth) and the type of laborers (village-tied, patron-tied, migrant, and so forth).[15] The most interesting aspect of Table 8.2 is the stability of interdistrict ranking in terms of real wages. Yearly pairwise rank correlation coefficients were found to be highly significant (at 1 percent level).[16] This helps one in identifying the districts where the agricultural laborers are more vulnerable to exogenous shocks as compared with other districts. Concentrating on the bottom five districts in these four years, a total of eight districts appear vulnerable: Faridpur, Jessore, Kushtia, Bogra, Khulna, Pabna, Rangpur, and Tangail. The first three districts make the list in all four years. While average annual real wage data could not capture the vulnerability of the two famine districts as identified in this study (Mymesingh and Sylhet), they remain critical problem regions because of a high degree of susceptibility to flood (regular and flash), which may have a devastating effect on income and employment of all households, particularly of the agricultural laborer households. The above analysis suggests that there are ten districts in Bangladesh where the government should carefully monitor the nominal wages and rice prices throughout the year. Any sign of trouble as reflected in a sudden shift in real wages will warrant immediate response in terms of additional supply of foodgrains (to check upward movement of rice price) and/or expenditure for additional employment generation (to check downward movement of wage income of the vulnerable wage-dependent families). These are an integral part of a package of famine prevention and famine relief policies.

An attempt to discern long-term trends by fitting ordinary least squares time trend to the district level real wages of agricultural laborers failed. In general, most districts show no trend over the period 1953–1976. There were six districts with negative trend (linear) coefficients, but unfortunately the corresponding R^2 was very low in each case. The remaining ones had positive trend coefficients, and at least in the case of three districts (Mymensingh, Faridpur, and Jessore) the R^2 was reasonably high (0.81, 0.68 and 0.85 respectively). The reason that this evidence on positive trend is focused is not so much that it necessarily speaks for a relatively stronger position of these districts compared with others; rather it is noted here that such interpretation may be quite misleading. The average underlying trend often hides the magnitude of year-to-year fluctuations; as a result the vulnerability of a region to natural or man-made crisis is not revealed. This is exactly what happened here. It is true that the three districts mentioned came out with a positive real wage trend, but it was shown earlier that in recent years they all belonged to the bottom five among all districts in terms of the absolute level of real wage of agricultural laborers. Furthermore, they are among the top in terms of coefficient of variation of annual average wage (real) rates over the period 1953–1976. Besides, the trend regression analysis revealed that the standard error estimate of these districts was among the highest.

Seasonal Variation in Real Wages of Agricultural Laborers

In Chapter 2 a stylized description of the agricultural labor market was presented. It was pointed out that while supply of and demand for agricultural wage labor did play a role in the determination of wage level, there were a number of other factors that had a significant influence on the process of wage determination. In particular, it was emphasized that institutional factors play a dominant role in determining off-peak season wage level, although these influences are also modified by the reality of supply and demand for labor. In short, seasonal variations of supply and demand for agricultural labor combined with prevailing institutional norms and the physical norm of minimum acceptable wage level (famine wage) explain seasonal variations in real wage rate of agricultural laborers. Needless to say, what happens in the agricultural sector is also influenced by the general economic environment, particularly by the extent of employment opportunities in the nonagricultural activities in both rural and urban areas.

To recapitulate, real wages referred to here are wages in rice equivalent obtained by applying the monthly average wholesale price of coarse quality rice to the corresponding nominal wage rate (daily). In order to isolate the seasonal pattern in real wages, the underlying trend was eliminated by taking a twelve monthly moving average. Seasonal wage relatives were obtained for the period July 1953 to June 1976 by taking the ratio of actual monthly wage to the corresponding moving average value. In order to obtain monthly seasonal wage indexes for different periods, the averages of each month were calculated. The results of this exercise are summarized in Table 8.3 and Figure 8.4.

Considering the entire period under consideration, it is found that January is the period of highest wage relative and September the lowest.

Table 8.3. Seasonal Variation in Real Wages of Agricultural Laborers in Bangladesh.

Year	Month of Highest Wage Relative	Month of Lowest Wage Relative	Ratio of Lowest to Highest Wage Relative
1953–1954	December	September	0.70
1954–1955	May	June	0.75
1955–1956	January	May	0.61
1956–1957	February	June	0.53
1957–1958	November	July	0.57
1958–1959	December	April	0.71
1959–1960	December	April	0.76
1960–1961	December	January	0.91
1961–1962	December	September	0.81
1962–1963	May	April	0.86
1963–1964	April	November	0.81
1964–1965	July/December	February	0.85
1965–1966	February	September	0.62
1966–1967	March/April	August	0.72
1967–1968	March	July	0.70
1968–1969	May	July	0.79
1969–1970	March	April	0.52
1970–1971	January	March	0.76
1971–1972	January	May/June	0.79
1972–1973	December	April/May	0.75
1973–1974	February	September	0.76
1974–1975	July	October	0.67
1975–1976	November	July	0.64
1953–1976	January	September	0.85
1953–1960	January	June	0.83
1960–1965	December	September	0.92
1965–1970	January	July	0.77
1970–1976	December	April	0.85

Source: M. Alamgir, *Famine 1974: Political Economy of Mass Starvation in Bangladesh,* Statistical Annexe, Part I (Dacca: Bangladesh Institute of Development Studies, 1977), pp. 54 and 68.

The month of lowest wage relative has apparently varied from period to period but that of highest wage relative has remained confined between December and January. The latter is not surprising since it coincides with the harvest season of the most important crop, that is, *aman* (both broadcast and transplanted) and of a number of other minor but reasonably labor intensive crops such as sugarcane (November–March), ginger (November–January), turmeric (November–January), potato (December–February), and *Bhadoi* chillies (September–December). These two months also fall within the sowing periods of local *boro*

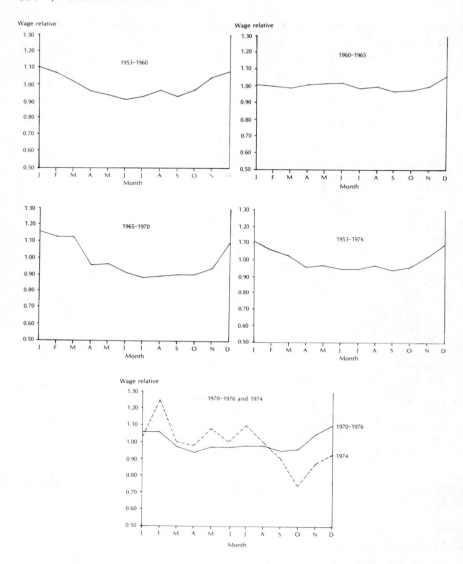

Figure 8.4. Seasonal movement of real wages of agricultural laborers.

(November–December), HYV *boro* (January–February), wheat (November–December), *masur* (October–December), *rabi* chillies (December–January), and sugarcane (October–March). Needless to emphasize that December and January is a period of all-round intense agricultural activities in rural Bangladesh. It is, therefore, not surprising that many areas have to fall back on female laborers and migrant laborers as well as the temporary returnees from town to meet the seasonal peak demand for labor.

The lowest monthly wage relative is found to occur primarily in a period when there is no major sowing or harvesting activity (April, June, and September). One does not really expect July to be a month of lowest wage relative unless, of course, in the period under consideration sowing of *aus* and jute was delayed due to late rain, which automatically pushes back the major part of harvest of these two crops into the month of August or even later. This is what appears to have happened during at least three years in the 1965–1970 period.

Seasonal variations in real wages of agricultural laborers come out rather neatly in the first diagram of Figure 8.4, which represents the period 1953–1976. Between the two high peaks of monthly wage relatives in January and December the other months of relatively lower relatives fall, thus making a gentle "U" shape with two local peaks around May and August. May is a sowing month for *aus* (March–May), *tossa* jute (April–May), mesta jute (April–May), *bhadoi* chillies (May–June), turmeric (March–May), ginger (March–May), and a harvest month for local *boro* (April–May), HYV *boro* (May–June), and *rabi* chillies (March–May). On the other hand, August is a major harvest month for *aus* (July–August), white jute (July–August), and tossa jute (August–September).

As for the periodic averages, the most important thing to note is the average seasonal amplitudes (average absolute deviations of monthly wage relatives from one):1953–1960, 0.05; 1960–1965, 0.02; 1965–1970, 0.09; 1970–1976, 0.05 (0.0458); 1970–1976 (without 1974), 0.05 (0.0525); 1974, 0.09. These figures confirm what one can see directly from Figure 8.4. The 1960–1965 period shows the least seasonal fluctuations in the real wage of agricultural laborers. Probably the introduction of the Rural Works Program, providing off-season employment in rural areas, had some effect in smoothing the seasonal fluctuations in real wages. The behavior of real wages in 1974, the famine year, clearly defies the normal expectations regarding seasonal fluctuations.

The last column of Table 8.3 presents the ratios of lowest to highest price relative. It supports the thesis presented in Chapter 2 while discussing the labor market that the real wage rate during the off-peak period is not necessarily pushed down to the minimum possible (for example, the famine wage level) level because of implicit contracts and social ties. The figures presented here suggest that for the entire period under consideration the real wage rate during the off-peak period has remained within fifteen percentage points of the peak period wage rate. The above minimum possible wage rate did not cost anything in terms of loss of employment given the nature of the demand function for labor (Figure 2.2 of Chapter 2). In this context the difficult years can be isolated easily from Table 8.3 by looking at the magnitude of the ratios mentioned above. Clearly, on seven different occasions the off-peak seasonal wage relative fell below the peak relative by more than twice the average level of the period as a whole.[17] They are all known to be difficult years for one reason or another, mainly natural disasters cutting into employment opportunities and relative food scarcities pushing normal seasonal peak prices up further.

It appears that beginning in 1971–1972 a gap between lowest and highest wage relative has widened. While it may be premature to read too much into this movement, one cannot ignore the possibility that this is a vindication of what many observers, including myself, have been saying regarding the weakening of the traditional bonds in the labor market that influenced seasonal variations in real wages of agricultural laborers. For one thing, the phenomenon of migrant labor is reducing the hold of local labor on maintaining a floor to the off-peak season wage rate. Furthermore, in many cases family labor is being utilized more intensively than before. Finally, the labor pool is being swelled by sharecroppers who have been evicted because the landlord finds it cheaper to employ hired labor, by new entrants into the small and marginal farmer groups, and, last but not least, by the landless laborers who have recently lost control over whatever small amount of productive assets they owned.[18]

The above analysis of seasonal variations in real wages of agricultural laborers provides a basis for formulating policies to protect this group from the grip of famine. The seasonal pattern has clearly revealed the periods of low real value of labor power. Clearly, during such periods it may sometimes be necessary to organize either direct transfer of food resources (public distribution of food or foodgrain, as the case may be) and/or indirect assistance in raising purchasing power (works programs). Even in a normal year, a comprehensive antipoverty program would call for measures to eliminate/reduce seasonal fluctuations in calorie intake per capita through various forms of interventions.

Wage Equations—Causal Analysis

An attempt is made here to explain the variation in annual average real wages of agricultural laborers in Bangladesh. The idea is to identify a set of macroeconomic variables that influence the level of wages. For this a regression analysis was carried out where a number of linear functions were estimated. The dependent variable was real wage rate of agricultural laborers (W_{AR}) and the independent variables were GNP at constant 1959–1960 factor cost in Taka million (X_{1R}), agricultural (X_{2R}), industrial (X_{3R}) and other sectors (X_{4R}) value added in same unit, acreage under HYV in thousand acres (X_{5R}) and real wage rate of construction workers in Taka/day (X_{6R}). The following generalized relationship was postulated:

$$W_{AR} = F(X_{1R},\ X_{2R},\ X_{3R},\ X_{4R},\ X_{5R},\ X_{6R}) \qquad (8.1)$$

What equation (8.1) hypothesizes is that the level of W_{AR} will be determined by the general economic prosperity (X_{1R}), demand for labor in other sectors of the economy (X_{3R}, X_{4R}), which actually reflects the potential for labor transfer out of agriculture, expansion of employment opportunity within agriculture through the introduction of HYV (X_{5R}), and finally by the expansion of off-peak season employment in construction (for example, rural works programs), which is best embodied in the real wage rate of construction workers. It was necessary to introduce one supply variable, annual agricultural labor force. Unfortunately, no data are available, so it was dropped. While one would have liked to estimate a joint function, intercorrelations among explanatory variables made it rather difficult to introduce them all at once. Alternative specifications were estimated by dropping one or more of the colinear variables. The period covered was 1956–1957 to 1973–1974. The reason why earlier years were not included is that data for real wage rate of construction workers were not available. It may be pointed out here that this set of data on the wages of construction workers is different from that presented in Figure 8.2. This is a set of data for helpers in construction, which the Bangladesh Bureau of Statistics has been compiling separately since the late 1950s.

By any criterion the exercise has only been moderately successful. The estimated equations presented in Table 8.4 do not reveal the presence of positive autocorrelations. The degree of explanatory power of the various equations is moderately high as given by the value of corrected R^2. The construction wage rate variable turns out to be significant in all equations except (5) at some acceptable level. As a matter of fact, all variables except X_{4R} are found to be significant in one equation or another. But by and large, the levels of significance are low. The unexpected outcome is the negative sign of the coefficient of X_{5R}, the HYV acreage variable.

Given the earlier statements made about the complexities of the agricultural labor market, this is probably what one could do with a

Table 8.4. Wage Equations: Regression Results (dependent variable W_{AR})

	Independent Variables						Constant	$\bar{R}^2$	SEE	DW
	X_{1R}	X_{2R}	X_{3R}	X_{4R}	X_{5R}	X_{6R}				
1.	0.000033^c (1.800)				−0.000092 (1.222)	1.6726^c (2.256)	1.208^a (4.315)	0.51	0.1903	2.58
2.		0.000075 (1.420)		0.000014 (0.477)	−0.000086 (1.141)	1.6237^c (2.126)	0.9607^a (2.278)	0.48	0.1950	2.35
3.			0.000379^c (1.917)	0.000009 (0.314)	−0.000170^c (1.922)	1.0544 (1.257)	1.412^a (7.155)	0.54	0.1844	2.23
4.		0.000086^c (1.852)			−0.000081 (1.120)	1.6589^c (2.250)	0.9274^b (2.300)	0.51	0.1892	2.13
5.			0.000406^b (2.360)		−0.000173^c (2.030)	1.0429 (1.290)	1.433^a (7.996)	0.57	0.1779	2.06
6.				0.000033 (1.154)	−0.000067 (0.867)	2.0068^a (2.706)	1.484^a (6.974)	0.44	0.2025	2.30

[a] 0.01 level of significance
[b] 0.05 level of significance
[c] 0.10 level of significance

Note: Variables: W_{AR} = Real wage rate (Taka/day) of agricultural laborers;
X_{1R} = GNP at constant 1959–1960 factor cost in Taka million;
X_{2R} = Agricultural value added at constant factor cost;
X_{3R} = Industrial value added at constant factor cost;
X_{4R} = Value added of other sectors at constant factor cost;
X_{5R} = Acreage under HYV in thousand acres;
X_{6R} = Real wage rate of construction workers (Taka/day).

macro-level analysis of the variation in annual average real wage rates. The value of R^2 suggests that there are many omitted variables that influence W_{AR}. Actually micro-analysis reveals that it is not always possible to capture quantitatively the influence of institutional variables on the level of wages although they are undoubtedly significant. This emerges clearly in the case of X_{5R}. Normally one would expect that the HYV rice being more labor intensive would exert a positive influence on real wages of agricultural laborers. But empirical evidence reveals the opposite. For a relatively short period in the 1960s a positive association between real wage rate of agricultural laborers and acreage of HYV could be discerned (Figure 8.1). This relationship, clearly, does not hold for the entire period under consideration. Micro-studies by Clay and Arens and Beurden reveal evidence of weakening of the positions of agricultural laborers due to changes in the mode of wage payment (from traditional share payment to cash wages and/or cash contracts), pressure exerted by migrant laborers and eviction of tenants, and the general effect of the processes of pauperization in the rural areas.[19]

EMPLOYMENT IN RURAL BANGLADESH

Labor Force Participation

In a country such as Bangladesh, even under normal circumstances, poor households suffer due to lack of adequate employment opportunities, more so during a famine. Thus, it matters very little whether wage rates are held above the famine level through institutional pressure or not because without effective employment there cannot be effective demand for foodgrains and consequently the affected families are likely to undergo calorie deprivation. It was noted earlier that historically governments in South Asian countries have resorted to emergency relief works programs in order to transfer purchasing power to the people during a famine. These efforts have been ad hoc without a serious attempt to understand fully the causes of underemployment and unemployment of the potential work force. The problem is endemic in rural areas of Bangladesh. This is why we focus our attention there.

In order to appreciate the problem of unemployment and under-employment and its bearing on famine, one needs to analyze the conditions of both supply of and demand for labor. As compared with the wage analysis presented above, one will have to go a step further and examine the factors that lie behind supply and demand in the labor market. What one is concerned with here is the economic activity of the population; this refers to work for profit, wage or salary directly and/or indirectly irrespective of whether the work is carried out on a self-employment or hired-employment basis.

Data from eight villages of Bangladesh on labor force participation rate among different types of households are presented in Table 8.5.[20] These figures are broadly in line with those obtained from the latest national census of 1974.[21] The participation rate differential by tenurial status shows the expected pattern with the owner farmers being at the bottom and either tenant farmers or the landless laborers at the top. The observed differential between landless laborers and tenant farmers is a reflection of the employment opportunities in the open labor market in the area under consideration. As expected, the labor force participation rate is higher among small farmers (less than 2.5 acres) as opposed to medium and large farmers. The degree to which these two rates differ reflects the vulnerability of the poorer households to fluctuations (seasonal and annual) in the labor market. Apparently, the poor households in the famine area are more dependent on the labor market than those in the nonfamine area. The differential in the labor force participation rate among important occupational groups in any area is not as sharp as that among landholding or tenurial status groups.

It is interesting to note in Table 8.5 that the labor force participation rate is much higher in the famine districts than in the nonfamine districts. Since the overall availability of employment opportunities and the level of economic activities are lower in the famine area relative to the nonfamine area, the higher labor force participation rate in the former would have to be explained in terms of the perceived need of the rural households, which forces them into the labor market although return to labor (per unit and total) may not be very high. To be more precise, the work leisure preference map of households and consequently the labor supply schedule in the famine area is significantly different from the nonfamine area. This is, however, not to deny the importance of a number of other factors, such as level of income, age structure, sex ratio, urbanization, and student participation in determining the labor force participation rate. There is yet another factor that deserves to be mentioned. This is the differences among areas and groups of households in the participation of young children (age 5–9 years) in the work force although they are not counted as such.[22] Once adjustment for this factor is made, regional differences are likely to be reduced. To sum up, one can say that if the labor force participation rate is used as a criterion for determining the emphasis of employment promotion policies, then the small and marginal farmers, tenant farmers, and landless laborers in the famine area of Bangladesh should get priority. The following analysis of unemployment and underemployment confirms this view.

Table 8.5. Labor Force Participation Rate Among Survey Villagers

Household Groups	Famine Area	Nonfamine Area	Total
Tenurial Status			
Owner farmer	31.6	23.2	26.5
Owner-cum-tenant farmer	32.0	28.2	29.6
Tenant farmer	33.3	38.1	36.1
Landless laborers	35.4	25.7	31.7
Landholding status (operational)			
Less than 2.5 acres	34.0	25.3	29.8
2.5 acres +	27.9	25.6	26.7
Occupational status			
Farming	31.9	25.4	28.1
Wage laborers	34.1	26.1	29.5
Trade and business	34.2	25.7	28.8
Transport workers[a]			
Salaried workers	32.8	23.2	27.8
Others	36.5	36.4	36.5
Total	32.6	25.4	28.5

[a]Sample observations less than 10.

Structure of Employment and Unemployment

There is little controversy that the rate of unemployment is high in Bangladesh, although reliable estimates are difficult to come by. Admittedly, the most difficult task is to define unemployment and underemployment in rural areas of developing countries such as Bangladesh. In the current literature one comes across a wide range of concepts of unemployment that produce different estimates. It is, however, agreed upon by many that irrespective of the concept used, instead of limiting oneself to a single aggregative estimate of unemployment one should try to obtain separate estimates by region, sectors, occupation and education, and also by whether the people are self-employed, wage laborers, or a hybrid of the two. For wage laborers, one should obtain information about the mode of wage payment and the type of laborer (for example, village-tied, patron-tied, or migrant laborer).[23] Such differentiations are necessary for the formulation of appropriate employment promotion policies. The specific contents of employment promotion policies will depend on the concept of unemployment used:[24]

1. Is he/she considered unemployed because he/she does not work for a normal/optimal unit of time given exogenously? (*Time criterion*)

2. Is he/she considered unemployed because his/her income falls short of a desired minimum? (*Income criterion*)
3. Is he/she considered unemployed because he/she is willing to do more work? (*Willingness criterion*)
4. Is he/she considered unemployed because he/she could be withdrawn from his/her present work with total output being maintained with minor changes in technique and/or organization? (*Productivity criterion*)
5. Is he/she considered unemployed because he/she does not "recognize" himself/herself as employed? (*Recognition criterion*)
6. Is he/she considered unemployed because his/her income is not conditional upon his/her work? (*Conditionality criterion*)

The above concepts of unemployment have been critically evaluated by a number of authors.[25] It has been correctly emphasized by many authors that employment promotion policies in a country such as Bangladesh should be formulated on the basis of a careful analysis of the structural characteristics of the rural labor market. This assumes even greater importance if one looks at these policies as integral components of a package policy for famine prevention and relief.

One can now agree that for policy formulation one needs a segmented approach to the problem of unemployment and underemployment in rural areas, the segments identified to be based upon the structural characteristics of the labor force and labor market. A review of the alternative concepts of unemployment and underemployment with a view to formulating famine prevention and relief policies suggests that *time* and *income* are the two most important dimensions. This does not necessarily ignore the other two useful aspects, willingness and productivity. If the *time* norm is set on the basis of the perception of the society about the optimal amount of work, it should subsume the willingness aspect in the sense that those who are less than fully employed should be willing to work more. On the other hand, to the extent to which income of an individual/household is linked to its productivity, the *income* criterion will take care of the productivity criterion although not quite the same way in which the latter is phrased.

Using the time criterion alone, unemployment and underemployment can be defined in three different ways. First, a *mandays concept* under which unemployment is defined as the difference between the supply of manpower measured in mandays and the actual number of mandays worked by all working adults. Supply is given by the product of the number of working adults and the desirable minimum number of days of employment in a year. Second, a *manpower concept* whereby unemployment is defined as the number of working adults employed gainfully for less than the desirable minimum number of days/year. Finally, a *household concept* that defines unemployment as the number of households working less than the desirable minimum number of days/year/working adult. The importance of this concept lies in the fact that the household is the normal accounting unit and the well-being of individual members (working or nonworking, working full-time or part-time) is closely linked with the average status of the household. This point emerges clearly in applying the income criterion to measure unemployment and underemployment. It may also be pointed out that uneven incidence of unemployment may make household units more unequal than individual members, which would have policy implications.

According to the income criterion, employment and unemployment is defined in terms of adequacy of income, both originating from the work done and also unearned income (including transfers) if any, to meet an objectively defined minimum consumption requirement. This income level has been termed poverty income. Following this criterion, two different concepts of unemployment can be defined. First, a *manpower concept* under which an individual is unemployed if his family income is equal or less than the poverty level. Second, a *household concept* whereby unemployment is measured by all households earning poverty income or less. As will be seen later, this is identical with the headcount measure of poverty.

One can go a step further and establish a link between time, income, and the poverty line to define a hybrid criterion of unemployment and underemployment (*time and income*). Accordingly, one can define a *manpower concept* by which unemployment will be measured by the working adults employed for less than the desirable minimum number of days/year (irrespective of their earnings) and those employed for more than the desirable minimum number of days but their household earning being poverty income or less. Furthermore, one can also define a *household concept* whereby unemployment is measured by all households employed less than the desirable minimum number of days/year/working adult and those working above this level but earning poverty income or less.

In this study, only a modest attempt has been made to estimate unemployment and underemployment of rural households in the survey areas. Information was collected on the distribution of working days of earning adult members in various occupations. No attempt was made to assess the willingness or availability for additional work of the working members of households. Since data were also available on the income of the household, it was possible to apply, time (mandays, manpower, and household concepts), income (mandays and household concepts) and time and income combined (manpower and household concepts) criteria to estimate the extent and pattern of unemployment and under-employment in survey villages by various household characteristics. It should be noted that unemployment and underemployment are jointly estimated. To estimate the supply of manpower (measured in mandays) two different criteria of desirable (in full employment sense) minimum number of days of work in a year was applied. The first criterion gave a figure of 343 days, which was arrived at by subtracting the number of days of allowable leave (22) with full pay in the case of industrial workers from the total maximum (365). Admittedly, applying the criterion for industrial labor to rural labor is somewhat misleading but in the absence of a better objective standard this has been tentatively accepted. According to the second criterion, the minimum norm selected was 290 days a year. In addition to the twenty-two days allowable nonworking time a year mentioned above, this figure also adjusts for one day a week rest and recreation. Needless to say, that neither of these norms refer to the willingness criterion. In Tables 8.6 through 8.11, applying the two norms discussed above, two different rates of unemployment in mandays R_1 and R_2, have been arrived at. For calculating other concepts of unemployment and underemployment, the 290 days norm has been used. Household characteristics considered here include, tenurial status (Table 8.8), occupation (Table 8.9), size of household (Table 8.10) and landholding (operational) class (Table 8.11). The poverty line is defined as the level of per capita income adequate to purchase a bundle of food and related items that is considered adequate to satisfy the minimum need of a person. In the context of rural Bangladesh minimum is defined as 2100 calories and 45 grams of protein requirement. The items included in the minimum consumption bundle are rice (coarse), wheat, potato, sugar/gur, pulses (masoor), vegetables, fish (chinghri), meat (beef), milk (cow), fats and oil (mustard), and fruits (banana). In 1973–1974 prices, the bundle was found to cost Tk. 917 per adult in rural Bangladesh. However, the figure varies slightly from region to region. Poverty level income in different survey regions was Ramna, Rangpur, Tk. 870; Gaorarang, Sylhet, Tk. 884; Kogaria, Rangpur, Tk. 935; Dewanganj, Mymenshingh, Tk. 792; Nazirpur, Patuakhali, Tk. 981; Laskarpur, Sylhet, Tk. 869; Komorpur, Khulna, Tk. 1089; Charbaniari, Khulna, Tk. 917.

In Tables 8.6 through 8.11 the unemployed and underemployed on the basis of time criterion (except for R_1) are those who work for less than 290 days a year. Those who work for less than 100 days a year have been identified as severely underemployed. Mildly underemployed are those who find work for a period between 100 and 290 days a year.

Table 8.6 presents an overview of the unemployment and underemployment problem of rural Bangladesh. According to the mandays

**Table 8.6.   Alternative Estimates of Unemployment and Under-
employment in Rural Bangladesh, 1973–1974**

Alternative Concepts of Unemployment and Underemployment	Famine Area	Nonfamine Area	All Area
Time criterion			
Mandays			
R_1	35.2	30.2	34.4
R_2	23.6	17.7	20.3
Household			
Unemployed and underemployed	67.4	57.9	62.1
Mildly underemployed	59.2	54.6	56.6
Severely underemployed	8.2	3.3	5.5
Manpower			
Unemployed and underemployed	66.0	59.0	62.0
Mildly underemployed	50.5	52.9	51.8
Severely underemployed	15.5	6.1	10.2
Income criterion			
Household	85.7	77.5	81.2
Manpower	83.5	78.0	80.4
Time and income criterion			
Household	94.1	89.0	91.2
Manpower	93.2	87.9	90.2

concept, the magnitude of unemployment and underemployment lies
somewhere between 20 and 34 percent of the work force depending on the
time norm. The rate of unemployment is significantly higher in famine
areas than in nonfamine areas. This is more true when the time criterion
is applied to households. For policy analysis, households need to be
focused on since they constitute the target unit. Even a fully employed
individual member of a household has to share the consequences of
unemployment and underemployment among other members. Over 60
percent of the survey households were unemployed and underemployed,
57 percent mildly underemployed, and 6 percent severely underemployed.

Needless to say, the position of the severely underemployed households is the most precarious as they are among the first victims of
famine. It is, therefore, worthwhile to analyze who they are. As can be
seen from Table 8.7, there are eighty-eight households (out of 1613 in
seven villages) that could be classified as severely underemployed. The
majority of these households are owner farmers and owner-cum-tenant

Table 8.7. Profile of the Severely Underemployed, Underemployed Poor, Fully Employed Poor, and Underemployed Nonpoor Households of Rural Bangladesh

Household Characteristics	Severely Underemployed		Underemployed Poor		Fully Employed Poor		Underemployed Nonpoor	
	Number	Percentage	Number	Percentage	Number	Percentage	Number	Percentage
Tenurial status								
Owner farmer	54	61	406	48	261	55	116	72
Owner-cum-tenant	23	26	205	24	83	18	29	18
Tenant farmer	3	3	59	7	5	1	2	1
Landless laborers	8	9	169	20	122	26	14	9
Landholding (operational)								
Small	67	76	597	71	347	74	91	57
Medium	19	22	219	26	110	23	54	34
Large	2	2	23	3	14	3	16	10
Size of household								
Up to 5	53	60	387	46	160	34	71	44
6 to 8	25	28	291	35	190	40	64	40
9 +	10	11	161	19	121	26	26	16
Number of earners								
1	44	50	357	43	283	60	40	25
2	30	34	250	30	124	26	79	49
3 +	14	16	232	28	64	14	42	26
Occupation								
Farming	72	82	498	59	236	50	128	80
Laborers	8	9	235	28	117	25	7	4
Trade and business	4	5	51	6	54	11	19	12
Transport	—	—	2	a	3	1	—	—
Salaried earners	1	1	42	5	48	10	5	3
Others	3	3	11	1	13	3	2	1

Table 8.7. (continued)

Household Characteristics	Severely Underemployed		Underemployed Poor		Fully Employed Poor		Underemployed Nonpoor	
	Number	Percentage	Number	Percentage	Number	Percentage	Number	Percentage
Asset sale								
Did not sell asset	54	61	479	57	279	59	120	75
Sold asset	34	39	360	43	192	41	41	25
Distress sale	31	35	292	35	136	29	35	22
Income (Taka)								
Less than 2000	34	39	450	54	230	49	3	2
2000–3000	17	19	195	23	116	25	22	14
3000–4000	7	8	103	12	66	14	14	9
4000–5000	7	8	50	6	26	6	14	9
5000–6000	8	9	25	3	19	4	18	11
6000–7000	6	7	6	1	5	1	10	6
7000–8000	4	5	3	a	3	1	12	7
8000–10,000	1	1	1	a	5	1	15	9
10,000–12,500	3	3	6	1	1	a	16	10
12,500 +	1	1	—	—	—	—	37	23
Total	88	100	839	100	471	100	161	100

Note: Small holding is less than 2.5 acres; medium holding is 2.5 to less than 7.5 acres; large holding is 7.5 acres and above.

a negligible

farmers (87 percent) and their holdings are small. They are largely self-employed in farming (82 percent). Half of these households have only one earning member but this is somewhat compensated for by the fact that in a majority (60 percent) of the cases the size of household is relatively small (up to 5 members). It is not surprising that in this group 39 percent sold assets in 1974 of which 34 percent represented distress sale. It is interesting to note that although 72 percent of the severely under-employed households earned an average income of less than Tk. 5000, they are spread over all size group of income. What this implies is that among the upper income (and landholding) groups there are some households that live off of either pure rental/interest income or operate farming operations primarily through hired hands (including supervision).

What emerges clearly from the analysis of the severely underemployed households is that they are a relatively small proportion of the total but, in the context of Bangladesh, the absolute number is quite large. These are families who are hanging on to their small amount of productive assets desperately trying to make a living out of them except for a few who come from large landholding/income groups. If one were to improve their well-being in situ one would have to provide them with more effective employment by improving their access to inputs and credit and productive assets. This is a situation in which one can talk in terms of a limited form of land and water reform that would restrict the beneficiaries to the small holding household engaged primarily in farming. This would keep the administration of land reform manageable in a country such as Bangladesh. However, one should hasten to add that the socio-political realities demand that the restricted land reform be accompanied by measures to promote the income and employment opportunities of the landless laborer whether severely underemployed or not by pure time criterion. Measures for them should include direct income transfers, rural works programs, expansion of nonagricultural rural activities, effective labor organization to protect real wages, and the like.

The total magnitude of the unemployment and underemployment problem emerges more sharply by the income and income and time criteria, which also reflect the magnitude of rural poverty. Following these two criteria, three separate groups with different types of unemployment and underemployment can be identified. The first and perhaps the most important group, in terms of required policy focus is the one where households earn less than poverty income and work less than 290 days/year/working adult. The second group consists of households that work more than 290 days/year/working adult but earn poverty income or less. Finally, there is the group of households earning more than poverty income but working less than 290 days/year/working adult. This order should probably be maintained when one determines priorities in employment promoting policy focus.

The poor households clearly require income augmentation through employment promotion. The task is not simple but there is scope for this group to improve both the productivity of the currently employed work force and to increase the amount of work done to use up the available slack. There are 839 households in this group which constitutes 52 percent of the total households in seven villages for which detailed employment data are available (Table 8.7). Relatively speaking, households in this group are more homogenous than the severely under-employed although it covers a much larger set. They come primarily from similar backgrounds as the severely underemployed except that, as expected, the landless laborers are represented in full force. There is no amibguity in terms of income as almost the entire sample has an annual average household income of less than Tk. 6000. One important fact is the relatively large representations of the medium farmers who, inciden-tally, come mainly from the 2.5 to less than 5 acre category. Clearly, the lower middle strata farmers are in no happy position and they are not necessarily immune to famine. While a narrowly based employment promotion strategy will make the severely underemployed the target group (omitting the affluent members, of course), a famine prevention and relief strategy in Bangladesh has to be, of necessity, broad-based covering at least all of the underemployed poor. The suggested em-ployment promotion policies would be a combination of those mentioned above for the severely underemployed, the landless laborers, and the small and marginal farmers.

The plight of the small farmers, marginal farmers, and the landless laborers is confirmed by the data showing the distribution of the fully employed poor by different characteristics (Table 8.7). Data on this group is more revealing than data on the other two groups shown in Table 8.7 in the sense that it brings out the vulnerable position of petty traders, salaried earners, and other minor occupational groups. Needless to say, they are all hardworking people, but unfortunately their productivity and income is low.[26] Since, they are apparently employed full time or more, the immediate problem is not to get them more work, but to make them more productive either in their current trade or elsewhere. The need here is to follow the earlier set of policies along with an added-emphasis on skill development activities that would absorb workers in higher return jobs in the nonagricultural sectors within the rural areas. There is, however, one aspect of policy for this group that requires some discussion. It may be necessary to relocate spatially some members of these groups in order to promote their income earning potential. This is a challenging task by itself that will call for careful planning of population redistribution (however small the scale of operation may be). Some comments also need to be made on the group of households that work on an average less than 290 days/year/working adult but earn more than the poverty income. One may feel tempted to say that from the point of view of the principal focus of this study, the problem is not very acute and as such does not require immediate attention. This view is probably encouraged somewhat by the evidence presented in Table 8.7, which shows that, while there are some indications of predominance (if not overwhelming) of small landholding groups, the households are somewhat evenly distributed across different income groups. In order to recommend any policy for this group, further analysis will be necessary. Since a sizable proportion of households in this group come from the medium and large landholding class (44 percent) and upper income (annual average household income above Tk. 6000) groups (45 percent), it would be helpful to apply the willingness criterion to determine the proportion of households that are involuntarily underemployed. Besides, there are households whose income level, although above, is very close to the poverty line. Available data suggest that about a quarter of the underemployed nonpoor households are not very far above the poverty line. Therefore, the policymakers should worry about this group also.

One can turn around the information presented in Table 8.7 and analyze the unemployment and underemployment of rural households by major characteristics. Table 8.8 looks at households classified by tenurial status. Irrespective of the concept of unemployment and underemployment used, the tenant farmers seem to be in the worst position, closely followed by landless laborers. The question of tenants being exploited by the landlords through both land and capital relations has been raised before. The position of the landless laborers appears to be stronger than that of tenant farmers. But this is an illusion in the sense that, while the average income and employment of the landless laborers may be higher, their vulnerability arises from larger variance in both. Since they are dependent on the market for selling their labor power and acquiring in exchange wherewithal for purchasing subsistence requirements, market fluctuations affect them directly. Unlike the tenants, they are unable to accumulate food resources directly in order to hedge against any violent swing in market behavior. However, both of these groups are forced to work hard, and seek employment all the time to remain above water. That is why only a negligible fraction (as compared with owner farmers and owner-cum-tenant farmers) appears to be severely underemployed by the pure time criterion. The picture changes somewhat if one looks at the estimates of unemployment and underemployment on a working adult (manpower) basis. The income criterion

Table 8.8. Alternative Estimates of Unemployment and Underemployment in Rural Bangladesh by Tenurial Status, 1973–1974

Alternative Concepts of Unemployment and Underemployment	Owner Farmer	Owner-cum-Tenant Farmer	Tenant Farmer	Landless Laborers
Time criterion				
Mandays				
R_1	29.8	39.5	49.9	24.6
R_2	17.2	28.7	40.9	11.1
Household				
Unemployed and underemployed	59.3	67.7	85.5	58.6
Mildly underemployed	53.2	60.9	81.2	56.2
Severely underemployed	6.1	6.8	a	a
Manpower				
Unemployed and underemployed	57.2	70.9	88.6	55.7
Mildly underemployed	46.4	60.7	77.3	47.5
Severely underemployed	10.8	10.2	11.3	8.2
Income criterion				
Household	76.0	84.5	92.8	89.5
Manpower	74.7	84.0	94.7	87.9
Time and income criterion				
Household	89.2	93.0	95.7	93.8
Manpower	87.2	92.3	97.3	93.8

aSample observations less than 10.

and the time and income criterion tell the familiar story about rural Bangladesh. A large proportion of households in all tenurial groups are highly vulnerable to exogenous shocks. Owner farmers appear to be in a relatively better position. This is true for all size groups of farms. An important implication of this finding is that a tenurial reform allowing for "land to the tiller" may improve the situation by way of reducing the vulnerability of this society to famine.

Among different occupational groups, farmers and agricultural laborers show a higher incidence of unemployment and underemployment by all criteria than other groups (Table 8.9). A sizeable proportion of farmers are severely underemployed. This is primarily conditioned by their small size of productive asset. On the contrary, the landless laborer suffers from lack of adequate work. However, as mentioned before, this should not make one lose sight of the problem of unemployment and underemployment among other occupational groups. As expected, the employment status of households is significantly influenced by the size of

Table 8.9 Alternative Estimates of Unemployment and Underemployment in Rural Bangladesh by Occupation, 1973–1974

Alternative Concepts of Unemployment and Underemployment	Occupation					
	Farmers	Agricultural Laborers	Trade and Business Workers	Transport Workers	Salaried Workers	Others
Time criterion						
Mandays						
R_1	37.1	28.0	26.1	19.9	18.0	19.4
R_2	25.9	15.0	12.9	5.5	3.4	5.0
Household						
Unemployed and underemployed	66.3	63.3	47.2	46.3	43.6	48.0
Mildly underemployed	58.7	61.2	44.1	46.3	41.8	36.0
Severely underemployed	7.6	a	a	a	a	a
Manpower						
Unemployed and underemployed	66.0	65.3	51.1	a	40.6	45.7
Mildly underemployed	53.6	61.0	41.7	a	31.4	34.8
Severely underemployed	12.4	4.3	9.4	a	9.2	a
Income criterion						
Household	77.7	92.4	82.7	a	72.0	85.7
Manpower	78.3	89.7	84.6	a	69.7	83.0
Time and income criterion						
Household	91.2	94.2	89.8	a	76.0	92.9
Manpower	90.6	92.8	89.6	a	80.8	91.5

aSample observations less than 10.

household, which is shown here as a proxy for number of earners (Table 8.10). The incidence of unemployment and underemployment is negatively correlated with the size of the household when only the time criterion is used. But the result is opposite under the other two criteria. The apparent contradiction is resolved by the fact that the negative relation is a reflection of the presence of a large number of "hardworking poor" in the sample.

Finally, data presented in Table 8.11 show little intergroup (by size of holding) variation in the rate of unemployment and underemployment measured by time criterion. Actually, the medium holdings (operational) show a higher rate than the other two types of holding. This, however, does not hold for the cases of severe underemployment, which is higher for small holdings than others. The expected negative relationship between type of holding and the incidence of unemployment and underemployment emerges nicely when the income and time and income criteria are used.

In order to complete the picture of employment and unemployment in rural areas, it is worthwhile to take a look at the general occupational

Table 8.10. Alternative Estimates of Unemployment and Underemployment in Rural Bangladesh by Size of Household, 1973–1974

Alternative Concepts of Unemployment and Underemployment	Size of Household		
	Up to 5	6 to 8	9+
Time criterion			
Mandays			
R_1	33.6	32.4	30.9
R_2	21.7	20.3	18.5
Household			
Unemployed and underemployed	64.8	61.8	56.6
Mildly underemployed	57.3	57.5	53.5
Severely underemployed	7.5	4.3	3.1
Manpower			
Unemployed and underemployed	65.3	61.9	58.3
Mildly underemployed	51.9	52.1	51.4
Severely underemployed	13.4	9.8	6.9
Income criterion			
Household	77.6	82.8	86.2
Manpower	77.3	81.8	82.4
Time and income criterion			
Household	87.7	93.8	94.2
Manpower	88.4	91.2	91.0

Table 8.11. Alternative Estimates of Unemployment and Under-employment in Rural Bangladesh by Size Group of Landholding (Operational), 1973–1974

Alternative Estimate of Unemployment and Underemployment	Type of Holding		
	Small	Medium	Large
Time criterion			
Mandays			
R_1	30.2	36.7	31.6
R_2	17.7	25.3	23.9
Household			
Unemployed and underemployed	61.6	63.2	60.9
Mildly underemployed	55.6	58.8	57.8
Severely underemployed	6.0	4.4	a
Manpower			
Unemployed and underemployed	60.8	64.5	61.9
Mildly underemployed	49.3	55.4	58.6
Severely underemployed	11.5	9.1	a
Income criterion			
Household	84.5	76.2	57.8
Manpower	82.0	82.1	56.4
Time and income criterion			
Household	92.7	88.7	82.8
Manpower	91.0	90.5	82.9

Note: Small holding is less than 2.5 acres; medium holding is 2.5 to less than 7.5 acres; large holding is 7.5 acres and above.

aSample observations less than 10.

structure of the rural households. Table 8.12 shows that most of the households are engaged in farming or wage labor. Therefore, these should be the areas of concentration of the employment promotion policies of the government. There are many owner farmer and tenant farmer households whose major occupation is actually wage labor. The degree of dependence on the labor market for the major component of earning is inversely related to the size of operational landholding, not an unexpected finding (Table 8.13). In this context an important finding is that rural households often tend to maintain second and third lines of defense in terms of minor occupation. As expected, farming and wage labor turn out to be the two dominant principal minor occupations for rural households (Table 8.14). However, among farming, transport, and other occupational households, over 40 percent do not have any other occupation. Their well-being is very closely related to the degree of fluctuation in their current level of activity. Therefore, for many households in these

Table 8.12. Occupational Structure of Rural Population in Bangladesh (percentage distribution)

Occupation	Household	Working Adults
Farming	59.7	61.4
Wage labor	23.4	20.3
Trade and business	7.5	7.5
Transport	0.4	0.3
Salary earners	7.3	8.8
Others	1.8	1.6
Total[a]	100.0	100.0

[a]Total may not add up due to rounding error.

groups who are unable to accumulate any asset as a safeguard against bad times, subsidiary employment opportunities would have to be generated.

The phenomenon of a single occupation household is closely related to seasonal fluctuations in major occupational activities in the rural household, particularly the lack of adequate alternative employment opportunities for small and marginal farmers and landless agricultural laborers during off-peak season. Seasonal fluctuations in the real wages of agricultural laborers have been discussed before. Some data on seasonality of employment in rural Bangaldesh are presented in Table 8.15. Since the data are obtained from two isolated villages, generalization with respect to specific pattern of seasonal fluctuations in employment for the country as a whole is not possible. But when one considers the figures presented here along with other studies by Habibullah,[27] Muqtada,[28] and Cain et al.,[29] one cannot but be impressed with revelations regarding the vulnerability of rural households, particularly agricultural laborer households to seasonal fluctuations in employment. These findings vindicate our analysis of seasonal fluctuations in real wages of agricultural laborers. Actually, all households with little staying power have been found to suffer from seasonal fluctuations in calorie intake due to the seasonal pattern of crop production and employment. Such data have been compiled by the two nutrition surveys carried out in Bangladesh during 1962–1964 and 1976. Again, all evidence, with minor exceptions, points to the July–October period as the most difficult one. It is clear that except for the recognized peak period in each region, there is need for expanding employment opportunities within or outside agriculture during the rest of the year.

It is apparent from the above that the thrust of the employment promotion policies designed to prevent famine should be to smooth the

Table 8.13. Percentage Distribution of Households by Major Occupation and Household Characteristics

Household Type	Occupational Groups						
	Farming	Wage Labor	Trade and Business	Transport Worker	Salary Earners	Others	Total[a]
Tenurial status							
Owner farmer	67.3	16.0	8.0	0.2	7.8	0.8	100.0
Owner-cum-tenant farmer	81.0	9.1	4.1	0.3	4.7	0.9	100.0
Tenant farmer	65.2	20.3	8.7	—	15.8	—	100.0
Landless laborers	10.2	60.3	11.4	1.2	11.4	5.5	100.0
Size group of landholding (operational)							
< 0.5 acres	22.0	51.9	11.5	0.7	9.7	4.3	100.0
0.5 < 1.0	52.3	25.8	12.3	0.7	8.4	0.7	100.0
1.0 < 2.5	76.3	9.6	6.6	0.3	7.1	0.3	100.0
2.5 < 5.0	88.1	2.1	3.6	0.3	5.4	0.6	100.0
5.0 < 7.5	86.6	3.1	4.1	—	6.2	—	100.0
7.5 < 12.5	87.0	—	2.2	—	10.9	—	100.0
12.5 +	100.0	—	—	—	—	—	100.0

[a]Total may not add up due to rounding error.

Table 8.14. Percentage Distribution of Households by Major and Principal Minor Occupation

Household Type		Principal Minor Occupation					
	Farming	Wage Laborer	Trade and Business	Transport Worker	Salary Earner	Others	Total[a]
Farming	43.0[b]	25.0	16.6	4.9	7.2	3.4	100.0
Wage laborer	60.5	28.3	4.2	0.3	4.5	2.4	100.0
Trade and business	59.7	16.5	22.1	—	4.7	—	100.0
Transport	28.6	28.6	—	42.9	—	—	100.0
Salary earner	75.8	12.9	2.4	—	8.1	0.8	100.0
Others	32.1	14.1	—	—	3.6	50.0	100.0
Total	50.5	24.0	12.7	3.1	6.3	3.5	100.0

[a]Total may not add up due to rounding error.
[b]Diagonal elements indicate households with single occupation.

343

Table 8.15. Seasonality of Employment in Rural Bangladesh (number of days employed per month per head)

Month	Agricultural Laborers	Month	All Rural Workers
January	20	Magh	21
February	20	Falgun	18
March	22	Chaitra	15
April	23	Baisakh	20
May	21	Jaistha	20
June	20	Ashar	25
July	18	Sraban	24
August	23	Bhadra	18
September	22	Aswin	11
October	23	Kartik	19
November	23	Agrahyan	23
December	22	Poush	21

Source: Agricultural laborers from S.R. Bose, "Trend of Real Income of the Rural Poor in East Pakistan 1949-66," Pakistan Development Review 8(3):481 (Autumn 1968); all rural workers from Rushidan Islam, "Approaches to the Problem of Rural Unemployment," Paper presented at the Third Annual Conference of the Bangladesh Economic Association, Rajshahi, Bangladesh, June 19-21, 1977.

Note: Employment of all rural workers is shown against Bengali months, which start with Baisakh (15th April–15th May).

employment cycle over the year and also to ensure some minimum income for the workers. Famine relief measures should concentrate on providing relief through works programs against food wages. A counter-seasonal pattern of rural works programs and Food-for-Works program will help reduce fluctuations in the consumption stream of the poor households. Furthermore, as it has been repeated a number of times before, promotion of nonagricultural activities in rural areas remains crucial. All these, however, are not supposed to imply that there is no scope for expanding employment opportunities within agriculture or for smoothening the crop cycles. It is quite conceivable that wide spread diffusion of HYV rice will further increase overall labor force absorption in agriculture and it will also smooth the seasonality since there exists scope for expanding employment in off-peak season activities such as weeding. Furthermore, one may conceive of increasing cropping intensity by improving water management. In any case, one could tailor adjustments in current cropping pattern that would smooth the seasonal demand for agricultural labor. However, these technocratic solutions will not necessarily solve the problem at hand unless accompanied by necessary institutional reforms that would secure access to employment and/or productive assets for the vulnerable groups in the rural areas.

Performance of the agriculture sector to date in terms of expanding employment opportunities has not been very satisfactory. It has already been pointed out that the overall employment elasticity of HYV turned out to be lower than anticipated and the rate of diffusion of HYV has been slower than expected. The nonagricultural sector has not been able to take up much of the slack labor from the agricultural sector. As a result, dependence on agriculture for livelihood has remained as large as ever.

Employment in 1974

There should be no doubt now that for many households the employment situation is precarious even in a normal year, but the year 1974 was particularly bad. First, a shift in the relative price of jute and rice in favor of the latter resulted in substitution of jute acreage by rice (local and HYV *aus*), the exact extent of which is not known. Since jute is a more labor intensive item than rice, a shift of cultivated acreage from jute to rice meant a loss of employment. This loss has been calculated under alternative assumptions in Table 8.16. A large part of this employment loss occurred during the July–October 1974 period since this was the harvesting season. As is known, the period was also the height of the famine. Figures in Table 8.16 show that, whichever estimate is considered as plausible, the extent of loss of employment of hired hands was large. This loss was partly compensated for by the additional employment generated by replanting of *aman* that was destroyed by flood.[30]

Second, the above finding needs to be looked at in the light of the information generated by the village survey on the percentage decline in employment of hired laborers between July–October 1973 and July–October 1974 as presented in Table 8.17. On the whole, there was a decline in employment of hired laborers of about 5 percent during the period under consideration. But this total hides the fact that the famine area suffered a decline of 25 percent, while the nonfamine area actually enjoyed an increase of 2 percent in employment. The landless laborers were adversely affected in both regions.

INCOME OF RURAL HOUSEHOLDS

Level and Structure of Income

At the beginning of this chapter, some data were presented on rural and urban income per capita from national accounts statistics. The village survey data provides more detailed information on the level and structure of income of rural households. The level of income

Table 8.16.   Estimated Loss in Employment in 1974 Due to Decline in Jute Acreage

1. Expected jute acreage in 1974 = 1780 thousand
2. Actual jute acreage in 1974 = 1417 thousand
3. Decline in jute acreage in 1974 = 363 thousand
4. Employment loss (in mandays) per acre due to shift of one acre from jute to
   aus = 47 for traditional variety of aus (hired labor component is 32)
        24 for HYV aus (hired labor component is 13)
5. Loss in total employment in 1974 due to decline in jute acreage:

Assumption I: All area shifted to traditional aus.
   a. Loss in total employment (000 mandays) = 1,7061
   b. Loss in employment of hired labor (000 mandays) = 1,1616

Assumption II: All area shifted to HYV aus.
   a. Loss in total employment (000 mandays) = 8,712
   b. Loss in employment of hired labor (000 mandays) = 4,719

Assumption III: Shift is distributed in the same proportion as the distribution of traditional and HYV aus in total aus acreage in 1974.
   a. Loss in total employment (000 mandays) = 1,2392
   b. Loss in employment of hired labor (000 mandays) = 7,759

Source: 1. Estimated by applying the predicted share of jute acreage in total *aus* season acreage to the total *aus* season acreage of 1974. This share was predicted on a basis of a trend regression covering the period 1965–1966 to 1970–1971, which could be considered as normal.

2. Government of Bangladesh, Bureau of Statistics, *Statistical Yearbook of Bangladesh, 1975,* p. 99.

3. 1 − 2.

4. Bangladesh Institute of Development Studies survey data of 1969–1970 from Phulpur in Mymensingh district.

5. (3) × relevant figure in (4).

Table 8.17.   Percentage Decline in Employment of Hired Laborers Between July–October 1973 and July–October 1974 as Reported by Survey Villagers

Area	Landowners	Landless Laborers	All Villagers
All area	5.0	18.7	4.6
Famine area	33.9	34.5	24.5
Nonfamine area	−7.7	6.4	−2.4

indicates the normal level of protection against hunger and malnutrition afforded to an average household in any group and the structure of income helps one to trace precisely the sources of variability of income. The structure of income is obviously closely linked with the structure of employment. It is important for the policymakers to see this link in order to develop an idea about the relative rates of return (or productivity) from various types of work. This is the point that emerged sharply in the discussion above on unemployment and underemployment measured by the income criterion or the time and income criterion.

Levels of per household and per capita (unadjusted and adjusted for adult unit) income in rural Bangladesh for the year 1973–1974 are presented in Table 8.18. Two sets of estimates, one with imputed family labor and the other without, have been worked out. For the purpose of the present analysis, the relevant figures are per capita adjusted income without imputed family labor. It is, however, interesting to note that survey data on per capita unadjusted income without imputed family labor gives a much lower figure for all areas (Tk. 536) than what is implicit in the overall national per capita income estimate of the Bangladesh Bureau of Statistics for the year 1973–1974 (Tk. 889).[31] How high or low the figures are in Table 8.18 can be guessed if one compares them with the poverty line, which is Tk. 917 per adult unit in 1973–1974 prices.

For the eight survey villages, the per capita (adjusted without imputed family labor) income fell short of the poverty income by 27 percent. There was no difference between the famine and nonfamine areas. Apparently in a normal year, the two areas are at par in terms of per capita income, but the problem for the famine area arises from the variability of annual income due to greater susceptibility to natural disasters. Both size of operational landholding and tenurial status appear to have significant influence on the levels of per capita income. The average per capita income for all tenurial groups falls below the poverty line, but the tenants and landless laborers are very precariously placed with their income deficit being 43 and 52 percent respectively. The average income of only the large farmers exceeds the poverty income. Data by occupational status again indicate an income deficit for all groups. Relatively speaking, farming, trade and business, and salary earning households are better placed than the other groups. Table 8.18 confirms the earlier finding on the basis of employment status that the vulnerable groups in rural Bangladesh are tenant farmers and landless laborers (by tenurial status), small farmers and a part of medium farmers (by size of operational landholding), and wage earners, transport workers, and other minor occupational groups (by occupational status).

The structure of income of rural households follows an expected pattern (Table 8.19) with agriculture being the dominant component (60

Table 8.18. Levels of Per Household and Per Capita Income in Rural Bangladesh, 1973–1974 (in taka)

	With Imputed Labor			Without Imputed Labor		
		Per Capita			Per Capita	
	Household	Adjusted[a]	Unadjusted	Household	Adjusted[a]	Unadjusted
Area						
Famine area	1548	354	285	2982	673	536
Nonfamine area	4061	706	563	3858	671	535
All area	3460	673	538	3429	672	535
Tenurial status						
Owner farmer	4421	959	768	4023	754	601
Owner-cum tenant	4874	948	775	3913	664	530
Tenant farmer	2533	634	500	2410	523	413
Landless laborers	1322	362	291	1686	437	345
Size of operational landholding						
Small	2272	577	366	2599	603	481
Medium	2499	1300	1220	4552	697	558
Large	17642	1799	1460	10167	1067	848
Occupation						
Farming	3984	725	582	4024	740	591
Wage labor	1866	442	352	1691	405	320
Trade and business	3586	742	539	3524	731	575
Transport worker	2797	614	502	2724	598	489
Salaried worker	4662	774	620	4532	753	601
Others	1706	473	379	1531	436	346

aPer adult unit (adult male = 1.0; adult female = 0.9; and children = 0.5).

Table 8.19. Structure of Income of Rural Households

| | Percentage Distribution | | | | | |
| | Without Imputed Family Labor | | | With Imputed Family Labor | | |
Components	Famine Area	Nonfamine Area	All Area	Famine Area	Nonfamine Area	All Area
Agriculture	69	61	64	61	61	60
Crop production	55	48	52	46	48	47
Share/rent	4	7	6	5	7	6
Others	10	6	8	10	6	7
Wages	12	13	13	14	13	13
Income from cart/boat	2	1	1	2	1	1
Trade and business income	7	11	9	8	11	10
Salary income	9	9	9	11	9	10
Imputed family labor	—	—	—	4	5	5
All others	12	5	8	2	1	1
Total[a]	100	100	100	100	100	100

[a]Total may not add up due to rounding error.

percent), followed distantly by wage income (13 percent), and trade and business income (10 percent).[32] Pure rental income is about 6 percent of the total income, which implies that if "land to the tiller" policy was to be followed then the per capita income (adjusted without imputed family labor) of the part tenants and tenants could increase by 21 percent.[33] This figure may go up even further if productivity goes up following tenurial reform. It was found that 23 percent of the rural households depend on wage labor as a major source of income (Table 8.12) but wage income accounts for only 13 percent of the total income.

About 80 percent of the total rural household income originates from agriculture, either directly or indirectly. Crop production accounts for most and, therefore, what happens to rural families at any point in time is tied to the health of the crop production activity. This remains true for all groups of households (Tables 8.20 through 8.22). Table 8.20 shows that both tenant farmers and landless laborers derive an important part of their income in the form of wages. Their interests can be promoted by encouraging them to form trade unions so as to be able to bargain from a position of strength. During a period of famine, relief works programs would be an important vehicle to inject purchasing power into these groups. It is important to note that landless laborers derive 16 percent of their income from other agriculture (livestock, poultry, forestry, and fishing). Therefore, promoting other agriculture will promote the well-being of this group and reduce its vulnerability to famine. An urgent

Table 8.20. Structure of Income of Rural Households in Bangladesh by Tenurial Status (without imputed family labor)

| Components | (Percentage Distribution) | | | |
	Owner Farmer	Owner-cum-Tenant Farmer	Tenant Farmer	Landless Laborers
Agriculture	69.4	78.7	60.1	17.6
Crop production	54.1	69.9	50.0	0.7
Share/rent	9.0	0.9	1.0	0.7
Others	6.3	7.9	9.1	16.2
Wages	7.7	7.4	21.0	50.5
Income from cart/boat	1.8	1.6	1.4	2.3
Trade and business income	10.0	6.2	9.8	12.6
Salary income	10.7	4.7	6.1	12.0
All others	1.1	1.3	1.7	5.0
Total[a]	100.0	100.0	100.0	100.0

[a]Total may not add up due to rounding error.

Table 8.21. Structure of Income of Rural Households in Bangladesh by Size Group of Landholding (without imputed family labor)

	Percentage Distribution						
	Size Group of Landholding (acres operational)						
Component	Less than 0.5	0.5 < 1.0	1.0 < 2.5	2.5 < 5.0	5.0 < 7.5	7.5 < 12.5	12.5+
Agriculture	38.7	54.9	68.4	76.5	78.8	80.9	96.7
Crop production	16.3	37.1	57.1	68.0	65.4	65.1	92.5
Share/rent	12.0	10.2	3.7	1.5	4.8	9.8	0.8
Others	10.4	7.6	7.6	7.0	8.6	6.0	3.4
Wage income	32.4	21.8	9.4	3.9	4.6	0.6	—
Income from cart/boat	1.5	0.9	1.5	1.1	1.4	1.6	1.2
Trade and business income	13.4	9.1	9.0	8.4	8.3	8.3	—
Salary income	10.7	11.8	10.3	9.1	6.0	8.2	2.0
All others	3.3	1.5	1.4	1.2	0.9	0.4	Neg.b
Total[a]	100.0	100.0	100.0	100.0	100.0	100.0	100.0

[a]Total may not add up due to rounding error.
[b]Negligible.

Table 8.22. Structure of Income of Rural Households in Bangladesh by Occupation (without imputed family labor)

Components	Percentage Distribution Occupational Groups					
	Farming	Wage Labor	Trade and Business	Transport	Salary Earned	Others
Agriculture	84.3	19.0	45.1	10.3	27.0	17.2
Crop production	68.2	10.1	13.1	9.3	18.0	11.4
Share/rent	7.0	2.9	2.7	—	4.4	1.1
Others	9.1	6.0	29.3	1.0	4.6	4.7
Wage income	4.6	77.1	2.9	4.5	2.4	4.8
Income from cart/boat	1.4	0.4	0.4	82.6	—	—
Trade and business income	5.3	1.5	50.3	2.6	1.5	—
Salary income	3.4	1.7	1.2	—	68.2	0.4
All others	1.0	1.7	—	—	0.9	77.6
Total[a]	100.0	100.0	100.0	100.0	100.0	100.0

[a]Total may not add up due to rounding error.

need for diversification of sources of income is brought out clearly in Table 8.22 for three major occupational groups, farmers, wage laborers and, transport workers. These groups derive an overwhelmingly large proportion of their income from one source, each of which, as mentioned earlier, is subject to large variation. Salary earners are excluded because their major component of earning is more or less guaranteed. This table also reveals the importance of other agriculture as a source of income (29 percent) for the trade and business occupation group.

Distribution of Income

While the absolute level of income is important to determine the average level of well-being of a group of the population, a knowledge of the distribution of income is equally important to appreciate the relative deprivation of the various groups and their relative strength to face a calamity such as famine. Besides, the movement of real income per capita of the rural and urban poor is related to the pattern of income distribution and its changes over time. Total income remaining the same, a more unequal distribution will indicate a worsening of the living conditions of the lower-income group. A similar statement can be made of comparison between two regions.

Available data from income expenditure surveys carried out by the Bureau of Statistics reveal that the distribution of rural income in Bangladesh as measured by Gini coefficient worsened between 1963–1964 and 1973–1974 (from 0.33 to 0.38).[34] Data from the village survey show a much higher degree of inequality (Gini coefficient = 0.46, Table 8.23) than what is indicated by the national expenditure survey mentioned above. This is true whether income is defined to include imputed family labor or not. Lorenz curves of total income are presented in Figure 8.5. There is not much difference in the degree of inequality between famine and nonfamine areas, but the figure for individual villages varies widely (Table 8.24). Inequality in total income is contributed mostly by inequality in agricultural income. It is hypothesized by many that the principal source of inequality in agricultural income is inequality in the distribution of landholding. National data do indicate that the worsening of the rural income distribution between 1963–1964 and 1973–1974 was associated with a worsening of the distribution of landholding (both ownership and operational). Village level data as shown in Table 8.24 were used to relate Gini coefficients of total income and agricultural income with those of owned landholding, operational landholding, and total assets. The estimated coefficients of the regression equations had the right sign but they were not statistically significant at any conventional level. This does not necessarily rule out existence of a relationship between these variables rather it calls for more observations to test the hypothesis.

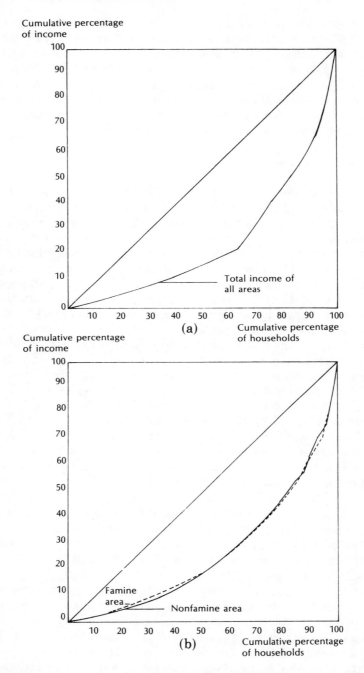

Figure 8.5. Lorenz curves of income distribution of rural households in Bangladesh, 1973–1974.

Table 8.23. Size Distribution of Income in Rural Bangladesh (percentage of total income)

Area	Percentage of Households							Gini Coefficient	
	Bottom 5%	0–20%	20–40%	40–60%	60–80%	80–100%	Top 5%	Total Income	Agricultural Income
Without imputed family labor									
All villages	1.64	6.55	6.55	13.72	20.51	52.67	23.89	0.4586	0.4667
Famine area	1.89	7.58	7.58	12.02	20.01	52.81	25.81	0.4586	0.4766
Nonfamine area	1.45	5.78	7.89	13.66	20.93	51.74	22.20	0.452	0.4508
With imputed family labor									
All villages	1.70	6.78	6.78	14.39	20.56	51.49	23.58	0.4446	0.4443
Famine area	2.17	8.68	8.68	12.95	20.62	49.07	25.43	0.4110	0.4113
Nonfamine area	1.45	5.81	8.59	13.16	20.89	51.55	21.57	0.4415	0.4488

Table 8.24. Gini Coefficient of Income, Landholding, and Total Assets of Survey Villagers

Villages	Gini Coefficient				
	Total Income	Agricultural Income	Owned Landholding	Operational Landholding	Total Assets
Ramna, Rangpur	0.4275	0.3651	0.660	0.5560	0.6289
Gaorarang, Sylhet	0.3433	0.3821	0.6023	0.6449	0.5745
Kogaria, Rangpur	0.4016	0.4174	0.5912	0.5033	0.5725
Dewanganj, Mymensingh	0.4996	0.5282	0.6384	0.6018	0.6191
Nazirpur, Patuakhali	0.3967	0.3973	0.5593	0.6044	0.5456
Laskarpur, Sylhet	0.4120	0.4138	0.4760	0.5074	0.4630
Komorpur, Khulna	0.3434	0.3607	0.5648	0.2894	0.4987
Charbaniari, Khulna	0.3990	0.4377	0.4495	0.5630	0.4478

It is interesting to note that considerable inequality in income distribution shows up within each household type according to various criteria (Table 8.25). As for variation in inequality between groups under the same classification, the largest is revealed among different tenancy groups. There is very little difference in the degree of income inequality between groups classified either by size of operational landholding or by number of earners. Among all the different types of households shown in Table 8.25, the highest degree of inequality under almost all circumstances is shown by owner farmers, which is a clear indication of the importance of distribution of landholding in determining the distribution of rural household income in Bangladesh.

Level and Structure of Poverty

A high degree of inequality along with a low level of average income has resulted in widespread poverty among the rural population in Bangladesh. Earlier studies indicate that the situation has worsened over time. An analysis of rural poverty is carried out here in order to establish a link between poverty and famine. It is rather obvious by now that famine victims come from among the poor. So one needs to know the magnitude of poverty as well as structural characteristics of the poor. This information along with that on unemployment and wages as presented earlier, can be used to determine the nature of preventive and remedial policy measures against poverty and famine. What is being suggested here is that, in countries of South Asia, the spectre of famine can not be eliminated without eliminating poverty. There is no denying that it is a formidable task since it goes beyond merely ensuring adequate supply of foodgrains.

It can be seen from Table 8.26 that 79 percent of the survey households are poor. There is not much difference between the poor and nonpoor households in terms of size of household or number of earners. But, as expected, on a landholding (ownership, operational, and cultivable), assets (total), and income (total) scale there is considerable difference between the two groups. However, the average size of debt of the poor households is lower than that of the nonpoor households. What is important to note is the significant difference between famine and nonfamine areas. Apparently the poor of the famine area are poorer and consequently more vulnerable than the poor of the nonfamine area. The difference is indeed very large in landholding and total assets, which are the two important indicators of well-being from a long-run point of view.

The structure of income of the poor households (Table 8.27) clearly suggests that policy emphasis should be toward protecting wage income and other agricultural income along the lines suggested earlier. It seems

Table 8.25. Gini Coefficient of Income Distribution of Rural Households by Selected Characteristics (income in Taka)

Household Type	Famine Area		Nonfamine Area		All Villages	
	(a)	(b)	(a)	(b)	(a)	(b)
Land ownership status						
Owns land	0.4776	0.4461	0.3851	0.4531	0.4422	0.4521
Does not own land	0.2282	0.2854	0.3384	0.3449	0.3183	0.3282
Tenurial status						
Owner farmer	0.3909	0.4417	0.4735	0.4871	0.4562	0.4713
Owner-cum-tenant farmer	0.4800	0.4550	0.3446	0.3545	0.4001	0.3983
Tenant farmer	0.2790	0.3633	0.1791	0.1869	0.2883	0.2877
Landless laborers	0.2507	0.2642	0.3691	0.3769	0.3138	0.3199
Size of farmer (operational)						
Small	0.3682	0.3290	0.4366	0.4467	0.3940	0.3975
Medium	0.3537	0.3768	0.3933	0.4087	0.3855	0.4000
Large	0.2723	0.1708	0.3200	0.3350	0.3607	0.3460
Occupation						
Farmers	0.4211	0.4537	0.4117	0.4271	0.4281	0.4423
Wage laborers	0.1990	0.1738	0.3782	0.3872	0.3256	0.3194
Trade, transport, and business	0.4614	0.4398	0.4413	0.4424	0.4598	0.4407
Others[a]	0.3623	0.3746	0.4661	0.4739	0.4501	0.4529
Number of earners						
One earner	0.3425	0.4244	0.4296	0.3845	0.4171	0.4397
Two earners	0.4086	0.4413	0.4399	0.3961	0.4318	0.4576
Three or more earners	0.4296	0.4219	0.3760	0.4622	0.4000	0.3883

Note: (a) With imputed family labor.
(b) Without imputed family labor.
[a]Others include Salary earners and all others.

Table 8.26. Profile of the Rural Poor in Bangladesh, 1973–1977

	Famine Area		Nonfamine Area		All Areas	
Total percentage of households in poverty	79.5		77.5		78.5	
Selected characteristics of poor households						
Size of household	5.43	(5.6)	7.52	(7.2)	6.48	(6.4)
Number of earners[a]	1.82	(1.8)	1.89	(1.8)	1.86	(1.8)
Landholding (acres)[a]						
Ownership	1.08	(1.61)	2.07	(2.35)	1.58	(1.99)
Operational	1.18	(1.61)	2.51	(2.58)	1.85	(2.10)
Cultivable	0.89	(1.36)	1.67	(1.92)	1.29	(1.65)
Total assets (taka)						
Per household	6278	(9042)	16537	(17294)	11444	(13252)
Per capita	1156	(1625)	2199	(2397)	1765	(2068)
Total income (taka)						
Per household	1996	(2983)	2493	(3858)	2246	(3429)
Per capita	368	(536)	331	(535)	346	(535)
Average size of dept[a] (taka)	154	(461)	589	(859)	373	(711)

Note: Figures within parentheses are for all households.

[a]Per household

358

Table 8.27. Structure of Income of Poor Households, 1973–1974

	Percentage Distribution		
	Famine Area	*Nonfamine Area*	*All Areas*
Agriculture	59.8	61.9	61.0
Crop production	45.4	47.6	46.6
Share/rent	2.1	5.2	3.9
Others	12.3	9.1	10.5
Wage income	19.3	18.8	19.0
Income from cart/boat	1.6	0.9	1.2
Trade and business income	8.0	9.9	9.0
Salary income	8.6	7.5	8.0
All others	2.6	1.1	1.7
Total[a]	100.0	100.0	100.0

[a]Total may not add up due to rounding error.

that participation of the poor in other occupations is very low as compared with the average for the entire sample (Table 8.19). This clearly suggests another area of action both in terms of widening the scope of subsidiary occupations as well as raising productivity of these jobs by further skill training, if necessary. The productivity raising aspect is very important because, more so than other occupational groups, the minor groups need to accumulate in good years since during a famine period they suffer a drastic shortfall in demand for their products and services.[35]

Incidence of poverty among different groups of households in rural Bangladesh, as shown in Table 8.28, only confirms what was concluded earlier regarding the profile of vulnerable groups on the basis of employment status. While poverty exists in all groups, the relatively more vulnerable groups are tenant farmers, laborers, small and marginal holders, transport workers, and other minor occupational groups. In this context, perhaps it is more illuminating to consider Table 8.29 showing the income gap of the poor households classified according to major occupation. The staggaring finding is that 68 percent of the wage laborer and other minor occupational group households had an income gap of 50 percent and above in 1973–1974. In all other groups, at least one-third fell in this category. This situation hardly needs any further comment.

Decline in Real Income of Wage Laborers in 1974

Given the above poverty profile of the rural households in Bangladesh it is not surprising that the flood and famine of 1974 had such a devastating effect. Clearly, as was contended earlier, the well-being of a majority of

Table 8.28. Incidence of Poverty Among Different Groups of Households in Rural Bangladesh, 1973–1974

	Proportion of Households in Each Group		
	Famine Area	Nonfamine Area	All Areas
Tenurial status			
Owner farmer	74.7	72.3	73.4
Owner-cum-tenant	70.8	84.1	78.6
Tenant farmer	81.1	92.9	87.3
Landless laborers	92.9	81.9	89.2
Size group of landholding (operational)			
(in acres)			
< 0.5	89.4	77.8	84.3
0.5 − < 1.0	89.6	79.8	84.5
1.0 − < 2.5	79.8	74.3	77.6
2.5 − < 5.0	66.4	79.1	74.6
5.0 − < 7.5	30.8	83.1	70.6
7.5 − < 12.5	20.0	71.1	56.6
12.5 +	12.5	50.0	35.0
Occupation			
Farming	72.7	74.0	73.3
Wage labor	96.2	89.3	92.8
Trade and Business	87.0	77.2	81.2
Transport	100.0	60.0	71.4
Salary earner	68.4	71.7	69.8
Other	95.7	62.5	87.1
Size of Household			
Up to 5	81.3	67.8	76.3
6 to 8	81.5	79.1	80.1
9+	67.0	86.4	80.2

families in the country oscillate between the poverty line and famine line. In a good year, the income gap is narrowed but given the size of the gap for most households there is little or no possibility of its ever being eliminated unless a concerted effort is made to raise the productivity and income of the poor. In a bad year, the income gap widens and people get closer to the borderline of starvation. Many may cross this line and die, but usually such deaths are not noticed and they are attributed to natural causes. What becomes very clear from the analysis of the relevant facts presented in this book is that the Bangladesh population is unable to withstand any violent fluctuation in foodgrain availability (as conventionally defined), foodgrain price, or real income. The allowable margin is apparently very small and a large unfavorable swing in any one or a combination of the three elements mentioned here is likely to trigger a period of prolonged foodgrain intake decline resulting in excess deaths as happened in Bangladesh in 1974.

Table 8.29. Income Gap of Poor Households Classified According to Major Occupation, Rural Bangladesh, 1973–1974 (proportion of total households in each region)

	Percentage Shortfall of Income of the Poor Households from Poverty Line											
	All Area				Famine Area				Nonfamine Area			
Occupation	Up to 10%	10–25%	25–50%	50% and Above	Up to 10%	10–25%	25–50%	50% and Above	Up to 10%	10–25%	25–50%	50% and Above
Farming	0.0349	0.0765	0.2417	0.3805	0.0475	0.0970	0.2673	0.3149	0.0235	0.0578	0.2184	0.4404
Wage Labor	0.0313	0.0458	0.1663	0.6843	0.0335	0.0622	0.2105	0.6555	0.0291	0.0291	0.1214	0.7136
Trade and Business	0.0451	0.1278	0.2030	0.4361	0.0556	0.1481	0.2593	0.4074	0.0380	0.1139	0.1646	0.4557
Transport	0.1429	—	0.1429	0.4286	0.5000	—	0.5000	—	—	—	—	0.6000
Salary earner	0.0698	0.1163	0.2093	0.3023	0.0789	0.1053	0.2368	0.2632	0.0566	0.1321	0.1698	0.3585
Others	0.0645	—	0.1290	0.6774	0.0870	—	0.1739	0.6957	—	—	—	0.6250
Total	0.0383	0.0744	0.2165	0.4555	0.0495	0.0898	0.2486	0.4074	0.0276	0.0597	0.1856	0.5017

That the famine was inevitable becomes clear when one looks at the data presented in Table 8.30b, which show the percentage decline in total wage income between July–October 1973 and July–October 1974. The condition of the landless laborers needs little elaboration.

Table 8.30a. Percentage Decline in Real Wage Rate of Agricultural Laborers Between July–October 1973 and July–October 1974 as Reported by Survey Villagers

Area	Landowners	Landless Laborers	All Villagers
All area	6.2	74.0	43.1
Famine area	−37.6	74.2	32.7
Nonfamine area	13.8	74.0	46.7

Table 8.30b. Percentage Decline in total Wage (Real) Income Between July–October 1973 and July–October 1974

Area	Landowners	Landless Laborers	All Villagers
All area	8.1	78.2	45.8
Famine area	9.0	83.1	47.7
Nonfamine area	7.2	75.7	44.1

A MODEL OF RURAL HOUSEHOLD ECONOMY

It was pointed out in Chapter 2 that the operation of different markets in a famine-prone economy culminates in a low level of income and foodgrain consumption for the majority of rural households. It was also highlighted that such an economy is composed of interdependent systems. This section presents a simultaneous equation model of income and employment determination of rural households. The model attempts to capture the essence of operation of product and factor markets in rural Bangladesh. In addition to income (production) and consumption components, it includes a credit market. The dynamic aspects of the new theory of household are brought in through a household size equation, a land transaction equation, and a market surplus equation to link successive periods. It tests sharecropping theories by including a tenurial status variable where appropriate to see if it effects input use in crop production. It also tests whether tenurial status affects the ability of the farm household to build up noncrop agricultural activities, i.e., whether more secure tenurial status ensures food security and allows diversification of farming. The market interrelatedness is included in the following way: Peoples' assets give them preferential access to employment opportunities in an economy with surplus labor as well as access to credit via collateral, as in conventional models. Thus the model incorporates simple views on rationing and how this is achieved where job opportunities are limited. The model is applied to the data generated by our village survey. Since employment data were not collected from one village, they were left out of consideration, giving us a sample of 1613 households.

The Model

The model consists of fourteen equations, including two identities. It integrates the static consumption and production (income) systems of rural households with the credit system. Furthermore, a number of dynamic relations are incorporated in the model: household size, net land sale, and net marketed surplus of paddy. The dynamic relations are intended to take account of links between successive periods, which would indicate an improvement or worsening, as the case may be, of the status on individual households. The model, along with variable definition and parameter estimates, is presented in Table 8.31.

Consumption System. It is assumed that household utility is a function of food and nonfood consumption, and leisure, that equals total time available less work time. Then maximizing such a utility function subject to a full income constraint (where full income depends on time and nonearned income) would yield food, nonfood, and leisure demand equations where demand was a function of prices and income. We assume that some aggregate utility function exists; this is a debated point but appears better than assuming identical utility functions for individual members of the household. Utility level is scaled by household size; also, the full income constraint depends on household size, and hence time availability. Thus household size becomes an argument of the demand functions.

It is convenient to estimate demand for food and leisure only leaving nonfood (including saving) as a residual, since the latter is heterogeneous and in this instance we lack data to estimate nonfood demand functions. Demand for leisure can be estimated as labor supply, which in turn can be split into supply to own farm, to wage labor in agriculture, and to nonfarm acitvities.

For empirical implementation, the above relations need to be modified to capture some of the peculiarities of the rural scene in a country like

Bangladesh. This is necessary because there is no single theory of demand under rationing in that peoples' adaptation to disequilibrium is imperfectly understood. In product, factor, and credit markets, rural households are always responding to disequilibrium situations with respect to prices and quantities supplied and demanded. Market clearing is achieved through the intervention of nonprice variables. The following model reflects such considerations, although the final estimating equations have been further adopted to the nature of data available.

In the food demand equation, the arguments on the right side are household size $(x10)$, total household income $(x13)$, credit availability–borrowing $(x9)$, land rented in $(x15)$, land rented out $(x17)$, and village dummies $(x29, x30, \ldots, x34)$ as shown:

$$x1 = f^1 (x9, x10, x13, x15 \ x17, x29, x30, x31, x32, x33, x34) \qquad (8.2)$$

Rice available for consumption of the household $(x1)$ through production and market exchange is taken as proxy for food demand. This variable is likely to be correlated with household size; therefore, in estimating equation (8.2), $x10$, was dropped from the right side of the equation since it swamped other variables of interest. Income is expected to have a positive effect on food demand. Land rented in or out is included separately from other income variables because the income is in kind—i.e., a cropshare—and hence has a more direct impact on food availability than ordinary income. Land rented out should have a positive coefficient; land rented in should have a negative one. Net borrowing can have two opposite effects, and the final outcome will depend on the relative strength of the two. As a resource, it could augment command over food and thus have a positive sign. On the other hand, it could be used to meet other expenditures (e.g., marriage, festivities, land purchase) and thus come up with a negative coefficient because such expenditures are associated with both borrowing and depleting own resources. Obligation to repay credit could also depress consumption. In this equation, village dummies are used to capture differential price effects. We followed this procedure because it is difficult to obtain direct observations on price and wage covering the entire accounting period (a year).

As for labor supply, it is assumed that self-employment on farm $(x2)$ is rationed by cultivable operational landholding $(x18)$. Tenurial status $(x 21, x22,$ and $x23)$ affects employment through its effect on input use (see the literature on sharecropping on this). Other determinants of self-employment on farm are taken to be size of household and village dummies, the latter of which include land quality and input price effects.

The complete relationship is specified as

$$x2 = f^2 \ (x10, \ x18, \ x21, \ x22, \ x23, \ x29, x30, \ x31, \ x32, \ x33, \ x34) \tag{8.3}$$

It is important to note that in this and the following two employment equations, the dependent variables are specified as actual number of days employed. These are essentially equilibrium values, and thus the usual identification problem exists. However, given that in the short run the labor supply function is likely to be stable while labor demand function will shift because of seasonality, weather, and other exogenous influences such as increased expenditure on rural works programs, change in availability of complementary inputs, and so on, the functions identified are labor supply functions.

In equation (8.3) one would normally expect both household size and landholding to have positive coefficients. For household size, two factors may operate in the opposite direction. First, there is often a positive association between family size and the family's position in the social hierarchy (upper strata in the society usually tend to maintain extended family links). This may deter the household members from working on their own farm. Instead, they may seek employment in nonfarm activities, which is considered more acceptable, or they may have political interests. Second, larger households may seek nonfarm employment more aggressively than otherwise to supplement household income. Such employment often demands full-time commitment, which means that a great deal of household labor has to be withdrawn from own farm work. This is possibly the case of families who hold relatively small productive assets and who may find it profitable to rent it out entirely or partly and opt for nonfarm work. In this case, the operation of such forces may be strong enough to produce a negative coefficient for household size in equation (8.3).

We assume that nonfarm employment ($x3$) is rationed by occupational status, which is a proxy for access to training in specialized skills, education, and so on. It also depends on landholding, which may limit access to off-farm employment, since care of one's own land involves supervision and may prevent long absences. Other arguments in the nonfarm labor supply function are household size and village dummies, as shown in the following equation:

$$x3 = f^3 \ (x10, x18, x24, x25, x26, x27, x28, x29, x30, x31, x32, x33, x34) \tag{8.4}$$

As for other labor supply equations, one can suggest that the sign the coefficient of household size in equation (8.4) will be positive. In the case of occupational dummies, it is relatively easy to speculate that in relation to farmer household (reference dummy), wage laborer families will have a lower level of nonfarm employment (that is, the coefficient will be negative) and others a higher level (positive coefficient). In all three labor supply equations, village dummies stand as proxies for wage and employment opportunity differentials.

Wage employment is considered to be a residual category. People unable to supply labor in other categories are forced into this category, although even here there is an element of rationing introduced by tenurial status to the extent to which better jobs go first to the clients of large farmers. Wage labor is a function of household size, income, tenurial status, and village dummies.

$$x4 = f^4 (x10, \ x13, \ x21, \ x22, \ x23, \ x29, \ x30, \ x31, \ x32, \ x33, \ x34) \qquad (8.5)$$

As in the case of self-employment in farming, household size is expected to have a negative coefficient reflecting household status effect. The income coefficient is expected to be negative also.

Production System. The production system of rural households includes agricultural and nonagricultural activities. The households are expected to maximize profit (net income) functions subject to the production function, fixed asset endowments, and a given set of prices of input and output. For our purpose here, we identify and estimate directly the net income equations for crop income ($x5$), other agricultural income ($x6$), and nonagricultural income ($x7$). It is important to separate different types of income because the underlying production functions are probably different although they are all assumed to be linear in inputs. In a rationing model in which access to land and credit is not free, certain activities may be more profitable than others, and we need not expect marginal productivities to be equal in all activities.

Crop income is hypothesized to be a function of cultivable operational holding, self-employment in farming, amounts of land rented in and out, nonfarm assets ($x16$), net borrowing, and village dummies. All lands are considered to be of the same quality, most probably an abstraction from reality. Labor in this instance is primarily adult male (age 10 and above) labor since in Bangladesh constraints on women's labor cause women not to contribute to crop labor. Nonfarm asset is a composite variable that includes implements, bullocks, and so on. The crop income equation can now be written as

$$x5 = f^5 (x2, \ x9, \ x15, \ x16, \ x17, \ x18, x29, \ x30, \ x31, \ x32, \ x33, \ x34) \qquad (8.6)$$

In equation (8.6) one would expect positive coefficients for net borrowing (working capital effect), cultivable operational holding, and nonfarm assets. As for the influence of land rented in and out, the farmer would reduce crop income for a given cultivable operational holding while the latter would raise it because of institutional crop share arrangements. Accordingly, land rented out would have a positive coefficient and land rented in would have a negative coefficient. An interesting question is whether the sum of these two coefficients is significantly different from zero and, if so, whether it is positive or negative. A net negative effect would imply that, because of poorer incentives, sharecropped land is less productive than owned land. This might be evidence for the question of tenurial reform. Village dummies are expected to capture price effects and also effects of any regional differences in crop production technology, soil fertility, or cropping pattern.

The arguments in the equation for other agricultural income include household size, nonfarm assets, land rented out, tenurial status, and village dummies. It is expected that nonfarm assets and land rented out will have positive effects on other agricultural income. Normally one would expect a positive coefficient for household size also if it stands as a proxy for labor of women and children—e.g., care of animals is often allotted to children. However, a large household allows a larger share of landholding to be brought under one's own cultivation, thus reducing rent income, which is an important component of other agricultural income. Tenurial status may shift the relationship, in that security of tenure may increase food security in cereals and allow diversification into noncrop agriculture, a luxury not affordable by those near subsistence or with insecure tenurial status. The role of village dummies is similar to what was mentioned previously (that is, they capture price and technology effects). The other agricultural income equation is as follows:

$$x6 = f^6 \ (x10, \ x16, \ x17, \ x21, \ x22, \ x23, \ x29, x30, \ x31, \ x32, \ x33, \ x34) \quad (8.7)$$

Nonagricultural income is assumed to be a function of household size, nonfarm employment, nonfarm assets, occupational status, and village dummies. Nonfarm employment and nonfarm assets will have positive coefficients. Household size is introduced to capture women's and children's unmeasured contribution in home crafts; therefore the expected sign of the coefficient is positive. Occupational status in this instance will signify the influence of accumulated human capital assets. Finally, village dummies will capture the effects of prices as well as scope of nonfarm activities. The nonagricultural income equation is as follows:

$$\begin{aligned} x7 = f^7 \ (x3, \ x10, \ x16, \ x24, \ x25, \ x26, \\ x27, \ x28, \ x29, \ x30, \ x31, \ x32, \ x33, \ x34) \end{aligned} \quad (8.8)$$

In addition to crop income, other agricultural income, and nonagricultural income, rural households earn a part of their total income from wage labor on farms. Agricultural wage income constitutes a significant proportion of income of a great many rural households in Bangladesh. Wage income does not originate directly from households' own production activities; rather, it is related to the activites of other households who hire in labor. It is obvious that wage income will be largely and positively influenced by wage employment. The village dummies will reflect the influence of differential wages. An additional variable land, is introduced to see if own-farm responsibilities limit work outside, or if it increases access to wage employment because of patron–client relationships. The sign of the coefficient will tell us which effect predominates. The wage income equation is thus written as

$$x8 = f^8 \ (x4, \ x18, \ x29, \ x30, \ x31, \ x32, \ x33, \ x34) \tag{8.9}$$

Credit System. Net borrowing is expected to depend positively on family size because of both need and ability to repay from wage or salary income. The sign of the coefficient of landholding is unclear a priori: larger landholdings imply greater needs for working capital and greater ability to borrow via collateral effect. However, large landholders are also likely to have more internally generated funds. For consumption loans, one expects a negative relation with landholding (needs) but also a positive collateral effect. Thus the effect of landholding on total net borrowing is not predictable and we may further expect possible non-linearities in the relationship. At very low incomes, people's demand for credit is to meet subsistence rises, and self-finance is possible at high incomes. We do not deal with this type of curvilinear relation in the present model, which has been restricted to a linear form.

The village dummies capture the effect of differences in the credit market situation with respect to the price of credit and quality and quantity of credit available. Our hypothesized relationship for the credit system is

$$x9 = f^9 \ (x10, \ x18, \ x29, \ x30, \ x31, \ x32, \ x33, \ x34) \tag{8.10}$$

Dynamic Equations. We do not extend analysis into full intertemporal choice, since this involves issues as how the family utility function is derived, and how children who may begin as arguments of the function eventually change the utility function. Rather, we postulate simple equations based on current variable values for household size, net land sale ($x9$), and net marketed surplus ($x8$). Household size, as we have seen, enters into a number of current period relations, and it also enters recursively into the static system for the next period, mainly through labor supply. Net land sale and net marketed surplus are resource variables that affect the initial endowment of the household for the next period; as such, they do not enter any of the current period relations. We isolate these two particular resources, because land is crucial to food security, and net marketed surplus is the main source of cash income to many households.

It is hypothesized that family size depends on landholding, tenurial status, nonhousehold work employment, and food availability. Land-holding will exert two types of influence, both positive, on household size. The first is the result of a close association between landholding status and extended family status. The second is landholding's positive effect on fertility through its effect on income and nutritional status. This second type of influence will be further strengthened by the fact that large landholding may lead to increased desired family size to meet own-farm demand for labor (including that for supervision). Food availability affects family size through its positive effect on fertility and negative effect on mortality. Nonhousehold work employment will capture the residual effect of overall demand for labor in directly remunerative activities facing the household. As for tenurial status, one may speculate that groups other than owner-farmers will have smaller families and that the strength of the relationship may very well be related to the degree of insecurity of land tenure. Considering these factors, one can write the household size equation as follows:

$$x10 = f^{10} (x1, x14, x18, x21, x22, x23) \qquad (8.11)$$

Land sale is taken to depend on income and borrowing for current position. Past land sales ($x19$ and $x20$) are included to allow for lagged adjustment.

$$x11 = f^{11} (x9, x13, x19, x20) \qquad (8.12)$$

It is hypothesized that net marketed surplus of paddy is influenced by family size, net borrowing, cultivable operational holding, and amount of land rented in and out. A large family size raises consumption demand and thereby reduces marketed surplus; the coefficient is expected to have negative sign. To the extent to which net borrowing financed working capital, it will have a positive effect on net marketed surplus both because of higher output and because of need for repayment in cash. Similarly, cultivable operational holding, through its influence on out-put, will affect net marketed surplus positively. The coefficient of land rented in is likely to be negative, while that of land rented out is likely to be positive. However, as in the case of crop income, the interesting hypothesis is whether there is a significant difference between the two coefficients in absolute magnitude, i.e., whether the net effect of land rental system on marketed surplus is zero. The marketed surplus function postulated here is as follows:

$$x12 = f^{12} \, (x9, \, x10, \, x15, \, x17, \, x18) \tag{8.13}$$

As indicated earlier, there are two identities. One shows that total income equals the sum of crop income, other agricultural income, nonagricultural income, and wage income. The other shows that total nonhousehold work employment equals the sum of self-employment in farming, employment in nonfarm work, and wage employment. Thus

$$x13 = x5 + x6 + x7 + x8 \tag{8.14}$$

and

$$x14 = x2 + x3 + x4 \tag{8.15}$$

The model structure can be summed up as follows:

Farm household size depends on long-run characteristics and in turn affects employment, and hence income and net supply of rice for consumption.

Family food availability depends on income and credit availability.

Net marketed surplus influences the degree to which farm households participate in credit markets, can hire labor, and enter the supply side of the food market.

Credit is a resource that may augment current production and income and thereby consumption, or it can influence consumption directly.

Net land sale either augments (if positive) or depletes (if negative) the family resource base.

Income determines how a family participates in the product markets and in the labor market.

Income itself is a function of household resource endowment and employment.

Employment opportunities also affect labor supply and are linked to demographic status—e.g., family size affects labor supply.

To recapitulate several special features of the model:

Price terms are not directly introduced, village dummies have been used although they also reflect employment conditions, village infrastructure, land quality, etc.

The model and all relations are specified as linear even though in some instances nonlinear versions might be superior (e.g., in a credit equation).

Some variables act as proxy for others—e.g., household size acts as proxy for unmeasured family labor.

Methodology of Estimation

The structural parameters were estimated using two-stage least squares (TSLS). We acknowledge that, if farmers adjust inputs depending on the unobserved error term, there may still be simultaneity bias problems in estimating net income functions that are related to production functions. One can pass over the issue, hoping that inputs are chosen before output is observed.

The significance tests used are single-coefficient tests or simultaneous tests, but in this exercise the significance level has not been adjusted for the number of tests undertaken. This is less satisfactory than doing a joint test. The problem with joint tests is that it becomes hard to examine single coefficients, and in a somewhat exploratory model of this type, individual coefficients are of interest. Purists will understand that we accept more coefficients as singly significant than a simultaneous test adjusted for number of tests might accept. Finally, R^2 from TSLS shown against each equation in Table 8.31 mean relatively little, as they are based on instruments: they are presented by convention.

The Results

Consumption System. Of the four equations in the consumption system, the estimated food availibility equation is different from what was specified previously, in that village dummies are not included. This is because when they were introduced the level of significance of other coefficients and also the explanatory power of the equation were reduced while the dummies themselves did not seem to matter at all. Although it is difficult to explain, clearly spurious correlation among explanatory variables is introduced when we put in village dummies. Therefore, they were dropped from final estimation of the model. For the remaining explanatory variables, however, the estimates represent the expected relations, a positive and significant coefficient for income and the amount of land rented in, and a negative and significant coefficient for the amount of land rented out. As for credit, the result obtained here is a negative coefficient that is not statistically significant at conventional levels. One could, therefore, tentatively conclude that while credit probably exerted both of the expected influences, the negative influence coming from the need to finance other expenditures had a slight edge. It is important to note that the combined effect of land rental arrangements is negative (sum of the coefficients of land rented in and out) and statistically significant.

The employment equations give rise to some interesting results. It seems that the negative effect of family size predominates its relationship with wage employment and self-employment on farms. It is possible that by controlling for social status one would have obtained a positive coefficient for family size in the wage employment equation. Increased family size increases employment in nonfarm work because the higher availability of male labor allows more earners to be employed outside, and probably also because the labor of women and children on the farm can free male earners for outside employment. This also ties up nicely with what we mentioned earlier as the second reason why household size may have negative influence on self-employment on farms and wage employment (social status effect).

The coefficient of landholding has the expected positive sign in the equation for self-employment in farming and negative sign in the equation for nonfarm work. It should be noted that the influence of household size and landholding in the employment equations is not exactly symmetrical in the sense that positive or negative effect on self-employment on farms and wage employment is not counterbalanced by a negative or positive effect on nonfarm employment, which essentially reflects limited scope for nonfarm work in rural Bangladesh. It is, however, partly also explained by complete withdrawal from effective employment by adult members of the upper strata of the society. It would also be a feature of rationing: households with large landholdings have more own-farm opportunities and also preferential access to other employment. In the case of wage employment, we had introduced a total income variable rather than a landholding variable alone. The sign of the coefficient is negative as anticipated although not statistically significant.

Looking at the influence of tenurial status, one finds that owner-cum-tenants spend more time in self-employment in farming than either owners or pure tenants. The coefficient of owner-cum-tenant dummy is positive and significant (at the 5-percent level). This is in keeping with their entrepreneurial spirit, which caused them to rent extra land. On the other hand, there is no significant difference between owners and pure tenants. It seems that tenants do not necessarily devote less labor per unit of land than what they would do if they owned the land. This, however, may also reflect the landlord's ability to extract a minimum application of labor time (in operation and supervision) from the tenants. An important implication of this finding would be that, controlling for technology, there should be no difference in land productivity under different tenurial arrangements. The coefficient of agricultural laborer dummy is large, negative, and highly significant, which confirms the obvious—they work for themselves but not on their own land.

The above is again brought out in the wage employment equation, where estimates show that tenurial status makes little difference except for the group of agricultural laborers. The coefficient is positive and highly significant. Comparing coefficients of agricultural labor dummy variable in equations for wage employment and self-employment in farming, one finds that in relation to owner-farmers, agricultural laborers perform wage employment roughly the same number of days more than they spend less in self-employment in farming. The high level of significance of the coefficient in the face of insignificance of the other two coefficients—for owner-cum-tenant farmers and tenant-farmers, respectively—imply that small operational holders belonging to these tenurial groups do not have preferential access to wage employment. On the contrary, it seems that a mutually convenient dependent relationship has developed between large and medium landowners and landless households, which provides labor input security to the farmer during peak periods and food security to landless households.

We indicated earlier that, for nonfarm employment, occupational status dummies will capture the effect of specialized skills and education. This came out clearly from the results in that, compared with farmers, wage laborers have lower and other groups higher access to nonfarm employment. All coefficients are highly significant except for transport workers, which is significant at the 10-percent level. As expected, trade and salaried worker groups show very large effects of skill and education. Wage laborers, on the other hand, have very little access to nonfarm employment. This confirms the view that rural laborers in a country like Bangladesh are tied to agriculture, that is, they are not doubly free in the Marxian sense.

All village dummies have significant but small coefficients in the self-employment equation. In the case of wage employment, there were no significant intervillage differences except in one village. Differences in nonfarm employment opportunities among villages do not follow any particular pattern.

Production System. Turning now to the production system equations, we find that in the crop income equation, both self-employment in farming and cultivable operational landholding have highly significant positive coefficients. These results were not unexpected. But, while the coefficient of nonfarm (including farm other than land) assets turned out to be positive, it is not statistically significant, probably because error in variable biases the coefficient toward zero. It includes bullocks and ploughs, which will raise crop income, but other assets—such as other animals, transport equipment, artisans' assets, fisheries equipment, etc. —which do not. There are significant intervillage differences that originate from differences in land quality, from susceptibility to natural disaster, and from differences in the overall production environment.

Unexpectedly, the coefficient of net borrowing has a negative sign in the crop income equation. This can be explained by an underlying nonlinearity in the credit relation. The relation between credit and income appear to be U-shaped because needs raise demand as income falls and collateral effects increase access to credit as income rises. There is yet another plausible explanation: that crop income is reduced because in some cases at harvest time creditors literally wait on the side of the field to collect a share of the crop as their repayment (part or total).

Land rented out has, as predicted, a positive effect on crop income, and land rented in has a negative effect. The sum of the two coefficients is negative and significantly different from zero, which supports the hypothesis that land rented in is less productive than owned land because of the poor incentives for sharecroppers to adopt land-augmenting technology. Given the productivity difference between owned and rented land, it can be shown that the proportion of output from rented land marketed is higher than on one's own land. One objection to land/tenurial reform is that it reduces the supply of agricultural products to industry—but here the productivity effect compensates.

The result of other agricultural income shows that land rented out is the predominant influence. It has a highly significant positive coefficient. The coefficient of family size is not significant at conventional levels, but the negative sign suggests that the effect of increased family labor in increasing land operated under the family's own supervision— which reduces rent—outweighs the positive effects of family labor in other agriculture. Nonland assets have a significant positive influence (one can rent out bullocks and ploughs and can earn income from milch cow, fisheries, forestry, etc.). An important result is that tenurial status has significant influence on other agricultural income: owner-cum-tenants earn less than owner-farmers, and agricultural laborers and tenants earn less still. The difference increases with remoteness from landownership, which is not surprising since rental income from land is the most important component of other agricultural income. It also shows that groups with less access to owned land (i.e., less secure economic status) are less able to build up and support stocks of livestock and poultry and are also less likely to possess significant amounts of forest resources. There are significant intervillage differences in other agricultural income. These differences are not as pronounced as in the case of crop income, but they are mostly in the same direction, which implies that other agricultural income supplements crop income.

In the case of nonagricultural income, all coefficients have the expected sign and effect. Nonagricultural income depends heavily on nonagricultural employment. In addition, family size has a positive effect, which is evidence in favor of the view that unrecorded labor of women and children may contribute to nonagricultural income (their effect on releasing male members of the household for nonagricultural employment is captured by the nonagricultural employment equation). As expected, nonfarm assets have significant positive effects on nonagricultural income. As mentioned before, village dummies pick up the effect of differences in the demand condition, which appear to be highly significant for most of the villages. Among occupational dummies, only the coefficients of trade and transport work are significant, while the others are not. Somewhat unexpectedly, after the effects of other variables are accounted for, it seems that little variation is left in nonagricultural income to be explained by occupational status dummies.

The wage income equation reveals that wage employment is the most dominant factor. The coefficient of landholding is significant and positive. This indicates that, although landholding may not be positively related to access to wage employment, it has a positive influence on wage rate. Some intervillage differences probably reflect different wage rates.

Credit System.   The credit system consists of only one equation. Regression results suggest that the net borrowing equation has very low explanatory power. Two problems seem to have influenced results. First, people are by nature secretive about credit transactions whether they be lenders or borrowers, and hence error in variable bias is introduced here. Second, the nonlinear asset relation is probably at work. Keeping these points in view, we find that family size has an expected positive effect on borrowing, which probably reflects both needs, and a greater ability to repay through more potential earners. The coefficient of cultivable operational holding is negative and significant at a relatively low level (10 percent). As expected, significant intervillage differences indicate supply side differences.

Dynamic Equations.   Finally, results of the dynamic equations are quite encouraging. For example, the estimated family size equation confirms the view that landholding, food availability and employment opportunities have positive and highly significant effects on family size. What is perhaps most noteworthy is that tenurial status matters and that the difference in coefficients becomes more marked with greater degrees of insecurity of status. More specifically, the difference between owning and not owning land comes out very clearly, whereas the difference between owner-farmers and owner-cum-tenant farmers is not significant.

Table 8.31. Regression results: Rural Household Model (TSLS)

Explanatory Variables	Dependent Variables											
	x1	x2	x3	x4	x5	x6	x7	x8	x9	x10	x11	x12
x1										0.000127[b] (2.035)		
x2					8.1277[a] (7.501)							
x3							5.9607[b] (2.232)					
x4								5.4186[a] (32.771)				
x9	-0.920 (0.402)				-1.4353[a] (3.410)						-0.0000184 (0.883)	0.0077[a] (3.156)
x10		-16.427[a] (3.103)	13.818[b] (2.004)	-14.991[b] (2.108)		-15.609 (1.260)	152.83[a] (5.001)		105.71[a] (4.022)			-3.121[a] (4.635)
x13	0.7943[a] (31.137)			10.00505 (0.913)							-0.000000276 (0.123)	
x14										0.00274[a] (3.081)		
x15	161.72[a] (3.305)				-547.74[a] (9.210)							-2.3835[a] (4.477)
x16					0.00917 (0.446)	0.0135[b] (2.006)	0.0372[b] (2.189)					
x17	-217.75[a] (5.883)				125.74[a] (3.623)	428.03[a] (38.51)						2.5459[a] (9.134)
x18		44.799[a] (11.959)	-12.746[a] (2.665)		561.59[a] (11.181)			14.241[b] (2.116)	-33.794[c] (1.811)	0.5449[a] (10.115)		6.5107[a] (12.595)
x19											0.0977[a] (3.086)	
x20											0.0481 (1.279)	

Table 8.31 (continued)

	(1)	(2)	(3)	(4)	(5)	(6)	(7)	(8)	(9)	(10)	(11)	(12)
x21	21.027[b] (2.092)		−3.0427 (0.236)		−96.133[b] (2.075)							−0.2360 (1.245)
x22	6.085 (0.316)		6.2504 (0.298)		−167.75[c] (1.889)							−0.7384[b] (2.123)
x23	−106.04[a] (10.437)		90.291[a] (8.346)		−178.14[a] (3.7314)							−0.6686[a] (3.614)
x24		−58.404[a] (5.739)			255.26 (1.532)							
x25		196.70[a] (12.845)			858.80[c] (1.752)							
x26		102.77[c] (1.883)			1111.9[c] (1.775)							
x27		251.37[a] (13.499)			923.87 (1.436)							
x28		208.63[a] (6.917)			−376.53 (0.664)							
x29	−35.713[a] (2.628)	80.348[a] (5.180)	9.2230 (0.244)	3008.5[a] (16.468)	203.80[a] (3.345)	1101.7[a] (5.344)	420.55[a] (8.439)	188.96[a] (3.673)				
x30	−72.837[a] (5.102)	−14.614 (0.960)	−0.5511 (0.028)	587.98[b] (2.458)	92.892 (1.413)	531.62[a] (3.202)	170.74[a] (3.183)	−233.60[a] (3.223)				
x31	−111.97[a] (6.978)	18.510 (1.031)	−15.041 (0.740)	1287.8[a] (5.647)	58.773 (0.814)	101.77 (0.567)	−73.608 (1.243)	59.375 (0.720)				
x32	−65.759[a] (4.526)	57.800[a] (3.333)	−1.275 (0.061)	288.37 (1.1600)	−185.23[b] (3.094)	345.09[a] (2.107)	−244.81[a] (5.249)	−281.49[a] (3.768)				
x33	−67.503[a] (4.647)	140.40[a] (8.045)	−17.966 (0.769)	1085.9[a] (4.821)	276.19[a] (4.411)	−478.79 (1.571)	−45.197 (0.908)	−181.45[b] (2.400)				
x34	−53.050[a] (2.895)	14.705 (0.669)	−82.021[a] (3.349)	−2.5565 (0.009)	−150.32[b] (2.084)	406.76[b] (2.221)	71.433 (1.323)	−220.67[b] (2.328)				
Intercept	413.34[a] (4.120)	236.8[a] (6.550)	−13.03 (0.289)	203.2[a] (4.696)	−585.8[b] (2.324)	428.8[a] (4.155)	−1439.0[a] (4.444)	−123.4[a] (3.080)	−135.5 (0.773)	4.305[a] (14.717)	0.0195[b] (2.111)	−0.6848 (0.231)
R^2	0.3681	0.2866	0.3751	0.0042	0.3653	0.5179	0.3273	0.5281	0.0491	0.3935	0.0055	0.2377

(Based on instruments)

Note: Figures within parentheses are t-statistics. [a]Level of significance: .01. [b]Level of significance: .05. [c]Level of significance: .10.

There are relatively few observations for land sale in the sample, and it is a last-ditch response to a crisis since land is so scarce. Hence one can understand the very low explanatory power of the equation—quite possibly, land sale is almost a qualitative variable. A family in dire need will decide to sell and often sells much of its holding, and hence a profit model may be preferable to a linear regression. The coefficients of income and credit have the right sign, but they are not statistically significant at conventional levels. Past land sales affect current land sale with the coefficients on last year's sales being more significant than those of sales two years ago—i.e., there is some evidence that land sales are a sign of distress, where families selling one year tend to remain in difficulties the next year, and where the decline in significance of sales two years ago possibly indicates that the family has sold all its land.

Like the land sale equation, the explanatory power of the net marketed surplus equation is not very large, but the estimates of structural parameters are of the expected sign and highly significant. We find that the' coefficients of land rented in and out are roughly equal and of opposite sign. It means that a "land-to-the-tiller" policy will not necessarily have an adverse effect on the supply of marketed agricultural output to the industrial sector, as many fear.

The interdependence of production and consumption and of different markets has been borne out by data from Bangladesh. It is established that the well-being of typical rural households as reflected in food availability, employment, and income depends crucially on the amount of cultivable operational holding, tenurial status, nonfarm assets, occupational status, and the general agro-ecological and socioeconomic environment of the village. What is likely to be the family's future is given by its credit, marketable surplus, and land sale status. These findings are clues to a wide range of policy options for the decision-makers. Many of these have already been brought out in this and earlier chapters. A more systematic exposition of a policy framework is presented in the next chapter.

Variable Definitions

There are twenty exogenous variables used as instruments, fourteen endogenous equations defined by twelve equations, and two identities.

Endogenous variables

$x1$ consumption of rice per household (lb/year)
$x2$ self-employment in farming in mandays
$x3$ employment in nonfarm work in mandays
$x4$ wage employment in farming mandays
$x5$ crop income in taka
$x6$ other agricultural income in taka

x7   nonagricultural income in taka
x8   wage income in taka
x9   net borrowing in taka
x10   size of household
x11   net land sold in 1974 in acres
x12   net marketed surplus of paddy in maunds (= 82.29 lbs)
x13   total income in taka
x14   total nonhousehold work employment in mandays

Exogenous variables
x15   amount of land rented in in acres
x16   nonfarm assets (those excluding land) in taka
x17   amount of land rented out in acres
x18   cultivable operational landholding in acres
x19   net sale of land in 1973 in acres
x20   net sale of land in 1972 in acres

Tenurial status dummies:
x21   1 if owner-cum-tenant farmer
        0 otherwise
x22   1 if tenant-farmer
        0 otherwise
x23   1 if landless laborer
        0 otherwise

Occupational status dummies:
x24   1 if wage earner
        0 otherwise
x25   1 if trade or business
        0 otherwise
x26   1 if transport worker
        0 otherwise
x27   1 if salaried worker
        0 otherwise

Village dummies:
x29   1 if village Laskarpur
        0 otherwise
x30   1 if village Komorpur
        0 otherwise
x31   1 if village Charbaniari
        0 otherwise
x32   1 if village Ramna
        0 otherwise
x33   1 if village Gaorarang
        0 otherwise
x34   1 if village Gobindaganj

NOTES AND REFERENCES

1. For some earlier studies, see S. R. Bose, "Trend of Real Income of the Rural Poor in East Pakistan 1949–66," *Pakistan Development Review* 8(3):00–00 (Autumn 1968); M. Alamgir, "Some Analysis of Distribution of Income, Consumption, Saving and Poverty in Bangladesh," *Bangladesh Development Studies* 2(4):737–818 (October 1974); Ed-

ward J. Clay, "Institutional Change and Agricultural Wages in Bangladesh," *Bangladesh Development Studies* 4(4):423–440 (October 1976); Azizur Rahman Khan, "Poverty and Inequality in Rural Bangladesh," in *Poverty and Landlessness in Rural Asia*, International Labour Office (Geneva: International Labour Office, 1977), pp. 137–160; Jenneke Arens and Jos Van Beurden, *Jhagrapur: Poor Peasants and Women in a Village in Bangladesh* (Birmingham: Third World Publication, 1977), pp. 94–104; M. Alamgir, *Bangladesh: A Case of Below Poverty Level Equilibrium Trap* (Dacca: Bangladesh Institute of Development Studies, 1978).

2. All figures in this and the following paragraph are quoted from Alamgir, "Analysis of Distribution of Income," pp. 747–749.

3. Bose, "Trend of Real Income," pp. 452–488.

4. M. Alamgir and L. Berlage, Bangladesh: *National Income and Expenditure 1949/50–1969/70* (Dacca: Bangladesh Institute of Development Studies, 1974), pp. 58–69.

5. Alamgir, *Bangladesh*, p. 7.

6. Data on nominal wages of agricultural laborers are collected by the Directorate of Agriculture of the Government of Bangladesh and the other wage data are collected by the Bangladesh Bureau of Statistics. For further details on the quality of some of these data, see Alamgir, "Analysis of Distribution of Income," pp. 751–753.

7. The following deflaters were used here. Fisheries workers and agricultural laborers: consumer price index for agricultural laborers. Urban unskilled workers: consumer price index for industrial workers at Naryanganj. See ibid., pp. 752–753, 757. Industrial workers and construction workers: cost-of-living index of all industrial workers. See Government of Bangladesh, Bureau of Statistics, *Monthly Statistical Bulletin* 4(10):58 (October 1977).

8. A linear trend fitted to the data on real wages for the period 1949–1976 produced an R^2 of 0.0269.

9. See also Kirsten Westergard, "Bangladesh Mobilization Study: Village Level Analysis," mimeographed, Centre for Development Research, Copenhagen, 1977.

10. Admittedly, the agricultural laborers have other sources of income. But data presented later in Table 8.6 show that wage income represents 77 percent of total income (without imputed family labor) of a laborer household. It should be noted that annual wage earnings were calculated on the basis of an assumed 259 days of employment a year. See Alamgir, "Analysis of Distribution of Income," p. 798.

11. Arens and Beurden, *Jhagrapur*, p. 103. The data refer to wage rate only and does not take into account the total number of days employed.

12. For more on the aspects covered in this paragraph, see Alamgir, and Berlage, *Bangladesh*, pp. 38–50; Alamgir, "Analysis of Distribution of Income," pp. 753–755; Government of Bangladesh, Ministry of Agriculture, *Bangladesh Agriculture in Statistics, 1973* (Dacca: Ministry of Agriculture, 1974), pp. 57–69.

13. See M. Alamgir, "The Dimension of Undernutrition and Malnutrition in Developing Countries: Conceptual, Empirical and Policy Issues," Development Discussion Paper No. 82, Harvard Institute for International Development, February 1980.

14. Arens and Beurden, *Jhagrapur*, p. 102. The authors lived in the village of Jhagrapur in the district of Kushtia in Bangladesh for over a year.

15. See Clay, "Institutional Changes in Bangladesh"; Arens and Beurden, *Jhagrapur*.

16. Rank correlation coefficients were 0.75, between 1972–1973 and 1973–1974; 0.91, between 1973–1974 and 1974–1975; 0.87, between 1974–1975 and 1975–1976; 0.86, between 1972–1973 and 1974–1975; 0.79, between 1973–1974 and 1975–1976; and 0.76, between 1972–1973 and 1975–1976.

17. These periods are 1955–1956, 1956–1957, 1957–1958, 1965–1966, 1969–1970, 1974–1975, and 1975–1976.

18. See Alamgir, *Bangladesh*, pp. 90–122; Clay, "Institutional Changes in Bangladesh," pp. 426–438; Arens and Beurden, *Jhagrapur*, pp. 94–104. One should point out here that the seasonal wage gap would have been larger but for the downward pressure on the general wage (real) level as shown in Figure 8.1.

19. Clay, "Institutional Changes in Bangladesh," p. 438; Arens and Beurden, *Jhagrapur*, pp. 102–103; Alamgir, *Bangladesh*, pp. 19–37.

20. The reference period is July 1973–1974. Total labor force data were collected from all eight villages but, as explained in Chapter 4, detailed employment data were collected for seven villages. Census definition of labor force has been followed here. Labor force is defined as the population above ten years of age falling in the following categories: (a) the regular workers on the payroll, (b) apprentices learning trade in any establishment, whether they are paid or unpaid, (c) hired workers, (d) owners or proprietors of an establishment and any of their family members if they also work in the establishment.

21. See M. Alamgir, "Population Growth and Economic Activity of the Population in Bangladesh," a contribution to the country monograph on *Population Situation—Bangladesh* prepared under the auspices of ESCAP/Bangladesh (forthcoming); A.F. Md. Habibul Huq, "Labour Force Analysis: Bangladesh 1974," *Bangladesh Development Studies* 6(2):163–190 (Summer 1978).

22. Another crucial omission is the work done by female members of the household, most of which, according to current accounting practice, is excluded from economic activity. This is clearly wrong; it ignores the problem of the women population in terms of getting adequate return and security for the contribution made in the various phases of production of goods and services. For more on women at work, see Mead Cain, Syeda Rokeya Khanam, and Shamsun Nahar, "Class, Patriarchy, and the Structure of Women's Work," Working paper No. 43, The Population Council, New York, 1979.

23. This classification has been adopted from Arens and Beurden, *Jhagrapur*, pp. 96–97. Village-tied workers are those who find employment within their own village or in neighboring villages. "They do not have a fixed relationship with one and the same patron," p. 96. The patron-tied workers include two groups—those working for households with whom they have no kinship ties and those who permanently sell their labor to a member of the extended family. According to the authors, "Patron-tied laborers have more security and status than village-tied laborers and migrant laborers. Patron-tied laborers are more closely connected with the existing rural power structure," p. 96. Finally, migrant laborers are "those who leave their village frequently and go quite some distance . . . searching for employment," p. 96. Arens and Beurden feel that "the issue of migrant labour is crucial as the influx of outside labourers might increasingly upset traditional employment patterns," p. 97.

24. Further details on the alternative concepts of unemployment can be found in A. K. Sen, *Employment, Technology and Development* (Oxford: Clarendon Press, 1975), Chapter IV; A. K. Sen, "Poverty, Inequality and Unemployment: Some Conceptual Issues in Measurements," *Economic and Political Weekly*, Special Number, November 1973, pp. 1457–1464; Raj Krishna, "Unemploymnt in India," *Economic and Political Weekly* 8(9):475–484 (March 13, 1973); K. N. Raj, "Trends in Rural Unemployment in India: An Analysis with Reference to Conceptual and Measurement Problems," *Economic and Political Weekly* 11(31–33), Special Number, August 1976, pp. 1281–1292; Raj Krishna, *Rural Unemployment—A Survey of Concepts and Estimates for India*, World Bank Staff Working Paper No. 234, April 1976.

25. Ibid.

26. This view is supported by another study by Abdullah Faruk. See A. Faruk, *The Hardworking Poor* (Dacca: Dacca University Bureau of Economic Research, 1976).

27. M. T. Habibullah, *The Pattern of Agricultural Unemployment* (Dacca: Paramount Press, 1972).

28. M. Muqtada, "The Seed-Fertilizer Technology and Surplus Labour in Bangladesh Agriculture," *Bangladesh Development Studies* 3(4):403-428 (October 1975). For a recent critique of Muqtada's work, see Rizwanul Islam and Rushidan Islam Rahman, "Surplus Labour in Bangladesh Agriculture—A Comment," *Bangladesh Development Studies* 6(2):221-226 (Summer 1978); and also "reply" by Muqtada in the same issue.

29. Cain, Rokeya, and Nahar, "Class, Patriarchy and Structure of Women's Work," pp. 19-27.

30. In the absence of hard data it is somewhat difficult to make an estimate of the total employment generated due to replanting of *aman*. Nevertheless, on the basis of the survey data, a guess estimate can be attempted. In the eight survey villages, a total of 632 areas of cultivated land was damaged of which over 270 acres or 43 percent of the damaged areas *aman* crop was replanted, generating 4107 mandays, that is 15.2 mandays/acre of additional employment. According to Government of Bangladesh, Water Development Board, *Annual Report on Flood in Bangladesh 1974* (Dacca: Water Development Board, April 1975), p. 81, in 1974 a total of 746,240 acres of *aman* were partially damaged. Assuming that 43 percent of this area was replanted, the resulting additional employment turns out to be 4701 thousand mandays. This nearly compensates in full for the loss of employment due to a shift of jute acreage to *aus* under assumption II in Table 8.16.

31. Government of Bangladesh, Bureau of Statistics, *Statistical Yearbook of Bangladesh 1979*, p. 341. This statement remains true after account is taken of the fact that the rural income is lower than the national average because, given the large weight of rural areas, the national average is usually much closer to the rural income than urban income. Relevant data for earlier years can be found in Alamgir, "Analysis of Distribution of Income," p. 743.

32. These figures are based on total income with imputed family labor.

33. This figure was estimated from the following information. Owner-cum-tenant and tenant account for 27 percent of total rural household income with per capita adjusted income without imputed family labor being Tk. 645. If an additional 6 percent of the total income accrues to this group, the per capita level would go up to Tk. 783, that is, up by 21 percent.

34. Alamgir, *Bangladesh*, p. 15.

35. A. K. Sen, "Starvation and Exchange Entitlement: A General Approach and Its Application to the Great Bengal Famine," *Cambridge Journal of Economics* 1(1):33-59 (March 1977).

Chapter 9

No More Famine?

A SUMMING UP

Nineteen seventy-four was a year of global food shortage; along with many other countries, Bangladesh suffered heavily. The situation was aggravated by a number of factors; some were rooted in the historic evolution of Bangladesh society, and others emanated from mismanagement of the food system in the face of a severe natural calamity, flood. As a result, Bangladesh experienced one of the worst famines of its history.

Given the controversy surrounding the subject, we have defined famine very cautiously in Chapter 1 and applied this definition to analyze major famines of South Asia. Famine is a complex socioeconomic phenomenon, best understood in terms of a community syndrome. What distinguishes it from hunger, starvation, undernutrition, and malnutrition is the occurrence of excess death. There can be general, local/regional, or class famine depending on the factors that trigger the causal sequences. Historically, famine has moved from being general to local/regional to class. This should not be considered a necessary sequence however, because there are exceptions to this in some regions of the world.

The economies of South Asia are famine-prone in the sense that a large proportion of the population lives under the constant threat of famine—

although the complete sequence of events characterizing famine are not unleashed as frequently as they were in the past. Bangladesh is typical in that the society is in the below-poverty-level equilibrium trap in which the per capita foodgrain consumption of a vast majority of the population oscillates between the poverty and famine line. In the past, famine occurred when the existing equilibrating mechanism broke down under the pressure of a combination of factors—that is, the buffering mechanisms (formal and informal) on the production and consumption sides proved inadequate to prevent excess death.

Famine in present-day South Asian societies cannot be explained in terms of a decline of foodgrain availability or failure of exchange entitlement alone. Rather, its roots must be traced to a combination of both superimposed on a set of social relations that are inherently exploitative, in the sense of being biased against the poor. Therefore, an analysis of the sociopolitical context of famine is as important as looking at figures on food availability and/or at the movement of real income of different classes in the society. The sociopolitical context has local, regional, national, and international dimensions, all of which need to be kept in view when one diagnoses famine and formulates famine prevention and relief policies. The analytic framework in Chapter 2 considered all these aspects.

In medieval India, peasants were impoverished through feudal exploitation. Localized famines occurred frequently as a result of drought, but Bengal was largely free from famine. Famine caused depopulation and migration, often dislocating production activities. There were very few buffering mechanisms either on the production side or on the consumption side. A feudal ruling elite organized very little relief, and such efforts were never carried beyond the capital city.

During colonial rule, famine frequency, intensity, and coverage increased manyfold. Bengal experienced perhaps its worst famine as early as 1770, when about ten million people perished. The presence of a unified administrative superstructure did not help in averting large-scale excess mortality in Bengal and elsewhere in India on many occasions. British colonial policies—particularly those relating to land-impoverished small farmers and agricultural laborers who were subjected to surplus extraction by various intermediaries and money lenders—trade, and industrial policies had an adverse effect on the small cottage-based enterprises and artisans. Ironically enough, while improved transport and communication facilitated famine relief efforts, it also aided traders in speculation. The government's strict adherence to free-trade policy made the consequences of famine worse (in terms of suffering) than they would have been with some direct market intervention on behalf of those lacking food resources. However, during the second half of the nineteenth century, the British colonial administration made headway in three directions, mostly at the prodding of the home government in London. First, after each major famine a commission was appointed to look into the causes. Second, famine codes were developed at the provincial level to help organize relief efforts. Finally, construction of large-scale gravity irrigation canals was undertaken in western and southern India.

In the few famines that have stricken Bengal since the beginning of colonial rule, excess mortality has been very high. The Great Bengal Famine of 1943 took a toll of somewhere between one and a half and three million people. An understanding of this famine is important for an understanding of the causes and consequences of the 1974 Bangladesh famine.

The condition of the Bengali peasantry had been slowly deteriorating since the beginning of the nineteenth century; therefore they became very vulnerable as 1943 approached. The overall food situation as measured by per capita foodgrain availability from domestic production was satisfactory until the middle 1930s. Since then Bengal has been largely an importer. However, it was not availability alone but the lack of purchasing power that became a critical problem. The Permanent Settlement of 1793 over the years created sharecropping and landless laborers and, as we observed earlier, rack-renting, subinfeudation, and usurious interest rates became common features of Bengal agriculture. The buffering mechanisms available during a difficult year were drawing down of old stocks (if any), early consumption of winter crops, and curtailment of consumption.

As analyzed in Chapter 3, a number of exogenous shocks disturbed the low-level equilibrium that existed in Bengal in 1943. There were locational and seasonal shortfalls in foodgrain availability and a drastic decline in real income (exchange entitlement) of a large proportion of the population. In explaining the 1943 famine this way, we have deviated somewhat from such authorities as Sen, who downplayed the importance of foodgrain availability decline, although his point about aggregate annual per capita availability is correct. This was a class famine: it hit hard the agricultural laborers, fishermen, and similar occupational groups. Available evidence suggests that the rate of destitution was high, and rural Bengal became more polarized than ever before. The only beneficial result of this tragedy was a worthwhile report by the Famine Inquiry Commission. Unfortunately, successor governments in India and Pakistan did not seriously follow up on the commission's recommendations.

All districts of Bangladesh were affected during the 1943 famine, although to varying degrees. The semifeudal production relation emerged as the dominant relation in Bangladesh agriculture. Peasants continued to be exploited by rich farmers, money lenders, merchants, political intermediaries, and also government functionaries. A high rate of population growth combined with a slow growth of income resulted in a near stagnant per capita income in the 1950s and 1960s. The real wage of agricultural laborers showed no improvement during this period. There was considerable fluctuation in per capita availability of food-grains over the same period. More importantly, in any normal year availability differed significantly across districts and seasons. Beginning in the early 1960s, foodgrain imports increased sharply. In addition, Bangladesh suffered from natural calamities, notably flood and severe cyclonic storms that destroyed property and lives. It seems that the frequency and intensity of such natural calamities increased manyfold in recent decades as compared with earlier decades. Furthermore, loss of agricultural productivity has been taking place due to soil erosion and salinity intrusion.

During the early 1970s, Bangladesh experienced successive shocks of natural disaster (cyclone, drought, flood), war, administrative and economic mismanagement, international inflation, and global food, fertilizer, and oil crises. These factors, combined with the existing inequalities of socioeconomic relations, culminated in the 1974 famine. Following the analytic framework presented in Chapter 2, a careful analysis of the 1974 famine was carried out in Chapters 4 through 8.

In the early part of 1974, rice prices increased sharply, and people slowly started moving toward smaller and larger towns on the way to Dacca, the capital city, in search of food. The movement from rural to urban centers accelerated after the flood that occurred during the monsoon of 1974. Occasional starvation deaths were reported as early as January 1974. There were some local initiatives in small towns to open langarkhanas to feed the destitutes, but such attempts were soon abandoned since no encouragement was received from the political and administrative leaders, who waited until the end of September before declaring famine. By that time the number of deaths had reached monumental proportion; dead bodies were a common sight in many urban centers, including Dacca. Although all parts of the country were affected, the hardest hit seemed to be the three districts of Rangpur, Mymensingh, and Sylhet. These were also among the severely affected districts in the 1943 Great Bengal Famine. Rangpur in particular suffered most, as it was hit by flood three times that year, uprooting people from villages and disrupting normal economic activities.

The worst months of the 1974 famine were July through October, the same months as the 1866, 1770, and 1943 Bengal famines. Like the 1943 famine, the 1974 famine was a rural phenomenon. People traveled long distances for food. In many cases their "wandering" period exceeded six weeks, and some people covered distances of over one hundred miles. In this movement, many families were separated and many households were totally uprooted from their place of origin. As in other famines, a large proportion of rural households were forced to sell some kind of asset in 1974. Distress sale of land was very common. In Chapter 4, survey data showed that 12 percent of *langarkhana* inmates and 2 percent of the villagers surveyed sold owned land in excess of 50 percent. The government estimate of 1974 famine mortality was low (26,000), but other available evidence suggests a much higher figure. Our own estimate, which is admittedly weak, puts excess death during the period July 1974 to January 1976 at one and a half million.

The profile of *langarkhana* inmates gives us a clue to the profile of the worst sufferers during the 1974 famine. It was revealed in Chapter 5 that 32 percent of the sample inmates owned no land and that 89 percent owned less than one acre (including zero holders). It should surprise no one, that victims of both the 1943 and 1974 famines came from the agricultural labor class and petty occupational categories. The laborer group as a whole suffered the highest rate of excess mortality. Again, among survey village households both total and child mortality rates for those with fewer than 2.5-acre operational landholdings, were almost double the rate for the above-2.5-acre category.

The response of the Bangladesh government to the 1974 famine was no different from that of the Bengal government in 1943. Twice-earned independence from foreign domination had brought about little change in the ruling elite's attitude toward the suffering of the common people. As expected, the first response of the Bangladesh government was to downplay the severity of the crisis. When public clamor for action reached a high pitch, the government came up with a modest relief effort. As discussed in Chapter 5, the relief came too late, was inadequate, and was very poorly managed. The international community's response fell far short of the need of the hour. A number of factors worked against Bangladesh. For instance, prospective donors were unhappy with the way the massive flow of aid soon after liberation was utilized. According to some observers, Bangladesh had been crying "wolf" for too long to arouse sympathy any more. There was worldwide tension about food, fertilizer, and oil crises. Above all, the Bangladesh government was only seeking emergency aid for flood damage; like the government in Ethiopia, it was reluctant to publicize the famine. Furthermore, the U.S.A.'s delaying of food shipments seriously handicapped the Bangladesh government in organizing famine relief. We are, however, assuming here that, had a larger amount of foodgrain been available, the Government would have organized adequate famine relief more expeditiously. While it seems that the international community, particularly the United

States, was unwilling in 1974 to bail the government of Sheikh Mujibur Rahman out of the crisis, the government functionaries themselves showed little sensitivity to the impending tragedy, even though ominous signs could be seen everywhere long before the actual tragedy occurred.

How did the Bangladesh society adjust to the postfamine situation? The famine set in motion forces to restore the original low-income–low-foodgrain-intake equilibrium. There was migration of labor to cities, but reverse migration wiped out the temporary labor shortage that appeared in some places. The wage mode changed, as in many areas kind and contract wage gave way to money wage. Between January and November 1974, landlessness increased by about 3 percent. Recent data on land-lessness suggest that the process of pauperization in rural Bangladesh has continued beyond 1974. Transactions in land during this period left middle and large farmers better off. Our analysis of survey data revealed that 5 percent of village households experienced a deterioration of their socioeconomic standing as measured by landholding status between January and November 1974. The position of the sharecroppers weak-ened as their number and proportion increased, but the area rented declined. By and large, all evidence points to the fact that the position of the existing rural elite was further strengthened as an aftermath of 1974 famine, which also implies that semifeudal production relations became more entrenched in rural Bangladesh.

Coming back to the causal sequence leading to the 1974 Bangladesh famine, we find that the explanation cannot be sought in per capita foodgrain availability as calculated from official data. The official figure was actually higher for 1974 than for other years in the 1970s. However, this was an overestimate. The true per capita availability in 1974 was probably lower than a required minimum because of substantial leakages through smuggling, abnormal storage loss, and private and trading stock buildup. Throughout 1974, the stock of foodgrain available to the government was never adequate for effective market intervention. It is clear that the government failed to predict the crisis; therefore, its level of preparedness was low. Furthermore, when the tragedy was unfolding, the relevant government machinery was unable to build up stock from domestic and foreign sources in time. The domestic procurement opera-tion in early 1974 was a dismal failure.

On the foodgrain import front, Bangladesh was confronted with a number of serious problems. The import plan prepared toward the end of 1973 underestimated the food gap since it was based on an optimistic output projection that did not materialize. The government's ability to procure foodgrain from abroad was limited by a foreign exchange shortage, the abnormally high price of rice in the international market, an inability to obtain short-term credit, the noncooperation of the international community, and the particularly hostile attitude of the U.S. government, which delayed food shipment and forced Bangladesh to suspend jute export to Cuba.

While admittedly the output projection for 1974 was optimistic, the actual per capita net output of rice was higher than in other years of the 1970s. For reasons mentioned earlier, this could not be translated into availability. Furthermore, this system of accounting overlooks the seasonal dimension that played an important role in accentuating the suffering of the people in 1974. Both *aus* and *boro* crops were below trend, the latter was 18 percent below trend in famine districts having been destroyed by early flash flood. It is interesting to note that, in 1974, the most perceptible damage due to flood was done to the *aman* crop, but its impact was not felt during that calendar year. It is clear that the natural pattern of seasonal availability of foodgrain was disrupted in 1974 by shortfall in *boro* output. Besides, there is evidence that surplus farmers retained marketable foodgrains longer than usual. Government foodgrain distribution did not follow the usual counter-seasonal pattern in 1974. Available evidence suggests that per capita availability of foodgrains during July–October 1974 was lower than that of an average year. More importantly, the government distribution system, which normally discriminates against the poor in rural and small urban centers, was even more descriminating in 1974. Although nothing definite can be said, supporting evidence indicates that there was considerable interdistrict variation in foodgrain availability per capita in 1974. To sum up, one can safely state that foodgrain availability decline was partially responsible for the 1974 Bangladesh famine.

The effect of foodgrain availability decline was further accentuated by a sharp increase in the rice price and a sharp decline in real income of the disadvantaged groups in the society during 1974. The average annual retail price (Tk./md. = 82.29 lbs) of medium quality rice increased more than fivefold between 1969–1970 and 1974–1975; its effect on consumer welfare is easy to imagine. The early 1970s had witnessed an irreversible upward shift in the base price of rice. In one year alone, between 1973–1974 and 1974–1975, rice price doubled. As expected, the 1974 famine coincided with a violent upswing of rice price. The general trend in rice prices in the 1970s can be associated with the 1971 war, natural calamities in 1972, 1973, and 1974, smuggling, deficit spending by the government, foodgrain availability decline, increase in import prices of rice, and population pressure. Factors such as flood, shortfall in imports and government offtake, abnormal storage loss, breakdown in internal distribution system, interference by government with the internal movement of foodgrains, and speculative hoarding by traders and surplus farmers should be added to those already mentioned to explain the 1974 increase in rice price. For most of 1974, the monthly average rate of price increase for all types of rice was about 21 percent. Foodgrain import price doubled between 1972–1973 and 1973–1974 and remained at the same level in 1974–1975.

The foodgrain price increase should be viewed in the context of a general inflationary pressure in the economy for postliberation Bangladesh. With 1969–1970 as the base, the general wholesale price index increased to 454 in 1974–1975. Among other factors, decline in output and availability of goods and services and increase in money supply played a very important role in sustaining the inflationary price spiral. Government fiscal operations and borrowing by the public sector from banks were mostly responsible for the unprecedented expansion of money supply. On the whole, the government failed to implement appropriate stabilization policies. Consumers and investors alike lost faith in the economy. There was a mad rush for pre-empting the supply of all commodities and for making quick money through speculation. Inflationary expectations raised income velocity of money significantly. Internal resource mobilization was at its lowest point and the government's ability to influence either the real or the monetary sector was reduced to a minimum.

The analysis in Chapter 8 suggests that the sharp decline in real income of the vulnerable groups in 1974 was only a continuation of the past trend reflecting essentially the inequity in Bangladesh society. The village survey data show that during the critical months of 1974 (July–October) real wage income of landless laborers fell by 78 percent as compared with the same period the year before. This indeed would be a severe blow to any family. There was a fall in both wage rate and employment. That year was also characterized by a sharp decline in jute acreage with adverse effect on employment. Under alternative assumptions about shift of acreage from jute to *aus* crop, the total loss of employment could be anywhere between 1.2 and 7.8 million mandays.

In South Asia, a key to understanding famine is to understand the society, particularly how employment and income of rural households are determined in the given social context. One should, if data permits, go a step further in order to analyze the level of food security (measured by the availability of rice for consumption) at the household level. Such an analysis will provide a guide for necessary policy changes that will enhance food security for all by increasing productivity and promoting equity (understood as equitable distribution of food resources).

The real income per capita in Bangladesh did not improve during the 1950s and 1960s over the 1940s; there was a sharp decline in the early 1970s. Roughly speaking, a similar trend is observable in real wages of all types of laborers. Between 1969 and 1974, real wage earnings of agricultural laborers declined by 40 percent. It is not surprising that our estimates showed that throughout 1974 agricultural laborer households were calorie deficient in most of the districts of Bangladesh. During the August–November period all districts were below an acceptable minimum. District level averages, however, do not reflect intradistrict and intrafamily differences in calorie intake.

According to many authorities, famine in South Asia is famine of employment. They rightly point to the ever increasing number of unemployed and underemployed as the potential pool of famine victims. Our survey data reveal a very high incidence of unemployment and underemployment in Bangladesh no matter which of the alternative concepts is used. About 8 percent of the households and 15 percent of manpower are severly underemployed, meaning they are employed on the average less than 100 days a year. According to a combined time and income criterion, over 90 percent of manpower/households are unemployed and underemployed. The incidence in all cases is higher in famine areas that in nonfamine areas. From the point of view of analysis of famine, the severly underemployed group deserves most attention. Though their percentage is small, their absolute number is indeed large. This group is drawn mostly from the small farmers. On the other hand, 29 percent of households are fully employed but they earn poverty income and less. Small and marginal farmers and agricultural laborers constitute the bulk of this group. Clearly, the rate of return for their labor is very low. Rural households tend to have one or more minor occupations in order to supplement their income, but about 40 percent of households reported having no minor occupation. A serious problem arises from the highly seasonal nature of agricultural activities in Bangladesh. Alternative employment opportunities are very limited during the off-peak season for small and marginal farmers and landless laborers.

The employment situation is also reflected in the level of income of rural households. All survey villages taken, the level of per capita income is 27 percent below poverty income. The income levels of tenants and landless laborers fall short of poverty level by 43 and 52 percent, respectively. The average position of all occupational groups appear to be the same. Not only the level of income but the distribution of income as well is a matter of serious concern. Over the decade 1963–1964 to 1973–1974, income inequality in rural Bangladesh increased significantly. This was due largely to inequality in agricultural income. Our survey data show considerable intervillage difference in income inequality. Again distribution of income is more unequal among land owners than among those who do not own land. This can be attributed to the fact that income inequality in the first group originates from inequality in land ownership.

Given low average income, a high degree of inequality of income distribution will mean a large proportion of the population below the poverty line. The situation has clearly worsened over time. For 1973–1974 the proportion of rural households in poverty is placed at 79 percent. As expected, poor households are poor in income, landholding, and assetholding, and the poor of the famine area are poorer than the poor of the nonfamine area. Among different groups in the society, tenants, agricultural laborers, small and marginal holders, transport workers, and other minor occupational groups are relatively more vulnerable. If one takes income gap from poverty line into account, then clearly the worst position is that of laborers and minor occupational groups.

The income and employment status of rural households is translated into their relative food security status. With limited data available we were able to generate a food security profile of rural households for 1973–1974 expressed in terms of household stock and availability of rice for consumption. The discussion was presented in Chapter 6. To sharply focus on the relevant issue, we classified households by their state of foodgrain deprivation. It was found that 36 percent of rural households were in some state of deprivation in the sense that their foodgrain consumption level fell below a given minimum. Among these, 24 percent were severly deprived—food gap was in excess of 50 percent. It is interesting to note that the proportion of food (cereal) deficit households are concentrated among small land holders. On the other hand, among different tenurial groups tenant farmers are most vulnerable, more so than landless laborers. As against the food security in grave emergency extended by dependency relationship, the tenants are subjected to continued high level of foodgrain deprivation through exploitative production relations.

An econometric model clearly showed the interdependence of consumption, production, and income and the interrelatedness of different markets in the rural economy. It was established that the food security status of a household is influenced by its landholding, other asset holding, tenurial status, and occupation status. Controlling for these factors, food security status will vary with village status.

It is difficult to accept morally but not difficult to understand why so many people live under constant threat of death from starvation. We are well into the last quarter of the twentieth century, which is characterized by significant breakthroughs in many spheres of life. We should be able to conquer famine and go a step beyond to eliminate hunger, undernutrition, and malnutrition. It should be understood, though, that the problem is not purely a technological one; it has an important soci-opolitical dimension. In a region such as South Asia, technological advance must go hand in hand with social change and evolution of political will so as to ensure food security for all.

It is unlikely that the ultimate objective of attaining food security for all in South Asia can be realized overnight. But a beginning has to be made now in terms of formulating policy and implementing it by stages. The Bangladesh case study of famine clearly drives home the point that delay in initiating an action program may prove very costly; we may again be pushed into the tragic situation of counting the dead. Being a famine-prone region, South Asia requires action on three fronts other than the long-recognized goal of increasing production: (1) identification of famine indicators and establishment of a famine forewarning system; (2) creation of a food security reserve; and (3) formulation and im-plementation of long-term policy changes that will effect an equitable distribution of food resources. These aspects are discussed briefly in the following sections.

FAMINE INDICATORS AND FOREWARNING SYSTEM

As a component of a global/regional/national effort to eradicate famine, one must develop a perception of appropriate famine indicators, be able to interpret them properly, and develop a mechanism that will generate necessary information to provide early famine warnings and/or to indicate the imminence or existence of a famine. From the approach adopted here to analyze famine, we suggest a set of sequential famine indicators as shown in Figure 9.1. These indicators are classified as follows:

1. A. Early famine-warning system indicators
   B. Prefamine syndrome indicators
      B1. Primary indicators
      B2. Secondary indicators
      B3. Tertiary indicators
   C. Famine syndrome indicators.

A closer look at these indicators will reveal that they are derived directly from the causal sequence of famine presented in Chapter 2. This is why we call these sequential indicators; it is very important to follow the sequence since it reflects the stage of the crisis.

Early famine-warning system indicators are designed to forewarn the government and other relevant national and international agencies about

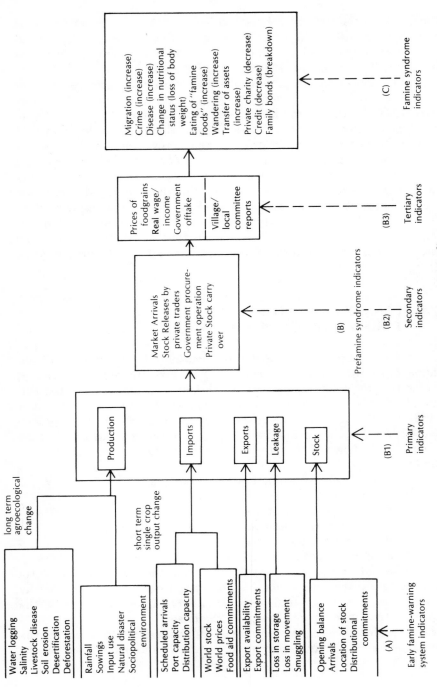

Figure 9.1. Sequential famine indicators.

an impending food crisis. The idea is to give sufficient lead time to these agencies so they can take necessary steps to prevent famine. Prevention of famine is the task at hand at this stage. These indicators are grouped separately on whether they affect production, imports, exports, leakage, or stock.

To predict the level of output, one needs to have an idea about planted area and yield. They are subject to the influence of short-term single crop output change factors and long-term agroecological changes. Monitoring of planted area can be based on sample field survey, aerial survey imagery by aircraft systems, or LANDSAT imagery. Given that separately all three have their weaknesses, serious at times, it is desirable to integrate them into a combined system. Planted area should be adjusted for damage caused by natural disaster, which can also be estimated by any one of the methods described earlier. The short-run yield prospect can be monitored by obtaining information on rainfall (for example, early, intermediate, or late monsoon rain or, say, in the case of Bangladesh, October rainfall is said to be very crucial), input use, natural disaster (which may not completely damage an area but can reduce yield), and other weather factors (for example, temperature, wind velocity, and so forth).

What is necessary, therefore, is a well-developed rainfall and other weather variable monitoring system and a close watch on supply and demand for fertilizer and pesticides in the national and international markets. However, the weather variables must be integrated in an analytic framework to provide a basis for crop yield forecast. A number of methods are available for crop forecasting: crop growth simulation models, crop-weather analysis models, empirical statistical models. The crop-weather analysis models are quite popular and useful. They are mainly multiple regression yield models in which yield is functionally related to climatic, weather, and other variables. FAO has recently devised a crop forecasting method based on agrometeorological information developed especially for drought-prone regions of Africa and preliminary work indicates its applicability to other regions.[1] The method is based on a water budgeting principle: water balance for each crop (difference between precipitation received by the crop and the water lost by the crop and the soil) is established by decade intervals (ten days) over its vegetative cycle. Data required are normal precipitation (P_N), actual precipitation (P_A), number of rainy days, potential evapotranspiration (PET), and crop coefficients. This information is used to prepare an index of crop stress (index value = 100 implies no stress) at various stages of a growing period. This method will forewarn if there is a problem with normal crop development because of insufficient water supply. Although this is very valuable, one should take account of other indicators mentioned earlier for complete crop yield forecasting.

Long-term agroecological change may adversely affect crop yield and thereby precipitate a food crisis. It is important to monitor these indicators because they can bring about irreversible change in the carrying capacity of a region. Indicators to be monitored are: area affected by waterlogging, extent of salinity in surface and groundwater and area affected, rate of soil erosion, desertification and deforestation, loss of soil fertility through chemical degradation, nature and intensity of livestock disease, and level of environmental pollution.

A country/region that suffers from chronic food deficit should also carefully monitor indicators related to imports. The first important indicator is the pipeline of scheduled import arrivals—timing and quantity. In 1974 both caused problems for Bangladesh. At the time of impending crisis, the natural question is, have the ships carrying foodgrain left the port of origin as anticipated? Related to this are the constraints of handling capacity at the receiving ports and the physical distribution system. Therefore, appropriate indicators are indexes of port capacity and distribution capacity. Along with these, the early warning system must gather information on world stock and prices of foodgrain, ocean freight rates, and food aid commitments. A close watch on these variables in 1973 would have found the Bangladesh government better prepared to meet the 1974 food crisis.

We have emphasized the point many times that in order to prevent famine, it is necessary, though not sufficient, for the government to accumulate adequate food resources under its own command. Relevant indicators are opening balance, arrivals, location of stock, and distributional commitments. There should be a tie in between import plan and stock, on the one hand, and distributional commitments, on the other. One should watch whether the current distributional commitments of the government are likely to reduce the available stock below what could be considered critical operational level.

Other early warning system indicators are expected to keep track of the debit side of the food accounting system. For example, abnormal losses in storage and movement should be monitored. Similarly, smuggling is important for some regions. Since direct measures are not easy to come by, surrogate indicators such as border prices and movements of a few major commodities known to be exchanged for foodgrain could be monitored. Our study suggests that the distribution of interdistrict price correlations may be a valuable smuggling indicator as well as indicative of general abnormalities. This would be relatively easy to monitor since district prices are collected already.

Prefamine syndrome indicators tell us whether the preventive actions initiated after early famine warning signals were received have been effective. If these indicators suggest otherwise, further actions will have to be initiated. The nature of these actions will, of course, depend on the degree to which earlier actions have been successful. At this stage, both preventive measures and relief preparations may be called for. The prefamine syndrome indicators could be divided into primary, secondary, and tertiary indicators. Primary indicators are production, imports, exports, leakages, and government stock position. While these should all be separately monitored throughout the year, it will be more meaningful to combine them into per capita national and regional foodgrain availability indicators by major seasons, which may coincide with individual crop cycles. As far as possible, the production components of foodgrain availability indicators should be actually realized and not anticipated (projected) values. Admittedly, it is not easy to collect data on cereals available for consumption immediately following a harvest. The value of this indicator will depend on the ability of the concerned government to establish an effective mechanism for generating appropriate data.

The secondary indicators monitor the reactions of the food system to the status of the primary indicators. Among different secondary indicators, level of government procurement is most useful since data are reliable. In most countries, there is no direct basis for estimating market arrivals, stock releases by traders, and private stock carryover from one crop season into another. However, if the government procurement machinery is reasonably well developed then it can be utilized to monitor information on market arrivals and stock releases by traders. Since we do not have a good basis for monitoring secondary prefamine syndrome indicators, any sign of worsening movement in them should immediately be investigated thoroughly so as not to be taken by surprise by later developments.

The primary and secondary indicators are synthesized into a set of tertiary indicators that include foodgrain prices, real wages, government offtake in market economies, reports from village/local committees, and arrivals in rice mills in both market and centrally planned economies. It is relatively easy to obtain observations on synthetic indicators. But these are extremely important since we have seen that in a country such as Bangladesh, if adverse movements of prices and wages continue for sometime, then famine becomes inevitable unless such movements can be arrested by appropriate action. Finally, when famine syndrome indicators become visible to the naked eye, it is time to organize vigorous relief to save lives. Famine syndrome indicators are observed both at social and physical levels. The latter is related to individual food intake producing specific biochemical-chemical signs.

It is important that the sequential famine indicators are monitored regularly with as much care as possible. The current effort of FAO to develop a global famine forewarning system should be further strengthened, which is possible only if the participating countries take the task seriously and commit resources to establish a national early warning system and operate it efficiently. Needless to say, the activities of the national units should be coordinated at the regional and global level. Regional and global coordination is necessary since food trade flows must balance; it is no use for a country to develop a national plan in isolation. It seems that a regional approach is useful because relevant information can be exchanged quickly between subregions and a regional plan can be formulated and implemented in case of trouble. Regionalizaiton of the early warning system can be brought about under the auspices of FAO.

Setting up an early warning system and/or monitoring the complete set of indicators discussed here do not ensure that famine or food crisis can be averted. Prevention of famine depends on the political will of the national government to adopt necessary measures and on the desire and ability of the international community to respond to a crisis. By all accounts in 1974, the Bangladesh government ignored all early warnings and the response of the international community was lukewarm. It was also an unfortunate coincidence that in 1943 the U.S. government was reluctant to come to the aid of the Bengal famine victims for fear of displeasing the British colonial government of Sir Winston Churchill.[2]

In this context, it is interesting to examine what happened in Bangladesh following the drought of 1978, when a shortfall in the August and October rainfall occurred. Knowledgeable observers, including FAO, predicted that the winter *aman* crop would be adversely affected. The Bangladesh government appeared reluctant to subscribe to this view on the plea that it did not have a firm basis to estimate the likely effect of the shortfall in rainfall on *aman* crop. In the face of continued drought (below normal rainfall reported in four out of the first five months of 1979), the controversy over the harvest of *boro* crop and the prospect of the *aus* corp persisted. The government became so sensitive to any suggestion that a food crisis was imminent, that its permanent representative to FAO went so far as to force FAO to drop Bangladesh from the list of countries likely to face food shortage as reported in monthly food outlook reports.

In reality the food situation worsened; it was reflected in the movement of synthetic indicators like rice prices—prices of *aman* and *boro* rice in late May were about 40 percent higher than a year before—and depletion of government stock. There were also some reports of starvation deaths from the district of Rangpur. These were combined with severe criticism of the government by oppositon political leaders and independent observers who demanded immediate action. It was only then that the government admitted a substantial shortfall in both the *aman* and *aus* output. It also betrayed its own intolerance of political criticism by passing a special presidential ordinance that, among others, banned all public discussion (which it deemed to be prejudicial) of the food situation in the country.

However, the government's response to the situation revealed some interesting facts about famine prevention and relief. The government was able to arrange for large import arrivals over the period July through November 1979 (actual arrivals during the first three months totaled 1.274 million tons). Unlike 1974, the international community was very cooperative in helping Bangladesh obtain a necessary food supply. There was apparently no problem of shipping, which was also easily arranged. On its part, Bangladesh proved that it could, if it wanted to, handle about 400,000 tons of import a month without any serious breakdown in port clearing facilities, internal transport network, and storage facilities. Within this short period, the amount of food shipment handled was unprecedented. This combined effort of the Bangladesh government and the international community is reminiscent of the massive wheat shipments to India in the wake of the 1967 Bihar famine. Another action of the Bangladesh government that helped avert a repetition of the 1974 tragedy was the opening of about fifteen hundred "feeding centers." Since the government had not declared the situation a famine, it chose not to call thes centers *langarkhanas*. Despite a slow response by the government in the earlier stages of the crisis, famine was averted due largely to massive food shipments from abroad. The importance of political and administrative will at national and international levels to fight off a food crisis could not be better demonstrated.

FOOD SECURITY FOR ALL

The question that confronts us now is how to ensure food security for all households in a region. This is not only a question of overall availability of foodgrain, but also of its distribution among households. For the moment we ignore the problem of inequity in intrafamily food intake distribution. The task involved has several dimensions. First, how to make up for unanticipated shortfall in supply. Second, with or without such a shortfall, how to ensure that all households have adequate purchasing power to buy a required minimum of food.

Unanticipated shortfall in supply can be made up by additional imports and by drawing down of an emergency reserve, assuming that normal stock is already committed and that normal interdistrict re-allocation have occurred. In a situation such as that of Bangladesh, an emergency stock of foodgrain can be used to intervene in the market to exercise a moderating influence on price and/or to directly transfer food resources to seriously deprived families. One has to resolve three issues, though. First, what should be the size of the emergency food security reserve? Second, where should it be located? Third, what should be the basis for distribution? These questions sound simple, but nothing short of an involved analytic framework can provide satisfactory answers to all. As a first approximation, though, one could apply some rules of thumb to resolve these issues. For illustrative purpose, we discuss them with reference to Bangladesh.

The purpose of an emergency food reserve should be to avert large-scale starvation deaths. We have seen that even in a normal period 24 percent of rural households are severely deprived of foodgrain; it is absolutely essential that their basic food security be enhanced to prevent them from being among the first victims in case of a natural or man-made calamity. From historic analysis, we find that the longest continuous spell of food crisis could be August through October, that is, three months, which is also a reasonable lead time for obtaining additional unplanned imports. We assume that in a crisis these households will have little or no access to food resources and, therefore, will have to be supplied with at least 220 oz/day per capita (their current maximum level) for a minimum of three months. At the projected rural population level of 1980, the required reserve works out to be about 400,000 tons. Adding 100,000 tons to this for open market operation, the food security reserve comes to about 500,000 tons. This figure is comparable with some of the estimates by several international organizations such as FAO and the World Bank. We admit that the 100,000-ton figure for open-market operation is somewhat arbitrary, but this is a very important component of a food security reserve. Even before food transfer to target households takes place, there is a need for doing something to keep market prices in check particularly where there is a sharply rising trend. It is assumed that food surplus countries can be persuaded to transfer food resources in excess of their current food aid commitment so that food security reserves for a region such as Bangladesh can become operational.

The second issue is where to locate the food security reserves. We have seen that in 1974 as well as in 1943 almost all districts of Bangladesh were affected by famine although there was some variation in intensity and that there were problems with interdistrict movement of foodgrains. Therefore, reserves must be located in places that enable the government to rush food to the needy in case of an emergency wihtout much loss of time. We classified Rangpur, Mymensingh, and Sylhet as being relatively more severely affected by flood and famine in 1974. One should probably also add the coastal districts of Barisal, Noakhali, and Chittagong, which are very vulnerable to cyclones. Furthermore, there are three other districts—Faridpur, Pabna, and Kushtia—with unusually low per capita availability of foodgrains in both 1973 and 1974 (see Table 6.29). This gives us nine districts that should probably be considered for inclusion in a priority list for the location of an emergency stock of foodgrains. More careful analysis will be necessary to identify the number, size, and precise location of additional storage facilities. A famine map prepared for Bangladesh by Bruce Curry at the University of Hawaii and the work done at the Food Security Unit of FAO may provide further guidance. It is desirable that detailed famine maps be prepared for relatively more famine-prone regions of the world. Our analysis shows that certain areas are more vulnerable to famine, that it is often the predictable conclusion to known causal sequence.

A number of tasks are involved for distribution. First, a list of beneficiaries of emergency food distribution would have to be prepared. This can be done by village/local committess. Second, although it is convenient to fix a per capita quota, it may be beneficial to allow a certain amount of flexibility to the village/local committee, who know better about individual household needs. Third, the village/local committee should be assisted in building a reasonable makeshift storage facility. Fourth, in cases where the village is located at a disadvantageous point in relation to the site of food security reserves, help in shipment will be necessary. Fifth, this type of emergency food release at the village level would have to be coordinated with other indigenous relief efforts to make the whole operation more effective. Sixth, food should be distributed without charge because it is unlikely that the target group will have the necessary purchasing power under the circumstances in which such distribution arrangements are being made. Seventh, to the extent to which it is possible, it may well be that some independent monitoring of village efforts is undertaken—to avoid the possibility of village elites and leaders acting the same way as government agencies and ignoring warnings through negligence or political reasons.

In making the above points, we oppose free cooked food distribution by settingup *langarkhanas* because they never functioned well in the past. This was particularly borne out by the 1974 Bangladesh experience. We emphasize reliance on local organization for the distribution of foodgrain in an emergency situation. No government can estabalish overnight a network of distribution centers that can reach village levels. Again, under no circumstances can they be a permanent feature given the cost implications.

We have so far looked into the question of food security reserve from the point of view of an individual country. There is considerable merit in widening the scope of such a reserve interregionally and internationally. The ASEAN countries have already established a food security reserve of fifty thousand tons. There is talk of setting up an international reserve that is estimated by FAO at sixty million tons. In view of many impediments, it is unlikely that an international foodgrain reserve will materialize in the near future. Instead, it may be worthwhile to explore the feasibility of obtaining better coordination of national food security reserves on a regional basis backed up by a modest regional reserve to meet only extreme emergencies. To promote such an idea for South Asian countries appears to us to be very desirable.

One of the key elements in food security for all is purchasing power for all. Given existing income inequality and the prevalence of poverty, income redistribution seems to be an effective means for raising the purchasing power of those who have little of it. This will require policy intervention to change reward structure, factor returns, and asset distribution. In South Asian societies where distribution of political power is heavily biased against the poor such policy interventions to the level of required effectiveness are unlikely to be undertaken by the elite. Political mobilization of the poor is not in the cards now but in the long run it is unavoidable. At that point the dominant elite will possibly have no other choice but to make major concessions in terms of committing resources to enhance the food security of the poor. In the meanwhile one can only hope that some redistribution will be allowed.

That the purchasing power of the poor can be raised by increasing their productivity and by creating new avenues of employment has been said by many. The measures to be included here are the familiar ones: distribution of subsidized inputs (superior to output price support policy as much of the literature indicates that this policy leads to capital bias and benefits large farmers more), provision of extension services, marketing facilities and credit, promotion of small-scale rural industry, and public works programs. Given that in South Asian countries low purchasing power is related to unemployment and underemployment, public works programs assume great importance. However, the public works programs need to be designed so as to benefit the deserving only. This can be achieved by maintaining a master roll of the poor, offering a lower than market wage rate or food wage. Another measure that merits serious consideration is elimination of rationing privileges for the urban rich, extending them (to the extent to which budgetary resources will permit) to the rural poor (presumably the urban poor are already covered), thus raising their real income.

LONG-TERM POLICIES

All of the famine prevention and relief policies discussed have long-term ramifications. Our analysis of Bangladesh data points toward the need for an in-depth look at some of these policies. In addition, there is a basis for considering such measures as land reform and tenurial reform, issues that are often hotly debated.

It was found that landholding and family size interact to produce a social status effect that reduces self-employment on farms. Again the demand and opportunities created by large family size induces adult male members to seek nonfarm employment. The result is that large landholdings and other absentee holdings are often undersupervised and underutilized and crop income per acre falls. These findings, along with others that clearly show that income and thereby cultivable operational holdings exert an overwhelming influence on food security of households, suggest that the issue of land reform should be carefully analyzed. The results are also encouraging in that land reform seems unlikely to drastically reduce marketed surplus.

The patron-client (labor bond) relationship seems to exert an influence via lower wage rate received by wage laborers than small farmers, although one might wish to look at seasonal wages and seasonal participation to confirm that different access rate from tenancy is important. Unionization of landless agricultural laborers could improve their bargaining position. In the context of a polarized rural social structure such as that of Bangladesh, a certain degree of support and encouragement must be forthcoming from the government if the interest of the poor and disadvantaged groups is to be promoted. But given the class base of the Bangladesh government, one can only be cautiously optimistic about this possibility. It is clear, however, that under the present state of the rural economy, laborers will remain dependent on agriculture, especially crop production, as a main source of livelihood. That their condition can be improved by expanding nonfarm employment opportunities is borne out by our results.

We found evidence that the present land tenure system of Bangladesh is not neutral with respect to its effect on productivity of owned and rented land as well as on food availability to households, but there is no significant difference in marketed output. The productivity differential arises mainly from differential access to or use of inputs other than labor. Data suggest that tenurial reform combined with a better input distribution system will raise output, income, and food security of rural households, particularly of the currently disadvantaged groups, without necessarily having an adverse effect on the volume of agricultural output marketed.

Families who sell land are mostly in a desperate situation. Since they can be easily identified, it is possible to formulate certain policies to support them in difficult circumstances. One may consider providing specialized short/medium term credit at concessional terms. A second policy measure could be establishing land banks to whom individuals sell (mortgage) land and then lease it back for cultivation. This will hopefully slow down the process of pauperization and polarization that is going on in rural Bangladesh today. Without a land bank, people tend to sell to large land holders, which increases their hold on small and marginal farmers and landless agricultural laborers through patron-client relationships.

We cannot, with clear conscience, live with the specter of famine hanging over many parts of the world. There can be no peaceful coexistence between man and famine. Recent increasing global tension around issues that are actually nonissues would be largely eliminated if the value of human life was duly appreciated by the policymakers. It is not technological capability but social and political relations within and between countries that stand in the way of ensuring food security for all. The most challenging task of the future seems to be how to make national governments and the international community more sensitive to the needs of the poor so that more resources are committed to prevent famine. This is only the beginning—the ultimate objective of all activities combined should be to improve the quality of life. Unfortunately, we seem to be failing in making a beginning of the beginning.

NOTES AND REFERENCES

1. M. Frere and G. F. Popov, *Agrometerological Crop Monitoring and Forecasting,* FAO Plant Production and Protection Paper 17, Rome 1979.
2. For an interesting account see M. S. Venkataramani, *Bengal Famine of 1943: The American Response* (Delhi: Vikas Publishing House Pvt., 1973).

Index

A

Absorption function, 255n

Africa, and calorie requirements, 8n

Age, and famine mortality, 143, 144. *See also* Children; Elderly

Agra, scarcities in, 77

Agricultural credit, 215-219. *See also* Credit market

Agricultural income equation, 367

Agriculturalists' Loans Act, 76

Agriculture. *See also* Food production; Rice production and famine-prone economy, 16

and labor market, 20

semifeudalism in, 48

Ahmed, Raisuddim, 209, 211, 213

Ahmednagar, famine in, 56

Ajmer, famine in, 75

Akbar, Ali, 137

Akbar reign, famine during, 55

Alamgir, M., 308

Algeria, cash aid from, 177

Aman, crop, 201-202. *See also* Rice production

and Bangladesh famine of 1974, 389

employment generated by, 382

fertilizer for, 209

harvest distribution, 304n

and HYV technology, 220

monitoring of, 398

output during, 1961-1976, 204

price of, 224

price analysis for, 288

production levels for, 203

and real wages, 319

Anjumane Mofidul Islam, 129, 130, 140

Arens, Jenneke, 314, 325

Arthur, W. Brian, 140, 158

Asaduzzaman, M., 211, 213, 289, 291

ASEAN countries, food security reserve of, 401

Asia, and calorie requirements, 1

Assets of famine victims, 166-168. *See also* Distress sales

evaluation of, 193n

lost during famine, 186

Aus crop, 201-202. *See also* Rice production

Marginalization, and famine syndrome, 46,47

Market. *See also* Capital market; Labor market; Rice market
  crisis moderating role of, 43
  free-trade concept of, 63, 65, 67, 73, 80
  imports in, 39, 41, 211, 212, 264, 281, 397

Masur crop, and real wages, 321

Mauritania, 9n

Men, in langarkhanas, 152-153

Merwara, famine in, 75

Mia, Karimuddin, 119

Middle East, and calorie requirements, 8n

Midnapore Cyclone, 92

Migration, 384
  during Bangladesh famine of 1974, 131, 133, 386
  and famine, 57, 46, 47, 181
  reverse, 181

Migrant labor, phenomenon of, 322, 381n

Ministry of Relief and Rehabilitation
  press releases of, 177
  on seed grants, 179-180

Monegar Choultry, 61

Moneylenders, 187. *See also* credit market
  and capital market, 24
  during famine, 48
  role of, 68-69

Mortality
  during Bangladesh famine of 1974, 130
  cattle, 75, 194n
  and famine, 5
  in famine of 1899-1900, 75
  of famine victims, 157-158
  of Guntor famine, 64
  of Kashmir famine, 54
  occupational pattern of, 158

Mortality, excessive
  of Bangladesh famine of 1974, 140-145
  of famine syndrome, 150n
  of 1943 Bengal famine, 84, 87

Murkerji, Karunamoy, 79, 82, 85, 86

Mukherjeee, Ramkrishna, 79, 85, 87

Muqtada, M., 341

Mussulman population, famine among, 67

Mymensingh
  famine in, 103, 386
  famine relief in, 170-171, 172
  famine vulnerability of, 317, 400
  langarkhana in, 174, 175
  per capita net output in, 241
  rice prices in, 276
  rice production of, 242

Myrdal, Gunnar, 8n

Mysore, famine in, 61, 69

Mysore Famine Code, 73

N

Nanavati, Sir Manilal, 90

Narayangonj
  rationing systems for, 227
  rice market of, 296, 297, 299

Nazirpur
  high interest rates in, 164
  severely deprived households in, 251

"New world order," 2

Niger, 9n

Noakhali
  famine in, 86
  famine vulnerability of, 400
  rice production of, 242

Nonagricultural income equation, 367

Nutrition crisis, 4

Nutrition surveys, 341

O

Occupation
  of famine victims, 152, 156
  and household income, 352
  and incidence of poverty, 360, 361
  and mortality, 158
  and underemployment, 338
  and vulnerability to famine, 392

Occupational structure,
  in rural Bangladesh, 341

Offtake, government, 226-228
  during famine period, 244-245
  monitoring of, 397
  shortfall in, 248, *See also* Shortfall

"Orissa Famine," 66

Mohiuddin Alamgir, a Visiting Scholar at the Harvard Institute for International Development, received an M.A. in economics from Dacca University, Bangladesh, and an A.M. and Ph.D. in economics from Harvard University. Since 1976 he has been Research Director of the Bangladesh Institute of Development Studies. Prior to that, he held various positions in the Pakistan Institute of Development Economics, in Karachi, and in the Bangladesh Institute of Development Studies, in Dacca. Dr. Alamgir has been a consultant to a number of international organizations, including the World Bank, the U.N. Economic and Social Commission for Asia and the Pacific, the U.N. Food and Agriculture Organization, and the U.N. Environment Programme. He was the President of the Bangladesh Economic Association in 1974-1976 and a council member of the International Economic Association in 1974-1976. A member of the Third World Forum and the Association of Third World Economists, he has written extensively on a wide range of topics in economic development and policies, including planning, manpower and education, trade, urbanization, agriculture, rural development, national income, and savings. Some of Dr. Alamgir's publications are *Bangladesh: National Income and Expenditure; Saving in Bangladesh; Bangladesh: A Case of Below Poverty Level Equilibrium Trap;* and *The New International Economic Order and UNCTAD IV.*